1942

1942

WHEN WORLD WAR II
ENGULFED THE GLOBE

PETER FRITZSCHE

BASIC BOOKS
New York

Basic Books
Hachette Book Group
1290 Avenue of the Americas, New York, NY 10104
www.basicbooks.com

Printed in the United States of America

First Edition: September 2025

Published by Basic Books, an imprint of Hachette Book Group, Inc. The Basic Books name and logo is a registered trademark of the Hachette Book Group.

The Hachette Speakers Bureau provides a wide range of authors for speaking events. To find out more, go to www.hachettespeakersbureau.com or email HachetteSpeakers@hbgusa.com.

Basic Books copies may be purchased in bulk for business, educational, or promotional use. For more information, please contact your local bookseller or the Hachette Book Group Special Markets Department at special.markets@hbgusa.com.

The publisher is not responsible for websites (or their content) that are not owned by the publisher.

Print book interior design by Bart Dawson

Library of Congress Control Number: 2024054708

ISBNs: 9781541603219 (hardcover), 9781541603233 (ebook)

LSC-C

Printing 1, 2025

This book is dedicated to my students.
We traveled well, I think.

David M., Victor, Jonathan, Jeffrey S., Glenn, Joe,
Sace, David B., Molly, Bryan, Alex, Jason T., Will, Thilo,
Amanda, Andrew, Jason H., Jeff H., Kristin, Tyler,
Eric, Scott, Peter, Christopher, and Rhiannon

Man's yesterday may ne'er be like his morrow;
Nought may endure but Mutability.

—PERCY BYSSHE SHELLEY, "MUTABILITY"

CONTENTS

Contents

PART IV • PUSH DOWN THE ROAD

PART V • PULL UP THE ROAD

PART VI • OCCUPATION

INTRODUCTION

This is what the war did. It handed you over to war, from one war to another war. It deployed millions of soldiers far away from home. "Do they send you to France" like in the last war? "No, they do not send you to France. They send you to Tunisia, and then they send you to Sicily," remarked one fictitious American infantryman; "God knows where they'll send you after that." The war sent air forces that brought mayhem to ends of the earth. Looking up at "the military planes that cross my sky," and out again at "little brown-eyed" children in the garden, a suburban housewife wondered "what I might see in this little lane" when bombers returned to raid English towns such as her own. "All the bleeding and choking, all the groaning and dying will have to be done personally"—that is what people were told about their homes, "the most dangerous of all places" in "the next war." With powerful binoculars, thousands of civilian spotters took up lonely positions in the hills and along the coasts to watch for enemy planes: "The Safety of Millions Depends on Eyes Like These."[1]

Evacuation specials pulled out of the war, transporting refugees to unknown destinations. In the famous war movie *Casablanca*, a camera zooms in on the globe, following routes of escape from "Paris to Marseille, across the Mediterranean to Oran," and "then by train, or auto, or foot, across the rim of Africa." The actors themselves were so many of Europe's fugitives. Evacuees in one place worried about the war catching up with them in the next. There was no real safe harbor, and ships out at sea were sunk with few survivors stranded in lifeboats.

Deportation trains pulled right into the war when authorities arrested citizens as conspirators or when the Japanese purged Chinese communities in Malaya and the Germans snatched Jews from their homes to murder them in Poland. Neighbors sometimes helped the soldiers hand people over, confirming how the war converted personal features of spite and envy into ready arms.

After territories were conquered, the war spread out when food supplies ran short and people starved and when soldiers ran after residents to conscript them into forced labor. The war enveloped the villages and towns that insurgents raided to expel the entrenched occupiers, each group using violence to force civilians to take sides in the combined effort to drain the sheltering seas. A dreadful shriek of detonations, the war was all people knew or saw or heard. Everywhere they read newspapers or passed on rumors, the war took on forms that were more monstrous and closer up.

World War II was the "greatest cataclysm of violence in human history."[2] Sixty-five million people, or more, were killed in about two thousand days, four times as many as in World War I. The untidy sum was about 3 percent of the world's population. The Second World War was not merely a deadly enlargement of the First: civilians made up two-thirds of the dead, whereas in the Great War it had been mostly military men who died. Of the 2 billion people on earth in 1939, about 120 million ended up wearing a uniform as soldiers in the war, an astonishing number but small when compared to hundreds more millions who waged the war as workers, extracting resources and manufacturing equipment, or who found themselves displaced through famine, bombardment, or land-clearing operations. No belligerent suffered the losses of the Soviet Union. Twenty-seven million inhabitants were killed in a population of 170 million, including ten million Red Army soldiers, a figure representing more than half of all military deaths in the war. Ten percent of World War II's dead were Jews, whose communities in eastern Europe were obliterated in the Germans' "Final Solution." Dead civilians stand out as the singular accomplishment of the war.

It was the year 1942 that scattered pages from the book of Revelation far and wide, here monsters of violence and visions of affliction and doom, there programs of hope and salvation.

The war engulfed the entire globe in 1942, when, after Pearl Harbor, all the major belligerents had taken sides in the Axis, dominated by Germany and Japan, or with the Anglo-American and Soviet Allies. It was fought across the continents and seas and in the air. Technology made these stretches possible: before the war, Pan Am Clippers flew routes from Hong Kong to San Francisco and New York to Lisbon, and submarines reached halfway across the earth. The war between the Axis and the Allies also gave geopolitical significance to areas such as the Indian Ocean where supply lines across the Pacific and around Africa converged. Everywhere the global conflict heightened a sense of local vulnerability. From Caracas, for example, the enemy could snip the "G-string" at the Canal Zone to "rip" the "soft underbelly" of the US Gulf states.[3]

It was not so much locations but ideas that made the war global. Each side, the fascist newcomers in the Axis and the variously "democratic" Allies, believed the war to be a great fight for freedom. Each took up battle in the name of humanity against the other's wickedness. This self-appointed stewardship of the world's moral order drastically escalated the level of violence meted out to the enemy.

The war connected a global public that narrated far-flung events as parts of an intimate, agonizing melodrama. As an epic battle between the Allies and the Axis, Stalingrad riveted the attention of the world in the fall of 1942. It was like watching your own city—as if "Edgewater, Hoboken, Newark," and Union City "were in enemy hands." But it was the universal ideas of the war that locked people all over into some aspect of the struggle as they recognized the parts their own trials played in the wider conflict. These ideas centered around freedom. As a result, Japan's victory over Britain in Singapore in February 1942 shook race relations in South Africa and the United States. The entire world monitored struggles for self-rule in India, and Indians knew their struggles reflected other campaigns for liberation across the globe. In this sense, there were not foreign wars in World War II.[4]

The idea of "one world, one war" created shared audiovisual space. Statesmen addressed global audiences directly to appeal to the world's conscience and judgment. Listeners tuned in to the news as well as foreign programs, the BBC and Radio Moscow in German-occupied territories, or Radio Free India, which broadcast from Berlin. Listening was an act of connection as people followed the progress of the war according to coordinates as far away as Stalingrad or Singapore. In Fort Hare, in South Africa, Nelson Mandela remembered how his friends would "huddle round an old radio" at night to listen to Churchill's speeches. Even crossword puzzlers added more foreign clues so that ten across, four down, became a basic two-step of the world war. Particularly on the Allied side, an international repertoire of movies and songs gave the ideas of the great military effort an immediate and homespun quality.[5]

As the war welded together conflicts into world struggles for freedom and sovereignty, second fronts cracked open in 1942 well beyond the primary military zone between the Axis and Allied armies. In its familiar form, the second front was the one the British and Americans were pressured to launch in Europe against Nazi Germany so as to relieve the beleaguered Soviet Union. The Allied invasion of North Africa in November 1942 remained an incomplete effort, but global coordination among the Allies was only one dimension of the war. Second fronts flared whenever ideological confederates took up their own aims of freedom and liberty in rearguard battles around the world. The whole earth seemed to be on the march, "not in one place, but everywhere."[6] In crisscrossing conflicts, partisans fought Japanese and German occupation troops and British imperialists in India, and they labored against racial injustice or defended ethnic privileges or religious rights at home, in Detroit, in Calcutta, in Johannesburg. War kept handing war over from one place to another.

There was an awesome moment of enlistment when citizens all over the world claimed the war as their own, insisting this is "our war too" to wage a "people's war" for political justice and self-rule. These parallel wars, more apparent in the Allied sphere than in the Axis one, provided connective tissue to the all-out war. They also cut deep against the bias of existing structures of power. African Americans saw Nazis marching in Detroit, and many preferred to fight "crackers" down South than Germans over in Europe. Anticolonial wars, between "haves" and those who "have been had," disrupted the empires without necessarily contradicting Allied aims in the war.[7] Indeed, the promise of self-rule in the "Atlantic Charter" proliferated as much as it directed the fighting because it translated local conflicts about power into a universal idiom of right and wrong.

Far more numerous than fighters were the enemies they designated, usually ethnic or racial minorities who found themselves corralled in categories and circumstances that they had not created. Everywhere, second fronts against local civilian populations of Jews or Chinese or Ukrainians added to the combustion and confusion of the war. The killing kept moving back to home, where most of the dying was done.

If the disaster of World War I was remembered as a military one (trench warfare), the disaster was primarily civilian in World War II (the bomber). After the war, Hiroshima and Auschwitz became the most identifiable emblems of the civilian dead. The vast number of deliberate noncombatant deaths made World War II a completely different war from World War I or the Napoleonic Wars. In what was understood as modern "total war," ideas of citizenship, equality, and national belonging enrolled civilians in the war. They also became targets in the effort to destroy popular morale and industrial capacity. In fact, the British and Americans invested more resources to build air forces to "dehouse" or kill civilians than on any other aspect of the war. Long-range bombers killed more than two million civilians, women and children mostly.

In a war as much about racial and ethnic domination as territorial control, civilian populations found themselves on the front lines wherever they lived. The war did not just divide the world; divisions all across the world became parts of the war so that domestic enemies were added to foreign ones. "Wait for Me" was the most famous Russian song of the war. Like Vera Lynn's "We'll Meet Again" or Bing Crosby's "White Christmas," it regretted the soldier's leave. "Wait for me, and I'll come back"— "soldiers copied" the line into their notebooks, and girlfriends "read it over at night." However, there was another song in 1942 that was also written by Konstantin Simonov, "Kill Him!" "Kill" the assailant who had burst through the door to slap the "wrinkled face" of "your mother," to trample "your father's picture," and to corner her, "whom for so long you did not dare even kiss," and stretch her "naked on the floor."[8] In occupied territories, assaults against enemy civilians made for the deadliest, longest "second front." Indeed, it was the cohort of young men who slaughtered women and children, the majority of the war dead. Rape was the way women remembered the war in the Philippines, in Germany, and elsewhere.

The calamity of civilians who had been starved or discarded did not occupy a clear part in the war or in the stories about the war. Thucydides pointed out long ago in *History of the Peloponnesian War* that there was no virtue in the lawlessness of the plague or civil war, which killed off the strong as well as the weak. Narratives elevated the war, but they obscured and defaced it because refugees and evacuees did not fit well into righteous or militant storytelling. The fate of Jews was misunderstood because they were romanticized as partisans or forgotten if they were not. Stories created a vital component of the fighting and sacrificing, but the sacred unity they drew together was always incomplete and frequently restrictive.

All the roads of the war ran over all the stories of the war. Luckless evacuees scattered the militant marchers, who composed such a striking image of the one billion people who took part in World War II. And soldiers on the front often felt like stunned, displaced refugees themselves, or they ran away. The sturdy causes of the war such as antimilitarism or antifascism eventually overran many more people than they enrolled. The world at war in 1942 is about the forceful mobilization under great ideological banners, but also the sharp contrary forces that shredded social solidarity and tore apart ideological unions.

To account for what the war did as it handed over soldiers and refugees and deportees from one war to another war, this book explores roads across the world. Roads lined up soldiers, but they also pushed around the war's castoffs, bombed-out townspeople or destitute villagers; you could read about the first sort of travelers in letters or books, but not about the others who were forgotten because they were not in uniform. They could not be heroic. After the prelude that sets the scene following Pearl Harbor, the second part of the book opens with the dramatic movement of armies across global meridians in 1942. Singapore at the beginning of the year stands for the great destruction of empires, while, more than four thousand miles away, Stalingrad at year's end shows the fantastic mobilization achieved by the Axis offense and the Allied defense. In the third part, the extradition of soldiers in battle, the shipwreck of sailors at sea, and flights of both the bombardiers and the people they bombed dramatize the relentless, capricious "winds of war" that kept sweeping through places. The war kept on coming, traumatizing the heroes, adding to the dispossessed, and everywhere enlisting more fighters.

The book shifts in the fourth part to investigate the roads on which the war pushed civilians out of their homes in very different events: the famines in Henan, China, and Bengal, India, and in Germany's deportation and murder of Jews in

Europe. Civilians also crowded roads because they were pulled into the war by new opportunities in the cities; I examine songs and worries and work in Richmond, California, and Johannesburg, South Africa, in the fifth part. Finally, the book takes up the occupied territories in the war with an analysis of collaboration and resistance in India under British rule, in the Philippines during Japanese occupation, and in Ukraine in Germany's new racial order. In the end, the war had too many sides for it to be told simply in terms of victory or defeat. The closer you got to the scenes of battle, the more vanquished there seemed to be.

Nineteen forty-two is the year when war advanced on the world with more war. Each of the new segments of war exposed terrifying, strangulating coils: the advance of Japanese armies in East Asia and German ones into the Caucasus in Russia and toward Egypt and Palestine. Debris of sunken ships washed up on Florida's beaches. The war bolted forward, and it lurched backward and skipped sideways as insurgents rose up to contest the territories the enemy had taken. Again and again in 1942 violence erupted out-of-bounds, with the main features composed by dead civilians, who had been driven out or bombed or simply murdered. There were so many stations to count in this new global war that it became difficult to bear the cross or reflect on martyrdom and resurrection. There was no victory in sight in 1942, only more battles.

What is more, the contested ground broke apart as anticolonial forces stood up to fight imperial rulers but also to defend communal liberties and protect ethnic or religious privileges. In India, South Africa, and the United States, the fight for freedom wielded a very sharp sword because the vigorous claims of majority rule threatened minority rights as well as foreign intruders. As most people around the world came to realize, the war was always also at home. It was in 1942 that the world learned of the German efforts to murder Jewish families, but other horrors endured by civilian populations such as bombardment, evacuation, forced labor, and famine remained largely unseen in the reporting of the war, in the cavalcade of newspapers and posters, because they did not fit into the militant picture of the war between the Allies and the Axis.

Nineteen forty-two was an alarming year without clear victors. It was forth-and-back with the course of events composing bewildering zigzagged shapes. The war extended forward, and it reached back in a series of convulsive detonations.

Indeed, for most of the time, the Allies were losing the war they would win in 1945. And when they did win it, the huge cost to do so ensured there was no return to the world of 1939 since all the maximum efforts had raised fundamental questions about freedom, empire, and citizenship. The Battle of Stalingrad at the end of 1942 halted the mighty German assault against the Soviet Union, but the surprising Japanese victory at Singapore at the beginning of the year cracked open an entire imperial epoch and charged insurgent popular and racial politics. So great was the cumulative violence against human beings that it undermined the fundamental theology of our age. This book puts emphasis not on end-time but on endless war times, not on Death, but on more, often noxious life-forms. Anchored more in the outcome of Singapore than in Stalingrad, this sudden, deep uncertainty about the future serves to highlight the competing ideals and the proliferation of violence across the fronts of the global war. The book shows what the war did, not how it came to an end, so that this exploration of 1942 is more about the world at war than it is about the provisional victory known as World War II. That said, thank goodness the Allies won.

The flames that burned through half the world's population make the experiences of 1942 relevant to any estimation of global dangers to social and political life today. The year 1942 illuminates 2042, with the later year serving as a marker of the turbulence of economic distress and climate change and the proximity of mass carnage. In an image crafted by journalist Dorothy Thompson in 1939, refugees composed "an advancing crowd shouting a great warning": "the jungle is on fire!" They abandoned the places where homes had been wrecked and came upon other places where they could not build new ones. The unforgettable impression of the imagery of fire confirms its overall relevance to modern times. Today, we imagine confronting future challenges to the planet with conventional notions of the successful effort to beat the military foes in World War II in mind, but we need to remember the profound unsettlement of the effort, the massive numbers of civilian dead and the constant reignition of racial and ethnic conflict, all the wars out of conventional bounds, which the victorious end of the war against Germany and Japan, V-E Day and V-J Day and the soldier's kiss on Times Square, hides from view. Nineteen forty-two is a warning, not a guide.[9]

Although the Allies won the war in 1945, and the Axis powers were defeated, victory hardly tied up the unraveling that occurred in 1942. The first year of the world war was shocking because one war kept giving way to another war, revealing the globe grabbed and contorted in a violent emergency as people watched the horizon, as they thought about children in the garden, and as they considered what "this little lane" would look like in the "next war." It was the year the war won the war.

World War II diligently sets up World War III with the last doomsday ready to be marked up. But 1942 does not point the way to the end of the war or to the end of the world; rather, it points to repeated postponement in rounds of renewed anguish and improvised repair. "There is disaster only because, ceaselessly, it falls short of disaster." Instead of the end point of Hiroshima, this book excavates the "big island," which is what the word "Hiroshima" means in Japanese, the wide space taken up by the war.[10]

PART I

PRELUDE

CHAPTER 1

Five Days in December

The afternoon of Sunday, December 7, 1941, was brisk and sunny in Pittsburgh. Families loitered on downtown streets to inspect the Christmas window displays at Gimbels or Kaufmann's. Moviegoers lined up at Loew's Pennsylvania to see *Birth of the Blues,* starring Bing Crosby. Across town, twenty-five hundred patriots jammed the Soldiers and Sailors Memorial Hall in the Oakland Civic Center to protest what they took to be the warmongering policies of President Franklin D. Roosevelt.

Set to begin at 3:00 p.m., the America First rally promised to be a raucous affair, and almost every seat was taken. It was just at the moment before speakers came onstage, around 2:30 p.m., that the first Associated Press reports of the Japanese attack on Pearl Harbor offered a dim sense that the United States was already at war. (The attack was launched at 1:55 p.m. eastern, 7:55 a.m. Hawaii time.) A local reporter who had arrived to cover the event informed the organizers about the sketchy facts. America First decided to go on with the antiwar protest.

First on the bill was Irene Castle who, with her first husband, Vernon, had made a name as a ballroom dancer. The couple had even been the subject of a 1939 movie with Fred Astaire and Ginger Rogers. Wiping away a tear, the remarried McLaughlin told the Pittsburgh audience that she had lost her husband in one war and did not want to lose her son in another.

The real crowd-pleaser was North Dakota senator Gerald Nye, who took the stage at 4:45 p.m. Described as "tall, dark, handsome," Nye had chaired the Special Committee on Investigation of the Munitions Industry from 1934 to 1936. What he feared was "the establishment of an economy here that is dependent upon war, an economy that affords prosperity through the flow of human blood." He got the rally going. "Never, never, never again must America let herself be made such a monkey as she was 25 years ago," he declared, before asking, "Whose war is this?" "Roosevelt's!" the excited crowd chorused back. Even after a piece of paper had been shoved in front of him confirming Japan's declaration of war, Nye continued his folksy harangue against the president. "Treason," the crowd roared back; "Impeach him." Only after about fifteen minutes did Nye read the note. "I have before me the worst news that I have encountered in the last 20 years," he ventured. An "excited murmur" swept through the rally, but Nye refrained from taking it seriously. "I can't somehow believe this," he exclaimed, and veered off to mention the *Greer*, an American destroyer that had been fired on by a German submarine on September 4, 1941, an incident that Nye believed was not unprovoked as Roosevelt claimed—"and that's cheating." Leaving the stage, Nye still felt cheated. Pearl Harbor was "just what Great Britain had planned for us," he insisted.

Returning to Washington, Nye bowed to circumstance and voted with his fellow senators to declare war on Japan the next day. On December 8, the Pittsburgh branch of the America First Committee, with fifteen thousand members, dissolved itself, but not without the local chairman feeling that "something precious to us has been torn away and ravished."[1]

Nye's appearance in Pittsburgh on Sunday was part of the America First road show, much bigger than the Castles' on Broadway had ever been. The America First Committee had been launched to enforce American neutrality, a big issue after September 1939 when Hitler invaded Poland, and Britain and France declared war on Germany, and to thwart Roosevelt's desire to provide Britain with any "aid short of war." However, America First really came into the public eye after celebrity aviator Charles Lindbergh joined the antiwar effort in April 1941. To America Firsters, the United States was moving closer to a war it could not win. "Does any sane person believe," former president Herbert Hoover asked, "that by military means we can defeat two-thirds of the military power of the whole world in even years and years?"[2] Together, Germany and also Japan, an aggressor in China, were all mighty. At the same time, Roosevelt sharpened the "material means" available to him by declaring an "Unlimited National Emergency" on May 27, 1941. Following Germany's invasion of the Soviet Union at the end of June, he proposed the extension of the unprecedented peacetime draft from twelve to thirty or more months. A wail of protest followed, with the extension passing the House of Representatives by a single vote on August 12.

When first introduced in September 1940, the draft quickly became homespun. According to a Gallup poll, the majority of young men had no personal objections to a year of military service. Since the size of the US Army ranked eighteenth in the world, the draft seemed an appropriate measure with Europe at war. Song and dance embraced the draft. Featured in the Abbott and Costello movie *Buck Privates*, the Andrews Sisters made "Boogie Woogie Bugle Boy" an instant hit at the beginning of 1941. It told the story of a famous trumpet player from Chicago who was at the top of his craft: "But then his number came up and he was gone with the draft." This goodwill changed with the extension of the draft. The Prairie Ramblers updated their recording of "I'll Be Back in a Year, Little Darlin'" to "I Won't Be Back in a Year, Little Darling." Soldiers themselves threatened to desert after their year was up. *Life* magazine reported on the graffiti scrawled around army posts: "OHIO," which stood for "Over the Hill in October."[3]

The declaration of an "Unlimited National Emergency" energized America First Committees, which soon numbered 450 chapters with eight hundred thousand members. Lindbergh along with Nye and others crisscrossed the country where the Irish, the Italians, and the Germans did not necessarily identify with Britain. Thirty thousand protesters filled the Hollywood Bowl on June 20, 1941, to hear Lindbergh. Hundreds of meetings and paid radio spots expanded the audiovisual space of the nation. Emboldened by the emergency, isolationism also took on a nativist aspect. Speaking in Des Moines on September 11, Lindbergh charged that "the three most important groups who have been pressing this country toward war are the British, the Jewish, and the Roosevelt administration," all of which served non-American interests. Having indicted Jews as warmongers,

America First found itself on the defensive. Even so, Lindbergh spoke to enthusiastic crowds in Fort Wayne, Indiana, on October 3, and his schedule of antiwar rallies stretched into the new year.

America First probably never had strong support of more than a quarter of the country. Its influence, however, was pervasive. As British ambassador Lord Halifax noted, the United States was divided against itself. In his estimation, Roosevelt had to "steer a course between (1) the wish of 70% of Americans to keep out of war" and "(2) the wish of 70% of Americans to do everything to break Hitler, even if it means war." Robert Sherwood, a White House speechwriter, recalled the period before Pearl Harbor more bluntly. "As the world situation became more desperately critical, and as the limitless peril came closer and closer to the United States," he wrote, "isolationist sentiment became ever more strident in expression and aggressive in action, and Roosevelt was relatively powerless to combat it. He had said everything 'short of war' that could be said." Yet "he had no more tricks left."[4]

Given these circumstances, the Allies were fortunate that Japan made the decision to go to war for them. The day after the Pearl Harbor attack, a front-page editorial in the *Chicago Tribune*, "We All Have Only One Task," reminded readers that this was the war "that so many of us have worked with all our hearts to avert," but the newspaper put the stress on "we all," united in an effort in which "recriminations are useless." "For all intents and purposes Isolationism and American Firstism are deader than a bombed soldier at Hickam Field," reported an observer in Chicago.[5]

"Well, it's here," remarked another Chicago resident. The reference was to the war and also to the end of the deadlock everyone felt between hating the dictators and fearing another war. Though involuntary, the decision came as a relief, but also introduced a feeling of disquiet since it swept Americans, and millions of others around the globe, into a new unmarked period of time, the uncertain vertigo of wartime.

Americans quickly learned the basics of what happened at Pearl Harbor: the sneak attack, the mass casualties at the naval base, the stricken airfields. What they did not know was that six Japanese aircraft carriers had launched the attack; they had little idea of Japanese military capacity. Nor was the public informed that the three carriers of the navy's Pacific Fleet had not been in port that Sunday—carriers would become the most important protagonists in the Pacific war. Even so, Roosevelt's fireside chat on December 9 was clear enough to anchor a profound sense of vengeance: through a "brilliant feat of deception, perfectly timed and executed with great skill," he said, "many American soldiers and sailors have been killed by enemy action. American ships have been sunk; American airplanes have been destroyed."

Roosevelt also stressed the global dimensions to the struggle in which the United States was one injured party among many. In his declaration of war on December 8, Roosevelt enumerated the other places the Japanese attacked, the Philippines, Malaya, Hong Kong, Guam, and Midway, making no distinctions between American and British possessions while stressing the unprovoked and perfidious nature of Japanese aggression. Maps in the *New York Times* and *Los Angeles Times* gave readers a powerful visual display of the far-flung attacks across the vast Pacific area. "The Japs are running wild all over Asia," one reader summarized.[6]

In his fireside chat the next evening, Roosevelt framed the attack to encompass the entire globe. Given the "actual collaboration" among Japan, Italy, and Germany, "all the continents of the world, and all the oceans," have been turned into "one gigantic battlefield" in which "Japanese successes against the United States in the Pacific are helpful to German operations in Libya," and any "German success against the Caucasus is inevitably an assistance to Japan in her operations against the Dutch East Indies." It was a quick lesson in world geography. Roosevelt framed the attack on the Hawaiian Islands in such a way to prepare American families for a long war in which their soldiers, sailors, and airmen would be fighting far from home.

Whether they wanted to avenge a dastardly attack on the United States or believed in the global mission to destroy the foundations of Axis militarism, Americans rallied. Although the requirements to allocate manpower made it necessary for the army to rely exclusively on the draft after December 1942, the expansion of the armed forces depended first on volunteers. The scene in Boston repeated itself across the United States: "Before the Navy and Marine recruiting station in the Federal Building opened at 8:00 am, there were 41 men, ages 17 to 43, waiting outside the door to join up and the offices have been swamped ever since. The Army reports that the number of recruits is '10 times normal.'"[7]

Typical also was the scene in Chicago where the *Chicago Defender*, a leading Black newspaper, reported, "Army Rejects Negroes." "Lewis Grady, 19, 6145 May Street, presented himself for service and was waved aside." Next in line was "twenty-year old Mitchell Jordan, 4318 Evans Avenue." "'Sorry, can't use you,' the officer informed him." It was not a week after Pearl Harbor when Sylvia Tucker of Detroit, determined to "heed the call" to donate blood as "a loyal American citizen and American mother," was told that regulations "barred Negro blood donors."

Although the American Medical Association and Red Cross protested that there was "no factual basis" to justify discrimination, the War Department refused to offend white southerners who, in the words of one congressman, could not imagine pumping "Negro blood into the veins of our wounded white boys" with all the "direful" effects "it might have on them or their children."[8] One African American leader rightly compared the policy to "the cult and curse of Hitler and Hitlerism." Black and white bisected wartime questions of life and death.[9]

The blockade of Black Americans from the wartime community continued a familiar story in which race persistently divided the "we all" the *Tribune* gathered together. "We must all stand united against this common enemy," editorialized the *Chicago Defender*, but "White America must first 'bomb the color line.'" That bombardment was slow in coming.

Hours after they heard about the attack, Americans began inspecting Japanese close at hand, making their way in Los Angeles to the district known as Little Tokyo. First, they cruised along First Street above which "gay Christmas decorations" fluttered until curious sightseers created such traffic jams that police closed off the street from Main to San Pedro "to prevent incidents." The next day, storefronts, banks, and department stores were mostly shuttered. Policemen patrolled the streets. Even at the end of the week, Little Tokyo remained "a deserted village." Charles Kikuchi headed for San Francisco on December 8 to "chase girls." "Holy Christ!" he later wrote: the city "was like nothing I ever saw before and everybody was saying that the Japs are going to get it in the ass." Japanese Americans reacted to Pearl Harbor "as Americans," yet were "painfully aware that faces turn to look at them" as they walked down the streets.[10]

The marking of Japanese Americans drew a further race line across "we all"—citizens of Japanese heritage pointed out, "I am an American," while Chinese residents insisted, "Me Chinese, Please, No Jap." It was not long before *Life* came to the aid of Americans confused by who was Japanese and who was Chinese. "LIFE here adduces a rule-of-thumb": after making physical distinctions between slender and squat, it summarized that Chinese have the "rational calm of tolerant realists," whereas "Japs, like General Tojo, show humorless intensity of ruthless mystics." (In response, the *New York Times* insisted that "whatever the slant of his eyes," it is "the slant of the heart that counts.")[11]

"It was the look in the white people's faces when I walked down the streets," recollected Chester Himes, the African American novelist. "It was that crazy, wild-eyed, unleashed hatred that the first Jap bomb on Pearl Harbor let loose in a flood. All that tight, crazy feeling of race as thick in the street as gas fumes"—the "blood-red hatred of all dark skin."[12]

The loathing of the Japanese remained palpable throughout the war, and, in some ways, the "infamy" of the attack held the country together. But Americans also recognized the larger threat posed by foreign invaders that forced them to confront questions of empire and the fate of subjugated people around the world. As a result, the war accentuated the planet's "dark skin."

ON NEW YEAR'S Day, Japanese newspapers published stunning photographs of the aerial attack on "Battleship Row" on Ford Island at Pearl Harbor. This was when Tokugawa Musei, a well-known radio personality, finally fell in with his country's war. "It was an unprecedented New Year's," he confided to the diary. "My heart swells with pride," he admitted, sorting the headlines from "the four newspapers our house receives."[13] They hurled Japan's power: "Advancing into the Southwest Pacific—the Rising Sun Flag" and "When Singapore Falls, India, the Heart of England, Will Quake."

For Musei, Pearl Harbor was more than a brilliant attack on the US Navy's Pacific base. It heralded Japan's war to liberate East Asia that over the past two or three centuries had been parceled out among the Western powers. Japanese knew well that it was the Stars and Stripes that flew over Manila just as the British raised the Union Jack in Singapore (and New Delhi, and Rangoon, and so many other places). In the very first week of the war, Japan broke through along a front stretching nearly halfway across the world from Hawaii in the East to Burma in the West. "THE WAR IS ON!" announced the *Japan Times*, nudging readers into a great drama in which war would be the means by which Japan seized control of events and built its own Asian empire.[14]

On December 8, the sun had barely risen when the first vendors appeared outside Tokyo's Shimbashi station with special editions calling out "*Sensô! Sensô!*" (War! War!). With their bells ringing, vendors soon spread out along Ginza Dori in the commercial district. In the excitement, streetcars emptied, and "a new wave of buyers swirled around the news vendors." By noon, huge crowds "flooded into the streets from shops, department stores, offices. Joyous relief and intense satisfaction shone in every face."[15]

"Patiently have We waited, and long have We endured," read the emperor's Imperial Rescript that was broadcast repeatedly over the radio. The "inordinate ambition" of the United States and Great Britain to "dominate the Orient" nullified "Our Empire's efforts of many years." They had demanded an almost complete cessation of what Japan considered to be its "manifest destiny," most concretely, its colonial activity in China, but, more generally, its claim to speak for an Asia for Asians, and they had enforced their own long-established imperial positions in the region with an embargo of oil and other vital imports to the island nation. "The situation being such as it is," the Imperial Rescript concluded, "our empire, for its existence and self-defense, had no other recourse but to appeal to arms and to crush every obstacle in its path."

The radio followed up the defiance with the martial song "Umi Yukaba."

Across the sea, water-drenched corpses;
Across the mountains, grass-covered corpses.
We shall die by the side of our Emperor,
We shall never look back.

There was a sense of common purpose in the struggle against Western imperialism. "Asia for Asians" was the new slogan. People rushed out to greet the new future with all its opportunities for the ambitious Japanese people. It beckoned just as the opening of the transcontinental West had for the United States. In the city of Yokohama, hundreds of citizens, anxious to keep up with events, purchased new radios or brought in old ones needing repair. In a demonstration entirely missing in the United States, tens of thousands of "extremely enthusiastic" people, their "hearts filled with joy," rallied in Tokyo's Hibiya Park across from the Imperial Palace on the following Saturday.[16]

When the attack on Pearl Harbor was announced, it was already December 8 in Japan. As the calendar indicated, Japan was ahead. It had taken the initiative in invading the outposts of

American and British empire and thereby established the meaning of the course of the events. The aim of securing hegemony in what had been a European-dominated East Asia stretching from China south to the East Indies (Indonesia) and west to India had already been announced in the Imperial Rescript, and the means for doing so, Japan's sponsorship of its own imperial device, the Great East Asia Co-Prosperity Sphere, which would liberate the peoples of East Asia from foreign rule and develop their long-stunted capacities, offered an attractive way to the future. Not Pearl Harbor, but the captures of Hong Kong, Manila, and especially Singapore were the big events that gave direction and meaning to Japan's war. The Japanese people were swept up in a tide of nearly uncontested enthusiasm in the aggressive "spirit of December 8."

An opportunity to overturn power constellations on the planet, the war was "the greatest turn that has ever been recorded in world history," a new chapter emancipating "the Asiatic nations from the bondage of the white man." "World history," the *Japan Times* concluded, was being made "so vigorously as to shake the very axle of the earth."[17]

Photographs published in the newspapers in December 1941 drew readers right into the war. They were all action shots: a Japanese naval squadron "knifing through the air on its way to wipe out enemy warships" and battleships zigzagging in a "frantic effort to escape Japanese bombs." Just two days after Pearl Harbor, Britain's capital ships *Repulse* and *Prince of Wales* were sunk off the coast of Malaya in the "smoke and spray" of "numerous bomb-bursts." Photographs of mechanized units, marching columns, and bicycle troops ("Pedal into Burma") composed motion pictures pulling readers into the relentless forward movement of Japanese forces. "Knifing," "blasting," "toppling" captions hounded the "swerving and swaying" enemy. From the start, the war was conceived in a highly aggressive way: banners "along the streets, in streetcars and restaurants," and really "everywhere," urged the army to "annihilate our enemies," to "slaughter them."[18]

However, the all-out success could not hide the glaring flaw of the attack. Japan assumed it struck at the heart of American power, dismissing the more realistic view, which was that Pearl Harbor was simply a remote appendage of an otherwise unscathed industrial giant—only four hundred thousand people lived in the far-off Hawaii Territory. The chief of naval operations, Admiral Harold Stark, later recalled having made this connection clear to Japan's ambassador before the war: "You too will have your losses," he reminded, and "unable to make up your losses," Japan "will grow weaker," while "we will not only make up our losses but will grow stronger as time goes on."[19]

Many senior officers in Japan's navy agreed—privately. Even Isoruko Yamamoto, the commander in chief of the Combined Fleet who planned the audacious preemptive strike on Pearl Harbor, opposed the overall military strategy. For someone who "bet on anything and everything," he was proud of playing a "full house" against America's "pair" on December 8. But as a poker player, he also knew he would be dealt other hands. "Anyone who has seen the auto factories in Detroit and the oil fields in Texas," he reflected, "knows that Japan lacks the national power for a naval race with America." Japan could "put up a tough fight for the first six months" in a war with the United States, "but I have absolutely no confidence as to what would happen if it went on for two or three years."[20]

The sense that time was running out had pushed the Japanese leadership into war in the first place. Japan was running out of resources. It had about a year's supply of oil. At the same time, military leaders watched Germany's spectacular conquests in 1940 and came to the conclusion that Europe's colonies in Asia were there for the taking. "Don't miss the bus!" they told themselves.[21]

The brilliant success of the Pearl Harbor attack served to validate traditional Japanese arguments prizing spiritual quality over material quantity. Yet observers admitted that the struggle might be a very long one—as aggressive naval and imperial powers, Great Britain and the United States had "dominated the world" for so long, controlling key points around the globe such as the Suez Canal and the Panama Canal, that "they will not submit without a struggle." The war could go on for "ten, twenty, and even a hundred years."[22]

The struggle would be long and thorny, and it would be global. Japan defined the war as the "Great East Asian War" against the Western empires in the name of one billion people, half the world's population, who "groan under their yoke." Between the "have" and the "have-not" nations, favorite vocabulary words for the upstart Axis, between "plutocratic-democratic map-makers of Washington and London" and the army of liberation mobilized in Tokyo to alter the face of the earth, "there has now opened a war for life or death." It was a planetary war of nations and races: "All the players are in the game and all the cards on the table. Nobody can back out," concluded one scholar writing about the conflict that lay ahead.[23]

Yet for Asians, the promise of the "Greater East Asia Co-Prosperity Sphere" turned into a "predatory enterprise" in which Japanese assumed the role of the European imperialists they had booted out of the Pacific. Already in China, Bengali poet Rabindranath Tagore warned in 1938 that Japan had erected a "tower of skulls." Racial hierarchies—"Asia for the Asians" with the Japanese on top but not "Malaya for the Malayans"—emerged as a central feature in Japan's "holy war." "The 'sphere' was actually a pyramid."[24]

"The enemy is coming, the enemy is coming. On Track 2 the enemy is coming. On Track 3 the enemy is coming!" Musei, the New Year's diarist, was startled to see his four-year-old son playing railroad conductor. The game suggested anxiety about the size and proximity of Japan's enemies, a subterranean current beneath public jubilation after Pearl Harbor. Yet residents headed to shops to buy aid-defense equipment—helmets, buckets, window strips. Assigned to air-raid shelters and drilled in firefighting, citizens prepared for the war. Indeed, the *hinomi*, or firewatcher, and neighborhood fire brigades that raced against each other had long been a part of urban folklore. "The enemy is coming, the enemy is coming" was a case of jitters as well as a call to arms.[25]

OVER THE SUMMER of 1941, Helmuth James von Moltke grew uneasy about the German invasion of the Soviet Union, which he followed closely as a counterintelligence officer in the High Command of the Wehrmacht. German troops advanced, but encountered stiffer resistance than expected. By the fourth or fifth week of the war, disappointing news from the front shredded Moltke's initial conviction on June 22, the day of the invasion, that "Russia would collapse from within." Gradually, he suspected that "we have touched something terrible and it will cost many victims." Moltke picked up *War and Peace* that summer with Tolstoy's description of the national spirit awakened by Napoleon's invasion of Russia in 1812 ringing alarm bells.

As he immersed himself in the novel, writing his wife that in the evenings he had "Tolstoyed a little more," Moltke came to the conclusion that a successful military outcome was doubtful. The Russians were fighting for their country and shared a patriotic story: "big words, very big words," made Russia "invincible." He calculated the effect of the words: "very, very heavy losses": "Every day costs 6,000 German and 15,000 Russian dead and wounded. Every hour costs 250 Germans and 625 Russians, every minute 4 Germans and 10 Russians."[26] By early December 1941, the German war machine came to a halt in the freezing-cold suburbs of Moscow.

On December 5, the Red Army mounted an unexpected and surprisingly strong offensive that pushed back German troops dozens of miles. Heinrich Hampe, with the Sixth Infantry Division, had gotten as far as a tram stop from which he picked up a "handful of old tram tickets" on which Cyrillic letters spelled out "Moskva," yet his unit quickly abandoned their forward position. Everywhere uncoordinated retreats along icy winter roads left behind the debris of corpses, broken trucks, abandoned guns, and "documents and letters" blown "across the steppes." Franz Halder, chief of staff of the Army Command, described Christmas Day as a "very difficult day." Then came "*a very difficult day!*" and "*another difficult day!*" followed by "a day of wild fighting." Wehrmacht armies eventually recovered, but the counteroffensive had bankrupted Hitler's blitzkrieg strategy. The Soviet Union had not been knocked out.[27]

Moltke could not think or write in peace. He was weighed down by the "hecatombs of corpses." "I slept very little for two nights," he wrote his wife, Freya, on November 13, "because I woke up at 3 and thought about Jews and Russians." The list he

tabulated in his head was appallingly repetitive: "Russian prisoners, evacuated Jews, evacuated Jews, Russian prisoners, hostages shot . . . again evacuated Jews, Russian prisoners."[28]

"Russian prisoners" referred to the hundreds of thousands
of Soviet soldiers who had died in Wehrmacht captivity; they
came to the attention of German authorities in the deteriorat-
ing war situation as a potential source of prison labor. The military crisis enveloped the eastern front, while partisan activity
endangered security in western Europe, a threat the Wehrmacht
attempted to deter with the "hostages shot" in France, Yugosla-
via, and elsewhere. And "evacuated Jews": since October, the
Reich had widened the scope of the war by deporting German
Jews to ghettos in the occupied territories. "One thing is quite
certain," Moltke reflected: "the Horsemen of the Apocalypse"
provided only a foretaste of "what is ahead of us."[29]

Moltke conveyed all the bad news in letters to "Pim," his wife,
Freya, who in his absence managed the family's Silesian estate
in Kreisau with their two young sons—"How may the milk be
doing and the sheep?" he made sure to inquire. In Berlin, however, Moltke compared himself to Cassandra, the lonely Greek
priestess blessed with the gift of prophecy but afflicted with the
curse not to be heard. "Will everything go under in chaos?" the
counterintelligence officer wondered. How can "I know this and
yet sit at my table in my heated flat and have tea? Don't I thereby
become guilty too? What shall I say when I am asked: And what
did you do during this time?"[30]

These questions steeled his opposition to Hitler. Arrested for
treason in January 1944 for helping draw up plans to regenerate
Germany after the Nazis, Moltke was executed at Berlin's Plötz-
ensee Prison on January 23, 1945, at the age of thirty-seven.
Freya died in Norwich, Vermont, on January 1, 2010.

"Evacuated Jews, Russian prisoners, hostages shot"—these issues pressed the atmosphere of crisis that prevailed when Hitler returned to the "Wolf's Lair," his headquarters at Rastenburg, East Prussia, on December 7, 1941. He had come back from a quick inspection trip to Mariupol and Poltava in Ukraine to confer with his generals after the Soviet counteroffensive, which had been launched a few days earlier. According to a staff officer, discussions revealed that Hitler "does not understand the state of our troops." Everything being done was just a "patch-up job." A week later, he issued the "no retreat" order in the face of what in some sectors appeared to be a rout.[31]

After Sunday dinner, around 9:00 p.m., Hitler was informed of the Japanese attack on Pearl Harbor, a place his staff first had to locate.

News of the attack came, as it did for millions around the world, over the radio. In this case, press chief Otto Dietrich had been monitoring foreign news. "A delirium of joy embraced everyone at headquarters"—"at least as far as one could see," noted Walter Warlimont, the deputy chief of operations. The news, Warlimont added, "left the lone bystander, who even in this hour still believed to be able to see, lonelier still."

The next day, December 8, Hitler decided to declare war on the United States in common cause with Japan in accordance with the spirit, though not the letter, of the Tripartite Pact, a defensive military alliance the two powers had signed with Italy on September 27, 1940, to create the Axis. The declaration of war was to be broadcast to the world in a public address to the Reichstag. That meant Hitler had to be in Berlin, and he left by overnight train for the capital that evening, but not before ordering Germany's navy to sink on sight any American ship.[32]

Since Hitler was late composing his speech, the Reichstag convened only at 3:00 p.m. on December 11. At some point, Joseph Goebbels, the trusted adviser, suggested that the Reichstag session be used as an opportunity to update Hitler's Gauleiter, the Nazi Party's district officials, about "broad military, foreign, and domestic political problems," a meeting that took place on December 12, 1941. There were thus two events planned, the big Reichstag address broadcast over radio and the little one with Hitler's political team in his private quarters.[33]

In his capacity as president of the Reichstag, another old Nazi, Hermann Goering, opened the parliamentary session with a moment of silence in honor of German soldiers fallen on the field of battle in Russia. Hitler cited the exact number in his address: 162,314, more than double the number killed in France and Poland. "You know me, my old Party companions," Hitler began, recalling that he had "always been an enemy of half measures or weak decisions." Identifying himself as "the child of a small, poor family," in contrast to Roosevelt's "filthy rich family," Hitler spoke up for the *Habenichts*, the have-not nations who "just want to live." This was a world historical moment that would determine the "life or death" of nations, "perhaps for ever." An Axis victory would pull down the "Anglo-Saxon-Jewish-Capitalist World" so that a "better New Order in the world" might rise. What was at stake was nothing less than "a historical revision on a unique scale."[34]

Goering closed the session with the idea of the "world war in the true sense of the word," a war between "the world of construction and the world of decay." Obviously, with Germany's declaration of war, all the major belligerents around the world had joined the fight. But the words "world war" were more than a quick shorthand about global scale; they referred back to an important prophecy that Hitler had made about the international situation on January 30, 1939. In words that were quoted back many times over the following years with almost theological authority, Hitler had prophesied the "annihilation of the Jewish race in Europe" in the event of a "world war." The accent on "true" in Goering's 1941 formulation implicated "the Jewish race."

For many observers, Germany's declaration of war promised only the elongation of the front across the globe and the prolongation of the war into an indeterminate future. "The war will now drag on forever," thought Paul Schmidt, Hitler's translator.[35]

The question remains: Why did Hitler declare war on the United States? British diplomat Sir Nicholas Henderson considered the declaration of war "Hitler's biggest blunder." Sebastian Haffner, who had tracked Hitler's career since the 1930s, thought the declaration an "act of lunacy."[36] With his "obliging declaration," Hitler passed over the golden opportunity "to work incalculable mischief" with the US commitment to give "precedence to the European war." Given the emotional desire to punish Japan, Roosevelt would have found it difficult to declare war against Germany on his own.[37] In effect, Hitler invited the Allies to fight the war they preferred: Germany first. What was important to Hitler, however, was that he had taken the initiative.

The world war had come. The big declaration was delivered on Thursday, December 11: the war against the United States. The second event, the Gauleiter meeting, took place on Friday afternoon in Hitler's private apartment in the Old Chancellery. There, he announced to the leaders of his party, about fifty in number, the decision that Germany would pursue the extermination of Jews across Europe, including German Jews. This was the political initiative of the Nazi Party. Most of Hitler's remarks focused on the war situation: the Soviet counteroffensive around Moscow and the new war in the Pacific. However, the part on the Jews was in the form of a directive, not a survey. Two sources give the gist of what Hitler said: the accounts of Joseph Goebbels, the propaganda minister and Gauleiter of Berlin, and of Hans Frank, governor-general in conquered Poland. They are not stenographic reports but are consistent with one another.

Goebbels reported to his diary:

Regarding the Jewish question, the Führer is determined to clear the table. He warned the Jews that if they were to cause another world war, it would lead to their own destruction. Those were not empty words. Now the world war has come. The destruction of the Jews must be its necessary consequence. We cannot be sentimental about it. It is not for us to feel sympathy for the Jews. We should have sympathy rather with our own German people. If the German people have to sacrifice 160,000 victims in yet another campaign in the east, then those responsible for this bloody conflict will have to pay for it with their lives.

Hitler's words referred directly back to the prophecy of January 30, 1939, in which a "world war" would result in the "extermination of the Jewish race in Europe." The prophecy had been formulated in the conditional future tense. On December 12, however, Hitler spoke clearly about intentions that were going to take place: Jews "will have to pay" with their lives; their destruction must be the "necessary consequence." There were also no bounds to the action; the table will be cleared in a single, immediate sweep. And there was no room for interpretation or hyperbole since the words were categorically "not empty," or metaphorical. The destruction of the Jews would require the effort to expunge sympathy and override exceptions.[38]

Frank's report was strikingly similar. He opened his statement with the summary that "one way or another we have to put an end to them." Frank called attention to the prophecy of January 1939. There would also be no halfway measures; "liquidation" was the goal. The final step was to approach the task without false or misplaced sympathy.[39]

It is not clear whether the decision to declare war on the United States and thus establish for Germany the conditions of "a world war" was made in order to fulfill the prophecy and murder all the Jews. It is a logically compelling conclusion, but seems unlikely. However, the declaration was certainly made with the prophecy in mind. For Hitler, and National Socialists, the declaration of war and the decision to exterminate the Jews became part of a single revolutionary effort.

In the days immediately following the Gauleiter meeting, strides to solve technical issues were also taken. On December 14, Hitler met with Heinrich Himmler, Reichsführer of the SS; Philipp Bouhler, chief of the Chancellery of the Führer; and Bouhler's chief of staff, Viktor Brack, who had coordinated the T4 program in which so-called defectives had been euthanized with gas over the course of the past year. (T4 stood for the Berlin offices on Tiergartenstrasse 4, a short stroll from the Chancellery.) It was Bouhler's Chancellery team that provided the experts who set up extermination operations in 1942. Hitler's Gauleiter conference set the planning process in motion; the T4 operation in the Chancellery offices was scaled up to expedite the destruction of "the Jewish race in Europe."[40]

It is not the case that Hitler decided to murder Jews on December 12, 1941. Already in the summer of 1941, "total liquidation began in the occupied Soviet lands. Selective mass executions of those seen as 'unfit for labor'" had also taken place. And beginning in October, German and Austrian Jews were being deported to ghettos in the East—the deportations preoccupying Moltke. The difference is that after December 12, 1941, the goal of the "extermination of the Jewish race" became systematic and directed centrally from Berlin. In place was now a comprehensive program of deportation and murder on German-occupied territory in the present time of the ongoing war.[41]

What actually concerned ordinary Germans around Christmas 1941 were events unfolding on the eastern front. The reversals of fortune in the "ice-hell" of Russia were far more consequential than the public suspected even after six months of war. On the evening of December 20, listeners got a sense of the disorder when Goebbels "delivered an address over all the German radio stations," announcing "a gigantic collection of winter equipment for the armed forces" to take place the following week. Germans were told "quite plainly that the situation was critical," so much so that what soldiers needed were suitable clothes. "The speech hit the people like a bomb." Local Nazis huddled together during the holidays to stitch together "10 x 10 cm quadrants" out of wool scraps to make blankets. Civilians donated their underwear as well as shawls, shirts, and pullovers, along with vacation stuff: skis and boots. The campaign was a splendid opportunity, scoffed one diarist, for all "ladies who had received fabulous fur coats from France to donate them [back] to our soldiers." Pleased with the totals, Goebbels regarded the collection as a spontaneous plebiscite in favor of the regime. Most Germans, however, felt that they had been brushed with catastrophe.[42]

Almost every day ambulance trains pulled into the main train station in Cologne in January 1942. The casualties on the eastern front touched nearly all families in the city. Listening to the radio, people learned to expect the most "strenuous challenges" for the New Year. Hitler pledged the home front to "make every, and, if necessary, even the last sacrifice." "Today there are only duties," boldfaced Cologne's party newspaper.[43]

In many ways the mood in Germany was apocalyptic, sinister, and portentous at the same time. The public felt backed into another costly war against formidable enemies, while leaders sought to outflank crisis in one sector with more war and unbounded action against the "real" enemies. The estimations contradicted each other in the abstract but actually meshed well in the energetic offensives the Germans undertook in the months that followed in 1942.

Germany fought the war across a long series of fronts across the globe. What the Allies feared most was a gigantic pincer strategy in which the Japanese and Germans would converge on the Middle East. Hitler himself proposed "exact coordination" between the two "gigantic military powers—Japan and Germany—far away from each other but standing together in battle," so that they would be able to leverage their forces to scatter the strength of the enemies who would exhaust themselves as they lurched from one place to another. However, this was a complete "wish strategy," since there was no coordination. Hitler's scenario did describe what happened to the Germans as the Allies launched counteroffensives at the end of 1942.[44]

As an epigram for audacious thinking, Goebbels quoted Nietzsche on the day of Japan's attack at Pearl Harbor: "what doesn't kill me, makes me stronger."[45] Always widely quoted, Nietzsche provided comfort!

IN FIVE DAYS in December, from the Japanese attack on Pearl Harbor on December 7, 1941, to Hitler's December 12 decision to exterminate "the Jewish race in Europe," all the belligerents entered a long and global war in which civilians would be the most numerous victims. The war had become a brutal prolonged world conflict.

"The equation at present" was quite "unbalanced," one American observer calculated in 1941: "80,000,000 Germans in one lump + the labor of n slaves + 8 years of intense rearming and organization + frenzied fanaticism versus 70,000,000 British in 4 continents + zero slaves + only 3 years of real rearmament and no industrial mobilization + dogged determination." In this grand, horrible struggle with the big lump and its slaves, "little by little, in every country of the world, in all the great cities, and in most of the accessible villages, the sights and sounds of war were to become the commonplace of the age." Splashy posters on the walls exhorted residents in Lagos and Calcutta to organize air defense and collect war funds; newsreels in local movie theaters chatted incessantly about new offensives. "Our world has grown closer and smaller," Sierra Leone's *Daily Mail* commented. Two great alliance systems, the Axis and the Allies, based in their territories around the world, waged war so that there were few truly neutral middle zones.[46]

(The blocs were incomplete at a few points: the Soviet Union and Japan, upholding their April 1941 nonaggression pact, did not fight each other. Most South American nations were not proper belligerents in the war, which also never stamped their histories the way it did the rest of the world. In the British Dominions, in Australia, South Africa, and Canada, antiwar and antidraft sentiment dating back to World War I limited military operations. The slaughter in the trenches a quarter century earlier cast long shadows on mobilization for war in 1939.)

Most everyone in the world was pushed aside or pulled into the conflict. "The coils of war increasingly strangle the world," observed Indian nationalist Jawaharlal Nehru. Soldiers and workers wondered what kind of war it was and whose interests it was fought for and who might gain even when it became clear that the Allies would win. The war displaced people, and it blinded them, and it also created new connections between places like Calcutta and Johannesburg and Detroit because there were so many wars waged. The world war was fought among empires—the United States, Great Britain, Germany, and Japan. And it was fought as an anticolonial struggle against empire, one that would continue well beyond 1945. World War II was also a war between the "haves" and "have-nots" abroad and between privilege and persecution at home. In many ways, World War II was a race war; the terms certainly suggest so: "Japs," "yellow race," "white man," "the Jew."[47]

World War II was about territory and dominion around the globe, but it was also about forms of social and political organization and about ways of seeing detail, recognizing suffering, and narrating the whole. This reconstruction of the building blocks of life made World War II a total war, one that mustered and killed larger and larger numbers of the earth's inhabitants in radical leaps that overran wild imagination.

CHAPTER 2

Drawing a Map

Less than a generation after the "Great War" of 1914–1918, five days in December 1941 suddenly created a global conflict stretching across continents and oceans, a replay, but much bigger than the earlier conflict. It was war in almost all the known places. The Allies had already decided on a "Germany first" strategy, but the spread of Japanese attacks required recalculations. What sort of shape would the war take, and along what fronts would danger lie? Old charts to territories had to be revised and new explanations and motives crafted. The planet included a great deal of inventory that needed to be sorted. Mapmakers got to work immediately.

In his fireside chat on December 9, 1941, President Roosevelt anticipated a "long war against crafty and powerful bandits." All the belligerents saw the conflict as a struggle between one side that had grabbed power illegitimately and the other that defended rightful claims. What made the war a total war was the weaponry and all-out mobilization of civilians. The war's moral reach was also all-encompassing, as all belligerents assumed roles as guardians of freedom. With competing visions of humanity, each side protected the human against the inhuman. Allied and Axis powers escalated violence because they pursued the aim of completely destroying the wickedness of others, rather than defeating political or military adversaries. The absolute difference between oppressors and liberators or between haves and have-nots is what totalized the war. Naming the war expressed its ethical stakes.

The "Greater East Asia Co-Prosperity Sphere" became the central aim of what was officially recognized as Japan's "Greater East Asia War" a few days after Pearl Harbor. Its guardianship of Greater East Asia and fierce resistance to the usurpations of the West gave energy and coherence to the war effort. In the Japanese view, the war with the United States and Great Britain was embedded in the larger struggle for self-determination in Asia. Neither whites nor Europeans had a right to claim the planet for themselves.

Pravda, the official newspaper of the Communist Party of the Soviet Union, applied what had been the central event in Russian history, the Patriotic War against Napoleon in 1812, to the all-out defense against the German invaders in what became known as "the Great Patriotic War." It was great because everything was on the line: the lives of the people, the Soviet Union, world socialism. A Communist tyrant, Stalin emerged as a patriotic Russian leader. For the poet Olga Berggolts, writing on the day after Germany's invasion, the war changed "in a blinding flash" where "You" and "I" stood. She wrote about her new love: "on that day too I did not forget / The bitter years of persecution and sorrow. But . . . you and I are one again, as before." For the Soviet Union, the world war began when German armies crossed its borders on June 22, 1941, allowing it to demonstrate its status as victim, not aggressor, as it had been in 1939 when it had followed Germany to invade Poland.[1]

Germany's war was always the "world war," just as it had been in World War I. It described the intercontinental geography of the conflict, but buttressed as well Germany's claim to be a world power with a right to contest the imperial claims of the Allies. Underneath, the "world war" also referred to Hitler's prophecy in 1939, with the great conflagration justifying the extermination of "the Jewish race in Europe."

In his speeches before Pearl Harbor, President Roosevelt sometimes referred to a second world war, but in April 1942 he admitted "toying" with the idea of a proper name for the new conflict. Perhaps it was "the Survival War," since "this war," he explained, "comes pretty close to being the survival of our civilization," of everything "we have lived for for a great many generations." His idea generated a flurry of new submissions. Some followed up Roosevelt's emphasis on danger: the conflagration should be called the "Anti-Dictator War." Other readers saw the war as the path to a more secure, happy future. Wasn't the present conflict a "War of Freedom" or a "War of Liberty"? Suggestions also registered the scale to the war: "Total War" or simply "Your War." Former isolationists, who had warned Americans against being suckered into another conflict, poked a finger in the eye of righteous patriotism. "Franklin's Folly" and "the Great Massacre" were among their ideas. Or else the war was exactly what soldiers suspected in their gut: a "Raw Deal," which turned Roosevelt's "New Deal" inside out. In the end, Gallup polling confirmed the public's preference for

"World War II," a name that stuck. For most people, it was just "the war."[2]

World War II was appropriate: after 1941, belligerents fought across the globe, from Alaska to Madagascar. The idea of the world's war also tallied up built-up fears, resentments, and desires, recognizing the historical moment. World War II looked back to the last war in 1914–1918, which now became known as World War I, and it anticipated a possible World War III. One form that cataclysm took was repetition through serialization.

As the game of names suggested, the United States was not prepared for armed struggle. The country had to figure out its role in the conflict and its place in the world. Roosevelt tried to provide guidance when, in his fireside chat on February 23, 1942, he asked Americans to "look at your map."

The White House announced Friday morning that the president would provide a "radio report" to the nation on Monday evening at 10:00 p.m. It would be designed, a spokesman explained, "to bring home to every American community and every American worker the effect on them of battle thousands of miles away." To that end, the president urged citizens to "have before them a map of the world or a globe" so that they might better understand him. Newspapers obliged by publishing maps "to clip and save."[3]

Americans anxious to get ready for Roosevelt's fireside chat stampeded booksellers to purchase maps on Friday. They cleared out shelves by Saturday. Rand McNally's "53-by-39-inch black-and-white world map at $2, and its 50-cent pocket map of the Pacific were among the rapid sellers." *Consumer Reports* recommended "Stanford's General Map" and Hammond's *World Wide Atlas*, but warned against Woolworth's 25-cent "Fold-O-Globe."[4]

With globes spinning and maps unfolded, listeners, estimated at 80 percent of the radio audience, waited for Roosevelt's lesson to the nation on February 23, 1942. He seated himself at a desk in front of a world map so he was able to turn half around and point out locations. However, Roosevelt could not show where American troops had deployed. After Pearl Harbor, there was nothing to move around: the Philippines had all but fallen; the Japanese occupied Singapore the week before. Roosevelt asked Americans to remember Washington's Continental army, which had faced "formidable odds and recurring defeats." "Every winter was a Valley Forge," Roosevelt recalled.

The president urged Americans to draw strength from "Washington's conduct" in "hard times," but stressed that "this war is a new kind of war." Modern weaponry made it different "from all the other wars in the past." Moreover, the "broad oceans" were no longer protective barriers but "endless battlefields" so that war actually encircled the world; military fronts stretched across "every continent, every island, every sea, every air lane." For illustration, Roosevelt asked Americans to "look at your map." With his finger he drew connections that the enemies threatened to cut. He pointed to supply lines to Australia and New Zealand, to the Persian Gulf and Mediterranean, to Great Britain and Russia; if they were severed, the Axis powers threatened the Middle East, Africa, and South America. In other words, there was no hemispheric defense at all.

The message on February 23 was that security and freedom depended on deployments in faraway places: indeed, Roosevelt used the word "distant" or "distance" seven times in his speech. "Look at your map": the exercise taught Americans to think in a globally minded way.

The world on the map behind Roosevelt's desk was displayed in a conventional Mercator projection with continents anchored far from one another in a big foursquare ocean. But the point of his address was to encourage Americans to see the world at war as a matrix of interconnections across the globe. Stress on the word "globe" implied that "Mercator's projection cannot tell this story." "No one can read the map of this war until he has comprehended the fact that the world is round," asserted *Life*. During the war, a new generation of cartographers insisted on decentered perspectives that showed true distances, sizes, and relationships among land- and sea masses. Trained as an architect and working in advertising during the 1930s, Robert Edes Harrison led the way. In his view, people misread maps because they approached them from a single direction in which North was always on top. He proposed to create two-dimensional maps revealing various impressions when the globe was rolled around this way and that in order to apprehend old shapes in new ways, sideways, or upside down. The new perspectives might at first startle or look "queer," but they avoided the standard distortions of Mercator's projection.

If one drew a map of the world centered on the North Pole, the Eurasian and North American continents appeared as an interconnected landmass; on Roosevelt's map, however, Europe, North America, and Asia were all widely separated by the Pacific and Atlantic Oceans. Mercator also projected the hemispheric unity of North and South Americas. But taking Madison, Wisconsin, the hometown of isolationist leader Philip La Follette, as the vantage point, one geographer drew an arc around the world at the distance of Buenos Aires; every European capital including Moscow fell inside the arc and was closer to Madison. What is more, from Japan's perspective, Dutch Harbor, Alaska, provided a much more direct route to the United States than Pearl Harbor. Occupying Norway, Germany shortened the route to the United States over Canada. However, neither empire fully understood these relationships because they were locked into Mercator projections.[5]

Indeed, conventional maps had always worked a spell on strategists. Already in *War and Peace*, his 1869 novel about Napoleon's invasion of Russia in 1812, Leo Tolstoy warned against putting trust in maps, which promoted the illusion that "all the possibilities have been foreseen." In one scene, Russians rejected the Germans' science of war: "There was a need not to think, not to stick pins in the map, but to fight, to beat the enemy." Holed up in his military headquarters at the Wolf's Lair, Hitler absorbed himself in ever more detailed maps that simulated accuracy and control, but provided few guides to the dynamic situation on the eastern front. He ordered "divisions and battalions back and forth" like a croupier, observed one staff officer, while "losing entire armies."[6]

The world war shoved off continents to make room for the globe and, with it, dispelled conceptions of American security. "Since Dec. 7 all of us have been studying the maps," editorialized the *New York Times*. "Moulmein is no longer a word in a Kipling poem." "There is only one front in this war," the paper commented in August 1942, the one from "the Solomons to the Volga." "A battle won or lost anywhere is won or lost everywhere." One world, one war—what emerged during the war was an understanding of the planet as an integrated organ as depicted in the famous 1968 photograph *Earthrise*. "We came all this way to explore the moon," and instead "we discovered the earth," recalled Apollo 8 astronaut William Anders. A few years after the war, the prospect of nuclear war made the planet the only reference point to security: "Doom is global by definition, not national."[7]

ALL THE BIG belligerent powers conceived of space in expansive ways. Americans eventually stationed themselves physically all around the world. Every point from Guadalcanal to Stalingrad sat on the same "ever-moving, endless, and indivisible front." Of course, not everyone found their bearings. Most sailors in the US Navy had never been to sea or "seen anything larger than the Ohio River." Shipping out to New Zealand, one Marine asked: "Where the hell is that?" "I've heard of it," someone replied, "but just where *is* it?" Its location "down under" simply promoted a debate about whether the earth was flat or round.[8]

Germans groped to get their hands around the world. "We thought that comrades in Karelia or the Crimea were endlessly far away," observed Hans Schwarz van Berk in the influential weekly *Das Reich*. In the meantime, "war has charged around in the world in great leaps" that can "only be followed with the aid of a globe." "The German eye and the German ear will have to accustom itself" to unfamiliar names and places. Yet the new geography was also unsettling. The latest joke: A small-town bookseller takes down a globe and points out all the countries at war with Germany. "'Holy shit,' replies the rube, 'does the Führer know about that?'"[9]

Japanese planners had traditionally oriented themselves to the north, to the colonies in Formosa and Korea and to China and Manchuria. Foreign-language courses emphasized Chinese. With the new war, South Asia with its rich resources—oil, rubber, tin—suddenly came into view. In the five months after December 8, 1941, Japan acquired a vast southern empire the perimeter of which was many times larger than the country's old sphere of influence. Japan was poised to disrupt the "entire Indian Ocean traffic system." But empire also meant a new order of difference: Muslims in Malaya and Indonesia and Catholics in the Philippines. To familiarize readers with the new inventory, the *Japan Times* published a series of informative surveys: "The Rivers of Java," "Climate of the Philippines," "Peoples of Sumatra," "Religion of Thailand," and "Geology of India." There was even a hopeful item on Australia's koalas. Despite the helpful atlas, soldiers found these tropical places to be hot and very far from home.[10]

All the major powers in the war drafted new geopolitical frameworks to manage global space. On August 14, 1941, Roosevelt and Churchill, after a secret meeting in Placentia Bay, Newfoundland, unfurled the Atlantic Charter, which outlined the war aims of the two allies even before the United States formally joined the conflict. The goals of the war were articulated in explicitly geographical terms with worldwide implications. The charter called for the restoration of "sovereign rights and self-government to those who have been forcibly deprived of them" and looked beyond occupied Europe to the future in which "all peoples" had the right "to choose the form of government under which they will live." The Atlantic Charter quickly became a way to think about the global future.

Both Japan and Germany based their new geopolitical visions, to cite the preamble of the 1940 Tripartite Pact, on a "lasting peace" achieved by redistributing world space in "a new order of things calculated to promote the mutual prosperity and welfare of the peoples concerned." Japan's Greater East Asia Co-Prosperity Sphere arranged space for the East Asian family; Germany's Generalplan Ost, which accompanied the invasion of the Soviet Union in June 1941, modeled the "regions of Europe" on the basis of race. Yet Axis space was delimited by regional perspective in which the emphasis fell on integrating continental blocks under the leadership of a dominant power. Neither Japan nor Germany boasted Britain's "steamship, train, and telegraph lines bursting like fireworks" over the globe in a "glow of progress," nor did they develop the United States' intercontinental air routes.[11]

ON HIS VOYAGE back home from Canada after signing the Atlantic Charter on August 14, 1941, Churchill's battleship, *Prince of Wales*, caught up with a convoy of seventy-two merchant ships sailing to Liverpool. Waving from the bridge, the delighted prime minister asked the captain to go around one more time to sail right through the convoy, which "looked almost like a town." Once the sailors realized it was Churchill, "cheers rang out from every ship."[12] But just what did Atlantic cheers mean?

Introduced on the front pages of American newspapers, the eight "peace aims" of the Atlantic Charter to restore sovereign rights against foreign domination could be dismissed as a "rehash of old ideas," "platitudinous declarations" that "do not cost us anything." At the same time, "the dramatic background of powerful battleships" and "airplanes roaring constantly overhead" cast Roosevelt as a world leader committed to "the final destruction of the Nazi tyranny." In "The Rendezvous with Destiny," the *New York Times* described the fateful "play of would-be gods and self-elected giants," the only "great Powers left in the world that speak with human voices, in the name of people." And what they had to say—"That All Men in All Lands

May Live Out Their Lives in Freedom" was the caption in the *Times*—drowned "out all sounds" as far as "Dakar and Teheran." The Atlantic Charter was a "democratic bomb."[13]

The costly war had put the future of the British Empire into doubt. It was the world's largest geographic unit, encompassing 13.7 million square miles (whereas the Roman Empire stretched across 1.7 million), more than a quarter of the land surface of the earth with 23 percent of the world's population. This expanse was why Churchill was determined to bring Roosevelt into the war—even to the point of signing off on the Atlantic Charter. It was also why the Atlantic Charter took on a life of its own as Britain's imperial subjects wondered about their own freedom. When addressing West African students in London on the day the charter had been published, Deputy Prime Minister Clement Attlee was pointedly asked what people the charter had in mind. "You will not find in the declaration," he replied to "long and prolonged applause," the suggestion that "the freedom and social security for which we fight should be denied to any of the races of mankind." The *Daily Herald*, a Labour newspaper, jumped on point: "ATLANTIC CHARTER: IT MEANS DARK RACES AS WELL."[14]

In Sapele, "fifteen questioners, including a young lady, fired their broadsides at me, demanding positive proof of Britain's sincerity of purpose and whether the Atlantic Charter was applicable to Nigeria or not?" At question time, after a lecture in Warri, someone asked "whether the Prime Minister had answered my cablegram." Audiences posed "the ever recurrent question of whether the Atlantic Charter was applicable to Nigeria or no?" What Nnamdi Azikiwe encountered as he set out with his Lagos football team, Zik's Athletic Club, on a "Goodwill Tour" across Nigeria at the end of 1941 was an extraordinary chain of voices in English and Yoruba, Edo, and Igbo, about the aims of the war, the charter itself, the democratic future of Nigeria, and the "New World We Intend to Build After the War."[15]

The seven-week Goodwill Tour featured "thinly veiled anti-colonial rhetoric in the guise of pro-war support." Zik's football team, later split into the "Bombers" and "Spitfires," attracted enthusiastic crowds and netted impressive gate receipts: sixteen pounds in Sapele, nineteen pounds in Benin, and twenty-five pounds in Warri, where "Old Man Football gripped everybody, young and old, black and white, rich and poor." What the tour proved was that British West Africans "are 100 per cent behind the Empire's war effort." But it had a larger purpose. Efforts had to be made so "the Allies should win this war," but "as the day follows the night," the war required a peace in which Nigeria got "democracy in action" at "the dawn of a New Africa." At each stop, Zik argued for the credibility of the Atlantic Charter and against the notion that it was idle "Atlantic Chatter."[16]

The grandest goodwill tour promoting the Atlantic Charter was Wendell Willkie's "One World" trip around the globe in fall 1942. The circumpolar route was featured on the inside covers of his 1943 publishing sensation, *One World*, among the fastest-selling books of all time: New York, Natal, Cairo, Jerusalem, Ankara, Tehran, Moscow, Chungking. "One World" was commissioned by Roosevelt to bolster support for the Allied cause at a time when it was not clear that there would even be a Cairo or Moscow to visit. Willkie, the Republican nominee for president in 1940 who had thrown his support in favor of the president's interventionist foreign policy, came to the conclusion that "true victory meant freedom not only from fascism but also from empire." The Atlantic Charter had to apply to India and East Asia and Africa, and not simply to Europe "under the Nazi yoke."[17]

In his "Report to the People," broadcast on October 26, 1942, on all four major radio networks with more than thirty-six million listeners tuned in, Willkie confirmed that people from Egypt to China asked about the Atlantic Charter. Again the "recurrent question": Did it truly belong to them? In Willkie's "new world idea," "there is no more place for imperialism"; "the big house on the hill surrounded by mud huts has lost its awesome charm." This unity of purpose reflected "a larger map that marks a single world," one overlaying the "splotches of color" of the different territories and their separate and unequal paths. "Everybody has been talking to the common man since the war began," noted the *New York Post*; with Willkie, "the common man talked back."[18]

Churchill talked back too. When pressed at the time to offer a clear path to self-determination in the colonies, he made clear that he had "not become the King's First Minister in order to preside over the liquidation of the British Empire." Indignant, he was "not going to accept less favorable terms" from a salesman like Willkie "than I could get from Hitler." For Churchill, the Atlantic Charter protected the sovereignty of the places the Axis had trampled. Britain's stewardship of empire could not be compared to Germany's occupation of Poland despite the chorus of voices on both sides of the Atlantic demanding that individual liberties take precedence over sovereign or states' rights.[19]

In Germany, Carl Schmitt, a political theorist regarded as the "crown jurist of the Third Reich," sharpened Churchill's suspicions about unbounded American moralism. For Schmitt, the Atlantic Charter divided the world into blocs of humanity and inhumanity. In this division, the universal became a total and uncontainable force impeded only by noncompliant out-laws represented as "the inhuman enemy." Locating the violence of the war precisely in the proclamation of goodwill, Schmitt anticipated the post–Cold War critique of US human rights policy as disguised imperial thrust. By contrast, Germany, in his analysis, organized different peoples in an integrated "Grossraum," or bounded living space. In fact, the Nazis rejected both the accommodation of ethnic differences and their assimilation to a higher standard. Schmitt had only German racism to offer in place of American imperialism, murder instead of melting pots.[20]

WITH ITS DECISIVE victories in the opening phase of the Great East Asia War, Japan instantly acquired an empire of 3.3 million square miles, one of the largest in modern times. With 20 percent of the world's population, it stretched from the puppet regime of Manchukuo in the North to New Guinea in the South, from the Marshall Islands at the international date line to Burma in the West. Japan's "voice of Asia" pronounced the principle of equality: "No nation will presume to violate the freedom of another nation," "no nation will exploit another," "no nation will force its culture upon another," and "no race will consider itself superior." It heralded the emancipation of "Asiatic nations from the bondage of the white man" who, with discriminatory laws and international police forces, had enforced "the will of the few against the desires of the many."[21]

However, Japan did not conceive East Asian Grossraum to be a confederation of equals. It was a greater whole in which each part contributed to regional cooperation and prosperity by accepting its "proper place" under Japan's leadership. This idea was consistent with "Asia for Asians" but not with "Malaya for Malayans." As they established themselves in "every corner of East Asia," Japanese administrators cast themselves as both mother and father of Asia, providing spiritual guidance as well as superlative military leadership.[22]

Japan and the older colonies of Formosa and Korea formed the center of the Co-Prosperity Sphere. This prewar construct was surrounded by a zone of client states, Manchukuo and the Nanjing Chinese government and, later, Thailand, Burma, and the Philippines. Other territories such as the Dutch East Indies, New Guinea, and Pacific islands including Guam were ruled directly by the army or navy. Everywhere the Japanese extracted resources, though never enough to meet needs, and impressed local labor. Across these administrative boundaries lived East Asian people with distinct identities: Muslims in Malaya and the Dutch East Indies, Catholics in the Philippines, Buddhists in Thailand and Burma, Confucians in China. An extensive Chinese diaspora tied the ethnically diverse region together commercially. Japanese ideas of Asian space did not align with the experiences of East Asians or fix their loyalties.[23]

The Japanese aim of consolidating East Asia against the European West was shaky from the start. With its victory over the Russian Empire in 1905, Japan starred in the confrontation between the imperial West and the subjugated East, but the violence of its own colonization of Korea a few years later and its intervention in China in the 1930s tarnished its claims to benevolent leadership. After 1942, it became clear to the Asian people it occupied that Japan had stepped into the role of the Western imperialists it had vanquished, sharpening their weapons and adopting their racism. Anticolonialism served the ends of Japanese empire so that Japan could assert domination while repudiating to the West.

Yet the fall of Singapore, a strategic British Crown colony, in February 1942, had far-reaching consequences even if Japan failed to reap the advantages. The collapse of the European empires in Asia and Africa was a central event in twentieth-century history; Singapore blocked any return to the prewar world in the postwar era. When Japan tried to mobilize the national aspirations of East Asians, it found willing partners. In November 1943, at the end of the second difficult year of the war, it organized the Greater East Asia Conference in Tokyo and, with great fanfare, proposed a Pacific Charter as an alternative to what it considered a restorationist Atlantic Charter. The joint declaration recognized the principle of independence and enshrined the principle of racial equality. Ba Maw, prime minister of Burma, felt brushed by the new era: "My Asiatic blood has always called to other Asiatics." We "have come together," he said, "to the voice of our mother."[24]

The real hero of the conference was Subhas Chandra Bose, whose fight for Indian independence highlighted the ideals of the post-Western era. "Netaji" (the Respected Leader or, as detractors noted, "Führer") was lionized in the Japanese press as the most true-to-life figure of new Asia. Long a charismatic figure in Bengali politics, a former mayor of Calcutta, and leader of the Indian National Congress, Bose emerged as an uncompromising militant, determined to break with the nonviolent strategy of Gandhi in order to resist British rule at every point. His journey to the conference revealed the possibilities of Japan's Pan-Asian vision. The "one world" Bose traversed from Calcutta to Kabul and Berlin in 1941 to seek Germany's help for India's liberation and back to Tokyo and Singapore via submarine in 1943 matched the thirty-five-thousand-mile journey traversed by Wendell Willkie on behalf of the Allies.

Bose enjoyed a rapturous welcome from among the two million Indians living and working in Southeast Asia. He spoke to overflowing crowds in Singapore's Cathay Theater on July 4, 1943, a date that prompted references to George Washington, another anti-British freedom fighter. Audiences were enchanted by his escapades and aroused by his Churchillian oratory. "Give me your blood, and I shall give you your freedom," he promised.[25] In a "breath-taking display of love and admiration," supporters chanted back "Jai Hind" (Freedom for India) and "Chalo Dilli" (To Delhi).

"Netaji" became a household name throughout Asia. Japan's Tojo felled the empires, but India's Bose stood for the liberation of nations across the "Global South." In Germany, Bose consorted with exiled anticolonial fighters, including Haj Amin al-Husseini, the grand mufti of Jerusalem, and Rashid Ali al-Galyani, leader of the failed anti-British revolt in Iraq in the spring of 1941. Later on in Malaya, he raised an army of forty thousand volunteers to invade India; almost half the Indian soldiers the Japanese had captured in Singapore joined Bose—a pretty good catch. After the war, the soldier of the Provisional Government of Free India came to embody the "good Indian" as much as the patriot who contributed to the War Fund or the Congressman who demanded the British "quit India." It was precisely the outlaw character of Bose's global adventure by foot, by airplane, and by submarine that made him such an outsize figure. Today Kolkata's international airport is named after Subhas Chandra Bose.

BOSE PROVIDED A glimpse into Hitler's study when the two leaders, each one an "old revolutionary," in Bose's words, met at the Wolf's Lair in May 1942. "The furniture was simple and just enough for a small group. The walls were covered with two maps, one showing the Euro-Asian continents, and the other the war front."[26] After the invasion of the Soviet Union, Hitler gazed frequently at the maps to survey the panoramas he had opened up. He spoke to his associates on the afternoon of July 16, 1941, about the transformation of the conquered territories in the East into a "Garden of Eden."

He started to "carve up" the "huge cake." "Specifically," Crimea "has to be cleared of all foreigners," that is, the actual inhabitants, and "settled with Germans." Made "accessible by means of an autobahn," it "will be our Riviera." Another look at the map: the Baltic territories had to be "incorporated into the Reich," while "the regions around Moscow and Leningrad were to be "levelled to the ground." The basic operating procedure of the occupation was to take "all necessary measures—shootings, evacuations—we will do it regardless" (*trotzdem*). Before the vistas could be filled with German vacationers and settlers, they had to be emptied out of Jews and "natives" by means of "mass death on an epic scale."[27] Hitler's annotated maps formed the basis of Generalplan Ost.

In subsequent surveys of the eastern empire, in which the German people would have everything necessary to "assert their position in the world," Hitler emphasized that "our first task," following the example of the Romans, was "to construct roads"; "the beginnings of every civilization express themselves in terms of road construction." Along the big highways, Hitler imagined German cities placed like "pearls on a necklace," each surrounded by a "belt of delightful villages." Families would move into "handsome, spacious" residences with rooms "crawling with children." In twenty years, he estimated, twenty million people would inhabit the new territories. In three hundred years, he envisioned a "flourishing garden" of "unusual beauty" inhabited by as many as 250 million, even 600 million, Germanic settlers.[28]

It was a fantastic vision, its detail painted like a postcard down to a scale of 1:25,000.

As for "the natives"? First, and this was an inalterable element, "we will completely drive out" the Jews. Slavs would be subjugated as a native labor force or left to die. Although Hitler's longtime confederate Alfred Rosenberg argued for "fostering" Ukrainian efforts to attain "self-rule"—the transcript noted Rosenberg's "real soft spot for the Ukrainians"—Hitler was uncompromising. "We have no obligations whatsoever to these people," he insisted: "to reform housing settlements, to catch lice, to provide German teachers, to bring out newspapers—no!" It was enough to learn to read the traffic signs "so that they don't get themselves run over by our vehicles!" "There is only one duty," he continued, to make the country German and "to look upon the natives as Indians." Hitler set the tone for the murderous policies of the party apparatus, "the most voracious animal in world history." "I am as cold as ice about these things."[29]

The "natives" Hitler talked about constituted the remnant left behind, the "helots" and "slaves" to toil for the Germans. In their debates, the party's biopoliticians drew up various drafts of the Generalplan Ost, calculating that 80–85 percent of the Poles, 75 percent of the White Russians, and 64 percent of "'western' Ukrainians" would be disposed of or die out to make room for the pioneers. More than one million Jews in the Soviet Union were murdered soon after German troops entered their communities.

There were two genocides in the German empire, one carried out against Jews and one envisioned against Slavs. What characterized the Third Reich as it charged into the postwar future was an audacious and lethal sense of the possible, "regardless."

Literary guests in the East such as Ernst Jünger, a novelist scouting for the Wehrmacht, or Curzio Malaparte, writing for Milan's *Corriere della Sera*, returned home with lurid visions of death. *Kaputt* was the title of Malaparte's reportage.

There was no East Europe equivalent to Japan's East Asia. However abusive Japanese occupation authorities became, many took seriously the promotion of indigenous Asian culture. Germans never addressed foreigners as brothers, as did the Japanese. In the eastern empire, the line of separation between Germans and others was absolute. A distinction can be made between older views of "lands and peoples" and a newer Nazi one of "spaces and races." Japanese empire builders encountered "lands and peoples," whereas their Axis partners lorded over inferior races. The Nazis were so obsessed with race that they genuinely worried about the end of white rule in Asia after the Japanese took Singapore, although Hitler stopped the hand-wringing with his insistence that the struggle for "life or death" made Germans "quite ready to make an alliance with the Devil himself," pretty much what Churchill said about Stalin after Germany invaded the Soviet Union ("If Hitler invaded Hell, I would make at least a favorable reference to the Devil in the House of Commons").[30]

WITH FRIENDS LIKE the devil, the stakes of the war were considered to be enormously high. Even as racialists, each of the belligerents saw themselves as a new chartist, as a planetary visionary.

In their rhetoric and in their choice of enemies, they were all globalists. All the wartime mapmaking, the Anglo-American Atlantic Charter, Japan's Pacific alternative, and Nazi Germany's Generalplan Ost set out to recast the world according to new ideas of freedom, race, and restitution. These were causes that divided up and reconnected people across the globe. The new maps that travelers consulted as they crossed the new spaces revealed a dangerously mobilized world divided and redivided by violence that extended well beyond the struggle among the Great Powers.

CHAPTER 3

Telling a Story

A compound of events such as the five days in December pitched contemporaries into what they took to be great drama, the making of world history. "To me," remembered a young American, "World War II was like a gigantic stage production. It was as if I was a character actor on a global stage, watching this huge drama unfold around me."[1] Thinking of the war as theater and themselves as onstage, the warriors were preoccupied with turning points to orient themselves in the course of events, to measure the distance from beginning to end, from defeat to victory.

The radio, which was the way people all over the world learned about the war, intensified the sensation of performance. Whereas before the war people browsed newspapers, in the war they tuned to radios that devoted more programming to news broadcasts—in the United States, airtime devoted to news increased from 5 to 20 percent.[2] The immediacy of radio turned listeners into participants. Simulating reports from the scene, radio raised expectations about plots, turning points, and victories in accordance with the familiar staging of acts in a theater. The medium shaped the cusp of events.

"Today, we haven't gotten up from the radio at all. Papa has taken his position in front of it." That "is how we take in the beginning," wrote Isa to her husband, Fritz, in the field on the first day of Germany's invasion of the Soviet Union on June 22, 1941. And audiences stayed put. "This time," continued Isa, "*I* am the stalwart one, listening to all the bulletins." Meanwhile, in Leningrad, on the dot at 6:00 in the morning on the same day, tenants woke up to "the sound of the communal radio in the corridor." "Neighbors were already standing there half-dressed, their faces tense and eager," piecing together the announcement about the German invasion. "Five times a day," Lidiya Ginzburg remembered, "people ran to the loudspeakers." Americans joined the "stalwart" radio audiences after December 7, 1941.[3]

For all the excitement of radio transmission, the ability of war news to suddenly make ordinary days sensational was not new. More than one hundred years earlier, events had fluttered like banners announcing further installments in an unfolding story. "No, never shall I forget," recalled Germaine de Staël, "the moment when I learned from one of my friends, on the morning of the 6th March, 1815, that Bonaparte had disembarked on the coast of France" five days earlier. "I thought that the earth was about to open under my feet."[4] The news in 1815 not only felt instantaneous but was understood in a comprehensible political and historical frame.

Since ancient times, war has been compared to theater, *Theatrum belli*. The battle of ideas in World War II made the theatrical imagery even more compelling since it made rhetoric as well as force an art of persuasion. The eventfulness of the war was regarded as a legible movement in which there were opening scenes and defeats, entrances and exits, and resolutions sequenced in a series of scenes and acts. But if Shakespeare's plays had five acts, in 1942, no one knew how many there would be or which one was taking place or what side would gain the upper hand and at what cost. Indeed, there were multiple unresolved dramas: between the Allies and the Axis, between colonial powers and subject peoples, and between rich and poor and Black and white on the home front. People listened for the decisive turning points that would mark the movement from one act to another. They looked for the big picture.

Soldiers themselves disputed the panorama of action. When Paul Bäumer returned home on leave in Erich Maria Remarque's well-remembered classic novel about World War I, *All Quiet on the Western Front* (1929), he tried to tell the regulars in the tavern about the confusion prevailing in the lines. "Details, yes," replied the schoolmaster, dismissing them. "Shove ahead a bit out there with your everlasting trench warfare," he urged. "This relates to the whole," he continued, which "you are not able to judge. You see only your little sector and so cannot have any general survey." He blew his nose and finished up: "Completely rolled up they must be," the French, "from the top to the bottom."[5]

Paul was right, no? And the schoolmaster foolish? Readers have read Remarque that way, but World War II was fought in such a way that the schoolmaster would prevail and keep soldiers such as Paul oriented. Planners sought to avoid trench warfare at all costs, not only because it degenerated into a bloody war of attrition but also because it promoted a demoralizing state of mind in which the big picture had been reduced to waste products of a terrifying machinery. Much of the strategy of World War II turned on attempting to "shove ahead." At the same time, fighting a *"Bewegungskrieg"* with tanks, bombers, and submarines instead of a *"Stellungskrieg"* was also a mental effort to keep the general survey, the big picture, in view.

Every evening the political commissar of the Red Army's 38th Rifle Division at Stalingrad would take out his prop to provide the soldiers with political education. It resembled a "magician's case." "When open, the words of the Soviet military oath, presented on red velvet, could be read on the left, a command from Stalin and the portraits of Lenin and Stalin were displayed on the right." Inside were topographical surveys and a world map. "This is how it worked," explained Izer Ayzenberg, a kind of schoolmaster: "One group takes a map, hangs it up, and circles with a finger the cities that our bombers and the German bombers are attacking. The soldiers show interest in other military theaters. They ask what's happening in Tunisia, and so on. Another group is playing checkers, another is reading brochures." At one point, "the agitator asks for attention and conducts a ten- or fifteen-minute talk." What the propaganda master attempted to do with his "magician's case" was to give the "little sector" in Stalingrad world historical significance. The aim was to create a credible theater that organized local action in time and space.[6]

From the very beginning, observers scanned the horizon of war to find the turning points so that the action remained sensible and plotted. Everybody did this, but it was the Allies who, in retreat, put great stock in the idea.

For the Allies, 1942 kept deferring a dramatic turn in the course of the war against the Axis. Until the turning point, anything was possible. It was "late," the *New York Times* wrote in February, but "not too late." "We do not know when the tide will turn. It will, nevertheless, have its turning." With the resumption of the German offensive on the eastern front and the fall of Tobruk in North Africa at the end of June, the turning point seemed far off indeed. Yet the consoling idea was that one act would give way to the next. "The period immediately before us is like a dangerous rapids, full of rocks and shoals and whirlpools," but "the tide that leads to fortune or disaster is near the flood."[7]

The victorious battles in North Africa in November 1942 appeared to represent a credible turning point. Churchill remained cautious: "Now this is not the end," he said at the Lord Mayor's Luncheon at Mansion House on November 10; "it is not even the beginning of the end. But it is, perhaps, the end of the beginning." Newspapers were more confident. Since the end of the summer, "men began to talk hopefully of its turning point when it became apparent that the Germans were not going to gain their objective in Russia this year," noted the *Los Angeles Times*. With the "splendid victory" in Egypt, it discerned "the first visible sign" of "the turning of the tide."[8]

Viewing the same events, German commentators did not report on a turning of the tide. In private, they contemplated defeat for the first time. Gallows humor proliferated. The optimist pointed out, "We are going to lose the war," to which the pessimist responded, "Yes, but when?" "In 1941, we made it to Leningrad, and in 1942 to Stalingrad," went the next joke, and "now we're flat on our back" (*Rückgrat*).[9]

Publicly, however, the propaganda chief, Joseph Goebbels, labored to rally morale. He used a different set of images than did the Allies to take account of the drama of 1942. Speaking at Linz's railroad station in March, Goebbels put forward an extremely fluid view of history. Every war and every revolution demonstrated that "no great historical development is characterized *only* by successes—*victories give way to* defeats, and defeats, in turn, give way to victories." Goebbels argued that no great challenge could be achieved without "sweat, tears, and blood," borrowing and reversing Churchill's famous promise of "blood, toil, tears, and sweat."[10]

After the Allied landings in North Africa, Goebbels introduced war in "the shape of a wave." He pointed out that history proceeded in a "zig-zag," in which *precisely* the greatest victories" are preceded by "the biggest challenges." In the same speech, to the merriment of listeners, Goebbels switched to football. In the German championship series, Gelsenkirchen's "Schalke 04 is not going to be playing Kitzbühl," a minor club, "but Munich or Stuttgart or—well, I don't know the favorite teams in football so well, but along those lines." The point was to "*always* dominate the ball" and to "push the forwards and midfielders up." In those circumstances, he admitted, "there is always the danger" that the opponents achieved "a *sudden breakthrough*" to score a "lucky goal." "That is more or less the situation in North Africa." "The second half begins and in the *first* two minutes the opponent scores a surprise goal, so to speak." But "it doesn't matter" in the end; "if you are *one* goal ahead you've won the German championship."[11]

In his zigzag argument, Goebbels rejected the Allies' claim that "time works for *us!*" as they mobilized industrial resources. He explained that "time does not go to work for one or the other side." "I could just as well say that the calendar works for me, or the third-class waiting room works for me. That's just nonsense." Without quite making sense, he stiffened morale.

Yet the zigzags had a dispiriting effect because zigs and zags did not provide reliable points of orientation in the war. Hitler addressed radio audiences an unprecedented four times from January to April 1942, and the cumulative effect of his special broadcasts was to leave listeners with the impression that "the war was now only just beginning." This was so because the war seemed to have veered off course. Goebbels himself admitted at the end of the summer that "the end cannot be seen at all." The *Endsieg*, or final victory, was out of sight and out-of-bounds. The soldiers were not coming home.[12]

With Germany's invasion of the Soviet Union, along with Japan's offensive in the Pacific and the entry of the United States into the war at the end of 1941, the war seemed to lose shape and duration. It was no longer a series of German victories, 4–0 or 5–0. Given all the new factors, reported one sailor at sea, "I automatically had to think about Napoleon."[13]

NAPOLEON. IT WAS impossible not to consider Germany's invasion without thinking about Napoleon's 129 years earlier, almost to the day. Army Group Center advanced along the same road to Smolensk and Moscow as had Napoleon's armies. In a race between the two armies, Hitler reached Smolensk, 412 miles beyond the frontier, on July 18, 1941, five weeks before Napoleon who, speeding up, arrived at Borodino on September 7, 1812, while the Germans arrived only on October 11. Napoleon's bulletin reported snow on October 24, a little more than two weeks after the Germans did (October 7). Napoleon had already abandoned Moscow, which he occupied on September 14, by the time the Germans reached the outskirts on December 5. But whereas

Napoleon retreated along the main route, Hitler's armies fought along various fronts in Russia without ever getting to Moscow for three more years.[14]

Both the compelling parallels between the two invasions and the significant differences made Napoleon and Tolstoy's 1869 novel, *War and Peace*, which pulled the Napoleonic Wars through the lives of three Russian families who calculate the odds but rally to the national cause, so good to think with in 1941 and 1942. Indeed, argues one historian, the legacy of France's misguided invasion of Russia in 1812 caused the Wehrmacht's "grueling defensive battles" in December 1941 to be transformed for the record into a "catastrophe of Napoleonic proportions." In this case, facts deteriorated in fiction's light. For all the arguments for why Hitler's campaign could not be compared to Napoleon's, the leading Nazi newspaper admitted that the parallel "practically forces itself" on observers.[15]

For Wehrmacht personnel transferred to the eastern front from France, the journey among the ghosts of the *Grande Armée* had begun at Napoleon's tomb at Les Invalides in Paris where the custodian reported that more German soldiers had visited "the great Corsican" in the first year of the occupation than French visitors had in the previous ten years. Once in Russia, "Napoleon's road was our road," the cobblestones laid by the emperor's troops and the sides flanked by "centuries-old birch trees, which stood like some old, elite Napoleonic guard." At Beresina, the site of the great disaster of the retreat, memories of "old school-room pictures" inevitably "sent a small shiver down our spines." "One of the men finds a bronze eagle of Napoleon's army, half-hidden by a road near the water's edge."[16]

The creepy feeling about advancing along Napoleon's road was fully justified. Much like the *Grande Armée*, most German soldiers marched on foot followed by horse-drawn supplies. Hitler might not have been Napoleon—he insisted he wasn't—but logistics seemed similar enough. One Wehrmacht general in Russia, it might have been Fedor von Bock, asked his first lieutenant, who was planning to visit a bookstore in Smolensk, for "the thickest book about Napoleon's campaign in Russia!" "Standing before the map" in the fall of 1941, Field Marshal von Kluge was seen holding Caulaincourt's *With Napoleon in Russia*, the general's memoirs published a few years earlier. In a great phrase, novelist Herman Wouk imagined Caulaincourt's memoirs passed along "like pornography in a boys' dormitory." Already in the opening pages, before the fighting in Smolensk, the French general surveyed the "exhaustion," the "want and the piercing cold rains at night," which "killed off ten thousand horses"; "many of the Young Guard died on the road of fatigue, cold and hunger." Then there was winter, which, Caulaincourt predicted, "will come like a bombshell." "The Napoleon legend haunts us," wrote a correspondent for the German news service who accompanied the troops into the mud and rain of Russia.[17]

No text was more sought after to make sense of the war in Russia than Tolstoy's novel. Read again and again, it offered a first run of the drama in 1941 and 1942. In their own novels, Irène Némirovsky and Vasily Grossman took Tolstoy as a model for the panorama and scale of the war. It was almost impossible to find *War and Peace* in a London bookstore. No other book was checked out from Vilna's ghetto library in 1942 as often as *War and Peace*—"despite the long waiting list for the multi-volume edition." To read it offered a way to vanquish the enemy in fantasy. In James Michener's *Tales of the South Pacific*, officers and nurses bored waiting for the war on the remote island of Efate all tried to get through the acclaimed novel. The ensign "stayed in his sack for the better part of two days, reading *War and Peace*. He didn't even get up for meals." Or for volleyball.[18]

Readers picked up Tolstoy to search for clues in the novel to discern the outcome of the present-day conflagration. Many took comfort in the "popular patriotism" of the Russian people. According to Konstantin Simonov, Tolstoy answered pressing questions about "what was bravery, what was cowardice? Who were the people who really counted in war?" The reason "people devoured *War and Peace*," explained Lidiya Ginzburg, who survived the siege of Leningrad, was that the book offered "a way of measuring their own behavior" in wartime. "The reader would say to himself: Well then, so what I am feeling is right: that's just how it should be." Even the Soviet generals at Stalingrad, Chuikov and Rodimtsev, calibrated their behavior to Kutuzov's in 1812. Tolstoy provided a draft to the "Great Patriotic War."[19]

Tolstoy also provided views on the terrific violence of war, the flight of panicked civilians, the soldiers choking the roads. "On all sides," Tolstoy wrote (and Grossman would later rewrite in *Life and Fate*), "there was the noise of wheels, the rumbling of flatbeds, carts, and gun carriages, the thud of hooves, the crack of whips, the shouts of drivers, the cursing of soldiers." "On the roadsides" were dead horses, "broken-down wagons, near which solitary soldiers sat waiting for something," and the "ceaseless moan of cries."[20]

Many readers were struck by the harsh lessons Prince Andrei had learned after the battles. "Take no prisoners," the long-serving officer lectured Pierre. "The aim of war is killing," and its instruments are "the ruin of the inhabitants," to rob them in order to supply the army. "We've been playing at war," and "we act magnanimously." But war was "not a game." Soldiers made their "greatest contribution to the fatherland" by perfecting "the art of murder," commented one German reader about Tolstoy's world, and Hitler's.[21]

The fumbling search for parallels between 1812 and 1941 actually highlighted Tolstoy's basic premise about the fog of war. With the invasion of Russia, World War II entered a new phase—what Churchill remarked on as the "deep, slow-moving tides" of a long engagement—one that made Germans and other belligerents increasingly alike amid its murky motions. Soviet counterattacks put an end to the blitzkrieg campaigns. Germany's invincibility gave way to messier calculations. It was not so much that the Allies gained what Germany had lost; rather, Germany's power to dictate the terms of the war dissolved into a confused repertoire of mixed motivation, unintended consequence, and accident. The various combatants now "engaged" with one another as if they were in a heavy fog. Tolstoy's *War and Peace* seemed to be the appropriate guide to the "inexhaustible openness of events."[22] The novel conveyed drama but withheld a five-act play.

To picture the "current of life" on the battlefield, Tolstoy asked his readers to set aside theory and embed with an infantry company. What followed were among his most quotable lines. "Sometimes," he wrote, "when there's no coward at the head who shouts 'We're cut off!' and runs away, but a cheerful, bold man who shouts 'Hurrah!'—a detachment of five thousand is worth thirty thousand, as at Schöngraben." Yet "sometimes fifty thousand flee in the face of eight, as at Austerlitz." Even *Life* magazine used the hurrah scene to introduce its feature article "U.S. Army Private Charles E. Teed of Effingham, Ill.," who typified the new "draftee trained to fight." "In war, as in every practical matter," the magazine editors quoted Tolstoy, "nothing

73

can define, and everything depends on countless conditions, the influence of which becomes manifest all in a moment, and no one can know when that moment is coming."[23]

It was this sort of incalculable situation that invalidated the pretension of narrative to explain the war, just as it invalidated confidence in the ability of strategists to control the battlefield or read the map. The day after the battle, reports smoothed over what soldiers had seen and experienced, which had been "complex, infinitely varied and grim." In the end, "a general report is compiled," and, as Tolstoy recognized, "everyone is relieved to exchange his own doubts and questions for this false, but clear and always flattering presentation." Soldiers no longer "sense the raw, vital material that used to be there," since they too "narrate according to the reports." Tolstoy believed his achievement in *War and Peace* was to undermine the acknowledged authority of the war story.

Tolstoy was suspicious of narrative because it "falsely imposes causal determinism and sense-making devices onto the violence of war." "If we allow that human life can be governed by reason," he asserted, "the possibility of life is annihilated." Like the plan before the battle, the cleaned-up narration of its conclusion deleted all the "villainies, deceptions, betrayals, thefts, forgeries" and the "cheerful, bold man who shouts 'Hurrah!'" and thereby deleted life itself.[24]

In many ways, the Germans were betting against the novelist and his refusal to let the hero bend the enemy and achieve victory. Clifton Fadiman put it this way in his introduction to Simon and Schuster's new wartime edition of *War and Peace* in 1942: If Hitler "should fail, a new Tolstoy may arise fifty years hence to chronicle the vast drama of his rise and fall." But if Hitler "should succeed, that new Tolstoy will not arise. For there will be no novelists and no poets."[25] The successful execution of deliberate force would annihilate "the possibility of life," the hurrahs and deceptions. Reading Tolstoy revealed how the war shaped the very conception of the story of the war.

Yet *War and Peace* also missed the war. It had nothing to say about fundamentals in 1941 and 1942. There was nothing in the events of 1812 that could compare to the Third Reich's violence against Russian prisoners-of-war or the implementation of the "Final Solution" against Jews. Pairs such as Pierre and Platon, French and Russians, and "Aryans" and Jews could not easily stand in for one another. The idea that action was the amalgamation of the trivial and ordinary on all sides, the proposition that "only unconscious activity bears fruit," and hence the assertion that "no one could be guilty" fortified in a logical way Tolstoy's resistance to the efficient role of the plan. But it offered no guidance to the material of 1942: documented state-sponsored plans to murder civilians in the communities where they lived.[26] Smolensk was not like Smolensk.

Theater rested on resolution. Time was on the side of the Allies with their industrial capacity, but "victory watchers" looking for turning points also realized that the war would go on for a very long time. The gross extension of the fighting time revealed scarred and nightmarish terrain that made it difficult to see its satisfying end. Even as the war in 1942 compelled people to take sides, its advance tilled more and more ruins that harvested neither total victory nor utter catastrophe. Civilization was not destroyed, and the earth did not burn up. As philosopher Maurice Blanchot surmised after the war, "There is disaster only because, ceaselessly, it falls short of disaster."[27]

On February 8, 1942, as a result of daylight saving time, Americans advanced their clocks from 2:00 a.m. to 3:00 a.m.

"Alarm clocks in the dark morning hours were a constant reminder that the nation was at war."[28] Fast-forward, people remained in the dark.

ACTION AND THE acts of the play, location, and its place on the map did not complement one another in World War II. In the field, the dramatic sequence of events that led to resolution broke down from the start. Drama self-destructed into waste, but there was always a longing for the big picture and the meaning it conveyed. One of the reasons readers turned so compulsively to the literature of war was that it shuttled between the chaos of the battlefield and the order of the salon.[29] A novel such as Tolstoy's depiction of war *and* peace mocked guides and maps while disclosing the authority vested in them.

In the action, Tolstoy repeatedly shows the warriors crossing the next river, sometimes to be swept away by the current, with each scene widening the scope of the war, elaborating on motive, and simultaneously withholding further clarity or potential resolution. "On the twelfth of June," he wrote about the prelude to war in 1812 in the opening of "Part Three," "the forces of western Europe crossed the borders of Russia, and war began—that is, an event took place contrary to human reason and to the whole of human nature. Millions of people committed against each other such a countless number of villainies, deceptions, betrayals, thefts, forgeries," such "as the annals of all the law courts in the world could not assemble in whole centuries, and which, at that period of time, the people who committed them did not look upon as crimes."[30] The road of the war led straight on to a fast-moving, dizzying, terrifying carnival of circumstance.

The first stop was unscheduled: Singapore.

PART II

MOVEMENT

CHAPTER 4

"Road to Singapore"

In March 1940, Paramount released *Road to Singapore*, a film that "lodged Singapore in the world's imagination" as a tropical back lot for young adventurers. Starring Bing Crosby, Dorothy Lamour, and Bob Hope, it was the first of the popular "Road" movies and launched Hope's career. Short on money, Josh (Crosby) and Ace (Hope) never make it to Singapore, but they reach an island somewhere in the "South Seas" where both fall in love with the "inevitable native girl" dancing "in the inevitable sarong in the inevitable cabaret." The "amiable nonsense" (the *New York Times*) did not make much money, though Crosby's song "Too Romantic" proved to be a hit for Decca Records. It was the Japanese Imperial Army that produced the surprise hit "Road to Singapore" the following year with the invasion of British Malaya on December 8, 1941. It was a fast-paced production, tearing away what was amiable and familiar and tossing aside the inevitable. The Japanese raced down the Malay Peninsula from the less well-defended North to conquer the prized British colony and the lucrative port of Singapore.[1]

"The road to Singapore" will be no "open highway," the *New York Times* assured, but on February 15, 1942, the Japanese grabbed the city. "Fancy 550 miles in 55 days," reflected Australia's General Gordon Bennett, "chased by a Jap army on stolen bikes without artillery." "The whole thing is fantastic," the charge down the road surrounded by "impenetrable jungle" ending with the capture of the "impregnable" island fortress at the southern tip of the peninsula—his notes sound a bit like the movie. With stout-hearted melancholy, Bennett's own troops took up one of the movie's songs, the jaunty march "Sweet Potato Piper" to accompany their retreat. For the fifteen thousand Australians taken prisoner, and for the families of the thousands who died in Japanese captivity, the "Road from Singapore" was long and bitter, demarcating Great Britain's betrayal of the dominion.[2]

The Road to Singapore was also paved in the United States. By 1941, the US automobile industry had fully recovered from the Great Depression; 3.6 million units were sold in that breakout year. When Pearl Harbor was attacked, almost every American household owned a car. The new global demand for automobile tires planted Malaya's vast rubber plantations. In 1900, 40,000 tons of rubber, mostly from Brazil and Africa, satisfied the world's needs. By 1920, global production had increased to 354,000 tons. British investment poured into the colony; a north–south railway opened in 1909, and the trunk road to Singapore, which connected the larger cities across dozens of bridges, was completed in 1939 at which time Malaya produced most of the world's rubber with about half of the 600,000 tons exported to the United States. Inside a generation, the colony had become one gigantic plantation with a half-million mostly Indian workers supplying the labor for rubber production. Indians and Eurasians staffed the built-up administration, railways, and customs, while Chinese businessmen dominated the mercantile sector. As a result of the influx of migrants, Malayans became a minority in their own country, constituting just under half of the colony's five million inhabitants. Sixty thousand Europeans, mostly Britons, sat at the top of the colonial heap. "If India was the jewel in the imperial crown," Malaya was the "industrial diamond."[3]

Journalists crowded the Road to Singapore to cover the story once the British came to "consider themselves on the verge of war with Japan." The Japanese occupation of southern Indochina on July 28, 1941, established a forward base with 140,000 troops for offensives against the Dutch East Indies as well as Malaya. A retaliatory embargo on American oil exports to Japan four days later raised the question of US intervention in the Pacific conflict. Beginning in August 1941, journalists such as Cecil Brown (CBS), O'Dowd Gallagher (London's *Daily Express*), Ian Morrison (the *Times* of London), Harry Standish (*Sydney Morning Herald*), and George Weller (*Chicago Daily News*) collaborated on one of the largest literary documentations of the war: the fall of Singapore, Japanese domination of the Pacific, and the end of British imperial rule.

The story was always about empire. There was the advance of the Japanese on Western imperial outposts (the occupation of Hong Kong on December 25, 1941, and Manila on January 2, Singapore on February 15, Batavia on March 5, and Rangoon on March 8, 1942), but there was also the collapse of the plantation. "Britain's Greatest Defeat," "The Battle That Changed the World," as noted in titles, was both military and political or imperial. As a result, Raffles Hotel and the New World amusement park (and its companions, the Happy World and the Great World) got as much attention as the naval base at Sambawang or the airfield in Khota Baru. The dinner guests in formal wear, the "boys" to fetch *stengahs*, and the taxi dancers on the side figured as much in the journalism as soldiers and pilots and sailors. Reginald Dorman-Smith, the British governor of Burma, called the journalists who had descended on the colonial cities "vultures" who feasted on the dying flesh of "gin-swillin' pucca sahibs."[4]

Already for Phileas Fogg, propelled "around the world in eighty days" by Jules Verne in 1872, Singapore was "like a park with lovely paths cutting through it." Following in Fogg's tracks sixty years later, Jean Cocteau found the jungle to be "trained, domesticated": "Everywhere one comes on playing-fields, tennis-courts, football and baseball grounds. Crowds of people lounge on lawns facing the sea." The Crown Colony was a triumph of "refrigeration and airconditioning": the new restaurant in Robinson's Department Store was air-conditioned, and so was the Cathay Cinema. With temperatures in the nineties, most Europeans started work early, and by five o'clock it was *pahit* time during which Chinese "boys" rushed from table to table serving gimlets and *stengahs*—the half measure of whiskey and soda. The war in Britain with rations and bombs "seemed a million miles away."[5]

Behind the "orderliness" of the colonial capital on the waterfront was an enterprising city of extravagant contrasts. Phileas Fogg, on his way to Hong Kong, noted that "a large number of passengers had come on board in Singapore—Hindus, Delonese, Chinese, Malays, and Portuguese." Onshore was the Indian neighborhood "with peppers and curry and tropical fruits" and Chinatown with its narrow lanes in a "tangle like snakes and ladders on a game board."[6]

The green parcels of the plantations and the colorful cities enforced an overwhelming separateness. Visitors could wander about Chinese neighborhoods for days without seeing a single "white face." And British residents in Singapore spent their time among themselves at the hotels and clubs in which only servants crossed the color bar. Europeans sat on one side of the football field; non-Europeans stood on the other. Neither the highest Malay civil servants nor the wealthiest Chinese businessmen had entry to the club, the "spiritual citadel" of British power precisely because, as George Orwell noted, the talk in these "Kipling-haunted" places revolved around encroachments on the whites. "Except for a measure of superficial cordiality," concluded Malaya's largest Chinese-owned newspaper, "the segregation of the races in every sphere of life" in this country was "complete." Europeans knew Singapore with a clear map of "chinks, drinks, and stinks" in their minds.[7]

Visitors found it difficult to "assimilate" to the British custom "to have every demand gratified by shouting 'boy'": "One whisky water, three gins, and jump to it, boy!" The role of the master and the place of the servant turned into a kind of household drama in the Malay phrase book for "mems": "This is not clean," "Wash these plates," "Wash them again," "Wash it properly"; "Come here," "Go there." The adult Chinese "boy" served as a butler in the household alongside the Javanese *ayah* (nanny), the Malay *syce* (chauffeur), and the Indian *kebun* (gardener). When in January 1942, the "boy" was injured by shrapnel while on an errand, his employer had trouble locating him in the hospital because "we didn't know his name."[8]

Europeans and Asians mingled in the "Worlds," the gaudy entertainment parks in Chinatown, but relationships were transactional. Almost all visitors to Singapore and soldiers on leave visited the cabarets and dance halls of the Worlds, but these somewhat disreputable places were not where European residents would take their wives or business associates. The nights were loud and smoky. Announcements broadcast in Malay, Cantonese, and English, and visitors danced to Filipino jazz bands and drank Tiger beers, while Chinese girls sang Hollywood hits. "Dance and Drink in Untiring Comfort," advertised the New World Cabaret; "Crowded Nightly!" it always "accommodated more people than anywhere else." At tables along the edge of the dance floor sat the taxi girls who against a twenty-five-cent ticket would dance a quick number.[9]

"This is Singapore," a combination of the Malay words for lion (*Singa*) and city (*Pura*). After journalists settled into Raffles or the Adelphi Hotel, they attended their first military briefing. The defense line seemed as tidy as the color bar, but most war correspondents salted the confidence of the authorities with private doubts. Reporting for the *New York Times* from China, Hallett Abend returned to the United States via Singapore in 1941. He passed on the conventional wisdom that the naval base and land fortifications made Singapore "nearly impregnable." However, poking around, Abend realized Malaya's vulnerability to an attack in the North across the Gulf of Thailand from Japan's air bases in Indochina. He predicted the course of attack: an attack on airfields such as Kota Bharu on the gulf or Alor Star near the Thai border would provide launching bases for a land offensive down the Malay Peninsula to Ipoh, Penang, and beyond: "If the Japanese should attempt a land drive upon Singapore," he noted, "those names will appear as frequently in our newspapers" as other war-torn towns around the world.[10]

According to the American military liaison, the British believed Singapore's military value lay in "the illusion of impregnability built up in the Japanese mind." Or the bluff rested on the illusion that any invasion could be held off until British or US warships arrived. But bluff was not strategy, and, observers pointed out, the naval base was a base without a navy, "sentry boxes without sentries." When CBS's Cecil Brown went to see the base for himself, he stood in the deep grass on the northern perimeter of the island and realized that the guns "point out to sea."[11] There were no fortifications of any kind on the Johore Straits separating the island from the mainland.

The background music to the military briefings was the contrived upbeat of war news from Europe. "German Military Power Is Weakening Noticeably," reported the *Straits Times* at the beginning of September 1941, by which time, the paper claimed, German casualties in Russia totaled 2.5 million, a figure it doubled to six million at the end of November. "In Europe you can sense the impending victory," wrote columnist John Gordon as the Wehrmacht approached Moscow. "No one in Britain doubts it." "Against the rock-like defense of Russia," "the rat is now throwing himself against the bars." "His day is racing to an end."[12] It was newsreel confidence.

All this was compounded by the persistent mockery of Japanese abilities. For many observers, the overriding fact was that the Japanese "could not beat China for five years." Most notorious was contempt for "Japan's bush-league air force." As one of the "economically weak states," a premise that disregarded the country's massive investment in heavy industry and its skilled workforce, Japan was considered deficient in aeronautical skills.

Hallett Abend disputed the assessments. He thought it "nonsense" to contend that the Japanese could not fly as well as Americans. Indeed, given the number of Japan's combat-ready bombers and fighters and large numbers of trained pilots, American strength "certainly does not seem formidable." Since the British believed that talented horsemen (and good breeding) made good pilots, there seemed little reason to rate Japanese flying ability that experts believed to be further impaired by the position of the eye sockets and the habit of wearing glasses.[13]

With the long-delayed arrival, a week before Pearl Harbor, of the British fleet at the naval base—the battle cruisers *Repulse*, which had been laid down in 1916, and the newly commissioned *Prince of Wales*, on which Churchill had sailed to Placentia Bay in August, in addition to four destroyers—the gloom of war receded. "Never before surely can two ships of the Royal Navy have been more welcome nor given more confidence," wrote a cheered Megan Spooner, the wife of Rear Admiral "Jack" Spooner, on December 2.[14]

The new confidence rested on old illusions. No aircraft carrier had been assigned to Force Z, and none was available: *Indomitable* had run aground in Jamaica on its maiden voyage on November 3, 1941, and *Royal Ark* had been sunk off Gibraltar ten days later. Early on Monday morning, December 8, Japanese bombers smashed the spirit of self-assured revelry and launched an invasion of Kota Bharu in the northeast, just as Abend had predicted. The bombs they dropped on Singapore "cut across the stillness of the tropic night like some frightful oath uttered in a polite drawing room," reflected Ian Morrison of the *Times*.[15]

In the beautiful "twilight of Monday, December 8th," as "the bright-red sunset silhouetted the palms on the shore," the battleships steamed out of the naval base to engage the Japanese up the coast. The captain of *Repulse* notified the company: "We are off to look for trouble. I expect we shall find it." For too long "the old ship" had been "deprived of her fair share of hitting the enemy."[16]

Spotted by Japanese aircraft, Force Z turned back to Singapore on the evening of December 9, but maintaining radio silence the commander refrained from calling in air support to engage potential Japanese bombers. Soon after eleven in the morning the next day came the attack launched by the 22nd Naval Air Flotilla based in Saigon: "I see them: 1, 2, 3, 4, 5, 6, 7, 8, 9," Cecil Brown wrote furiously. "The nine Japanese aircraft are stretched out across the bright blue, cloudless sky like star sapphires of a necklace." Over the next half hour, torpedo bombers commenced a second attack and then a third in which three torpedoes found their mark. *Repulse* listed and was abandoned; Brown's colleague O'Dowd Gallagher was "able to walk down the side of the ship to the sea," dropping into "the still-spreading fuel oil." Adrift in the South China Sea, Gallagher could see that the *Prince of Wales* had lost power and its ability "to beat off the determined killers who attacked her like a pack of dogs on a wounded buck."[17]

When the news of the loss of the capital ships reached Singapore that evening, guests deserted the veranda of the Raffles Hotel "as though the last waltz had just been played." "From Africa eastwards to America through the Indian Ocean and Pacific we have lost command of the sea," noted the chief of the Imperial General Staff. "I put the telephone down," remembered Prime Minister Winston Churchill after the war, and "I was thankful to be alone. In all the war I never received a more direct shock." As he turned and twisted in bed, "the full horror of the news sank in upon me."[18]

The fall of Penang, Britain's oldest colonial possession in Southeast Asia, occurred a little more than a week after the sinking of *Repulse* and *Prince of Wales*. It was now evident, as headlines in the *Straits Times* conceded: "SINGAPORE REAL ENEMY OBJECTIVE." The newspaper put on a brave front. The "news is not good," but "it is not such as to justify any feeling of despair."[19]

In the meantime, Raffles advertised its traditional holiday dinners and dances from "8 pm to Midnight" as well as its "Special New Years Eve Dinner & Dance." In 1941, however, it announced "Fancy Dress Optional." Robinson's Department Store advertised as well. "Have you seen our new windows," it asked readers two weeks after the bombings. "They are 'Renaissance' Meranti Calico—Cool and hygienic—our Silverware Dept. is completely reorganized. Our Ladies' Dept. has been changed around. Our Toy Dept. is doing well. Our Café is <u>still</u> air-conditioned via the window frames. We still have the red carpet down and we can still give you that famous 'Robinson's Service.'" The emphasis in the press was on "business as usual." The Japanese mocked this show of imperturbability: "You English gentlemen," they broadcast from Penang. "How do you like our bombing? Isn't it a better tonic than your whisky soda?" (Soda tonic—the Japanese never got it quite right.)[20]

One surprise followed another, but colonial life was imperturbable until it ceased to exist.

Masanobu Tsuji, an operations officer for General Tomoyuki Yamashita's 25th Army, described the initial invasion force as a "scratch team" whose deployment in Malaya was planned only in September 1941. However, officers were carefully selected from among battle-tested veterans serving in China. Tsuji set up a training school in Taiwan where even under the pressure of time he put officers and engineers through the paces of handling infantry, artillery, and bicycles in the jungle areas of the island. The training laid the foundations for the army's "brilliant improvisation." This was not "the hideous efficiency of the Japanese war-machine," as Churchill believed, yet the concert of Japanese actions and their speed and mobility clearly revealed "hideous" deficiencies in the war-making capacity of the British against a determined foe.[21]

The Japanese planned a two-pronged attack on British positions in northern Malaya. The first was an amphibious assault on the beaches of Kota Bharu, which means "little fort" in Malay, to secure the airfield. Launched in the early-morning hours of December 8, 1941, eighty minutes before the attack on Pearl Harbor, it was one of the most difficult assaults in the campaign; rough water, concerted machine-gun fire from Indian defenders along the shore, and effective air strikes delayed the landing at the cost of 320 Japanese dead, about 10 percent of the total number of soldiers killed in the entire campaign. By the end of the day, however, the Japanese had put sufficient numbers on shore to break the defenders; the airfield was abandoned with its runways intact and the town occupied the next day.

The second major prong was an attack on the southern Thai town of Singora on the Kra Isthmus that put the Japanese in the shortest striking distance of the air base at Alor Star and the main western road down the peninsula.

By the end of the first day, December 8, the Japanese had gained the initiative; most ominously, they had destroyed the majority of Royal Air Force (RAF) aircraft stationed in northern Malaya. No wonder the air arm was called "Rare As Fairies."[22] British troops who had been dispersed across central and northern Malaya to protect the airfields had neither airfields to defend nor air support to cover their operations. The whole premise of British strategy, which was to engage an invading enemy, was found to be completely hollow. In twenty-four hours, the Japanese had landed twelve thousand troops as well as four hundred trucks and tanks.

The Japanese assault on British positions in northern Malaya set the pattern for the rest of the campaign all the way to Singapore. The idea was to use jungle terrain to make up for the initial disadvantage in numbers. The attacker had the upper hand in the jungle: dense vegetation restricted visibility, which facilitated the movement of small formations around and even through static defenses, while the defenders had difficulty making effective use of artillery and coordinating troops to protect flanks or position reserves in depth. Since the Japanese operated in small, almost self-sufficient units, they were not tied to the roads as were the more motorized British infantry. By taking roundabout routes and launching night attacks, the Japanese spooked the British, whose senior officers attempted to hold the line, so much so that sergeants refrained from "playing hide-and-seek with the enemy in the bush."[23]

It was "a conflict between puzzled elephants and tribes of agile, inventive monkeys," thought Molly Panter-Downes, who reread Kipling's *The Jungle Book* for her *New Yorker* pieces. If the Japanese "come up against heavy opposition," the correspondent wrote indignantly, "they make no attempt to launch a frontal assault but creep round and attack from a flank. Similarly, when our troops advance, the enemy disappears into the jungle on either side." *Jungle Book* monkeys kept the pressure on the colonial elephants.[24]

What accelerated the "driving charge" down the north–south road were the extensive use of bicycles and the efficient deployment of engineers. "A division was equipped with roughly five hundred motor vehicles and six thousand bicycles," recounted Tsuji. This meant that "wherever bridges were destroyed, the infantry continued their advance, wading across the rivers carrying their bicycles on their shoulders" while sappers made repairs. That one of the main Japanese exports to Malaya and Burma was bicycles meant units could find spare parts and mechanics along the way. After they abandoned their trucks on the road, the British were forced to retreat or regroup on foot.[25]

Once the British forces were swept up in a general retreat, the only possible strategic decision was how to pace the withdrawal in order to gain time for reinforcements, although it was never clear who would come. Debates turned on "how much to mass forward, how many losses to endure, and then how quickly to retreat." Some commanders favored a retreat in "long steps" back to a fortified rear position from which to launch a strong defense. By contrast, Lieutenant General Arthur Percival, the general officer commanding Malaya, tended to contest "every bend in the road," retreating only "as the situation developed." On the island of Singapore itself, Percival's idea of fighting on the perimeter instead of withdrawing to more defensible ground prevailed. He regarded his task as "to hold this *fortress* until help comes—as assuredly it will come."[26]

Churchill demanded a last stand in the streets and on the beaches of Singapore. As he cabled his commanders on February 10, 1942, "there now must be at this stage no thought of saving troops or sparing the population. The battle must be fought to the bitter end at all costs." In fact, in the councils of war, Churchill had left no doubt about the centrality of the Mediterranean, not the vital importance of Singapore. "On no account must anything which threatens in the Far East divert us from this prime objective," he wrote in a March 1939 memorandum. Singapore's "bitter end at all costs" was a call not "to withstand a long siege" but to resist long enough to have died nobly, to preserve "the honor of the British Empire" and "our race."[27] The troops caught on, as one soldier volunteered:[28]

Never before have so many
Been fucked about by so few
And neither the few nor the many
Have fuck all idea what to do

The city came under constant artillery shelling from across the Johore Straits. Aerial bombardment continued as well. "Hardly a street did not have its gaping hole or a jagged dusty run to mark the path of a bomb or shell."[29] Hospitals and schools filled with casualties. After basic services broke down, Percival signed Yamashita's terms of surrender in the evening of Sunday, February 15, 1942, at the Ford factory on Bukit Timah Road. Nearly one hundred thousand British, Indian, and Australian troops, most of them dirty and hungry after the long retreat down the peninsula, were taken prisoner. Although exhausted and nearly out of ammunition themselves, the Japanese had won the military engagement against the British and acquired the economic resources of Malaya and geopolitical advantages of Singapore, which they renamed Syonan, "Light of the South."

Three additional scenes indicate the wider context of colonialism that justified, energized, and extended the world war. The treatment of Europeans, Indians, and Chinese theatricalized an often gruesome sorting process based on race and nationality.

After conquering Singapore, Japanese military authorities operated with the same racial categories that had characterized the old colonial economy. Europeans, both prisoners-of-war and civilians, remained separated from the rest of society, but now jailed as dishonored vanquished overlords. Indians, a largely immigrant laboring class, gained most favored status, as the Japanese promoted the cause of India's independence.[30] Making up the large majority of Singapore's population and regarded by the Japanese as economically indispensable but politically unreliable, the Chinese received both the carrot and the stick, mostly the latter. Malays were generally left alone, although attempts were made to broaden their acceptance of the Japanese way by appealing to their Asiatic identity and culture. Eurasians remained an in-between group, "blacky-whites." They still aroused suspicion, not on account of their blackness but for their whiteness, an emblem not of miscegenation but of misplaced loyalty.

On the morning of Wednesday, February 17, the Imperial Army assembled British and Australian soldiers on the downtown Padang (a kind of imperial playground surrounded by the buildings of colonial power) and marched them along Changi Road to Changi Prison on the eastern end of the island. Nearly all the hundred thousand military personnel from across the empire committed to Malaya had been captured, a stunning number and about 1 percent of the entire strength of the British army at the time.

The march to Changi was a scene the Japanese captured for posterity. Illustrating the false superiority of Europeans, it introduced the new history of East Asia the Japanese believed they were writing. A Japanese diary picked up on a battlefield much later revealed the new picture book. Aside from the "usual items"—maps, war songs, imperial proclamations—the diary included "a painting by the war artist Tsuruda Gorō of British and Australian troops, naked to the waist, sweeping the streets of Singapore—masters of the East performing the most menial tasks." Sketches of "British POWs, head and shoulders" and a portrait of the "triumphant Yamashita facing Percival across the surrender table" filled other pages. Such images of the white man circulated throughout South Asia during the war. For captors and captives, the march of prisoners displayed how the race war had remade Asia.[31]

At two o'clock in the afternoon on the same day, February 17, the Japanese separated Indian soldiers and officers out from the British and Australians with whom they had fought, gathering them in Singapore's Farrer Park. After a British officer handed over the jurisdiction of the prisoners-of-war to the Japanese Imperial Army, Iwaichi Fujiwara, an ambitious intelligence officer responsible for relations with nascent independence movements in Asia, addressed the prisoners in an effort to recruit them into the new National Indian Army (Azad Hind Fauj). Fujiwara, who styled himself as a "Lawrence of Arabia" for East Asia, explained that "Japan is fighting for the liberation of the Asiatic nations which have been for so long trodden under the cruel heels of British Imperialism." He presented Japan as "the liberator and the friend of Asiatics." The offer was to collaborate with the Japanese on behalf of India's independence.[32]

A mixed reaction greeted the announcement of the newly formed Indian National Army. Shouts of "*Inqilab zindabad!*" (Long live the revolution!) could be heard, but the crowd was mostly silent. On February 17, Indian soldiery divided itself into two groups along lines of loyalty to the empire and aspiration born of resentment as its subjects, and also in accordance with family tradition, rank, and religion. Of the fifty-five thousand men at Farrer Park, twenty thousand signed up to join the liberation army; the rest were marched off to prisoner-of-war camps, although over the course of the year another twenty thousand enlisted, about 70 percent in all. The figure is high, an indication of anti-British feeling but also of the practical desire to stay out of a prison camp.[33]

Pro-independence Indians in Malaya found the new setting congenial. Just days after the beginning of the Quit India movement, Indians held "bumper protest meetings." Flocking to Farrer Park on August 12, 1942, "patriotic Indians gathered amidst deafening cries of 'Gandhi' and 'Down with Britain.'" The streets of the Indian quarter "were crowded with Indians wearing clean white 'Khadi' clothes and putting on the famous 'Gandhi' caps." Japanese occupation provided Indians public space and voice. As the *Shonan Times* put it two months later, "Gandhiji's Birthday Celebrated as Never Before in Malaya."[34]

The Asians the Japanese proposed to liberate were themselves infiltrated with traitors, namely, Chinese patriots who feared the Japanese more than they disliked the British. On Wednesday, February 18, the Imperial Army ordered a sweep to clear out anti-Japanese elements in the Chinese community in what has become known as *Sook Ching*, or purification through purge. The administration of rough, murderous justice continued for weeks. A full-scale campaign in newspapers and on the radio ordered the registration of all "overseas Chinese" at five assembly points across the island in order to screen the population. The *Kempetai*, the security police attached to the Imperial Army, pretended to separate out particular individuals for reasons of "military necessity," but the arbitrariness of the process indicated a broader policy of retribution directed against the entire Chinese community. Nor was the press coy about the "purification" that advertised a world divided between ethnic friends and foes: Singapore "will very soon be wiped clean of all disturbing elements, including Chinese merchants hostile toward Japan."[35]

In Japan's empire as in Germany's, deportation was used as a euphemism for murder. Authorities also relied on denouncers whose nods and gestures sufficed to detain thousands of businessmen, shopkeepers, and schoolteachers as well as individuals who simply signed their names in English. Japanese policemen working for the *Kempetai* themselves realized the capriciousness of the screening process. Chinese who appeared on lists that the *Kempetai* had drawn up were immediately taken away. The rest of the detainees had to wait long hours before walking past the hooded informers. "Who could know who was good or bad!?" wondered one official. When he appealed to superiors, he found them "unbending": in a military operation, "this was not the time to think of military laws, or hold conferences to discuss the for and against." Following orders, the officer and his company of auxiliary police hauled the victims away and "slaughtered them down on the beaches."[36]

The horrifying scenes alarmed otherwise sympathetic residents. A leader of the local Indian Independence League asked whether the Japanese army had "lost its mind." "The British had already surrendered and the war was supposed to be over!" "The residents of Singapore and Malaysia respected the Japanese soldiers' bravery and their fine policy to liberate and protect the natives," he acknowledged. However, "regard for the Japanese army has turned into fear." The *Sook Ching* was the "biggest blot" on the Japanese in Malaya, concluded one of Yamashita's generals after the war.[37]

Officially, the Japanese admitted to killing some six thousand Chinese residents in the *Sook Ching*—in itself a mass killing. The Chinese community put the figure as high as fifty thousand. One historian places the number "near 25,000."[38] Whatever the figure, it was proportionally higher than the number of Poles murdered by the Germans in Warsaw during the first year of occupation, 1939–1940.

A new world stage emerged in Singapore's midday sun early in 1942. All the air-conditioning had broken down. The disarmed imperial soldiers, the newly ratified liberation fighters, and the massacred ethnic emigrants on the beaches signaled the real collapse of crucial structures of the British Empire that, in the short term, was supplanted by a much more abusive regime but, ultimately, opened the way to new forces shaped by the promise and the violence of national and racial self-determination against foreign domination of any kind.

AS THE WORLD watched the Japanese army conquer Malaya, it believed the pages of history had turned. "With an ear-splitting roar," novelist Hino Ashihei remarked, "we heard the old nation of Britain collapse." The future was open: "The sky of East Asia has been cleared once and for all." "For the untold millions of peoples" of Asia, half the world's population of two billion, the *Japan Times* explained, the victory in Singapore ensured that they "might be free!" The war has "only just begun," promised Premier Hideki Tojo.[39]

The Japanese exulted in their new roles on the world stage. On February 18, thousands of residents in Tokyo streamed into Hibiya Park to celebrate the victory. Crowds also gathered at the nearby Imperial Palace where, on the bridge over the moat,

Emperor Hirohito took his horse White Snow to accept the "Banzai!" accolades of his people. From this moment of victory, remembered French journalist Robert Guillain, bowing "became a kind of national tic" whenever people passed the Imperial Palace. "This little operation took place every day, anywhere, at any time, on every occasion," even in a trolley crossing Tokyo where "carloads of passengers suddenly rose and, standing in their places, made their little bow." There were "bows at the beginning of every show in the theaters, when the whole audience bobbed in a single movement toward a point on the wall marking the direction of the palace" and bows "to a wounded veteran dressed in a white kimono, to the draftees escorted to the station by their families, to soldiers returning from the front with urns bearing the ashes of war dead."[40]

The victory in Singapore was the biggest affirmative event in twentieth-century Japanese history; it delivered on the promise of Pearl Harbor. "ARMY UNITS LAND IN JAVA," read the headlines on March 3, 1942, and three days later "JAPANESE OCCUPY BATAVIA"; the future kept unfolding. On March 9, the *Japan Times* confirmed "JAPANESE TAKE RANGOON." In "a veritable cinema boom," people flocked to the movies to see the big pictures of the war, *Malay War Record* and *Victory Song of the East*. The number of cinema visits in Japan reached a peak in the year of imperial expansion in 1942. The experience of war as epic theater intertwined the lives of Japanese more and more tightly with the imperial future.[41]

The "ear-splitting roar" was heard around the world. Not Pearl Harbor but Singapore was the epochal event at the beginning of the world war with reverberations for Europe's empires long after it had ended. The taking of Singapore rang a loud alarm in London—you could hear it in the "sudden spurt of un-English chattiness."[42] Each piece of news in 1942 arrived with the loss of "a new bit of the Empire," wrote chief of the Imperial General Staff Alan Brooke. "The surrender of Singapore is the blackest page in our military history for all time," said one lord. "Ten of the blackest weeks in our national and imperial history," counted George Orwell. Churchill had "never received a more direct shock," although Churchill described many shocks during the war.[43]

According to one well-placed visitor in London, February 15, 1942, "sounded to Britons something like an earth-shaking rehearsal for Judgment Day," not because it revealed poor military estimates in Malaya and elsewhere but because it served as a verdict on the imperial project itself. Speaking from exile in Berlin, Subhas Chandra Bose was convinced that "the fall of Singapore means the collapse of the British Empire."[44]

Although shaken, London rallied to the defense of empire, acknowledging, as the *Times* did, that "British dominion in the Far East can never be restored—in its former guise." But the metropole held out hope for its colonies' reform and revivification. In the end, the empire builders resorted to a well-rehearsed script of "imperial response to peripheral calamity": "self-scrutiny, debate over national character, reform, and reconstruction to ward off decline," without an understanding of why imperial subjects had shown themselves to be so "passive, timorous and apathetic." In the words of one commentator, "differences of race, colour, language, and customs" across the British territories did not constitute fault lines of disintegration but provided the basic justification for imperial rule.[45]

Americans saw Singapore more like the Japanese. In a widely read *Washington Post* column immediately after the fall of Singapore, liberal journalist Walter Lippmann argued the case for the transformation of a war to preserve the British Empire into a "war of liberation." He did so on the basis of the universal principles of the Atlantic Charter and on the more hard-nosed premise that American security rested on Asian freedom. "The basic proof of this matter is that we are at war with Japan because we refused to sell out China." For the future, the Western nations must begin "purging themselves" of any taint of an obsolete "white man's burden." "Tory imperialism will die hard," Lippmann conceded, knowing Churchill's position, "but it must die" in order to defeat "Nazi and Japanese imperialism."[46]

Lippmann's appraisal was radical because he believed the Allies' geopolitical victory in the Pacific required far-reaching social transformation around the world. Pearl Buck, a Nobel Prize–winning writer who had taught for many years at Nanjing University, went further. To listen to "Indians or Chinese or Koreans or Filipinos," she wrote, was to realize that the war would be completely taken over by racial issues. The "barrier between East and West" allowed Japan to conquer colonial territories in East Asia "quickly and easily." There was now a global standoff between "the white man" who was "not willing to give up his superiority and the colored" who was "no longer willing to endure his inferiority." By ignoring race, Buck warned, the white world was preparing "a future of nothing but struggle and war on a stupendous scale" in order "to keep down colored people who are so vastly superior in numbers and our equals in skills."[47]

Singapore in 1942 confirmed many of the ideas of "one world, one war" by expanding the geopolitical struggle between the Allies and the Axis across half the world. It also revealed that the world war was not simply about how to cut up or defend global territories but about how to imagine power in territories around the globe. The war was about rule itself, imperial domination, national liberation, and ethnic power, so that civilians were both major protagonists and victims. The stakes were as much racial and moral as territorial.

CHAPTER 5

"On the Road to Mandalay"

The road from Singapore led to Rangoon, the delta port on the Burma side of the Bay of Bengal that the Japanese occupied on March 8, 1942, and Mandalay, halfway up the Irrawaddy River. The route pointed the way overland to Calcutta, India's largest city, where tens of thousands of mostly Indian refugees from Burma had brought firsthand reports of the collapse of British authority and the violence of ethnic conflict. As Japan's armies streamed across borders, Japanese residents along the entire western coast of the Americas from Lima to Vancouver suddenly appeared conspicuous and threatening. Newspapers in February and March 1942 were full of stories about the fifth columnists Japan had allegedly mustered all over the Pacific and the refugees it had scattered across Asia. War in early 1942 was fast-paced not just as a result of the suddenly expanding boundaries of the conflict—"Moulmein is no longer a word in a Kipling poem"—but also because of the growing numbers of civilian enemies, Chinese "purified" in Singapore, Japanese interned in California, Indians run out of Burma.

Japan's campaign in Burma ran the conquest of Malaya in reverse, this time south to north into the mountains. As the Imperial Army captured airfields and overran defenses, British forces retreated into more inhospitable and indefensible territory, the Burma bisected by two huge rivers, the Sittang and the Irrawaddy, into Kipling's backcountry where gentlemen hunted tigers in the Arakan Mountains, and finally up against areas demarcated as "unsurveyed" on the government map. The campaign also replicated the one in Malaya: rapid flanking charges by the Japanese combined with British inability to find a strategic line to hold and defend.

Ready to sacrifice Singapore in order to hold Rangoon, the British continued their strategy of fleeing a little in order to fight at last. Once the Japanese occupied Point Victoria and its airfield at the end of the southern leg of Burma on December 15, 1941, however, the British found themselves overrun and outflanked at every point. Japanese forces invaded Tenassarim, the southernmost province, in a week, reaching Moulmein, Burma's third-largest city and, since 1826, Britain's oldest colonial possession, at the mouth of the Salween River on January 31, 1942. With the fall of Rangoon on March 8, 1942, the British lost supplies and a port of entry, and when they set the oil fields near Yenangyaung on the Irrawaddy ablaze on April 16, they were left without fuel. From Moulmein in the South to Mandalay in the North, the arc of Kipling's poem, the Japanese covered the same distance as they had in Malaya, some five hundred miles, though it took them twice as long, about three months. To a group of evacuees, "the whole progress of their war" seemed "fantastically improbable and indecently quick."[1]

The invaders tore out the pages, one by one, of Kipling's books. The reporter's notebook was ripped too. "The Japanese are driving with incredible speed," Jack Belden scribbled from Myitkyina. "Everything is happening so quickly that I cannot write a coordinated story," signing off, "Must Go. Goodbye."[2]

When the British said "good-bye," they left behind a country more ethnically homogeneous than Malaya and, as a result, more politically self-conscious, with Burmese aspirations to independence that aligned more easily with Japanese promises of "Asia for Asians." Nationalist groups worked with the Japanese during the occupation and achieved nominal independence in August 1943. They were anti-British but also anti-imperial in that they exalted a purified vision of a singular Burmese and Buddhist identity.

After its separation from India in 1937, Burma achieved limited self-government with a prime minister and elected legislature, including seats reserved for Europeans. While divided among themselves, it was Burmese legislators who promoted independence. The first prime minister, Ba Maw, mocked the idea that the British expected the Burmese to fight Britain's war with Germany without the promise of full independence: "Would Britain dare go to Poland and say, 'Don't think too much about independence'"; the transcript recorded "laughter." "Instead of talking about independence," would they urge Poles to "work hard, think hard. If Hitler had said the same thing to Poland," Ba Maw asked, "what would my friends in the European group" in parliament say? The British thought that Asians' keen interest in independence was some sort of "fetish"— instead, Ba Maw mimed, "work hard, think hard." There was more laughter. Resigning rather than serving under the wartime governor, Ba Maw was arrested for seditious speech under the Defense of Burma Act in August 1940. He escaped from prison during the invasion and returned as chief of government under the Japanese occupation.[3]

Ba Maw's laughter resounded in the streets, where radical nationalists organized among students and labor leaders. They called themselves *thakin*, the Burmese equivalent of *sahib*, the deferential form of colonial address, to insist that Burmese were the real lords.

Standing their own ground in parliament and in the streets, the *thakin* articulated the vigor of Burmese independence and the depth of suspicions against foreigners that led them to champion Japan's thrusts against the European empires. Many decades later, Ba Maw remembered the Russo-Japanese War in 1905 and "the emotion with which we heard about the Japanese victories." "I was then just a little boy at school," he admitted, yet feelings were so strong that "we fought each other to be on the Japanese side" in war games; India's Nehru had also offered Japan "three cheers" as a boy. Later on, movie audiences in Rangoon stayed on to jeer Churchill and cheer Hitler rather than shuffling out during the newsreels, as did Malays in Singapore.[4] *Thakin* is the key to understanding Burma's political choices in World War II—the sense of triumph at the end of British rule and the welcome extended to Japanese occupiers, as well as the resistance to the Japanese in 1944, and throughout the stress on Burmese ethnic and cultural supremacy.

The Anglo-Japanese war was a calamitous double tragedy for the large Indian population in Burma. As the coolies and clerks of the empire, they occupied the status of second-class "blacks" in any British evacuation scheme, and as foreigners they were despised by Burmese as the servants of British masters whose power the war had destroyed. In the six months after the Japanese invasion of Burma, almost the entire community of Indians—one million in a country of seventeen million—fled the country, mostly on foot over unforgiving terrain, leaving behind livelihoods and losing their possessions and often their lives. The Indians were not the largest refugee group at the beginning of the war, as some accounts suggested; about five million French fled the German advance in the spring of 1940. But even the exaggerated numbers signaled the new kinds of burdens that war placed on civilians, even entire ethnic groups. By the end of the war, the number of displaced people around the world, well over one hundred million, was comparable to the population of the Soviet Union or the United States; in a much less populated world, there were as many refugees in World War II as there are today. The Indian refugees provided a glimpse into the magnitude of this disaster, although their stories were overshadowed by the tales of Europeans on the run in "their war." In India itself, the fate of the refugees became a political scandal deeply injurious to British rule that during the war became associated more with death than life.

The war correspondents who raced to Burma to cover the Japanese invasion became preoccupied with the refugees who overran them. It was a war story largely shaped by retreat and the civilians caught in the terrible rush. What Indian newspapers reported on as well was the conspicuous racism exposed by imperial collapse. In the background to the individual stories of heroism and harrow, two roads could be made out. There were in fact two main escape routes across land, one over the Arakan Mountains to the port of Aykab (and then by steamer to Chittagong in eastern Bengal) or, much farther north through wilderness, one to Kalewa, Tamu, and Imphal (and then to the Indian railhead at Dimapur in Assam). But there were two roads also because the refugee traffic seemed to divide into a "white road" reserved for "Europeans, Anglo-Indians and Anglo-Burmans" and a "black road" taken by the thousands of Indians desperate to escape the devastation and violence.

The scandal of white and black roads had already surfaced with the evacuation of Penang, which was ordered two days after the Malayan city had been bombed on December 11, 1941. Occurring just days after Pearl Harbor, it must have been a shocking moment of vulnerability. According to William Paterson, an editor with the *Malaya Tribune*, Europeans boarded ferries with luggage and automobiles, while his Asian friends were denied permission and left behind. "Evacuation of Asian civilians was not considered feasible, since there was no possibility of providing transport for large numbers," read the official history. Singapore's governor subsequently disavowed the "very discreditable affair," establishing a no-discrimination policy in further evacuations. Duff Cooper, the British minister resident, furiously denounced the new policy as an abdication of imperial responsibility. It would "evacuate the troops first and leave the women and children to the tender mercies of a cruel Asiatic foe." Incredulous, he imagined a scenario in which "trains traveling south were forbidden to carry passengers who appeared to be evacuees, that first-class carriages were to be taken off the trains in order to prevent Europeans from traveling, that motor cars traveling south were to be turned back." In the end, there was no policy at all, which only led to chaos.[5]

As it was, Asian refugees from Malaya lacked destinations. For Europeans the first choice was Australia, a country in which the idea of "White Australia" was so woven into the political fabric that the dominion agreed to accept no more than fifty

Chinese and fifty Eurasian women and children from Singapore. (In September 1941, when London asked about accepting British civilians in the event of an evacuation of Palestine, Canberra demurred if the refugees were Jewish.) In Singapore, as in Penang, there was a white sea route and no "black" route at all.[6]

For British to evacuate the colonies was an admission that it could no longer hold on to them. Evacuation shattered civilian morale and put an end to basic services on which Europeans relied. After the first bombings of Rangoon, the governor worked hard to persuade the "sweepers" and dockworkers to return to the city. In January, as the Japanese advanced on Moulmein, authorities barred male Indians from deck space on the steamships departing for India, which, in effect, meant that space was reserved for wealthy refugees and European women and children.

As war correspondents raced in their trucks south down the road to report from Rangoon, they encountered the refugees headed in the opposite direction. "Dock labourers, coolies and bearers plodded side by side with clerks and government servants, their womenfolk and children trailing beside them," observed George Rodger. "Some of the men pulled heavy carts," but most just carried "a small bundle of personal things." Indians were left to their own devices and hardly dared to "forage in the jungle where Burmans might be lurking."[7] When the uncontrolled "exodus" out of Rangoon began in early February, no provisions had been made to distribute food and medical supplies along the way, to ensure movement across the Irrawaddy River, or to countermand other bureaucratic barriers impeding the Indians. Once the British army evacuated, authorities restricted traffic on the road from Tamu to Petal to authorized vehicles. By the time the late-spring monsoon rains had turned the roads into mud, thousands of refugees had died of disease, and thousands more would die in the attempt to cross the treacherous passes.

Lucky enough to attempt the journey by automobile, "I did the map very carefully with calipers yesterday," as one character, Portman, reported in an English account of the exodus. "I should say six or seven hundred miles. Awfully hard though to judge the contours." Portman calculated ten miles an hour, about one hundred miles a day. Even so, there was the problem of seating since "Miss Allison," a nurse, was Anglo-Burmese. While Allison had made all the effort to appear English, even at work having refused to speak Burmese, the other evacuees did not want to sit next to her because they did not want to touch her. Once on the road, the car merged into the "stream of traffic," fixed there "like a link in a chain." There was nothing to do but to watch "the other chain of living and dead" walking on foot along the road and to "count the dead. There were twenty-three of them before noon."[8]

Terrors stalked the sides of the road. Cholera broke out in February, and it overtook refugees making their way from Prone outside Rangoon across the Arakan pass to the small port of Tuangap. A letter in the *Bombay Chronicle* reported on a group of Indians who were "left Prone on the 22nd February": "The road was strewn with the bodies of the dead and the dying. Cholera and exhaustion, hunger and thirst worked havoc with the ignorant and innocent refugees. . . . Men and carts had to pass over festering bodies and the stench of rotting corpses was unbearable. . . . We closely observed everything on the way and kept a record of the dead bodies seen. We counted 170." Travelers learned to watch the road and number the dead.[9]

Witnesses superimposed the whole drama of war onto the refugee treks that culminated in a "Beresina moment" when the bridge needed to be repaired. Later on in a hospital in Bengal, a British woman could only summon up images from the movie *Gone with the Wind* to describe "pallets touching each other, people moaning for water and sicking up and so on everywhere."[10]

"Touching each other . . . moaning . . . and so on everywhere"—Burma truly seemed to reveal the extensive decomposition of order in the empire. Working for *Time-Life*, Jack Belden wrote that the "road to India" was "flooded by the ebb-tide of the British Empire." He also used evocative words to depict the scene: *pushing, trampling, knocking over, stumbling, jumping, swirling*, all of which fused his anger: "The Americans are sitting in cars on their asses. The British Empire is walking on its feet. On its last feet?" The question registered deep shock at the helplessness of the living and the numbers of the dead.[11] For correspondents like Belden, the refugees rolled up the British Empire behind them.

By the end of summer 1942, more than six hundred thousand refugees had reached India, some by steamship from Rangoon and Aykab, most across monsoon-swept trails from Tamu and Palel to Imphal. As many as eighty thousand had died along the way of cholera, malaria, and exhaustion.

At the end of the rainy season, the first investigators retraced the route out of Burma. They got as far as the hill town of Mogaung, where "the eerie silence among the dense, overhanging forest vegetation" revealed "thousands of skeletons, the majority Indian," which "lay along the road or in nearby bushes." British soldiers who returned to Tamu discovered a city of the dead: "skeletons sitting, lying or propped up, just as they had been before dying," in "derelict cars," "at decayed tables," "in collapsed beds." "It had been the end of a long, hard

journey for many exhausted, diseased and hunger stricken people who had died rather than give-in," wrote the reporter for
Calcutta's *Statesman*.[12]

The refugees trickled into Bengal in a state of utter exhaustion, diseased and delirious. Soldiers on their way to the front
could see the "evacuation specials" as they came into the station on "Platform 2" in Basen Basu's 1950 novel about the war.
"New batches arrived daily" and "crowded into the station,
in the waiting room shed, in the corners of the market. They
gathered together in every nook and corner, in every hole," like
"heaps of rubbish." "Look," the recruits nudged each other to
ask why people had "run away from Burma to die here on the
streets like cats and dogs." "It is not we alone who will die in
the war," the soldiers concluded; "civilians will not escape." The
stories the survivors told also provided accounts of the injustice. According to the *Bombay Chronicle*, the refugees had been
treated as if "they belong to an inferior race." Gandhi himself
exclaimed, "One route for the whites, another for the blacks!"[13]

Malaya, Burma—wasn't India next? The Japanese Imperial
Army did not invade India in 1942 because it faced the same
obstacles that vexed the refugees: scarce supplies, rugged terrain,
and monsoon rains. Although the Imperial Navy attacked Ceylon, it failed to annihilate Britain's Eastern Fleet, which escaped
without being detected. As a precautionary measure to keep
the Japanese from gaining a perch in the Indian Ocean from
which to threaten southern Africa or the Suez Canal, the British
launched an invasion of Madagascar, where in May 1942 they
faced the resistance of Vichy France's soldiers, but, for the first
time in World War II, the Allies got there before the Japanese or
Germans.[14] In the end, the Japanese left the Indian Ocean never

to return, abandoning the idea of hooking up with the Germans advancing in the Caucasus. However, it was two years before the British returned to the offensive in Southeast Asia.

In the meantime, shadows of war settled over India. Since Pearl Harbor, the fear of bombing resulted in the mass flight of workers back to the countryside, which only the famine a year later reversed. Authorities closed the port in Calcutta for a year. A citywide panic gripped Madras. "The exodus was on an astonishing scale," concludes one historian. "Whole families left their homes, taking such belongings as they could in over-crowded trains, buses, cars and bullock carts that were piled to overflowing. Homes were almost completely deserted and most shops in the city closed." Even "dangerous" animals in the zoo were shot lest bombs allowed them to escape into the streets. The observer gleefully notes the stranger-than-fiction scene in which "polar bears were killed in Madras by the Malabar Special Police because a British Police Commissioner feared a Japanese landing," forever securing the polar bear a place in Indian history. The strange, sudden "shiver of 1942," the awful flight from Burma, the broken soldiers in retreat, the rumors about Japanese invaders, the assassinated polar bear, all served to undermine the foundations of British authority more than the Quit India movement in August 1942. "Though only a few voices are audible," the unrecorded rumors rose to a "chorus: invasion is imminent; the Japanese are coming; the British are set to flee." Fear and suspicion rather than any particular event transformed the empire from an enduring presence into a rickety phenomenon.[15]

India's "shiver of 1942" was a paradox. It dramatized a Japanese invasion that failed to arrive, giving the British Raj a reprieve that the great fright had diminished in value.

IN THE SIX months after the attack on Pearl Harbor, the armed forces of the Japanese empire had conquered one-sixth of the planet. Once they had eliminated Malaya and the Philippines as Allied outposts, the Japanese Imperial Army easily absorbed Burma and the Dutch East Indies into the Great East Asia Co-Prosperity Sphere. The majority of the Indian soldiers it had captured in Singapore, enlisted men in the largest volunteer army in the world, had gone over to the Indian National Army and the Axis side, which suggested the poor state of British rule in India. The fact that Japan did all this when most of its army watched from the sidelines in China was astonishing.

Yet the stunning achievement also indicated weakness. If four-fifths of the army was otherwise occupied, it was not at all clear how Japan would take on both the United States and Great Britain. What was bold in winter seemed reckless in spring; the "victory fever" generated by Pearl Harbor and Singapore gave way to strategic paralysis as the military considered the next steps in a plan of attack.

North, West, South, or East.

The Greater East Asia Co-Prosperity Sphere set conceptual limitations on further action since the *"Grossraum"* had a cultural and geopolitical anchor. However, the empire remained imperiled if it stayed on the defensive or simply consolidated its perimeter. Since the United States mobilized overwhelming economic and military power to regain the offensive, time worked against the Japanese. Strategists believed that the empire needed to launch aggressive attacks beyond East Asia to preempt Allied initiatives that would threaten the region. The empire found itself forced to look beyond and thus possibly endanger its own achievements. Imperial and military logic collided.

Tied up in China, the Imperial Army was wary of grandiose or long-term land offensives. Beginning in 1942, it acted as a check on the navy's ambitions. Even so, Japan had to make decisions about how to erode Allied power in order to forestall its rapid development. There were elements in the army that had always seen Japan's future in the North, but Japan already lost an engagement with the Soviet Union in 1939, and, in April 1941, it signed a nonaggression pact that in the new global war usefully protected an important Japanese flank. North was not an option in the spring of 1942.

Many historians believe that if Japan had continued its offensive in the West, it would have posed the greatest danger to the Allies.[16] India was a very big challenge given the size of the subcontinent and the strength of its army, but Japan could have interfered with British supplies to the Middle East by occupying Ceylon and possibly Madagascar. Such a move in the Indian Ocean would have reinforced Germany's ongoing two-pronged offensive in North Africa and the Caucasus that put the Middle East and its oil fields in striking distance. When Germany took Tobruk at the end of June 1942, it had done much to prepare such a coordinated Axis offensive. West into the Indian Ocean offered Japan (and Germany) the greatest global advantage. However, it was not to be. The Japanese Imperial Navy pulled away from Ceylon in early April and steamed home after five months at sea and as many as 6,200 miles from its bases.

South or East.

An invasion of Australia in the South was also infeasible given the commitments of the army, but Japanese strategists calculated how to cut American supply lines to the continent. Australia loomed as a huge military threat to Japan once the United States established bases, even as Japan, in the "Near

North" rather than the "Far East," loomed as a danger to Australians. The most efficient way to isolate Australia was to attack New Guinea (Japan already occupied the northern shore), New Caledonia, Samoa, Fiji, and the Solomon Islands (Rabaul on the nearby island of New Britain was also in Japanese hands).

However, Yamamoto, the architect of Pearl Harbor, remained faithful to the traditional naval plan to draw out the American fleet, including the carriers he had not destroyed at Pearl Harbor. He believed the best way to get at the fleet was to launch an attack on Midway, America's remaining outpost in the western Pacific. Such an operation would contribute to the isolation of Australia and eliminate the immediate threat posed by the US Navy in the Pacific. The problem with tiny Midway Island was that while it was difficult for the Americans to defend, it was even more difficult for the Japanese to invade and occupy, given the island's proximity to Hawaii (1,073 miles) and distance from Japan (2,549 miles). The debate went back and forth until the humiliating Doolittle air raid against Tokyo on April 18, 1942, a quixotic pyrotechnical display put on to remind the Japanese that the United States was very much in the game. The sixteen B-25 bombers launched from the aircraft carrier *Hornet* did little damage but had an immense psychological impact, clinching the argument for a full-scale naval operation against Midway. Subsequent attacks to impede American supplies to Australia remained desirable, but undefined. So Midway it was. Two days after the Doolittle raid, the ships of the carrier fleet began to drop anchor in their home ports in order to be readied for the next mission.

East.

CHAPTER 6

Spring Internment

The Doolittle Raid and Midway Island, and the redeployment of navies and seizure of bases, defined the expansion of the Pacific war in the spring of 1942. So did the *Sook Ching* massacre, the refugees in India, and the incarceration of Japanese in the United States. Military fronts were drawn geographically as well as racially.

The Japanese appeared everywhere. Roosevelt started the list in his address to Congress on December 8, 1941. In addition to the attack on the Hawaiian Islands, "the Japanese Government also launched an attack against Malaya. Last night Japanese forces attacked Hong Kong" and also Guam and the Philippine Islands. In the following weeks, newspaper readers updated the list: the fall of Hong Kong, Manila, Singapore, Batavia, and Rangoon. The occupations were followed by bombing raids on Darwin, Australia, on February 19 and Ceylon on Easter Sunday, April 5, 1942. Maps needed to get bigger in order to locate all points of Japanese attacks. The wide Pacific Ocean resembled a blown-up version of the Malayan jungle that Japanese soldiers infiltrated from the sea and air and all sides on land to outflank British defenders. Since Japanese forces seemed to be everywhere, therefore they had to be everywhere, and it followed that being everywhere was a characteristic of the Japanese enemy so that *any* Japanese *anywhere* figured as a potential agent of Imperial Japan. As Japanese victories added up, this logic grew more compelling to Americans, who soon regarded Japanese American citizens as the soldiers of a fifth column.

In his goofy style, "Dr. Seuss" published a cartoon for New York City's *PM* newspaper on February 13, 1942, just days before the fall of Singapore, to visualize the gathering threat. He marched an endless line of stereotypical Japanese with buck-teeth and round glasses stretching up the Pacific coast from California to Oregon and Washington, each one ready to pick up his own package of TNT at a little house marked "Honorable 5th Column." On the roof, a compatriot with a spyglass kept a lookout for the Imperial Navy across the sea.[1]

The idea of the fifth column did not take hold all at once. It had been Germans who preoccupied American fears about spies and secret agents before the war. The big movie on the topic of subversion had been *Confessions of a Nazi Spy* in 1939. But the combination of Japan's "sneak attack" and older racial animosities against Japanese was such that suspicions quickly acquired a common sense irrefutability, setting the stage for the internment of Japanese American citizens (*Nisei*, or second generation) and Japanese residents (*Issei*, or first generation) living on the Pacific coast. The same sense of danger and policy of exclusion applied to Japanese Canadians in British Columbia. In 1942, Japanese became "Japs."

The existence of a Japanese fifth column was first suggested by the secretary of the navy, Frank Knox, at a news conference on December 15, 1941, at which he reported on his inspection tour of the Hawaiian Islands immediately after Pearl Harbor. Toward the end of his statement, which dwelled at length on the lack of preparation by the army and navy, Knox stated that an additional reason for "the success of the Japanese was coopera-tion" from the islanders themselves, 37 percent of whom were of Japanese heritage, the vast majority of them American citizens. "The most effective fifth-column work in this way was done in Hawaii, with the exception of Norway," he added.[2]

The term "fifth column" originated in the Spanish Civil War to refer to nationalists inside Madrid ready to support the four military columns besieging the republican capital in 1936. It is a concept that makes sense in a civil war in which citizens are divided by ideology and help one or the other side either openly on the battlefield or furtively as a "fifth column" working behind the front. Knox's reference to Norway invoked those Norwegians who had come out of the woodwork to support the German invasion in April 1940. However, as exiled Norwegian politi-cians were anxious to clarify, the fifth column was made up not of Norwegian citizens but of their foster children, the "sickly" German and Austrian children taken in by Norwegian families in the hardship years after World War I who, as adults, put their Norwegian language skills to use as soldiers in the Wehrmacht or as tourists, journalists, and businessmen. The fifth column referred to ungrateful Germans in Norway rather than treason-ous Norwegians working for Germany—clearly, Knox did not understand this distinction. In any case, the coordinated activity in which he imagined Japanese American citizens taking part had no ready precedent.[3]

Before Knox's press conference on December 15, 1941, there had been no references whatsoever to a fifth column of Japanese Americans operating in Hawaii, not in the *New York Times*, not in the *Los Angeles Times*, and not in Honolulu's *Advertiser* or *Star-Bulletin*. The only news item about fifth columnists immediately after Pearl Harbor regarded Japanese residents in the Philippines. Moreover, from the beginning to the end of the war, Honolulu's police chief denied the existence of any evidence of domestic sabotage or espionage. This squared with prewar reports that had concluded "there is no Japanese 'problem' on the Coast."[4]

Otherwise, only sixty-seven-year-old Edgar Rice Burroughs, author of the *Tarzan* books, who lived in Honolulu and wrote a humor column, brought up the fifth column in order to mock the idea (before Knox): "Well, we've nabbed another fifth columnist! Early this morning a light was seen on a hillside flashing code signals, and it didn't take the authorities long to get up there. They found an old man milking his cow with the aid of a blue light," the wind "now revealing, now blotting out the faint beams of his light. Blooey went another fifth column scare." "Behind our kidding and joking," Burroughs affirmed, "there is an iron will," "a splendid army," and "a grand navy. So talk on, little man, and give us more laughs." In his columns over the course of 1942, Burroughs never returned to the subject. And in his lengthy address to the graduating class at Annapolis a few days after his press conference, Knox had a lot to say about the navy, but not a further word about a fifth column.[5]

If Japanese Americans in Hawaii did not organize a fifth column, and the Norwegians had not either, where did the story come from, and where did it get its legs? The *New York Times* article on Knox's press conference commented that Knox "declined to elaborate on steps" to prevent further fifth-column activities, although he praised the "high pitch" of morale in Hawaii. The correspondent, Charles Hurd, added his own reassurance: "Reporters gathered the impression that short work was being made of rounding up all Japanese and other questionable persons, including native Hawaiian Japanese, who technically are American citizens." The "impression" about "rounding up" and Hurd's insinuation that Japanese on the islands were suspicious enough to make citizenship merely technical and to have warranted "short work" suggested that there was an untold story. It was enough for Wallace Carroll, a United Press International reporter. He had arrived in Honolulu on his way back from Asia a few days after the attack, and, on New Year's Eve, he published his story on what he had "learned" during "my recent visit to Honolulu."[6]

Carroll detailed many things he heard just talking to people, none of them authorized and all of them unnamed: "Big arrows, pointing to military objectives, were cut in the sugar cane on plantations in the islands a few hours before the Japanese struck"; "Japanese vegetable dealers" tracked activity around Ford Island because "they delivered their produce to the ships"; and "Japanese truck drivers, I was told, drove from side to side of the road from Honolulu to Hickham Field to delay American pilots who were frantically trying to reach their planes." It was all right out of Edgar Rice Burroughs. Carroll expanded on imaginary fifth columnists in his last paragraph: "When I left Honolulu ten days ago, I was informed that Japanese members of the Territorial Guard were still stationed at reservoirs, power plants and other public utilities. Japanese-Americans still held posts in the post office and telephone service." The agenda for "short work" was clear. Carroll's "facts" were intended to put Americans "on the alert in other potential areas of danger." With these observations, the acclaimed journalist planted a minefield.

Carroll's sugarcane arrows and vegetable dealers formed the body of hearsay evidence about a Japanese fifth column in the influential January 24, 1942, Roberts Commission Report on Pearl Harbor, chaired by Supreme Court justice Owen J. Roberts. It focused on the army and navy command. However, the fifth-column story had been officially released and was recycled in more lurid detail by Martin Dies's House Committee on Un-American Activities in the weeks that followed. Like Carroll, Roberts and Dies had nothing to go on but hearsay, yet the nonsense filled columns of newsprint, and it puffed up alarmist declarations by local and state politicians so as to become common knowledge.

The stories remained upright because they were cast in the solid mold of anti-Japanese racism. In a few short weeks, fifth-column stories justified the full-scale deportation of all Japanese, citizens and so-called resident aliens, from their homes in three American states and one Canadian province, to inland resettlement camps that authorities unabashedly referred to as "concentration camps." The rapid escalation of anti-Japanese policy was part of a larger race war that connected events in Singapore with imaginary occurrences in Honolulu. The press coverage would have probably sputtered out inconclusively without the rigid racial typologies standing in for concrete evidence. In the end, internment—the term used at the time—was simply justified by the belief that "a Jap is a Jap."

There was little panic regarding Japanese residents in the first weeks after the United States' declaration of war. In fact, editorials acknowledged the loyalty of Japanese Americans. However, consideration of the danger they allegedly posed and the remedies necessary to contain it grew more intense after Carroll's reporting and the release of the Roberts Report; the month of January is crucial because, by the end of the month, internment had become an idea fixed in the public mind. This period also coincided with the time from the fall of Hong Kong on Christmas Day 1941 to the surrender of Singapore on February 15, 1942. Four days after Singapore, Roosevelt issued Executive Order 9066, giving the secretary of war and regional military commanders the power to "exclude" "any person" from designated "military areas" in "any region or locality." Public Proclamation No. 4 issued by John L. DeWitt of the Western Defense Command on March 29, 1942, clarified the exclusion to include all Japanese American citizens and resident Japanese aliens living in all parts of the three Pacific states; Canada had issued the order for the mass evacuation of Japanese from British Columbia a month earlier, on February 26, 1942. Exclusion from a place also always came to mean internment somewhere else.

After Pearl Harbor, Charles Kikuchi, a doctoral student at the University of California, Berkeley, remembered that there was "no immediate outcry" against Japanese. "Sporadic anti-Japanese editorials did appear but they were dwarfed by editorials and commentaries of a more tolerant nature." Newspapers demonstrated the "local cohesion" of communities with stories about the loyalty of Japanese Americans and their willingness to pledge loyalty. On December 16, a week after Pearl Harbor, the *Richmond Independent* gave Bay Area readers a big "welcome to loyalty." "There should be no general persecution," the editorial ran, "because of the accident of birth"; "every friend to America should be welcomed whether he traces his ancestry to Germany, Italy, or Japan." If readers needed reassurance, the county sheriff, John A. Miller, affirmed that "most every Japanese here is a loyal American and those few who are not we have every facility to take care of in a lawful American way."[7] The sheriff's confidence in the "lawful American way" illuminated the tremendous confidence Americans had in the Federal Bureau of Investigation. The 1930s had been the "golden age" of Hoover's "G-men," whose professionalized anticrime units took on the gangsters of the Prohibition era. Take "an alien," proposed Charles P. Stewart in his newspaper column. "He's like a visitor in an aquarium. FBI investigators peek at him constantly through the glass, and at the first questionable wiggle of a fin, out he's flushed." And "a Jap"—"pretty easy to spot," certainly not "much of a problem for the FBI."[8] The aquarium illustrated the obvious: Japanese stood out more than Italians or Germans in the general population, reducing any possible alarm.

The release of "Roberts' fact-finding report" on January 25, 1942, established the "fact" of disloyalty among some Japanese residents of the territory, and thereby posed the question of how to distinguish the loyal from the disloyal. Los Angeles mayor Fletcher Bowron used the immediacy of the radio to portray the city as "the hotbed, the nerve center of the spy system." To meet the threat, he advocated for the "removal of the entire Japanese population—alien and native born—inland for several hundred miles." Even if there was no doubt that the group as a whole "may be alright," newspapers conceded "definite uneasiness" over the ability to make distinctions. Bowron estimated that "50 percent or more of the second generation are loyal: but I do not think anyone is in a position to ferret out" the other 50 percent.[9]

One way out of the difficulty was to simply make the problem the solution. According to one observer, the "homogeneity of racial and cultural traits made it impossible to distinguish between loyal and disloyal." Better safe than sorry meant grouping Japanese together indiscriminately. The absolute category of race solved the problem of individual identification by discarding it altogether. "Don't kid yourselves and don't let someone tell you there are good Japs," added a California congressman— "perhaps, one out of 1000."[10]

Ostensibly tackling a "most difficult and delicate question," one writer for the *Los Angeles Times* provided a very simple biological answer. "Our Japanese-Americans" were citizens by an "accident of birth," but are "Japanese nevertheless." "A viper is nonetheless a viper wherever the egg is hatched," he explained, warming to the topic, "so a Japanese-American, born of Japanese parents, grows up to be a Japanese, not an American."[11]

By the end of February 1942, the County Supervisors Association of California put forward a resolution endorsing placing all Japanese and their descendants in a "concentration camp under the supervision of the federal government." (The term "concentration camp" was used frequently until April when it disappeared once actual evictions of citizens were underway so that conceptions were grandiose, while their implementation was described much more modestly.) To read the resolutions, the radio remarks, and editorials from late January to late February 1942 is to gain the impression that the scale of proposed precautionary measures expanded many times without any new evidence. The process fed on itself as the imaginary problem of identifying suspects led to collective racial solutions. Ultimately, the war provided the opportunity to enact broad racist measures that otherwise would not have been feasible.[12]

The policies the War Department implemented regionally on the coast the State Department adopted for the entire hemisphere. Already in April 1942, it oversaw the deportation of the first of 1,800 mostly first-generation Japanese from Peru (out of a community numbering 25,000 mostly *Nisei*) to internment camps in the American West where some inmates languished until 1948. Hundreds of citizens of Japanese descent in Panama (with the canal), Venezuela, Colombia, and Bolivia, which deported one-sixth of its Japanese population, were also "kidnapped" without charge by local authorities and hustled onto evacuation ships bound for the United States. (The 250,000 Japanese living in Brazil were protected by their numbers and the smaller community in Chile, a country that occupied a long strip of the Pacific coast, by the government's refusal to comply with US requests; neither country declared war on Japan until 1945.)[13]

What makes the anti-Japanese incarceration policy on the West Coast so stunning was the visible threat posed by German submarine attacks along the East Coast. Indeed, after Pearl Harbor, Canada's General Staff confirmed that the country faced increased "dangers along Canada's coasts," but "the East Coast far more than the West."[14] In the early morning of January 15, the captain of *U-123* crept into New York's harbor to see the blazing lights of Manhattan's skyscrapers: "I cannot describe the feeling in words," he recalled. "It was unbelievable and beautiful." A ferocious attack occurred four days later when German torpedoes hit the Canadian passenger liner *Lady Hawkins*, which sank in thirty minutes off Cape Hatteras: 251 people died, while 71 survived five days at sea in an overcrowded lifeboat. Ships continued to explode a few miles offshore. On the sunny Monday afternoon of June 15, thousands of vacationers at Virginia Beach watched four tankers burn over the course of two hours. Swimmers even felt the force of the blasts in the water. "Thick black smoke could be seen belching into the sky"; the glow from the flames was especially luminous at night. Beaches up and down the seaboard were "strewn with washed up oil, wreckage and occasionally the body of a sailor." After six months, German U-boats had torpedoed 233 ships with a loss of life of more than six thousand sailors and passengers, more than twice the number of fatalities at Pearl Harbor.[15]

The American place that contained the most Japanese, who represented more than one-third of the population, never considered internment: the Territory of Hawaii. There was the joke about the sailor who disembarked in Pearl Harbor to see all the Japanese-looking men wearing uniforms of the Home Guard. "My God, we're too late," he exclaimed. Practical considerations prevailed since, as General Delos C. Emmons, commander of the Hawaiian military district, pointed out, Japanese Americans "added materially to the strength of the area." The territorial government was also less responsive to civic pressure, and there were no white "nativists" in Hawaii where Anglos, referred to as *haoles*, or strangers, remained a wealthy minority. Honolulu's leading newspaper, the *Star-Advertiser*, went on record opposing internment in either Hawaii or California and, unlike the rest of the American press, prohibited the use of the word "Jap"; even stories on December 7, 1941, spelled out "Japanese." Life in the ethnic and racial mix of Hawaii Territory was not one big aloha, but historians point out that it was "about as far from 'representative' as one could get in 1940s America."[16]

"The civilized mind fails to comprehend the enormity of this crime," read the editorial. "Individually, Americans are apt to be good, open-hearted people." But as a mass in a time of crisis, they were "transformed into unreasoning brutes," as lynchings and race riots confirmed. The United States violated its own constitution when it interned "full-fledged American citizens" who "have been conspicuously law-abiding and well-behaved." That was the opinion of the *Japan Times*, which concluded that "the innocent of the world will not be safe" until Japan's victory "in our sacred war against America."[17]

There was astonishingly little domestic opposition to the deportation of the Japanese population. The American Civil Liberties Union was split on the issue, with some California branches arguing for legal action to uphold "civil liberties," while the national board deferred to the government's powers in wartime. Jewish and Black organizations did not address the issue. In the end, concluded Robert Hosokawa, "the frenzy on the coast whipped the racial coals which had been smouldering for a generation." In just a month, the frenzy led to the largest forced migration in American history, 120,000 people in a single year, 1942. The worst fears of Japanese Americans had come to pass: racial animosity trumped constitutional liberty.[18]

Japanese Americans tried reconstructive plastic surgery to lift an eyelid or wore buttons to identify themselves as Chinese, but in the end they were rounded up and interned based on race and ancestry. (A Japanese great-great-grandparent sufficed to make a person Japanese, a much stricter definition than the Jewish grandparent in Nazi Germany.) There was no alternative, and most evacuees reconciled themselves to the no-win situation, submitting to dispossession and internment in order to prove their loyalty.

As the date of evacuation approached, a note of melancholy crept into the story. Under the headline "Hundreds Hunt Bargains at Little Tokyo Sales," the *Los Angeles Times* noted all the stores "plastered with signs lettered both in Japanese and

English that screamed 'Sale'" and "jammed with pawing, questioning customers." "It was business in reverse," the newspaper noted. "The law of supply and demand was ignored. Japanese merchants, unsmiling and worried, mechanically sold their merchandise at prices set by their spirit of resignation and hopelessness rather than with the usual eye to profit."[19]

The first step on the evacuation route was usually an assembly camp in the coastal cities themselves. In the San Francisco area, the makeshift camp was located at the Tanforan Racecourse in San Bruno, where the prize thoroughbred Sea Biscuit ("Horse of the Year" in 1938) had been stabled. The Kikuchi family spent four months in "Stable 10. Stall 5," which smelled of manure and hay. A friendly volunteer described the departure from home:

The Japanese were their cheerful selves: stoicism is a wonderful thing for circumstances like these. Think of what these people have been doing: The past week standing in line, first to register, then for physical exams. The last frantic arrangements, selling, storing, dispensing with precious possessions, leaving pets and garden behind, then the last night, most of them up until 4 and 5 am packing, getting everything ready for the early morning departure, everything neatly labelled and properly boxed. . . . Then up at six or so and get the children ready, dress in your best clothes, come down in the pouring rain of a cold dreary day, stand in line and mill around in the confusion of departure for an hour and a half, then load into the busses and at least we're off. And all with a smile.

The idea that the Japanese prisoners were better men and women than their captors was typical, an attempt to retrieve American virtue out of this twentieth-century "captivity story."[20]

In fact, the western frontier provided the imagery of the trek to the inland resettlement camp, an "unlikely place of wind, sand, and heat." *Time* titled its story "Eastward Ho." According to the *Richmond Independent*, it was a "great adventure" to "begin work at new 'Colony' homes." The *Los Angeles Times* also cut a slice of American pie, gesturing at an injustice that editors had done so much to realize. From Santa Anita by train to Manzanar in the interior valley, "not a word of Japanese was heard." When young Japanese called out, their names were "'Joe,' 'Pat,' 'Betty,' 'Rose,' and the like." "Except for the slanted eyes," the paper commented, "the departure could easily have been that of an equal number of Americans of Caucasian blood." The impression was that a Jap was not a Jap after all.[21]

Japanese American internment stories provided an inventory of America, attesting to prisoners' loyalty and shaming American readers. Boy Scouts. Check. Baseball. Check. "Jitterbug jam sessions." Check. Dating and going steady "as these American boys and girls walked down the camp street romantically holding each other's hands." Check. The latest fashions could be seen "when the pretty Nisei girls walked by in ultra-modern play suits with abbreviated shorts and 'bra' tops and bare midriffs" (older *Issei* were "embarrassed at the unembarrassedness of their American offspring"). "This isn't Japan" was the refrain. In fact, camp residents in both the United States and Canada tended to speak more rather than less Japanese; returned in some ways to reclusive, inward-looking mentalities; and nursed a bitterness at the broken pledges of democracy. Mary Oyama vividly remembered the view from the Heart Mountain Relocation Center in Wyoming. "The watchtowers stood out bold in the moonlight," she wrote, and the searchlights picked out "the cruel barbs of the wire fence." Outwardly, though, Japanese American writers put on a positive American expression "when the only crime is my face."[22]

Beginning in 1943, evacuees slowly trickled back into American life. College-age students matriculated in the colleges that would accept Japanese Americans; some did, while others didn't. Draft-age men signed up for selective service. Husbands and fathers found jobs out east. But the return was difficult. On the one hand, the migrants reported back that "I attracted very little attention on the train," or, more hopefully, "we can eat in *any* restaurant in New York." On the other hand, their welcome could be cold. New York's mayor, Fiorello La Guardia, who in 1924 as a congressman had advocated granting proper immigration quotas to Japan, opposed the resettlement of any Japanese Americans in the city. This was at a time when his sister, Gemma, who had married a Hungarian Jew, was interned in Mauthausen. Opposition to the return of Japanese Americans to the West Coast was even more vociferous. Mayor Bowron of Los Angeles ratcheted up his rhetoric over the radio in April 1943: "There are not—and never can be—such a thing as Japanese-Americans," he concluded; they were "a race apart," and "they can never be American" or "feel the term 'American.'" "We want none of them."[23] However, in 1944, the United States Supreme Court prohibited restrictions on the free movement of citizens no longer in custody. For their part, politicians in Vancouver reiterated "our slogan": "No Japs from the Rockies to the seas." (By 1947, more Japanese Canadians lived in Ontario and

Quebec than had in British Columbia, and fully one-sixth of the prewar population, four thousand in all, were repatriated back to Japan.)[24]

A child's plea, "Mommy, I'm tired of this place, let's go back to America," provided Robert Hosokawa the lead-in to his account of his departure from Minidoka Relocation Center in Idaho to Independence, Missouri. He split the difference, but ultimately told a tale about Americans rediscovering the value they placed on liberty. "One church had a stormy session in a meeting of elders, because a suggestion had been made for my wife and me to worship there," he recalled, and "two war workers walked out of a restaurant because of my presence." Yet "people have gone out of their way to be kind to us." For Hosokawa, resettlement was an example of how wartime evacuation "scattered Americans with Japanese faces across the country, giving them a chance to prove their assimilability."[25]

In Gila, Arizona, during the first Christmas in camp, Charles Kikuchi "stopped to talk about the camp with a Negro workman who was digging postholes for the fence which is going around the place." The young man asked about conditions. He was surprised to discover that most *Nisei*, including Kikuchi himself, felt allegiance to the United States: "Boy, you are making a mistake. Why should you be loyal to a country that don't want you?" he asked. "This is a white man's country." Even so, he hoped the world war gave a chance to "all the colored peoples of this world" so that "I can get a good job just like a white man and I don't have to dig post holes to lock you Japanese up who are born in California." Kikuchi himself came to recognize the global context of racial struggles of which the "evacuation of the Japanese is just one small, but important part." He realized that "the defeat of the Axis is not going to solve any of the minority problems." But "if the ideals of the Atlantic Charter are carried through it certainly will make a difference to the Negroes, Mexican, Japanese, Chinese, and other non-caucasian groups living in this country" and everywhere else around the world.[26]

"Evacuation specials" transported deportees across all the theaters of war. In the United States, evacuation began in the context of what was widely regarded as a race war between the United States and Japan, and incarceration ended at a time when the war had ignited postcolonial struggles around the world to extend citizenship irrespective of race. In 1943, the Magnuson Act repealed the Chinese Exclusion Act of 1882, allowing Chinese residents to become naturalized citizens while restricting permissible Chinese immigration. The Immigration and Nationality Act of 1952 extended the same rights and restrictions to other Asians. It was only in 1948 that native-born Japanese and Chinese residents of Canada were granted the right to vote and treated as other Canadian citizens. Both birth naturalization and immigration remain contested issues to this day.

American concentration camps should not bring to mind the conditions in German ones or the terrible fate of Jewish victims. Internment gave way both to a kind of wistful regret after Japanese residents had evacuated and to harder ex post facto justifications when they tried to return home. Even so, the term "concentration camps" was deliberately used in 1942 to recommend the unconditional separation of Japanese from other Americans and to describe involuntary incarceration of a whole group of people. Not even Mexicans in California were treated in such an absolute or unforgiving way, and the treatment of Japanese was even tougher in Canada. Certainly, other conspicuous groups in wartime America such as Germans, Italians, or

Jews did not suffer the harsh lashes meted out to Japanese. The whole logic of internment followed the new contours of popular politics around the world that took on distinct shapes according to how individuals were grouped into communal, ethnic, and religious categories. It was all part of the demos at war. Given this sort of neighborly demography, the spiteful energy against foreign aggressors on the military fronts enveloped Americans at home. And the military gains of the Axis and the setbacks of the Allies became only more numerous in the summer of 1942.

CHAPTER 7

Summer Offensive

Harriet jobbed at the American embassy in wartime Cairo. She walked over to the map on the wall and asked her boss to take a look. "You see what it is, Mr Buschman: it's a giant pincer movement," and she pointed out "two black claws," "one in the desert and the other in the Ukraine, converging on the Middle East." Buschman stared at the map. One claw was still pretty far away, but measuring the distance from Berlin to Cairo, the German Wehrmacht had very nearly reached the halfway point. After the fall of Tobruk in June 1942, the other claw was much closer, poised about 250 miles away on the Egyptian-Libyan border. The map drove home the frightening advance of the war, rattling Harriet's composure.[1]

This was the moment when Germany might have tipped the balance to bring about an Axis victory in the world war. In the summer of 1942, the Germans were also beating a "three-month pulse of death," murdering Jews from across Europe at a "hyper-intense" rate in specially built death camps in the General Gouvernement. Some 75 to 80 percent of "all victims of the Holocaust were still alive" in March. By the end of the year, most had been killed. This was the war the Third Reich largely won. Developments on one front suddenly, pitilessly revealed another awful one besides so that the war resembled a terrifying "new plague."[2]

The pincers materialized in the early summer of 1942 as a result of two successful German offensives: one in Ukraine's Don Basin in which the Wehrmacht decisively regained the initiative it had lost in the winter war, putting it in striking distance of the oil fields in the southern Caucasus; in the other, a German expeditionary force, the Afrika Korps, kicked open the door in North Africa to capture Tobruk and threaten the Suez Canal. Suddenly, Germans were on the move again, pushing against the Middle East and tightening the pinch of Harriet's pincers.

The two offensives demonstrated Carl von Clausewitz's description of war as "an act of force to compel the enemy to do our will" through the deployment of "unconstrained and uninterrupted violence." But an aggressive war of movement provided another demonstration of Clausewitz's reflections "on war." At a certain point, the momentum of attack reached a "culminating point" in which the costs of advancing outweighed the return; the art of war was to achieve political and military objectives before this point. The North African campaign from 1940 to the end of 1942 provided a vivid example of how long supply lines degraded the assailant. The British were always in more danger pursuing the Germans in the western desert around El Agheila (812 miles from Cairo), while the Germans had trouble once they reached the eastern desert around El Alamein (1,110 miles from Tripoli). The campaign went back and forth four times before the British prevailed in October 1942 when the Germans were not able to hold on to their gains in Egypt because of supply problems.

In the Don River region in Ukraine, the Germans encountered the classic dilemma described by Clausewitz in *On War*. Although they occupied more territory and acquired more resources, they also had to calculate the costs of occupying the territory they conquered and of supplying the armies at points increasingly far from the rail terminus at Rostov. Moreover, new factors added to the accumulating costs for the assailant, not just quantifiable ones but the defender's "spirit of enterprise," "the character of the people and the Government" that in the critical phase rouses hardy "forces of protection." What Clausewitz had learned when French imperial forces defeated the Prussians at Jena and Auerstadt in 1806 and learned again while serving on Kutuzov's staff during Napoleon's disastrous campaign against Russia in 1812 was that the fundamental tendencies of war went beyond material force to include the spirit of soldiers *and* the patriots behind them.[3]

The "spirit of enterprise" could not be measured. It was an imponderable element at the level of battalions and the national level of the people and their affiliation to the endangered nation at war. This was Prince Andrei's revelation that the battle-scarred officer tried to convey to Pierre at Borodino in *War and Peace*: not just recognition of how the factor of time constantly remodeled space but acknowledgment of the emotional goings-on in the soldier and the unit. "Nobody can know the relative strength of the troops. Believe me."[4]

Germany fought the war in summer 1942 with the same guiding ideas that had accompanied Operation Barbarossa the summer before. It was a fantastical mixture of the hyperaggression of preemptive attack to annihilate Judeo-Bolshevism so as to ward off the catastrophe that had almost engulfed Germany in 1918 maximized by wild social Darwinist ideas about supermen and subhumans and by the application of modern technology. As late as the fall of 1942, Hitler imagined pitching "our tents" in Baghdad and building spacious colonial residences along four-lane highways. It was a compulsively territorial vision in which Jews were buried in the earth, slaves mined the ground, and pioneers plowed the fields.

Relentlessly sifting the soil to improve the race obscured a rational analysis of means and ends. In the European theater, Germans made better soldiers, killing more of the enemy before they themselves succumbed, than any of the other belligerents. The problem was that the German military fought a two-front war without aircraft carriers or an oceangoing fleet. The Luftwaffe bombed Warsaw, London, and Stalingrad but never developed long-range four-engine bombers. Surprised at the number of Ford trucks used by the Red Army, the Wehrmacht relied on hundreds of thousands of horses to pull artillery and supplies, more so in 1942 than in 1941. The Germans called their transports *panje* horses; the Americans called theirs "Jeeps." The Third Reich fought twentieth-century war looking like a nineteenth-century army. Resources and men were limited, putting the premium on speed, yet Germans fought a war in which the expansion of space constantly reduced the possibilities of time.

The terrible scare of the winter of 1941–1942 was reinterpreted in terms of fate. "It was a very difficult and a very hard test, the most bitter trial of all," admitted Hitler, but "we overcame this most difficult period." History had come and gone, showing that "worse things cannot and will not come anymore."

In the end, Goebbels argued, the Germans had rewritten the Napoleonic narrative by surviving a winter allegedly colder than Napoleon's and by holding the line rather than retreating. There was no German Beresina. Soon enough, the bravado returned. There was plenty of leftover capital from the great victory over France in 1940, and the endurance of the winter war added to it. In speech after radio speech, Hitler, Goebbels, and Goering reiterated: the worst was over, the hardest had been overcome, and therefore victory lay directly ahead. Indeed, admiring the Soviets for their "brutal and drastic measures," Hitler resolved to apply "similar methods." Both Stalin and Hitler believed the war would be won in 1942.[5]

In what was to be the last Soviet push in the "winter war," the Red Army attempted to break through German lines east of Kharkov on May 12, 1942. After a promising Soviet start, however, the Wehrmacht counterattacked, cutting off one pincer and surrounding the other. In a reenactment of the great *Kesselschlachten* (cauldron battles) of the summer and fall of 1941, the Germans captured 240,000 prisoners-of-war at the cost of only 20,000 casualties; Kharkov was the last time in the war the Wehrmacht was able to grab so many Red Army men. In less than four weeks, the Germans had crossed the Donets River near Izyum (June 10), opening the way to reach the Don River and the oil fields in the southern Caucasus. Farther north they took Voronezh on July 6, 1942, and Rostov on the lower Don at the Sea of Asov (Black Sea) on July 23. Except for a small Soviet strip at the bend of the river, more or less opposite Stalingrad on the Volga, the German armies had swept through the entire western side of the Don River.

Farther to the south, on May 23, 1942, the Wehrmacht retook Kerch, a strategic perch on the Crimean side of the eastern bridge to the peninsula. This allowed German forces to press Sevastopol, the important fortress on the Black Sea, which fell after a terrible monthlong siege on July 4. In Berlin, Klaus Budzinski, the twenty-year-old son of a sports journalist and his Jewish wife, identified completely with the Germans—his father had even bought a big swastika-emblazoned flag to celebrate Hitler's birthday for 4 marks, 95 pfennig—this even as Klaus helped pack things for his aunt Fanny on the eve of her deportation. "**Special Bulletin**," he bold-faced at the bottom of his diary entry for July 1, 1942: "Sewastopol, the strongest fortress in the world, conquered!" Writing in the diary was like listening to a rebroadcast of the great victories exactly one year earlier: "Special bulletin . . . special bulletin . . . Special bulletin."[6]

Kharkov, Rostov, Sevastopol—it was an "amazing" time for the "reborn" Wehrmacht.[7]

After Kharkov, the Germans moved across the plains at a pace of nearly thirty miles a day. The *Times* described the invasion as a "flood" pouring into the foothills of the Caucasus, or it was an "avalanche," or a "stampede." Cameramen for the German newsreels angled their shots to show lines of men and columns of tanks walking into the Ukrainian national flag in which the azure horizon led the way across the yellow plains of sunflowers and corn. With "deeply bronzed faces and arms caked in dust," the warriors inspired a new optimism among Germans in the summer of 1942.[8] All the signals reanimated the Germans' "spirit of enterprise" and reconfirmed their sense of racial and military mastery.

Once again "the Russian earth was on fire" and once again it trembled under the footfalls of the master race. Soviet officers in Vasily Grossman's novel *Stalingrad* could not "stop thinking about the first day of the war," with its ignominious retreats; "it keeps coming back to me." The sense of renewed disaster completely overshadowed the accomplishments of the Red Army's counteroffensive in the winter. With the new communiqués, "the Voronezh front, the Don front, the Stalingrad front, the Transcaucasian front," 1942 turned into a "bitter summer." "In those days of endless battles and unending retreats everything was black, black, and red, for the Russian people," Leland Stowe, the reporter for the *Chicago Daily News*, remembered about the grief and blood. The war in the South was "like a knife rammed deep in my stomach," confided Grossman to his diary.[9]

The original plan, Case Blue, was for Army Group South to take territory and destroy armies from the Don to the Volga in order to advance on the Caucasus. After the victory at Rostov, however, Hitler revised the sequential operations and split the group into two armies to speed up operations: Army Group A, charged with the mission to take the oil fields stretching across the Caucasus from Maikop to Grozny, and Army Group B, charged with the simultaneous mission to destroy the Red Army on the west bank of the Volga River and occupy Stalingrad before turning to reinforce the southern front. In other words, from the end of July on, operations resembled a pincer that opened from five hundred miles across at the beginning of the offensive to sixteen hundred miles as Army Group B moved east toward Stalingrad and Army Group A turned south into the mountainous neck of land between the Black Sea and the Caspian Sea. This expansion was a rash decision in a "war without reserves" that called for the concentration of force rather than its dispersion.[10]

Army Group B could not keep up the fast pace of July as it attempted to sweep the Red Army from the territories it still held on the western side of the Don River where it bent sharply from east (in the direction of Stalingrad) to southwest (to flow into the Sea of Azov at Rostov). Its operations required massive air support and reinforcements of the 4th Panzer Army that had to be stripped from Army Group A. Kalach on the eastern side of the Don just to the south of the bend of the river was finally captured on August 23, 1942, with spearheads from Army Group B reaching the Volga and the northern suburbs of Stalingrad forty miles to the east the same day. In the course of the fighting, much of the Red Army's 62nd Army had been destroyed west of the Don. The thinking was that the remnants would be annihilated as the Wehrmacht crushed it against the west bank of the mile-wide Volga River around Stalingrad. In the "super air raid" on August 23, the heaviest since the opening day of Barbarossa, six hundred bombers pounded the city, which burst almost completely into flames, killing twenty-five thousand people in a city of four hundred thousand. It was a bombardment announcing how, in Grossman's words, "German violence would triumph over the world."[11]

In the meantime, Army Group A swept into the foothills of the Caucasus Mountains, taking both Maikop and Pyatigorsk on August 9, 1942. By early September, Ewald von Kleist's forces crossed the Terek River near Mozdok where the assault reached its culminating point. The Wehrmacht stood just short of the military roads the czars had constructed across the Caucasus in the nineteenth century: the Ossetian Military Road and the Georgian Military Road that ran up the Terek Valley over the Jvari Pass to Tbilisi, midway between the Caspian and Black Seas, a distance of 180 miles. From Tblisi, the oil-rich region around Mosul, Iraq, was 700 miles due south. The Wehrmacht also failed to reach Grozny, 90 miles away; from Grozny, it was 700 more miles over Baku on the Caspian Sea to Tabriz and the oil fields in Iran. In September 1942, Kleist in Mozdok represented one claw of Harriet's pincer, with the other held in place by Rommel near El Alamein, Egypt.

The summer of 1942 was also like the previous summer as the Germans continued to pursue the deliberate murder of Jews on all the territory in the Soviet Union the Wehrmacht occupied. After the recapture of Rostov on July 23, 1942, special forces of the paramilitary *Schutzstaffel*, or SS, Sonderkommando 10a of Einsatzgruppe D, put its program into action: announcements posted on August 9, 1942, the assembly of Jews around the city on August 11, and the transport of the victims in trucks to the Zmievskaya Balka (Ravine of the Snakes), an abandoned quarry on the western edge of town, on the same day. About twenty-seven thousand men, women, and children were murdered in one of the SS's largest killing operations.[12]

Evacuated from Leningrad and sheltering in the resort town of Pyatigorsk, Elena Skrjabina, a student of French literature, and her two sons were among thousands of refugees tossed up by the war. In early August 1942, the war approached once again. Announcements on the radio broadcast reported on the "unbelievable bestiality perpetrated by the Germans in the territories they have occupied." Rumors passed on stories about "the crimes committed" against Jews. "Common sense does not accept it but you must not disbelieve everything," Skrjabina reflected. Her friend Lyalya feared for her husband, who was Jewish, and her two daughters, but she had neither money nor energy to flee. At one street corner, a group of poor Jews gathered, "begging the passing cars to take them." Since nobody paid them any attention, "they cry, so that there is a constant, uninterrupted howl." After three days, an army truck finally stopped and took them along. When she found a "discarded rifle" in her garden, Skrjabina realized that the Red Army had fled as well. On August 9, 1942, "everything grew hushed," a silence broken by the roar of one tank and then another, with the "black sign of the iron cross" illuminated by the setting sun.[13]

Five months later when the Red Army advanced to liberate Pyatigorsk, Skrjabina, who had compromised herself by working with the Germans, decided to flee with the Wehrmacht. She ended up in a forced-labor camp near Koblenz until the end of the war. What her diaries do not hint at is what became of people like her friend Lyalya. On September 10, 1942, the SS murdered the majority of Jews in Pyatigorsk, about fifteen hundred men, women, and children, in a factory on the outskirts of town. Smaller killing operations continued until the Germans abandoned the resort to the Red Army on January 11, 1943; twenty to twenty-five Jews were shot on New Year's Day near Mashuk Mountain, the site of the poet Lermontov's death in a duel in 1841. These sporadic killing operations underscored the determination of the Germans in Pyatigorsk as elsewhere in Europe to find and put to death every single Jew.

THE SECOND CLAW of Harriet's pincer was much closer, threatening to clamp down on Cairo. It appeared to represent the final "dong" in what was known colloquially as the "Ding-Dong" war to describe the back-and-forth of Allied and Axis forces across North Africa. First one side found advantage, then the other. There was even a "Ding Dong Daddy," an American pilot of a B-25 bomber. The funny term comes from *The Wizard of Oz*, the 1939 movie in which the Munchkins sing "Ding-Dong! The Witch Is Dead" to celebrate the demise of the Wicked Witch of the East, which occurred when the tornado dropped Dorothy's house on her, and the death of the Wicked Witch of the West, who at the end was splashed with water.[14]

A total of seven dings or dongs sounded out the war in North Africa. *Ding*, when the British advanced into the colony of Libya, the Italian empire's "fourth shore," to take Fort Capuzzo after the Italian declaration of war in June 1940. And *Dong* after an Italian counteroffensive swept over the fortress to push the front east beyond Sidi Barrani in September. Another *Ding* in January 1941: British and Commonwealth troops recaptured Sidi Barrani, destroyed the Italian 10th Army, and took Baria and Tobruk. Rommel's Afrika Korps rang a *Dong* in April 1941 after they landed in Libya to reinforce the Italians and quickly laid siege to Tobruk and forced the British back a hundred miles into Egypt. And a *Ding* in November 1941 when a renewed Allied offensive relieved Tobruk to establish the line at El Agheila. There was finally a very loud *Dong* when the Axis captured Tobruk on June 22, 1942, taking more than thirty-three thousand British and South Africans prisoner. However, the Allies held their new defensive line after the First Battle of El Alamein on July 3. The question in the summer of 1942, when Harriet walked over to the map, was whether there would be another Allied *Ding* or whether the Axis *Dong* at Tobruk had introduced the final act to bring the campaign to a close with a German victory.

The desert war was a tough battle of attrition despite the movement back and forth across the sea of sand, which conjured up great fantasies about the mobility of the tank. Yet armies were tied tightly to supply lines; tanks were thirsty for fuel, which had to come across the Mediterranean; and both sides fortified positions with coils of barbed wire and acres of minefields. There were flies but no water or food in the desert;

soldiers "learned to exist almost entirely on tinned food." "Except on the coast line, there was nothing," wrote Eve Curie, the scientists' daughter, in her reportage, *Journey Among Warriors*: "no houses, no villages, no ditches, no rivers, no inhabitants, no frightened columns of refugees—absolutely nothing but emptiness. It was like taking a blank sheet of paper to write a story on it." Crossing "in the sky, on the sand, there were modern machines: planes, guns, trucks, and tanks, manned by daring men." But so few operational tanks survived offensive operations that the debris field around the burned-out wrecks provided more telling impressions. Alan Moorehead, correspondent for London's *Daily Express*, rummaged around the closest dump. The interior fittings of the tanks had been "dragged out like the entrails of some wounded animal, for you would see the mess boxes, the tooth brushes and blankets of the crews scattered around together with their little packets of biscuits, their water-bottles, photographs of their families, hand-grenades, webbing, tommy-guns, mirrors, brushes and all the mundane ordinary things that fill a soldier's kit-bag."[15] Every ding and dong left miles of burned-out vehicles, discarded equipment, clothes, and paper—always paper— scattered on the desert floor.

The German soldier was better outfitted to camp out in the desert, but the two sides lived under the same conditions and wasted themselves retracing the same movements between El Agheila and El Alamein. It was not surprising that they shared a favorite song, Lale Andersen's "Lili Marlene." However, the Allies had an easier time with supplies that the Germans and Italians had to transport across the dangerous Mediterranean. Moreover, British soldiers had the opportunity to take leave in Cairo, the great city crowned in the distance by the pyramids the Germans never glimpsed. The city looked like a railway station as refugees departed and soldiers arrived. The streets were always full of English soldiers back from the front: "Their worn, thin, washed-out khaki was wrinkled with heat. Dark patches of sweat showed between their shoulder blades and under their arms."[16]

Then in the dry heat of the desert at the end of June 1942, the unexpected *Dong*: Tobruk, which came not long after the big *Dong* of Singapore and a string of British defeats in Greece. For Churchill, the fall of Tobruk, which had become an important Allied supply port on the Mediterranean shore of eastern Libya, and with it the capture of more than thirty thousand soldiers of the British Eighth Army, was "one of the heaviest blows I can recall during the war"—he already had had several. Singapore could be sacrificed but not the Suez Canal and its port facilities at the terminus of the lifeline around Africa. Former war secretary Leslie Hore-Belisha rose in Parliament on July 2, 1942, to press the question about the next one hundred days in light of the last during which "we lost our Empire in the Far East." Stalin also wondered about the resilience of his democratic allies: while he was holding on to Sevastopol, the British had run away from Tobruk.[17]

Harriet's pincer claws had not yet closed. It was with grim determination that Britain and the United States accelerated reinforcements in Egypt with air forces and tanks. "The next three months," the *New York Times* observed, "will be the worst months of the war."[18]

Historians contend that Hitler, the supreme commander who ultimately decided on priorities in what had become a two-front war, missed an opportunity by not weighting the claw in North Africa at the expense of the one in the Caucasus.

"Only Hitler's obsession with the assault on the Soviet Union," writes one, "prevented Britain's almost certain defeat" in the Middle East. Had Rommel received in June and July the supplies he obtained in November and December, the battle might have turned. Of course, the Wehrmacht's problems in Russia would have been aided by the addition of the same supplies the Afrika Korps needed.[19] "For a brief moment in mid-summer 1942, Germany saw second-chance glimpses of grand victory." *Time* even asserted that "we're losing the war." With knowledge that "more than 1,000,000 Jews have been killed" in "countries dominated by Germany," the *New York Times* contemplated the "new Black Death" that "blights the face of the earth and the lives of people wherever it spreads." "This loathsome thing" hovered "over Egypt" and "over Palestine." Rommel in Egypt, Kleist in the Caucasus, the Japanese in Burma—Axis leaders savored the moment for "the Goddess of military fortune only knocks once."[20]

Demonstrations against the king and his British handlers had broken out in Cairo on February 4, 1942, when students showed their colors by chanting, "We are Rommel's soldiers." Whether secular or Islamic, nationalists deeply resented Egypt's treaty with Great Britain that required it to render assistance in the event of war; after it was invoked in 1939, the British treated Egypt like a colony, the ambassador acting as its governor. There were few people in "Midaq Alley" who did not resent the racial vulgarities that had become the white man's shorthand. "Gyppos" named just about any Egyptian, while "wogs" referred to local clerks "*working on Government* service." Radio Bari, Italy's Arabic-language station, provided singsong to the vibes on the street:[21]

Bala Missiou, bala Miser. (No more Monsieur, no more Mister)
Kelloh barra, haide sikter. (Go away, get out of here)
Bissama Allah, oua alard Hitler (We want Allah in heaven, and Hitler on earth)

The disorganized British retreat from the small port of Mersa Matruh, just a day's march from Alexandria, on June 28 and 29, 1942, brought home to British officials in Cairo the immediate danger posed by Germany's Afrika Korps. The British navy quickly dispersed its ships to Haifa and Beirut. Jewish refugees rushed to trains leaving for Palestine "in a state of agitated anxiety," the busy porters offering their own farewells: "You go. Germans come." July 1 was known as "Ash Wednesday," or the "flap," a word everybody used to "put a stopper on their panic." On the grounds of the embassy and at military headquarters, the staff set about burning files. Black smoke and charred paper swirled like "black snow" around the old city.[22]

Ash Wednesday marked uncertainty, the deep divide between what the Allies hoped and what they feared. It was not so different from Moscow's "Big Skedaddle" on October 16, 1941, after the Germans had taken Kaluga in the South and Kalinin in the North; the sound of artillery could be heard in the capital, which came to a complete stop. The smell of scorched paper hung in the air as party and government offices burned their files.[23]

German propaganda announced the aims of the Wehrmacht in Egypt. "Rommel's victorious soldiers" sought "to liberate Egypt from the English yoke." It urged the population to "be ready for this day" by making "General Rommel's victory easy" and "Britain's war difficult." Although it was not known at the time, Berlin sent an SS unit to Athens ready to leave for Egypt in order "to take executive measures against the civilian population on its own authority." The SS had its sights on Jews in Egypt, where the number had risen to eighty thousand during the war, and Palestine, with nearly one-half million Jewish settlers, about one-third of the population.[24]

British plans proposed evacuating Palestine in the event of an emergency, while the Haganah, the Jewish self-defense organization, had no alternative but to stay put and fight. Watching Rommel, suspicious of the British, fearful of Palestine's Arabs who resented Jewish settlements, the Haganah armed its Jewish volunteers as best it could.

The precariousness of the Jewish search for security was dramatized in shipwrecks: the *Struma*, a former luxury yacht packed with refugees in unsanitary conditions, stranded at anchor in Istanbul because Britain's policy was to refuse more immigrants entry into Haifa. When Turkish authorities resolved to tow the ship back to Romania on February 24, 1942, a Soviet vessel torpedoed the *Struma* with the loss of all but one of the passengers. There was also the *Patria*, a French ocean liner seized by the British, which sank in the port of Haifa after it was bombed on November 25, 1940, by the Haganah in extreme protest against the policy of repatriating illegal Jewish immigrants to Mauritius. With many more Jewish refugees pushing against the majority of Arab inhabitants since 1933, Palestine itself was an overcrowded ship without a harbor.

The general condition was displacement. For some, history moved violently across their community; others fled their homes. Refugees were everywhere, packed together "in a state of agitated anxiety," rushing for trains, perishing in sea disasters, seeking shelter in new towns and ancient villages.

It became clear in July and August how thinned out Rommel's supply lines were; the British rearmed faster than the Germans and responded with their own "spirit of enterprise." The front stabilized in North Africa, and the discontent in Egypt never jelled. But for the rest of the summer, and into the fall, the Egyptian border and the Volga River, El Alamein and Stalingrad, marked the precipice.

"Run, Rabbit, Run," a popular song from 1939, caught the "before-the-beginning-of-the-end" mood that had prevailed since the fall of France and continued to pluck courage in defeat. "On the farm, it's rabbit pie day," went the lyrics of the Flanagan and Allen song: "Bang, bang, bang, bang goes the farmer's gun. Run, rabbit, run, rabbit, run, run, run, run." In the running iteration—run, run, run—the enemy was on the loose, but the song kept the rabbit from eluding the hunter's stride: bang, bang, bang. The song raised spirits in the music hall whenever the word "Adolf" was substituted for "rabbit." Churchill rehearsed the refrain during the Blitz. With Germans at the gate, Harriet and Simon climbed the pyramids "singing 'Run rabbit'" until they were "overcome with laughter."[25]

CHAPTER 8

America Prepares for War

S o far the news has been all bad," admitted President Roosevelt in his fireside chat to the American people on December 9, 1941, two days after Pearl Harbor. News did not get better in the following months. A few hundred miles south of the White House, tankers started exploding off Virginia Beach. Japan's Imperial Army drove into Burma, while the Imperial Navy scooped up islands in the South Pacific. Army Group A established base at the foot of the Caucasus Mountains, and Rommel's tanks scattered the Eighth Army across the Egyptian desert. From Singapore to Tashkent, dirtied refugees walked the story of the war.

With this script of bad news at hand, Roosevelt outlined "solemn tasks" in his State of the Union address on January 6, 1942. The objectives remained clear: "smashing the militarism imposed by war lords upon their enslaved peoples" and "liberating the subjugated Nations." To accomplish the long, hard task, he promised to overhaul the United States: "We must strain every existing armament-producing facility to the utmost." And "we must convert every available plant and tool to war production." Americans "stand ready" to "keep the wheels turning and the fires burning twenty-four hours a day, and seven days a week." Roosevelt backed up promises with details. The budget for the following fiscal year added up to "56 billion dollars," which was "more than half of the estimated annual national income." For American families that meant "taxes and bonds and bonds and taxes" in order to "fight an 'all out' war." (The idea was "all-in" for "all-out" war.) He went down the line items: "In this year, 1942, we shall produce 60,000 planes." "We shall produce 45,000 tanks," and "we shall build 6,000,000 deadweight tons as compared with a 1941 completed production of 1,100,000." The pledge was largely kept.

It is hard to imagine the leaders of any of the other belligerents representing the war effort precisely in this quantitative way. Roosevelt added that "I rather hope that all these figures which I have given will become common knowledge in Germany and Japan." They did.

Hitler astonished his associates with "extraordinary knowledge about tools and weapons." He numbered with his fingers "the horsepower needed for wheeled tractors to pull heavy field howitzers (85hp)," the "gearshift problems in the Tiger tank," the "night-flying capabilities of the Heinkel He-177," and "the size of underwater bombs necessary to blow up submarine-base sluice gates (3000 kilograms)." It is, therefore, curious that Hitler dismissed the United States as a country of "millionaires, beauty queens, stupid records and Hollywood" and mocked its industrial capacity. Hitler thought it was "an absurdity" to think that a ten-thousand-ton ship could be built in ten days. (In fact, the Liberty ship *Joseph N. Teal* was built in ten days in Portland, Oregon, from September 13 to 23, 1942, a record soon broken.) "I am just waiting for an American to take delivery of a ten-thousander at the time of order," Goebbels remarked, playing his audience for laughs.[1] Hitler had little appreciation for the importance of industry and production (as opposed to technology), which was not surprising given the central role that biology played in Nazi thinking.

To provide spiritual heft to Roosevelt's call to arms, the Museum of Modern Art (MOMA) put on an ambitious photographic exhibition, *The Road to Victory*, in the spring of 1942, "the season's most moving experience," according to the *New York Times*. It aimed to integrate industrial capacity into the national narrative to provide "a stirringly articulate portrait of America" in the unsettled times created by the war. Accompanying the oversize photographs, Carl Sandburg's legends were written in muscular prose to create a compelling portrait of American will and power. He introduced "endless numbers" of pioneers and "soldiers, sailors, fliers, farmers, builders, workers" who manufactured "tons and tons" of stuff by "hauling, pounding, boring, drilling, lifting." As visitors made their way through the bends of the exhibition, they followed the procession of the war and the nation itself.[2]

The first photograph viewers saw as they entered depicted a natural, prehistoric place, Zion National Park, Utah. The land was "virgin": "America was promises." The next panels revealed promise fulfilled as the "human tide of pioneers" cultivated and tilled so that "the earth is alive." With "their homes" and "churches, shops, schools," the new people made the country "the best, last hope of earth." The procession sped up from farmland to industrial park, skipping the Great Depression. At the bend of the procession, viewers were astonished by "power dams" and "generators" that provided "light and power to homes and factories," harnessing "billions of horses." Both the "day shift" and the "night gang" "rivet the steel sheets" and "sew" on "steel buttons" to the "clank and boom" of "the mighty song of steel."

All at once, December 7, 1941, the "day of infamy," interrupted the procession. The explosions affirmed the prior innocence of America, "the best, last hope," as well as its industrial capacity. "War—they asked for it," read the text, and "they'll get" the war.

War turned the promise of America into an obligation of firepower. "The fat of the land" made "killers in khaki riding smoke wagons" out of pioneers. "Tornadoes of hell and ashes" materialized out of the industrial landscape to drop "loads of death, tons on tons," to annihilate "the hideouts of the 'New Order.'"

According to critic Kenneth Burke, the exhibition left America and its war "remoralized." The "magnificent portrait of America" confirmed the trajectory of the nation's industrial development. One "million three hundred fifty thousand" Americans left farms in just the year 1941. After you added up all the soldiers and job seekers who arrived in the cities by the hundreds every day, one-sixth of the population was on the move. The war created the "military-industrial complex" that would irrevocably transform the United States.[3]

Bittersweet, ever-popular children's books corroborated the vast change taking place on the road to victory in the 1940s. In Virginia Lee Burton's *Mike Mulligan and His Steam Shovel* (1939), it is "the new Diesel" and "electric shovels" that will do the construction work to build the office buildings and highways that readers know development (the war) required. In *The Little House* (1942), Burton's main character is put on new foundations on a hill by a brook, yet roads, automobiles, and gas stations fill in newly surveyed urban tracts. The "little house" was left as a keepsake.

You could watch Americans switch gears on "the road to victory." The industrial plants grew everywhere "in overwhelming numbers, at an overwhelming rate." In the East Bay in California, Richmond had a population of 23,000 in 1940, many employed in the city's two new shipyards that had been built before Pearl Harbor. Construction began on three more shipyards over the course of 1942, by which time the population jumped to more than 100,000.

However, nothing compared to Ford's new Willow Run plant in Michigan. Reporters went out to look at the diesel and electric shovels that scraped the "cornfields, rhubarb patches, and horse pastures" twenty-seven miles west of Detroit to lay the foundations of "the most enormous room in the history of man" with 3.5 million square feet and 42,331 industrious occupants. Four assembly lines "merged to two as the aircraft took shape" and then just one, which, one mile from the start of the line, "fed out" completed B-24 bombers each with 1,550,000 different parts in as little as sixty-three minutes. The challenge was standardization and specification; the effort lay in the ability "to 'dovetail' individual efforts and make 'the whole jigsaw' fit together in a coherent pattern." In "one of the decisive battles of the war," the first of 8,685 bombers rolled out of the plant on September 10, 1942. "Some day the name of Willow Run should be as famous in U.S. history as Bull Run," exulted *Life*. "I knew we were going to win the war when I saw the big Willow Run aircraft factory outside Detroit," remembered one satisfied Canadian ally.[4]

At the end of the war, the United States, with 6 percent of the world's population, accounted for nearly 50 percent of its gross product, up from 25 percent in 1938 (and the figure for 2000). Every day there were eight pages of help-wanted ads in the *Detroit Free Press*, and once labor demand was balanced with supply, worker productivity, in the automated aircraft industry, was twice that in Germany and four times greater than in Japan. Full employment also meant higher wages. Among the belligerents, only the United States enjoyed income growth, and it did so significantly; alcohol and tobacco products led sales among grocery-cart items over the course of the war. Soaring rates of petty crime, juvenile delinquency, marriage, and divorce traced the ragged edge of this new affluence. As a result, journalists found that Americans were "wallowing in unprecedented prosperity" and simply not "prepared psychologically to accept the cruel facts of war." But after his release from a Japanese internment camp, Carl Mydans was astonished at the entire effort: the country was "moving along a kind of never-ending conveyor belt."[5]

MOMA's procession came to an end with a huge photograph, twelve by forty feet, filled, "every inch of it, with marching men." These were "the country boys, big city lads," and "home town fellers" who had built America and left their homes in order to defend it. In fact, minding the business of enterprise, the United States was left with an army that was only eighteenth in size in the world, trailing imperial powers such as Germany, Britain, and Japan but behind Portugal and Sweden as well. In 1939, the United States could muster 5 divisions to Germany's 136. One in 10 Germans trained for war but only 1 in 200 Americans.[6] After Pearl Harbor, the size of the army ballooned by a factor of 11, to about three million with a further 200-plus percent increase in 1943. The already strong navy quadrupled in size to 640,000 sailors from 1940 to 1942, and almost tripled again to 1.7 million in 1943. US Army Air Forces grew at an exponential rate that reflected unwavering Anglo-American faith in airpower; at the end of 1942, the air forces were thirty-seven times larger than they had been at the end of 1939 (1.6 million).

What made "the road to victory" so moving was that it "dramatized an American epic" in which individual spectators could see themselves in the whole. A great deal of American reporting on World War II attempted to validate the processional by following "everyman" on the road from civilian to army life. Stories tried to find the right focus or recipe to bake the new element of global war into the American pie.[7]

Life caught him as he was underway, in March 1942, but wrote up "U.S. Army Private" as if it had tagged along with Charles E. Teed of Effingham, Illinois, from the start, before he had drawn his draft number in 1940. It opened the portrait with a prologue imagining Teed on the field of battle in Russia in 1812. No scene from Tolstoy's *War and Peace* was quoted more often than Prince Andrei's reflections on his military experience in which he came to the conclusion that victory or defeat depended not on "military genius" but on the soldier in the ranks, on Charles Teed, who in battle *"shouts 'hurrah' or 'We are lost.'"*[8]

Life scaled the war to the ordinary citizen. Teed and his widowed mother opened the Heart Café opposite Effingham's courthouse in January 1940, just as the United States began to muster up for war. With the town astride the busy intersection of two railroads and two highways—US 40 and US 45—the Teeds decided to keep the restaurant open all night "to catch the tourist trade," the country on the move. In October, in the inaugural round of selective service, Teed drew a number that "wasn't low" and "wasn't high." In the hustle of running the business, Teed was surprised to receive a letter in July 1941 notifying him to report to training. Ten days later, Teed, like so many young American men, stood with his girlfriend at the railroad station waiting for the train that would take him to Rockford, Illinois. (Americans usually took the train to start the trip to war, which is the dramatic scenario by which visitors enter the National World War II Museum in New Orleans.) He "couldn't quite believe he was going into the Army." At Camp Grant, Teed was inspected, drilled, and taught "when to salute and when not to salute." "Everything was new and strange," but "from the beginning of his military career, Teed had things the Army needed and wanted—a strong, healthy body, a tractable disposition and a natural respect for authority."

The railroad eventually brought Teed to Fort Bragg in North Carolina. Teed took "a certain pride in doing things well." He figured out problems, read the *Soldier's Handbook*, and learned to use a compass well enough to make squad leader. Over time he hankered for "some action," but he could not imagine himself among the dead, "who always had the faces of strangers in his imagination." Making the marksman's rating at Fort Bragg, even keeping up with "current events," Teed attracted the attention of his company commander. Yet there were other men who also showed initiative; "it remains to be seen whether Teed will prove to be the kind of man who makes a good corporal or sergeant." All around, "Teed is a good soldier," *Life* concluded, "a better soldier than his country seems to think." The magazine settled Prince Andrei's question: the citizen-soldier from Effingham will "cry 'Hurrah!' rather than 'We are lost!' when his moment comes." (Sergeant Teed served in North Africa, Italy,

and France, earning two Purple Hearts. He returned to Effingham where he opened a TV repair shop and died in 1985.)

Building a military force depended on pulling millions of
men like Teed out of civilian life and drafting them into the
army, which unlike the navy or air forces relied mainly on conscription. Selective service turned away significant numbers
of young Americans: fully 10 percent of all those examined
were rejected for psychiatric reasons (including homosexual-
ity) alone, a total of two million men. More than twice as many
prospective soldiers were classified as unfit because they were
fathers or felons or did not measure up because they were under
five feet tall or lacked at least twelve of their natural thirty-two
teeth, "a grim testament to the toll taken on the nation's health
by the Great Depression."

Yet selection disguised the army's task of social and physical rehabilitation. Special army schools taught the elements of
reading and writing with primers such as *Private Pete Eats His
Dinner.* By 1945, there were more than 25,000 army dentists,
up from 250 in 1939. Over the course of the war, they "pulled
15,000,000 teeth and fitted 2,500,000 dentures" in "the most
momentous job in the history of dentistry." More so than the air
force or the navy, the army was quite diverse. Just like Teed, the
GI was amazed by the different sorts of Americans: "I had not
known their like before, nor have I met them since." In a single
company, you could organize "a dramatic troupe" or start up "a
hillbilly band." If a battalion needed a soldier who spoke Italian,
the colonel found him "just by shouting for one."[9]

A divisional training camp for thirty or forty thousand soldiers required mixed terrain for training and maneuvers and
decent year-round weather, as well as a location near towns,
roads, and railways. One after another, camps were either

expanded or newly built in the South that offered the prereq- uisites. At Fort Bragg where Charles Teed reported, the "land had to be cleared, hills leveled, valleys filled, trees uprooted, and roads surfaced." It took "a labor force of 28,500" work- ing around the clock for nine months to triple the size of the camp. The army built "a road that stretched 74 miles," it built "a reception center capable of handling 1,000 men at a time," and it built twenty "63-men barracks, and a new hospital." The first thing that conscripts like Teed smelled was fresh paint and new lumber.[10]

When selective service began, the army was closer to the Continentals at Yorktown than it was to the army (air forces) that dropped the atomic bomb on Hiroshima. In 1941, the army still handed soldiers the standard 1903 Springfield rifle. The weeks of training aimed at developing the basic ability to han- dle modern field weaponry, antiaircraft artillery, and mortars as well as to learn the basics of map reading. And the army had to create the uniform: common quarters, standard military cour- tesies, adherence to rank, and submission to a military regime in which there were no longer personal civilian "rights." Mili- tary service shaped an immense army of millions of men who wore "government issue" (GI) and shared a playlist of hit songs and curse words. The training camp built a great big new set of American life far away from the Heart Café.[11]

PRIVATE TEED HAD traveled to Fort Bragg by train, but *Life* left unmentioned what that transit meant to African Americans in the Jim Crow era. There were "many people, many faces" on MOMA's "road to victory," but they were all white. Black

Americans were overlooked and their patriotic contributions accepted without further comment.

In fact, Blacks were made unwelcome when they volunteered for military service and segregated out and relegated to subordinate roles when drafted. "We were fighting the Second World War," admitted writer James Baldwin, but "*We*: who was this *we*?" Something more needed to be said.[12]

"It annoys our white friends to have this repeated so often, I know," observed George S. Schuyler, columnist for the leading Black newspaper, the *Pittsburgh Courier*, after Pearl Harbor, but "democracy means rule by THE people. Not merely rule by the WHITE people." If the "ruling white minority," he explained, "stresses the preservation of 'our way of life' as the great goal," the restoration of sovereign rights, "the vast mass of colored folk" all over the world "seeks an entire new" life, and, he added, "I think they are going to get it," announcing an expanded, more "concrete" view of the war and its "generalities about freedom."[13]

When he considered the role of Black troops in the US military, Secretary of War Henry Stimson reflected on the nation "suffering from the persistent legacy of the original sin of slavery." For Stimson, sin meant stigma, not trauma, one that confirmed the "incompetency of colored troops" and refuted the "vain hope" for social equality because of the "impossibility of race mixture by marriage." For the military establishment, Black Americans were "basically agriculturalists," which explained their enslavement in the past and their confinement to service roles in the present-day army.[14]

Pushed by spokesmen such as Schuyler, held in place by officials such as Stimson, the issue of the role of Black Americans in the armed services was hashed out in high-level consultations held in Washington, DC. In June 1941, Roosevelt and Secretary of the Navy Frank Knox met with Walter White of the National Association for the Advancement of Colored People (NAACP) and labor leader A. Philip Randolph. When the meeting got to opening up navy ranks to African Americans, Knox protested the very premise of juggling numbers. "We can't do a thing about it," he explained, "because men live in such intimacy aboard ship that we simply can't enlist Negroes above the rank of messmen." For the boss of the navy, the cultural "beliefs" of white sailors who could not imagine close contact in confined spaces with bunks and hammocks put a veto on integration. A natural conciliator, Roosevelt simply refined stereotypes to find a compromise. He brought up the navy's "good Negro bands" and recommended assigning some to the battleships. "'White and Negro men aboard ship will thereby learn to know and respect each other and then we can move on from there.' Knox promised to look into the matter and to see what could be done." Not much changed.[15]

As far as the army was concerned, it protested against being turned into what one spokesman called a "sociological laboratory"; "military orders, fiat, or dicta" would not change deeply held attitudes in the ranks, although the army was well-known for issuing orders and was in fact engaged in a vast social experiment to make healthy, mechanically adept soldiers out of many sickly, unskilled civilians.[16]

The war effort *nationalized* America's race problem, making it an *American* rather than merely a *southern* issue. The war effort transplanted a regional racial attitude into national policy, but the war aims also cast in a much more principled way the North's often parochial criticisms of the South. The war pulled at both ends of this rope.

There was no *Life* portrait of an African American soldier. Such a figure can be assembled only thanks in large part to letters soldiers wrote to the National Association for the Advancement of Colored People, the well-established civil rights group, or to leading Black newspapers such as the *Pittsburgh Courier* or the *Chicago Defender*, newspapers generally barred from army posts in the South. Black men did not always pull a draft number because draft boards in the South did not want to enlist African Americans. Nationally, they "rejected blacks at a rate of 18.2 percent, compared to an 8.5 percent rejection rate for whites." Since most of the army posts were in the South, the majority of American infantrymen traveled Jim Crow to get to training. Northern Blacks often experienced officially sanctioned discrimination for the first time when the Illinois Central or the Atlantic coast railroad crossed the Mason-Dixon Line and resegregated passengers to complete the trip south. Going to training was the Great Migration in reverse. Dudley Randall, a poet from Detroit, called the line "the black river, boundary to hell," as he "set upon the southern road."[17]

The official history commissioned by the US Army reflected on the boundaries African American soldiers had to consider as they reported to training camps in the South in 1942: "Would he be served if he tried to make a purchase at the main post exchange, or was there a special branch exchange for Negro units? Which theater, which bus stop, which barber shop could he use? Where could he place a long distance call?" The color lines multiplied: "Was he free to enter the main Red Cross office? The gym? The bowling alley? Would the station cleaning and pressing concessionaire accept his soiled clothing? How would he be received in the nearby camp town?"[18]

The camps themselves honored Confederate war heroes, a deliberate attempt by the US Army to reconcile South and North during World War I. Built in 1917, Virginia's Fort Lee was named after the Confederate general; Fort Pickett in Virginia (1941) commemorated George E. Pickett who led the disastrous charge at Gettysburg. The unpopular brigadier general Braxton Bragg got Teed's Fort Bragg (North Carolina, 1918). Even in North Africa, signs between American tents read "Rebel Street" or "Mason-Dixon Line." "Back in the Bronx," remembered one Marine, "we just didn't look at people as either Rebels or Yanks, but those Southern boys sure did."[19]

To flip through the files of the NAACP for any of the war years would build on the Civil War story. When soldiers arrived at Camp Wheeler, the colonel informed the recruits that it did not matter whether they came from Chicago or Detroit; they were now in Georgia. Black soldiers felt as though they arrived on a plantation: "It was as if we were the slaves and the white officers in our outfit were the overseers." The army believed southern officers were in the best position to handle Black soldiers, especially those from the North who were regarded as sullen, even rebellious; overwhelmingly, however, according to the army's own polling, "Negroes preferred Negro to white lieutenants" and white "Northerners to Southerners." In a 1943 report from Camp Johnston in Florida, an army medic used plain speech, spare as the poet's: "The crackers here call you nigger in a minute & we have no Service club, heater or nothing to go to. The barracks are no where the place is made up of burnt lumber & and the floors are made of sand. So far we all wish we were dead & in hell cause this place will drive the average man crazy."[20]

In the war years, many southern whites believed that Blacks were becoming more assertive because of the rhetoric of freedom and democracy enshrined in the Atlantic Charter and because of better economic opportunities. During the war, "a Negro in uniform evoked hostility, fear, and suspicion." It was felt that "a Negro in the Army had been 'spoiled,' had forgotten 'his place,' and had become 'uppity.'" The determination to put Blacks back in their place animated southern attitudes well after the war. For their part, Black observers thought that "the South was more vigorously engaged in fighting the Civil War than in training soldiers to resist Hitler." Since the War Department upheld southern prejudices in formulating policy on the participation of Blacks in the army and northern white soldiers added their voices to the lopsided polls opposing sharing even the post exchange, James Baldwin's summary in *Notes of a Native Son* (1955) was entirely justified: "The treatment accorded the Negro during the Second World War marks, for me, a turning point in the Negro's relation to America." "A certain hope died," he wrote, "a certain respect for white America faded."[21]

It was with racial policy based on the "southern way of life" that the United States Army deployed combat troops first to Northern Ireland in accordance with standing war plans and, over the course of 1942, to Scotland and England as well as Australia. Britain's Colonial Office, with an eye to public opinion in the colonies, criticized American segregation, while the Foreign Office urged good relations with the US military.

However, Britons themselves showed little understanding for overt segregation policies; public houses were just that, public. The *Pittsburgh Courier* published a letter written by an indignant Englishwoman, Patricia Strauss. She pointed out that the English prided themselves on hospitality. When they sponsored dances to entertain American soldiers, "the village girls quite naturally danced with the Negro soldiers." There was only trouble when "some white American soldier feels it incumbent upon himself to interfere"; "the villagers take the part of the Negro soldier," she made clear. (In one story, pubs displayed signs, "For British Civilians and U.S.A. Negro Forces Only.") The villagers' view was eventually adopted by Britain's Ministry of Information when it prepared a film short, *Welcome to Britain*, intended for new arrivals. American actor Burgess Meredith, facing directly into the camera, offered the following scenario: "You hear an Englishwoman asking a coloured boy to tea. She was polite about it and he was polite about it. Now," he admonished, "that might not happen at home, but the point is, we're not at home, and the point is too, if we bring a lot of prejudices here what are we gonna do about 'em?"[22]

The war forced American racial attitudes into new international arenas that confirmed as well as contested their basic premises. Nonetheless, Blacks remained mostly in supportive noncombat roles when the army shipped them overseas. And it was Black attendants who cooked and served and cleaned on the US Navy battleships that intercepted Japanese naval operations in the Pacific, first in the Battle of the Coral Sea in May 1942, then in the Battle of Midway in June. The US Navy resisted any relaxation of a policy of strict segregation in which Blacks and whites slept, ate, and worked in separate quarters. Even the heroism of Dorie Miller, a messman on the *West Virginia* during the attack on Pearl Harbor who had come to the aid of wounded sailors and manned an antiaircraft gun, did not hurry along changes in navy policy. Although he was the first African American awarded the Navy Cross, when Miller was killed in action on the escort carrier *Liscome Bay* in November 1943, he died a messman; Miller, like other Blacks, had not been allowed to apply for ratings. Nearly one-half of all Black sailors remained stewards—the new name—at the end of the war in 1945.[23]

Race relations in American society changed in that they became the object of more scrutiny; once they lost their self-evident aspect, the old customs could no longer be part of the background. As a much more openly contested category, race was more easily dismantled, but it was also more energetically defended. During the war, race was no longer a feature, or a given, but political.

THE HOMESPUN DISPLAY at MOMA and the portrait of Teed offered an incomplete and whitewashed picture of American mobilization that ignored the prejudices that undid national union. In a similar fashion, the accounts about the first US battles heroicized the action by overlooking points of real weakness and sheer luck. There was very little blood in all the flag-waving. The first victories at Midway and Guadalcanal were tenuous and surprising, inconsistent in any case with the superlative exploits reported after battle. Nineteen forty-two was a perilous year because it was not clear whether America or its democracy would prevail in the challenges of total war.[24]

The United States Navy began probing the expanding Japanese perimeter in the South Pacific in January 1942, but the first major attempt to block the expansion of Japanese power was the navy's attempt to prevent a Japanese landing at Port Moresby on the southern coast of New Guinea. Although the Japanese had already occupied the island's northern coast in March 1942, Port Moresby, less than three hundred miles from the Australian mainland, was the prize. The Americans seized the initiative to stop the Japanese in the Battle of the Coral Sea (May 4–8, 1942). The United States Navy also prepared to engage the Imperial Japanese Navy in the western Pacific. This effort culminated in the astonishing American victory in the Battle of Midway at the beginning of June. A third move was to deploy the Marines to reoccupy Guadalcanal in the Solomon Islands (August 7, 1942)—the Japanese had invaded the South Sea island on July 6 and begun building an air base. Together, New Guinea, Midway, and Guadalcanal added up to the beginning of the American counteroffensive against the Japanese.

Midway (June 4, 1942) was an amazing naval battle, the biggest and most consequential of the war. The Japanese aim was to engage the US carrier force in a "decisive battle" and to cap the victory with the occupation of Midway Island, twelve hundred miles west of Hawaii. The surprise American victory resulted in the fateful destruction of four Japanese aircraft carriers, all of which had taken part in the attack on Pearl Harbor. In a single ten-minute interval of bombing, US forces disabled the offensive capacity of the Imperial Navy. Both sides made major mistakes, but good luck accompanied the Americans, while bad luck stalked the Japanese. The basic Japanese strategy was correct: strike the Americans hard and fast before their buildup achieved "crushing superiority," but planning was faulty due to inflexibility and overconfidence, a sign of "victory fever." The Americans themselves launched a series of suicide air assaults on the Japanese carriers, yet sidestepped disastrous defeat when a last wave of dive-bombers struck at the most inopportune time for the enemy.

Coming a few days later, the reports straightened the path from intention to victory and turned a "freak accident" into a "perfect coordinated" attack. With a "panoramic view" of the

Japanese carrier fleet, "the greatest army of surface vessels any of us had ever seen—they seemed to stretch endlessly from horizon to horizon"—the retrospective aviator's eye told the story and wrote up the conclusion: when "I looked back to *Akagi* hell literally broke loose." The panorama suggested foresight and clarity, an insupportable view that recuperated losses into sacrifice while hiding the folly of the operation behind sequence and pattern. The eye blinded itself to the "sheer cluelessness" of the fog of war.[25]

Guadalcanal, the third big operation undertaken by the United States in the year after Pearl Harbor, ended in victory, but the struggle for the island was open-ended as well. The accounts of soldiers and journalists made room for the elements of "war that are confusing, illogical, random, and fatal": "no orders came . . . pure terror . . . cacophony . . . too close! . . . shaken and exhausted . . . one man dead and one wounded—the first installment of the price we were to pay." "Each point and each river along that quiet green coast has its story to tell of men fighting against each other and the jungle," reflected Herbert Merillat on Guadalcanal.[26]

When the US Navy discovered that the Japanese were building an air base on Guadalcanal, the snap decision was made to invade the island, about twice the size of Long Island, and to block any further southward extension of Japan's military perimeter. Otherwise, no one had ever heard of Guadalcanal. Staffers at the navy's South Pacific Area Command gathered up old Admiralty charts from 1897 and German ones from 1908 to prepare an amphibious landing on August 7, 1942, exactly eight months after Pearl Harbor.[27] In the early morning, eleven thousand soldiers of the 1st Marine Division under the command of Alexander Vandegrift landed without resistance and seized the nearly completed airfield. From embedded positions on the northern shore of the island, the Marines fought a tough five-month battle of attrition against the Japanese army.

Beyond the surf and sand, the Marines encountered an almost impenetrable jungle. No account of Guadalcanal lacks a rich description of how the jungle besieged both armies who quickly felt abandoned without regular supplies or reinforcements. "We were orphans," trapped on the island, one Marine wrote; "no one cared, we thought."[28]

What tied the fighting on land, sea, and air together was the constant need to secure or prevent landings of supplies, which, in turn, determined the timing of Japanese attacks in which newly arrived reinforcements never quite assembled sufficient strength. Everything depended on landing men and matériel. Strategically, the US Navy came out ahead, although it lost more ships and sailors because the Americans put ashore sufficient supplies, whereas the Japanese did not. Guadalcanal posed in miniature the deadly serious problem the Japanese faced throughout the war, namely, to keep supplies flowing to and from the periphery throughout the war; almost from the start, they were harassed by US submarines and could not move resources reliably around the empire. At the same time, the Americans defended a fixed base at Henderson, whereas the Japanese were dispersed and forced to infiltrate through the tangle in order to mount attacks.

After a few weeks, both Tokyo and Washington realized that Guadalcanal was the decisive opening battle for control in the Pacific. Just as American newspapermen arrived to report on this focal point of the war, the Japanese evened up their forces and launched air and sea bombardments against the Marine positions with attacks across the "bloody ridge" south of their encampments at the airfield. Throughout September and October, Marines felt doom approaching. When Hanson Baldwin of the *New York Times* arrived on the island in mid-September, he was surprised that the Marines defended such a "narrow enclave" (a stable base in Japanese eyes). Looking around, he thought that "we are just holding onto Henderson Field," which at the time had fewer than a dozen operable planes, "by the skin of our teeth." After his return, Baldwin wrote up a résumé: the foe was "tough and hard and relentless," yet this "major campaign" was being fought by the Americans "on a shoe string." "We have done some of it well, some of it brilliantly," he noted, but "some of it very badly."[29]

At one point, the *New York Times* even chiseled an epitaph for the Marines. "Guadalcanal" was the simple header, repeated in the text: "Guadalcanal . . . we know that these American young men will do all that humanly can be done to stand their ground and to advance. . . . Guadalcanal. The name will not die out of the memories of this generation. It will endure in honor."[30]

"The enemy is hurting too," reminded Chester W. Nimitz, commander in chief of the US Pacific Fleet. Over the months, the seesaw battles threw the Japanese out of kilter. At the beginning they underestimated the American threat, which made them both overconfident and ill-prepared. Insufficient supplies hobbled the usefulness of reinforcements when they did arrive. Japanese air forces also suffered terrific losses in the four-hour bomber runs from Rabaul and back: the Guadalcanal campaign cost the Imperial Navy "two and a half times the number of planes and fifteen times the number of pilots lost at Midway." For all the sacrifices the Japanese made to dislodge the Americans from Henderson Field, they never gained control of the air. And on the ground, heavier American firepower overwhelmed attacking infantry. The technological imbalance only widened as Marines brought in construction equipment and trucks.[31]

The threat of starvation hovered over Japan's entire offensive operation: supplies first delivered by ship were later run in by submarines and in the end stuffed into oil drums floated near shore. Fighters on both sides lost weight, but the Japanese starved. As early as September 1942, Colonel Tsuji reported to Tokyo that remnants of the Japanese army on Guadalcanal were "thinner than Gandhi himself." Isolated in temporary encampments, living off half rations and later roots and berries and roasted lizards, the soldiers referred to Guadalcanal as "Starvation Island." A poet described the complete lack of infrastructure:

> Our rice is gone
> Eating roots and grass
> Along the ridges and cliffs
> Leaves hide the trail. We lose our way
> Stumble and get up, fall and get up.[32]

On the 2,047 square miles of Guadalcanal, twenty-five thousand Japanese infantrymen died, five thousand in combat, but nearly one-half succumbed to disease and starvation, an astonishing figure that compares only to death rates in their own prisoner-of-war camps. Marines suffered acutely from malaria, but they did not fall down and die on the trail. The Americans won the campaign with disproportionately fewer infantry deaths. At Guadalcanal, the myth of the invincibility of Japanese supermen died, but not the tough, even horrified estimation of the bloody costs of war.

The jungle island took on monstrous and grotesque forms in the battles.

Onshore, you could see the bodies and debris wash up. The waters around Guadalcanal earned the nickname "Iron Bottom Sound." Battleships simply disappeared without a trace. On the morning of November 13, the cruiser *Juneau* was hit by a torpedo and "vanished as though she had been a mirage." The losses around Guadalcanal and Savo Island were so catastrophic, and traumatic, that the US Navy refused to report for many years on the extent of the casualties or the horrendous fate of the sailors who had perished in the water. Accounts of the ten surviving sailors from the *Juneau* who clung for ten days to rafts and debris were first published in 1947: "the slow death from thirst, exhaustion, wounds, drowning, and sharks." "Sharks"—the monster of the sea sailors feared most rarely appeared in print during the war.[33]

"Our 'green hell,'" as veterans remembered it, was made up of all sorts of "fear-creators." "The sounds of man's own war in the jungle, the rattle of small arms fire, the roar of artillery," combined with noises of the jungle.[34] When Marines entered the wild after battle, they found the ground scattered with corpses. "Dead bodies were strewn about the grove," wrote Robert Leckie. "All of my elation at the victory, all of my fanciful cockiness fled before the horror what my eyes beheld." Even veterans of the Great War had never seen such "congestion of the dead." And Marines felt compelled to kill Japanese corpses a second time to make sure the bodies were dead. "I have never heard or read of this kind of fighting," admitted the Marine commander; "these people refuse to surrender. The wounded will wait until the men come up to examine them and blow themselves and the other fellow to pieces with a hand grenade."[35]

American soldiers died as well, and even alive their broken bodies suffered from what Leckie called "speculative dread": "vacant stares from pupils that already seemed darker, larger, and rounder than normal." In what was the first report on Americans fighting, John Hersey claimed a victory of sorts since Marines proved to be "as brave as any fighters in any army in the world." Actually, he left a searing chronicle of frightened "men running away" who reassembled in a file of "shock and blast victims," recalling John Singer Sargent's 1919 oil painting, *Gassed*. According to a naval psychiatrist, Guadalcanal was the "American Dunkerque."[36]

The state of siege in the jungle battered the warriors. In this "patch of destiny," explained *Time* magazine, "the Japanese cling, animal-like, to the jungle. The Marines prefer the ridges from which their weapons, particularly artillery, can dominate the valleys. But they go down into the tangle to hunt out their prey." "It is simply a matter of killing or being killed."[37] The men on Guadalcanal walked into an unfamiliar jungle, and they walked out more frightened, having discovered some of the monsters of the jungle even in themselves. There was no panoramic picture. The arc from disorientation to horror and a wobbly victory traced the course of the war in the year 1942 from Pearl Harbor to Stalingrad.

IN THE DEDICATION to his 1962 novel, *The Thin Red Line*, James Jones noted the "special qualities" that "the name Guadalcanal evoked for my generation." Like other Pacific islands such as Tarawa or Iwo Jima, Guadalcanal became a fixed part of the American war memory. For much of the rest of the world, however, what recalled the American presence in far-off places were

Coke bottles and swing music. (Coca-Cola delivered five billion cases to the US military during the war, more than one hundred billion bottles; it had sixty-three overseas bottling plants in 1945, up from three in 1939.) "GI Jive" registered the arrival of American soldiers around the world. In place of a peppy march like "Over Here" from the Great War, swing quickly became the officially sanctioned morale-building music of war-bond rallies and USO shows. It was Artie Shaw and his "crack navy band," not Roy Acuff and his Smokey Mountain Boys, who toured the South Pacific.[38]

There was syncopation between swing and movements of the war. Swing was for the swing shift after midnight. It was a polka come apart at the seams: "dance time TNT" or "the blues on roller skates." Filled with unanticipated beginnings and endings, "this fast-moving world of ours" became more "jazz-shaped"—that was the evocative word Ralph Ellison used to describe America's protean culture. Couples simulated pushing away and pulling toward and took up more space as they did than two dancers had ever occupied before.[39]

The army's magazine *Yank* reported on the invasion of swing as American troops reached Iceland, Northern Ireland, and Australia. The "Ulster Hep Cats" spoke for itself, but "in Iceland, too!" the editors exclaimed. And another night, "somewhere in Australia," there was not much noise to be heard in "the bivouac area" outside "a snapping twig as a small kangaroo hopped through the underbrush." In time, "a couple of guitars began to twang softly in the woods. A little while later a muted trumpet joined in, "then a clarinet, then two saxophones." Within an hour, the woods were rocking to "One O'Clock Jump." What is noteworthy is how *Yank* choreographed the conversion to swing: "At the start, the Aussies asked for quick steps, jazz waltzes, barn dances." But "after a while, the Australians began to see the light and in recent weeks their demands for 'Chattanooga Choo Choo' have been so numerous that the band is beginning to feel sorry it ever heard of that illustrious train." "All you hear over here is *our* music," one corporal summed up—"good American jitterbugging."[40]

The American-inspired sound was established before the war, but it played louder during the war. Over the holidays at the end of 1941, the Bantu Men's Social Centre, one of the few public places for Africans in Johannesburg, sponsored a "battle of bands," including Johannesburg's Haarlem Swingsters, Benoni's Swing Aces, and Pretoria's Jazz Ramblers, who, "playing with a finish and finesse," won first prize. In Sierra Leone's Freetown, the Cuban Swingers and the Blue Rhythm Band played the Sackville Saloon. Even in Japanese-occupied Manila, "raucous boogie-woogie blared" along Daitoa or Greater East Asia Avenue (formerly Taft). Around the world, swing announced the Americans.[41]

In some ways Nazi leaders were right when they listed the eccentric products the United States had to offer the world, including "stupid records and Hollywood," yet they made sure German radio continued to broadcast some sort of jazzed-up music. Critics of jazz belonged to "a world that had long passed," Goebbels insisted; the conventional tastes of old men had contributed to Germany's loss in the last war, whereas, with "the application of new, better standards, we intend to win this war." "It is sometimes funny," noted a German infantryman bunkered in Stalingrad, that "the best music" played while outside the artillery "crashed and banged."[42]

CHAPTER 9

Stalingrad

A ll Moscow talks only of war," Tolstoy wrote about 1812. "What did one talk about in 1942? Russia—always Russia," wrote *Times* correspondent Alexander Werth. Talk estimated the velocity of advance, the distance of retreat, and the duration of the war; it told about the new places in which people willy-nilly found themselves; it marked out zones of danger. Werth returned to Moscow in June, traveling with a merchant convoy from England to Murmansk and then by train to Moscow. "To me this will always remain a memorable journey." Sitting for six days in a "'hard' carriage," he met more ordinary Russians than he encountered when stationed in Moscow. Soldiers, railway workers, and evacuees, "all these people had something vital to say." The Soviet counteroffensive in December and January had "gone well," but not as well as travelers hoped, so they talked about the spring campaigns.[1]

Along the railway line, Werth could see bomb damage and soldiers milling around rubble. Overhead, he heard Hurricanes "swooping over us." Whenever the train stopped, passengers jumped out to collect "bunches of buttercups" dotting the meadows. As he settled in, conversations turned to war.

Werth found civilians to be "doubtful" about the war. Short on food, and driven from their homes, they were "full of forebodings." One of the passengers spoke up: "The Germans were too strong." An old man who had taught Russian in Finland before the revolution added "in an almost educated way" that "it's just no use pretending Hitler and his chaps aren't clever," although "the Volga and the Don and the Caucasus are still in our hands." As far as he knew, his three sons in the Red Army were still alive.

The railway men were better off with a ration that included 800 grams of bread as opposed to the 250 grams the old man received, and they also got some fish, cabbage or potatoes, and, importantly, matches and cigarette paper (seven sheets per month) for tobacco (twenty grams a day). They had worked all winter repairing the Murmansk line, and despite "great dangers," "most of the team had stuck it" out. Many men came from Ukraine. Fretfully watching the German drive to the south, one of them reflected that "it would be too bad if, after being evacuated to Krasnodar, my family had to be moved still further. There isn't much further to go in the Caucasus." (The Germans captured Krasnodar in August 1942.) Altogether, they felt cheated and impoverished in the North, remembering the bounty of Ukraine: "What cherries we had, and what melons." "And what water-melons," another man echoed.

The soldiers on the train were also a long way from home, but they spoke up with more confidence, perhaps because they were better fed. In one compartment, officers took up one of the interminable games of dominoes. "The double-six," Werth learned, "is called Hitler, because, the major explained, it's the most frightening of them all." A captain remarked that "the Germans had caused the death and untold misery to millions and millions of people: 'we must see it never happens again. They are a nation of brutes.'" Another officer was reading an army paper. The front page gave details about the "ninety-thousand Germans killed or taken prisoner" in the battle for Rostov. After a stop at a small station, someone announced the news of the one-thousand-bomber raid conducted by the Royal Air Force against Cologne; it became "the main subject of conversation, and Britain is very popular for the moment."

Werth's favorite companion was a little girl of ten who had been evacuated from Leningrad with her mother. Seeing she was hungry, Werth gave her "a large piece of Canadian milk chocolate I had brought from Iceland"; she gobbled it up, and her mother gave him "a little tin box filled with cranberries" as thanks. Tamara delighted the company with a song from school that "resounded through the carriage":

Hitler sam sebé ne rad,
Vzyat ne mózhet Leningrád
Vidit Nevski i sady,
I ni tudy I ni sudy, etc.

Werth supplied the full translation: "Hitler is cursing his fate; he can't take Leningrad. He can see the Nevsky and the gardens. But he's stuck. The gangster also had a try at Moscow, but was soon kicked back. All his labors are in vain. He's stuck, he's stuck again." Although Tamara recited songs and stories, she knew little about the war itself. She had heard of Africa—"foreigners live there—perhaps Germans." Germans were everywhere. And "I've heard of Hitler. Hitler will have to be killed," and "I've heard of Moscow, from which the Germans were chased away."

A little world at war populated the train from Murmansk to Moscow, but the train also stood for the wider world, Canada, Iceland, and Africa, swept up into the war. Stalingrad would sweep the whole world back again into Russia. There were only two stories that circled the globe again and again in 1942: Stalingrad and India, the fight between the Allies and the Axis and the struggle between imperial power and anticolonial insurrection, "No Retreat" on the Volga and "Quit India." India was the bigger story, stretching across the year and beyond, but Stalingrad burst into headlines as a fantastic nail-biting comet in September and October. The end of the Wehrmacht's advance, the ability of the Red Army to hold on, the engagement of both sides in the city's streets—Stalingrad riveted attention.

Headlines from Russia turned the mills of daily conversation. Writing from the French countryside, Léon Werth noted that "the only topic is Stalingrad." According to the Ministry of Information, people all over Britain seemed to think of Stalingrad as "their own native town." "During those grimmer summer months," wrote a journalist from Moscow, "our fate, and my fate, and everybody's fate" seemed to be "in the hands of the Red Army."[2]

The headlines fell into the pages of the diary kept by Charles Rist, a French economist:[3]

12 September: Astonishing resistance of the Russians at Stalingrad

21 September: Stalingrad still holding out

25 September: In Stalingrad, astonishing resistance, which surprises the entire world.

28 September: Stalingrad still holding out. You can say that the entire world is waiting for news about the siege.

11 October: Stalingrad still holding out, despite Hitler's prophecy.

14 October: Stalingrad has not been taken.

Stalingrad was a terrific drama because it reduced "the whole global struggle" to scale; the "narrowness of the frame in which the terrific action is crowded gives the picture an unequaled clarity." London's "We Can Take It" gave way to Stalingrad's "No Retreat."[4] In retrospect, it was only a matter of two or three hundred meters that separated the Germans from their objective of shoving the Soviet defenders off the western shore of the Volga.

Yet for all the spectacle of the riverfront struggle to either vanquish the Red Army in decisive battle or deny the Nazis the victory they coveted, the armies in Stalingrad were bait. In purely operational terms, one function the German 6th Army accomplished was to concentrate enough Soviet power on the Volga to relieve pressure on Army Group A in the Caucasus. At the same time, the Soviet 62nd Army in Stalingrad kept the Germans busy far forward along the Volga, while the General Staff prepared a much more ambitious counteroffensive, Operation Uranus, to be launched hundreds of miles to the west with the aim of sealing off the possibility of retreat back across the Don River in order to trap the 6th Army. The Soviet 62nd Army pulled the German 6th Army into Stalingrad while being denied the decisive role in its destruction.

Completed on November 23, 1942, Operation Uranus drove two pincer attacks from the north and south through the German flanks west of the Don River. They met at Kalach and pushed forward to Stalingrad along the same routes the Germans had advanced three months earlier. It was "the gravest blow suffered by the Wehrmacht during the entire war." What German soldiers knew as *"Stalingrab"* or "Stalin-grave" ended in the deaths of nearly 150,000 German troops (and twice as many among their other Axis partners) in addition to 90,000 taken prisoner. The number of Russian soldiers killed was far greater; 500,000 men of the Red Army fell in 143 days of fighting over the city.[5]

BEFORE THE ONSLAUGHT at the end of the summer, Stalingrad had seemed safely removed from the ravages of the fighting. Crowded with soldiers who played one game of dominoes after another, the steamer plied the Volga River from Astrakhan to Kuybyshev. A visiting journalist found the river "alive with ships, tugs, and barges." On the left, "golden-brown cliffs rise along much of its western bank and cast a reflection into the water when the morning sun is just right." The eastern side was flat, broken up into sandy plains and forests. When the steamer approached Stalingrad, passengers could hardly see the city that stretched for twenty-five miles along the river. Mamaev Kurgan, the hill that was the highest point in the city, separated the modern "business, administrative and residential" center, with two railway stations, the Red Army House, and the Univermag Department Store, from the industrial North: the Red October Plant, the Barricades Plant, the Stalingrad Tractor Plant, and, in the distance, workers' apartments in Spartakovka Garden City.

Passengers climbed up the embankment into the city rattling with "an ear-shattering din of crawling tanks and trains, of street cars, lorries, motorcycles, marching men and policemen's whistles." "Sidewalks and streets were jammed with soldiers and women in bright frocks and well-worn shoes. Here and there the groups stood before soda fountains, drinking lemonade." Soldiers found a music shop to have their "balalaikas repaired." In a beauty parlor, "half a dozen women in white frocks were doing the nails of six other women, several of whom were exceptionally attractive." In the northern districts, "the factories were producing at full speed." The "sound and fury" overhead announced "the protecting wings of Red Air Force bombers and fighters."[6]

In the late afternoon on Sunday, August 23, German aircraft suddenly appeared. They circled over the city and flew in low to drop their bombs in a series of relays lasting long into the summer evening. The earth of Stalingrad "crumpled and blackened. The city seemed to have been struck by a terrible hurricane." Thousands of residents were killed at once as stone buildings collapsed and wooden structures burned to the ground, and survivors pressed to the river's edge to find ferries to evacuate the city. The Germans had left their "calling card" announcing "to Stalingrad and to the world that the Wehrmacht was at the gates."[7]

On the same day, Wilhelm Hoffman, a German soldier with the 94th Infantry Division, reported the "splendid news" in his diary: "North of Stalingrad our troops have reached the Volga and captured part of the city. The Russians have two alternatives, either to flee across the Volga or give themselves up." Hoffman took note of one more thing on August 23. He was struck by the words of a captured Russian officer who asserted that "the Russians would fight for Stalingrad to the last bullet." Indeed, in the southern districts of the city, "the doomed divisions are continuing to resist bitterly. Fanaticism." "Something incomprehensible is, in fact, going on," the German concluded.[8]

The initial plans for the 1942 push into the Caucasus did not highlight Stalingrad, underlining instead the importance of destroying the Soviet armies that had retreated ahead of the Germans. Soon enough, however, Hitler staked his armies to the ground of Stalingrad. "No one will ever again drive us from that place," he promised in a speech broadcast from Berlin's Sportpalast on September 30, 1942. The line, an echo of previous speeches, convinced officers of the 6th Army that Stalingrad would become a "second Verdun," a prestigious fortress never to be abandoned. Hitler's insistence that "no one will take back the ground on which the German soldier has once set foot" led to his refusal to allow the 6th Army to break out after it had been encircled at the end of November. He gambled on its utter destruction, which occurred two months later.[9]

"The German invaders are driving toward Stalingrad," and they stand "at the gates of the North Caucasus"—this was Stalin's bitter résumé of the German summer offensive. He knew his Clausewitz, arguing that "every new piece of territory that we leave to the enemy will strengthen our enemy and weaken us." Resources were not infinite; nor could the option of retreat be left indefinitely open. "The conclusion is that it is time to stop the retreat," Stalin insisted. On July 28, 1942, he issued Order No. 227, "Not One Step Back!" The line was drawn at Stalingrad. In their desperate defense of the city, Red Army troops fortified themselves with the slogan "For us, there is no land beyond the Volga."

Russia did not end at the Volga, but in 1942 Stalingrad had come to stand for every village the Germans had violated and for every village to be defended. Indeed, "Mother Volga" intertwined itself with Russia, its clusters of tributaries appearing "on the map like a gigantic tree"—the "bare trunk at the bottom" at the Caspian Sea, "an immense crown of limbs and foliage at the top," where the Volga curved around Moscow to its source, some two hundred miles south of Leningrad. The Volga River also intertwined with Soviet history. In tidied accounts of the Civil War, Stalin had played the decisive role in breaking the 1918 siege of Tsaritsyn, renamed Stalingrad in his honor in 1925. Stalingrad's defenders imagined themselves in the legendary Red Army when "Stalin had said that Stalingrad would not surrender, no matter the cost." "You can die," they affirmed, "but you cannot leave Stalingrad."[10]

With Order No. 227, Stalin had put forward a classic dilemma as outlined by Clausewitz. "If we do not stop retreating," he reasoned, "we will be left without bread, without fuel, without metals, without raw materials, without factories and plants, without railroads." The backside of the same dilemma contained the difficult calculations that faced the Germans as each step forward dulled their "fighting edge." What happened in the summer of 1942 was that material resources no longer supported the fighting spirit of the German invaders, while the fighting spirit of the Soviet defenders began to compensate for material deficiencies.

Alexander Werth put his finger on the new quality to the war, what he called the "psychology of 1942." It was the indeterminate factor that Clausewitz had recognized: "the character of the people and the Government" that in critical phases has the effect of "rousing forces of protection" among the defenders.[11]

What roused the forces of protection was the plain evidence of the depredations of the Wehrmacht that the Red Army uncovered as they liberated districts occupied by the Germans. As minister of foreign affairs, Vyacheslav Molotov prepared a paper on "Nazi atrocities" to appeal to feelings of love for violated villagers and to inspire hate for German predators. This "psychology" fueled popular determination to wage a "lutte à outrance" that provided the legitimacy for Stalin's tough order, "Not One Step Back!" Death on the battlefield was accepted in order to preserve life in the village, the soldier's own home. Stalingrad on the "Mother Volga" stood in for parents, wives, and sons and daughters threatened by Germany's invaders. Writers and poets energetically translated German violation into Soviet violence. Even *Pravda*, the official newspaper of the Communist Party, appeared with a new masthead, "Death to the German Invaders!" instead of "Proletarians of all lands, unite!"[12]

Molotov's report provided details. It was as if the foreign minister himself walked into the wrecked villages. The purpose was to bring vividly to light "the dark Hitlerite hatred" evinced by the "base and criminal destruction of our towns and villages."

German occupation usually began with "the erection of a gallows," the report explained, often in view of toppled statues of Lenin and Stalin. "In the center of Orel," it reported, the Germans "hanged an old man who protested against plunder. Beside him they hanged several citizens who refused to assist the Hitlerites in robbing the population." "Everywhere in the villages," German soldiers helped themselves to cattle, grain, and other foodstuffs; "like petty thieves," they stole kitchen "utensils, clothing, underwear, footwear, furniture and toys." As the Red Army approached, the retreating Germans scorched the earth. They "burned down 960 houses out of 998" in the village of Dedilovo. "A 77-year-old peasant named Grigoryev was shot because he said, 'Don't burn my house!'"

In a sidelong observation Molotov's report hinted at the fate of Jews in the occupied territories. Beginning in August 1941, SS death squads followed the advancing Wehrmacht, eradicating Jewish residents in one community after another. "The Hitlerites did not confine themselves to murders of individual Soviet citizens"; "a horrible massacre and pogrom were perpetrated by the German invaders in the Ukrainian capital, Kiev," in which "52,000 men, women, old folk and children" were killed. The paragraph moved from the massacre of "Ukrainians, Russians and Jews" to the specifically anti-Jewish operation: "A large number of Jews, including women and children of all ages, was gathered in the Jewish cemetery of Kiev"—a reference to the murder of Jews in the Babi Yar ravines, which included old cemetery plots, on September 29–30, 1941. The account also furnished accurate and terrifying details: "Before they were shot, all were stripped naked and beaten. The first persons selected for shooting were forced to lie face down at the bottom of a ditch and were shot with automatic rifles." Then "the next group of people selected was forced to lie on top of them, and shot." Molotov's attention to the murder of Jews was highly unusual since Soviet accounts of the war almost always grouped together rather than singled out the suffering of different nationalities.

The power of Molotov's white paper rested on the ability of the Soviets to go behind (abandoned) German lines and report on the atrocities. Documenting the war "against the peaceful, unarmed population—women, children, and old folk"—they caught the Germans "red-handed."[13] The record hoped to document what Clausewitz referred to as "the burning pain of the blow" that induces the defender to "run to arms" in "a state of fury," rather than drop weapons "in terror and stupefaction."

As Germany's spring offensive advanced toward the Don River, Soviet writers returned repeatedly to the despoiled villages to rouse a sense of purpose and induce the obligation to take merciless revenge. Konstantin Simonov, who wrote the most endearing ballad of the war, "Wait for Me," imagined a sequel in which Germans invade the home the soldier had left behind. Published in *Pravda* on July 14, 1942, "Kill Him!" implored the soldier to avenge the assailant who, bursting through the door, slaps the "wrinkled face" of "your mother," tramples "your father's picture," corners the wife, "whom for so long you did not dare even kiss," and casts her "naked on the floor." "No one will kill this foe," Simonov instructed readers, "if you don't kill him first." Ilya Ehrenburg followed Simonov, unfurling a "map of Russia" with green forests and blue rivers "drenched in blood." The German is what stands "between us and life" and "books, and girls, and happiness." Therefore, "in order to live, we must kill Germans." Ehrenburg pleaded for violence. "Let us not rely on rivers and mountains," he argued, pointing to the map. "We must rely only on ourselves."[14]

Where did the sense of duty—let's call it patriotism—end and the threat of force, or terror, begin? Both elements were present and perhaps necessary. Without a doubt, Stalin's get-tough orders were plainly coercive and at least marginally effective as a deterrent. In cases of "chaotic retreat," Stalin ordered the formation of special "guard units" to execute "panic mongers and cowards." Thousands of public executions were in fact carried out. But in any evaluation of the "psychology of 1942," it would be a mistake to think only of the gun at the soldier's back without considering the German with "his black gun" at "your house" assailing "your mother, your wife." In fact, the "No Retreat" campaign appealed to soldiers who swelled the huge increase in applications for membership in the Communist Party. Doors to the party swung open to applicants who could show they had killed German soldiers in the "vengeance accounts" in which they had tallied up their scores.[15]

Vasily Chuikov, commander of the 62nd Army in Stalingrad, who admitted to shooting cowards, acknowledged the importance of home to bolster soldiers' morale on the front. He had thought about the circumstances when a soldier shouted "Hurrah!" or "We're lost!" Take the soldier "marching in a column along a dusty road towards the Volga." "He has a knapsack with provisions" and items "given him by his wife or mother for the long road." When the soldier hears "the thunder of explosions," the "weight of his thoughts" might make him "stop or slow down," or remind him that "if you don't stop the enemy in Stalingrad, he will enter your home and destroy your village!"[16]

Would the soldier turn and run or go on? The German invaders themselves considered these circumstances since they came across the same articles when they overran Red Army positions. They read Ehrenburg's exhortation calling on soldiers to consider "only the number of Germans you have killed," rather than days passed or miles traveled: "Do not waver. Do not let up. Kill." This is why Hoffman, the German infantryman at Stalingrad, thought about Soviet "fanaticism," Tolstoy's "unknown X," the "spirit of the army." Watching the battles, newspapermen around the world sorted the news dispatches and read them against Tolstoy. "Ten thousand men" or "one copy of *La Marseillaise*," the London *Times* was still wondering in 1942.[17]

RUN IN FAST motion, the battle for Stalingrad revealed the German 6th Army's steady progress. It quickly broke through the defensive perimeter the Soviets had dug around the city. By early September, the Germans fought their way into the city district, destroying the bulk of the 13th Guards Rifle Division that had crossed the river a few days earlier to reinforce the beleaguered 62nd Army. The invaders squeezed Chuikov's forces to a narrow strip along the central and northern shore of the Volga River. For the city's defenders, September 22 was a "day of death." They fully expected to be thrown into the river and slaughtered. At the same time, a confident Hitler assured the German nation that there was no question that "we will overrun and take Stalingrad." In mid-October, German forces pivoted to attack from the North, the "darkest days" for the 62nd Army that was pushed out of most of the factories and split in two. Hitler considered the battle for Stalingrad won. "We've got it really," he told his Old Fighters on November 8, 1942—except for "a few very small spots." Nine-tenths of the city was in German hands.[18]

When slowing the film down and taking it frame by frame, another picture emerges. The German assaults in September and October came at an enormous price without wiping out the Red Army. Looking for a rapid checkmate, the assailants described their situation as a stalemate, which they found bewildering and frightening as the second winter loomed. By the end of October, the battle for Stalingrad had entered its ninth week, whereas German assaults on defended positions in the summer had been wrapped up in a week or two. Exhausted and with insufficient supplies even before crossing the Don, Army Group B's whole offensive sputtered at the Volga.

Despite the aggressive German battle plan, the 62nd Army continued to hold out on the western bank of the river, while Soviet forces on the eastern side ferried supplies and reinforcements across the river and menaced the ground the Wehrmacht managed to take with unrelenting artillery fire. The Soviets pounded German positions with Katyusha rockets, while the Germans found themselves unable to deploy tanks or aircraft strikes in the confined space they were forced to contest. The conditions of urban street fighting allowed defenders to entrench themselves in rubble and to conduct small-scale raids that threw the assailants off balance. This continuous agitation turned Stalingrad into a "cauldron of small attacks" in which the Wehrmacht was caught in the same trap as the Red Army.[19]

Newspaper headlines documented the close quarters of the battle, and its lack of resolution. After the attack on the city center, Lagos's *West African Pilot* reported that "RUSSIAN FORCES STILL HOLD NAZIS AT BAY," a standoff that continued to apply weeks later: "SOVIET FORCES STILL HOLD NAZIS AT BAY." "STALINGRAD BATTERED," reported the *Richmond Independent*, but a few days later, it was "RUSSIANS BATTER NAZIS." The *New York Times* left its readers completely dizzy with its titles: "The Red Army Wavers" on September 3 but "Russian Check" two days later; the "Nazis Gain" and "Russians Retreat" until the "Russian Stem," the story for September 12. "Foes Gain," yet "Defenders Hold." On October 16, "Russians Fall Back," whereupon "Russians Stem Stalingrad Drive."[20]

It was precisely this seesaw that made the battle so compelling to watch on the front pages. When seen close up, in title form, Stalingrad was the "BLOODIEST BATTLE IN HISTORY," the "Greatest Battle" because it kept on going.[21]

For German audiences, who also received constant updates about Stalingrad, the Russians' ability to hold created growing anxiety rather than watchful satisfaction. Two days after the Wehrmacht launched its assault into the city center on September 14, Goebbels noted that the "railway station is in our hands."

Goebbels's unusually close examination of details indicated that the operational circumstances of the offensive had shifted dramatically. Even when "the railway station is in our hands," the German win belied the outstanding reality on the ground: "The kilometer gave way to the meter as a unit of measure." Just like Goebbels, military staff had been compelled to put aside charts for street maps. Newspapers published their own city maps to identify Stalingrad's major features. The global event became entirely local as it was reported, "Reds Retake Stalingrad Streets." "There was not any distance, only proximity," summarized Hans Doerr about the theater of action in Stalingrad.[22]

Chuikov cited Doerr, a major general, in his memoirs. He described his tactics as "hugging the enemy," to reduce its room for maneuver and deny it the security of advance. "A strong wave from the sea hits the coast with tremendous force," wrote one staffer for the 62nd Army, setting the scene of the German assault. However, in Stalingrad, he explained, waves "were broken into smaller streams" by buildings and rubble that served as breakers or obstacles. The farther the Germans advanced, the more resistance they encountered, splitting "their river into tributaries." Hugged by the Russians, the Germans learned "to crawl, not to walk."[23]

The German soldier thought about progress and bending the opponent's will to the point when "our soldiers will get back to Germany" for the Christmas holidays. "After all," Hoffman noted, the army was "used to moving forward." But in Stalingrad, he was quickly disillusioned, conceding that "our old soldiers have never experienced such bitter fighting before." With the defenders "established" in "houses and cellars," "you don't see them at all"; they "are firing on all sides." Hoffman complained about "gangster methods." Hoffman projected his helplessness to conjure up the invincibility of the Russians. They "are not men, but some kind of cast-iron creatures; they never get tired and are not afraid of fire," while "we are absolutely exhausted." To his Russian foe, Hoffman conceded a kind of dominion in this "hell." Without signs of progress, Wehrmacht officers and their men became "bitter and silent."[24]

Germany's *Bewegungskrieg*, or war of movement, in 1940 and 1941 and even in early summer 1942 had become an intractable *Stellungskrieg*, recalling the battles of attrition fought in World War I. Chuikov described the ground as "slippery with blood"; for the Germans, it was "a slippery slope to death."[25]

For the first time Germans contemplated defeat. Among the German people, voices struck despairing notes in November 1942: "Is this supposed to be the beginning of the end????" wondered twenty-three-year-old Lore Walb, a devoted young National Socialist. Each question mark served as an exclamation. "Even if maybe mistakes were made," she considered in a rare moment of self-reflection, "others also made mistakes." Grief-stricken, she asked, "Do we have to be completely ground down once again?"[26] Across occupied Europe, graffiti announced the end in unambiguous terms that every German soldier could understand. "1918=1943," read the scrawl on the wall. Nineteen eighteen was the "never again" in Germany's false recovered memory of the disaster at the end of the Great War when the very existence of the nation seemed to hang in the balance. It justified the entire preemptive repertoire of German operations against enemies at home and abroad since 1933, and it loomed "once again" in 1942 and 1943.

By the end of October 1942, Chuikov felt that German attacks had lost their punch. Even so, if the Germans "were being drowned in their own blood," the defenders' own "ranks were thinning and our strength ebbing." Reinforcements continued to make it over the river, but new troops had a "life expectancy" of only a few days. Propaganda celebrated the resilience of every soldier, who, sturdy in the face of "iron wind," had become "one of the stones of the city." As long fighting raged, phrases enforced the duty to die, the tomb in stone. Chuikov came to suspect that his mission to beat the enemy on the Volga no longer had the full support of the army command. What he did not know was that a much grander offensive was in preparation.[27]

Stalin ended his radio broadcast on November 6, 1942, the eve of the twenty-fifth anniversary of the revolution, with words from a popular Russian song. "There will be a holiday in our street too," he promised, a sneaky reference that became clear two weeks later when the Red Army launched Operation Uranus. News of the operation's success was announced to the Soviet people and the rest of the world on the evening of November 22, 1943, when, after four days of intense fighting, two huge pincers from the south and the north met at Kalach, trapping nearly three hundred thousand Axis troops on the eastern side of the Don River. *"Nachalos!"*—"it's started," exulted Werth in Moscow. He had the unrelieved joy of marking up his map with a blue pencil to show Soviet gains as opposed to redlined German ones; he also needed a larger chart to show what the Soviets had achieved hundreds of miles away from the northern factory district on the banks of the Volga. Goebbels studied the latest military maps as well. "The final chapter has not yet been written," he consoled himself, but plainly he knew the news from Stalingrad was "anything but good." Whatever spin Goebbels put on it, Operation Uranus, a huge flanking maneuver to trap the 6th Army against the Volga, was an unqualified success, the grand turn of events in World War II.[28]

As the Soviets ripped through the defensive positions of the Wehrmacht west of the Don, they set in motion a huge disorganized retreat toward the relative safety of Stalingrad. This time the retreat to the east was German, not Russian. From his vantage point, novelist Theodor Plievier, a German Communist in exile in the Soviet Union since 1934, set the scene based on captured letters and diaries and his interviews with German prisoners-of-war: "On both sides of the bridge" at Kalach, "along the sloping shore and on the flat land to the east, the gray mass waited—men, horses, vehicles, and guns." It was a melancholy, desperate procession: "Long trains of ammunition, rations, field kitchens, and ambulances moved across the bridge." Plievier imagined the astonished German generals watching the winter of the army: the "mist and drifting snow and sweat and blood and screams and bent backs." They "observed with precision every detail—the gray face, the filthy overcoat, the battered boots, the missing small arms, or blanket, or mess kit." However, the lieutenant could not see any of "the howitzers, the motorcycles, or the radio trucks." The equipment had been left behind.[29]

Although he had half-expected disaster, Plievier's lieutenant did not think "it would come so soon. And he certainly did not think it would come from the rear. "He had never imagined the flood would pour from the west and float him still farther eastward," farther from Germany.[30]

Trapped in the Stalingrad cauldron, the 6th Army could not count on rescue or resupply but for the completely inadequate food, fuel, and ammunition airlifted in by the Luftwaffe. The army was so exhausted that it could not imagine fighting its way out. Even if a vanguard had succeeded, it could hardly have provided an escape route for two hundred thousand men dispersed widely across the pocket. In any case, true to his word that no

German soldier gives up ground, Hitler rejected any idea of breaking out of Stalingrad. The 6th Army was ordered to defend its positions. Logistics and ideology condemned soldiers to their doom.

In Stalingrad, German time ran out. In the winter, the sun set around three o'clock. There was a desperate shortage of candles to illuminate the bunkers the soldiers had built for themselves. "Everything has changed," wrote Vasily Grossman: the Germans who in September danced "to the loud music of mouth-organs, and drove about at night with their headlights full on," "these Germans are now hiding among the stone ruins." "There is no sun for them" anymore. "Here among the dark, cold ruins, with no water, and only scraps of horseflesh to eat, they will meet with vengeance" under "the cruel stars of the Russian winter night."[31]

The soldiers were like castaways, thinking constantly about a sudden reversal in fortune, or rescue, or Hitler. Indeed, one of the reasons for the lethargy of the troops, for their sheltering instinct, was simply the desire to stay put to wait for the deliverance they believed Hitler had promised them. "Despite everything," wrote a private, "we will hold out because the Führer will knock us out of here and the promises he makes, he keeps." "Trust in him is limitless," concluded the censor.[32]

Scenes of utter abandonment overtook the survivors when the Red Army tightened the last circle around the city on January 10, 1943. "As far as the eye can see," wrote a correspondent in one undelivered letter, soldiers lie "crushed by tanks, helplessly moaning wounded, frozen corpses, vehicles abandoned through lack of fuel, blown-up guns and miscellaneous equipment." Finally split into two pockets along the Volga, the Germans surrendered the first one on January 31, the second on

February 2. The Red Army captured ninety thousand mostly starved, wounded, and exhausted Wehrmacht soldiers; five thousand survived captivity to return home.[33]

The ending preoccupied Hitler, Goebbels, and other Nazi leaders. In a private conversation on January 23, 1943, Hitler found sufficient words to describe the desperate situation: "The men have nothing to eat, they do not have any more ammunition, and, with hollowed-out eyes, they stare back into utter collapse." Goebbels stepped into his propaganda role by stepping back from the gruesome scenes to consider their "genuine, Classical" dimension. Although the Propaganda Ministry had collected soldiers' letters in order to tell the gritty story of heroes, it put them aside, convinced the unvarnished accounts would be too "unbearable" for the German public. It was without the authenticity of the witness that the Nazis inscribed the defeat at Stalingrad into the annals of German history. Speaking in a live broadcast from the Reich Ministry of Aviation on January 30, 1943, Göring immortalized the fallen heroes in his "funeral oration." "Like a huge monument," the Battle of Stalingrad rose above the struggles of Germany's past as "the greatest of all heroic battles in our history." "In one thousand years, every German will speak in awe about the sacred spectacle of this battle and will remember that despite everything it was there that Germany's victory was decided." "They died so that Germany might live," announced the *Völkischer Beobachter*.[34]

It was the antique scale of thousands of years that gave meaning to the sacrifices at Stalingrad. Hitler himself could not understand Friedrich Paulus, the commander of the 6th Army, whom he had promoted to field marshal at the last minute in a clear signal for him to fight to the death. "He could have freed himself from all sorrow and ascended into eternity," remarked

Hitler, "but he prefers to go to Moscow." Stalingrad deferred the moment when Germany's sacrifices would be redeemed into endless time. Such a deferral made room for many more deaths, many more defeats.

Grossman crossed the Volga several times to report on the defenders in Stalingrad. "Busy with the sleepless work of war, carrying shells under their arms like loaves of bread," and "singing softly, or mildly swearing at each other," these men embodied the Russian and Soviet spirit. What they endured were the "living minutes to a great Today which is about to become a Tomorrow of an immortal page of history," a calendar that stood in contrast to the oblivion enveloping the Germans.[35] As living monuments, the units that had fought at Stalingrad were distributed across the army in order to cement the new confidence of the Red Army.

However, it was not Chuikov's defenders, but dozens of fresh divisions deployed by Operation Uranus, that broke the Germans. In many ways, the military state and not patriotic spirit built the victory. Stalingrad was a decisive turning point since the German Wehrmacht never regained the initiative, but that conclusion became clear only later on.

A few days after the surrender, newspapers published the iconic photograph of long files of captured German soldiers trudging from the valley to the heights the Red Army had conquered. The image depicted the sheer force of destruction the Red Army had inflicted on the invader. Britain celebrated Stalingrad Day on February 20, 1943; three days later, listeners tuned in to the BBC's "163 Days: The Red Army's Glory at Stalingrad." It served as a final epilogue to *War and Peace* that had been serialized on the radio a month earlier.[36] Seeing their own fates bound together in urban dramas such as Leningrad and Stalingrad, the British people took the Soviets into their hearts.

"AN ELDERLY FARM worker" took off his hat, though "he walked alone across the fields." Playing outside a cottage on a "golden day," when "the trees were radiant with color"—we are reading the London *Times* here—children ran indoors, shouting "The bells! The bells!" On Sunday, November 15, 1942, for the first time since the fall of France, church bells rang out, on this occasion to celebrate "the success granted to the forces of the Empire and our allies in the Battle of Egypt." From Westminster Abbey, from the bombed-out Exeter Cathedral, where only the bell tower remained standing, from a village church in Prestwich, Lancashire, the bells could be heard around the world as the BBC broadcast the peals as part of its midmorning program. "Did you hear them?" the announcer asked listeners in "occupied Europe" to make the point that after noon the bells would fall silent "till they ring out for final victory."[37]

Axis forces never advanced beyond El Alamein or Stalingrad or the island of Guadalcanal in the Solomons. But they had been stopped only in long seesaw battles measured in hundreds of yards or half-hour intervals. The bright skies on November 15 hardly cleared "the black days of 1942 when the Japanese conquered all of Malaysia, occupied Burma, and threatened India while the German armies approached the Volga and the Suez." When George C. Marshall, chief of staff of the United States Army, reflected on how "thin the thread of Allied survival had been stretched," he used small units: "in those hours" in those "black days."[38]

It was two years before carriers of the US Navy reengaged the Japanese Imperial Navy at Leyte in the Philippines and more than a year before the Marines followed up the island victory on Guadalcanal with the conquest of Tarawa at the end of November 1943. It took the Germans less than six months to get to the outskirts of Moscow, and it took the Red Army almost two years to dislodge them from the Soviet Union. Six months elapsed after the landings in North Africa before the Allies pushed the Germans out of Tunisia and another year for them to reach Rome. Given the long effort to roll back the Axis, most battle-field deaths occurred after 1942. The bells were only the beginning of a long, slow struggle to erode and chip at the enemy "town by town, island by island, in terrible killing battles."[39]

Guadalcanal, El Alamein, Stalingrad—the heat of the three theaters of war around the globe had the effect of maximizing appraisals of what it would take to achieve victory. The Allies committed themselves to an extraordinary level of violence. In an editorial titled "A Long War" at the end of 1942, the *Richmond Independent* took stock of the years of battle to come. "The Nazis will crack up," the editors assumed somewhat light-heartedly, but, they added, "it will be a long, hard and expensive war against the Japanese." In spite of "terrific bombings" and "disastrous sea and air and land defeats," it was certain "they will fight on." There was only one way to beat Japan, and that was to "wipe out" "every soldier" in addition to "every general" and "every admiral." Richmond's *Independent* concluded with a quote attributed to "one American general": "The only good Jap is a dead Jap." The general was Admiral William F. Halsey who, as commander of the South Pacific Force, had asserted that "the way to win this war is to kill Japs, kill Japs, and kill more Japs," a defiant statement about mass destruction that gave an official stamp to popular sentiment.[40]

It was indicative of the totalizing logic of war that the end of the Battle of Stalingrad was accompanied by the Anglo-American commitment at the Casablanca Conference in January 1943 to the "unconditional surrender" of Germany and Japan. The Allies agreed to an intensification of the strategic bombing against Germany's war industry, which, everyone knew, meant bombing German cities. Even when President Roosevelt clarified "unconditional surrender" to mean not "the destruction of the German people" but "the destruction of a philosophy" based "on the conquest or subjugation of other peoples," he defined victory as the complete annihilation of militarism, the enemies' armed forces, and the supporting political and social institutions. There would be no negotiations with any government that might overthrow Hitler but defend Germany's 1938 borders. Critics pointed out that unconditional surrender forced the enemy to fight to the "last gasp," with far greater Allied casualties as a result, but the enemy's apparent willingness to do so was the underlying premise of the doctrine. Victory was defined as efficient destruction; popular emotions of anger and vengeance were helpful engines to escalate the violence. Long before the prospect of invading Japan or the use of atomic weapons, there was broad Allied support for large-scale bombing campaigns that deliberately targeted civilians.

For the Germans, Stalingrad crystallized the absolute war of destruction they had fought since invading the Soviet Union. In an ideological war, it was a matter of life and death. From the beginning, Wehrmacht soldiers carried out "their own final solutions" against civilians as well as combatants to bring the war to its desired end. In his declaration to the German people on the tenth anniversary of the Nazi seizure of power, on January 30, 1943, Hitler rejected the idea that the war would end with victors and vanquished. There would be only the "survivors" and the "annihilated."

The trails of destruction were very long. In his war book, in which the main character is "the gay and gruesome monster *Kaputt*," who left behind places that have "gone to pieces, gone to ruin," Italian journalist Curzio Malaparte found himself with the Romanian army on the highway to Odessa in fall 1941. "For miles and miles around there was only dead iron." On the roadside and in the cornfields, he saw "overturned cars, burned trucks, disemboweled armored cars," but "nothing living, not even a corpse," just "hundreds upon hundreds of miserable steel carcasses." Carcasses, not corpses. In March 1944, the scorched earth stretched farther. The *Observer*'s Edward Crankshaw made the long journey from Moscow to Smolensk by train. "For hundreds of miles, for thousands, there was not a standing or living object to be seen. Every town was flat, every city. There were no barns. There was no machinery. There were no stations, no water-towers. There was not a solitary telegraph-pole left standing in all that vast landscape."[41]

Over the course of the war, an estimated 7,000 military aircraft crashed in Holland, steel nails driven into a bit of ground that encompassed little more than 16,000 square miles. (Some 300,000 planes were lost in World War II, almost half the 800,000 manufactured.) The ocean floor was littered as well. In engagements with Allied forces, the Japanese, largely dependent on oceangoing trade, lost 2,346 merchant and 686 naval vessels; in the Battle of the Atlantic, German submarines sunk some 3,500 Allied merchant ships in addition to 175 warships at the cost of 791 of their own submarines with a total loss of more than 100,000 lives. So many merchant ships had been torpedoed that *Time* warned vacationers against going to Florida in the summer of 1942: "The troubled shore waters of the Atlantic are often coated with oil. Bodies wash ashore on beaches often enough to shock swimmers."[42]

PART III

FIGHTING

CHAPTER 10

On Land

Straightaway, Stalingrad was regarded as a turning point in the war, and rightly so as events confirmed; from the Volga, the Red Army advanced, while the Wehrmacht retreated. It was a massive turnstile as well. As many as three million soldiers fought at Stalingrad; alone the Soviet counteroffensive mobilized one million men in the Red Army. Another one and a half million soldiers lost their lives in the "most ferocious and lethal battle in human history." Nearly 10 percent of all battlefield deaths in World War II occurred at Stalingrad. As a military operation, the battle removed more men from their homes than any other event in the war and buried half of them in a faraway *Stalingrab*.[1]

Stalingrad was the grand emblem of the ideological war between the Allies and Axis. Both sides quite believed that "the fate of Stalingrad will decide the fate of mankind for all time."[2]

Indeed, all the way down to the fighting men in the companies, the sense of being on the just side of the war was remarkable. The violence of the war was itself rooted in the idea of the necessity of destroying the enemies of humanity, the Nazis or the Bolsheviks. In this war, the psychological or spiritual element to crush a monstrosity activated the men fighting it.

However, narratives of the war concealed the terrible costs inflicted on the soldiers on the battlefield. The enumeration of the superlatives of battle hardly recognized the plain suffering. The stories of war honored fallen fighters in monuments that provided their deaths a place in history. However, strong as they were, ideological commitments did not remove the painful experience of their displacement. In the American Civil War, for example, soldiers in the field, whether they fought for the Union or the Confederacy, voted in disproportionate numbers for ideologically uncompromising candidates in wartime elections, yet desertions had thinned their ranks.[3] Being a soldier came with an overwhelming desire to quit the field of battle and to go back home, the most common feeling among all fighting men.

John Hersey played the theme of extradition to great effect in his reporting from Guadalcanal. Following Company H "into the valley" to fight in "the Third Battle of the Matanaiku River," Hersey discovered that these "American boys" "did not want that valley or any part of its jungle." What they were fighting for was home; "fighting for pie" was the way Hersey put it, though he added that soldiers also fought for "the good pay, the comforts, the democracy." ("I'm fighting for my right to boo the Dodgers" is how a Texaco advertisement put it in 1942.) Wanting to "get the goddam thing over and get home" led to further developments in the valley. Under attack, the company had fled in panic. And there was the collateral conviction that "a marine killed because he must, or be killed." The strain of this sort of warfare generated the psychic exhaustion that afflicted all armies. And it sanctioned an enormous escalation of violence that brutalized men even as it hollowed them out.[4]

Soldiers composed voluminous records of their own exile. In their letters, they mended the distance from home. They contemplated reasons for their departure, the feelings of confinement in faraway places, and their roles in the machinery of killing.

THE ARMY BULLETIN read, "Two or three divisions destroyed." But as the correspondent inspected the site of the battle near Leningrad, a place where dead soldiers had fallen a few hours earlier, the field appeared very much "alive." Along a stretch of five miles, he found a "complete tangle" of "mangled bodies," tattered uniforms, discarded equipment, "and paper—lots and lots of paper," he added, "mostly the notebooks and letters of soldiers." Across five miles and over five years, eyewitnesses to the fighting followed trails of paper. After the invasion of Normandy in June 1944, Ernie Pyle reported from the beaches. "Human litter extends in a thin little line, just like a high water mark," he wrote. Mile after mile were "soldiers' packs. Here are socks and shoe polish, sewing kits, diaries, Bibles and hand grenades. Here are the latest letters from home." Aside from the packs of cigarettes that the soldiers had been issued before they started, most of the refuse on the shore consisted of "writing paper and air-mail envelopes." Already at Waterloo in 1815, visitors to the battlefield had been struck by "quantities of letters and of blank sheets of dirty writing paper." Paper had "whitened the surface of the earth." Soldiers' letters compulsively annotated the army bulletin.[5]

The amount of paper that soldiers carried with them was staggering. In the Wehrmacht's campaign against Moscow in the fall of 1941, the 2nd Panzer Division received 80 tons of mail in addition to 530 tons of regular supplies. Some twelve thousand Wehrmacht personnel sorted through twenty-five million pieces of mail a day. The army's postal service handled a total of forty billion letters and packages over the course of the war (the figure for World War I had been 28.7 billion). On the other side, five million Red Army soldiers wrote more than one million letters each day. The American serviceman wrote a letter home about once a day—more free time was spent on correspondence than on anything else. Censors read a sample of 1,000 letters in a single shift. "I wouldn't mind so much," one exclaimed, "if that damned corporal didn't write five identical letters to five different girls every day."[6]

The sheer volume of mail to and from home registered the pain of the soldiers' absence. More than anything else, letters communicated longing for the familiar. Taken from their families, neighborhoods, and livelihoods, civilians were the ones who filled ranks in the people's armies that the war assembled. Letters were the only connection to their old world, and correspondents expended great effort to keep the span in good repair, tabulating letters sent and received, rereading old letters, and lamenting delays in getting new ones.

"It is midnight, and I've just come back from the observation post," wrote Nikolai to his "dear wife"; "right away I want to write to you." The fighting had died down, and the soldier wanted to "forget everything" and "to send you, even if it is difficult across the distance, a true and faithful kiss," a "close, close" kiss. "Musja!" he added. "Every day I take out our picture and look at it." Nikolai reached out without quite reaching her: "Write me, Musja, write me more often, write me at length. I am waiting."[7]

Just as soldiers addressed letters to loved ones in a familiar place, they wrote about the strange places where they sheltered and the new tasks they carried out. The wartime front was not much wider than the narrow precincts of home. Soldiers described daily routines, the weather and food, and the sights and sounds around them. Although letters provide insight into how combatants experienced battle or thought about death and the broader purpose of the war, most correspondence did not elaborate on these themes or provide censors with reliable indices of morale. "My field of vision extends only about a hundred yards," remarked a German infantryman, and it "covers approximately a hundred men." Whether advancing or retreating, most men in the field rarely saw the maps commanders had at their disposal—"Where are we, exactly?" asked the jokester: "In Russia," replied the veteran. Men were simply "in the middle of this syrup." From such shortened perspective, battle was "mostly a series of unheroic things—little successes, little escapes, long periods of waiting." For many soldiers, repetition unraveled sequence so that "day after day" nothing new really happened, even if they did not stay in one place for very long.[8]

A single letter was not apt to say much about the big picture of the war or its ideological highlights. But, taken as a whole, a soldier's correspondence revealed the effort he undertook to explain his part in the war, and the words and phrases he used tended to justify the righteousness of his country's cause and specify the wickedness of the enemy he faced. In the first weeks and months of deployment, letter writers exhausted the vocabulary of banality before they searched for more plaintive or telling descriptions. Even if it was not all-embracing, the pressure of social conformity was part of the uniform of the armed forces. One of the reasons military establishments eagerly embedded journalists as close to the front as possible was to use reports on the soldier's life as a means to authenticate and stabilize the larger ideological meaning of individual effort. In this democratic age, the experiences of the "little man" served to motivate readers at home, but also soldiers at the front, who read about themselves.

Given "the rapid growth of new ideologies in the world," national existence depended on "thought warfare," commented a Tokyo newspaper; writers were necessary because they produced "paper bullets" to "move, stir and inspire the reader." In its official communications to troops, the Wehrmacht hammered away at the theme that "the field postal service is a weapon" and that correspondence should be regarded as a kind of "spiritual vitamin" for both the reader and the writer. With images that acknowledged at least implicitly the growing losses of the long war, one commander ordered the letter writer to choose his words as would "a blood donor for the belief and will of his relatives."[9]

In other words, soldiers were asked to write their own film scripts and narrate their own newsreels, both of which were powerful media forms. Their production was designed to absorb stray and disturbing facts into coherent messages. Censorship was another way to shape the format and content of letters.

However, letters could be a kind of contraband that revealed "real" conditions on the front. "Real" perspectives were the first chinks in the "big picture" of war. Amid the strain of combat, writers cried and confessed. By simply writing things up, soldiers pushed against the stock phrases, justifications, and sentimentalities. Correspondence expressed both the limits and the power of collective ideas in the gigantic military ensembles. As Tolstoy recognized when infantrymen cried "Hurrah!" or "We're lost!" all these elements shifted around in combat. Moreover, collective bonding and individual weakness were not necessarily opposites, since the rhetoric of arming up when passing along news from the front, of disarming oneself in reflection, and then rearming once again to get on with it steeled the links in chains of escalating violence.

With tens of millions of pieces of mail going back and forth every day, Goebbels, the Third Reich's propaganda chief with access to censors' reports, understood full well how difficult war conditions dispirited soldiers. During the Soviet counter-offensive in the winter war of 1941–1942, he admitted to his own diary that "what our soldiers write home about the front has really become indescribable," with references to Arctic temperatures, lack of supplies, and broken chains of command. The horror of fighting dismantled many of the reasons soldiers endured suffering. "Human weakness is at work here," Goebbels concluded, and "one is powerless to counteract it." Widely shared, the conclusion here is that experience in war overwhelmed loyalties of wartime; "being" determined "consciousness." It is an extreme view because it is so blunt; even Goebbels's exasperation at weakness contradicted his own general faith in ideological enlightenment.[10]

When soldiers wrote to produce the millions of pieces of mail, they relied on a fund of phrases and images shaped by the terms of the battle between friend and foe. Whenever they described tough and horrific experience, what Goebbels referred to as the "indescribable," they veered along a continuum that stretched from endurance (loyalty) to disillusion (flight). The textualization of experience in letters and diaries picked up familiar literary devices that tended to repeat patriotic ideas about individual duty and the nation at war and to sideline discordant or disruptive elements that cast the soldier out of the group. Both aspects are present, however.

In letters and diaries, soldiers themselves wanted to wrap up matters and find strong meanings and relatable stories in spite of horrible experiences. This was such a strong tendency that it could surprise veterans. As late as 2003, Okamoto Masa, a former "special attack pilot," admitted that "without this diary, I would probably have believed like everybody else that I was dragged unwillingly in the war," that deep down "I never accepted" the propaganda. Yet "this diary" told another story of genuine enthusiasm, one that became "essential to my self criticism" about his former robust wartime self.[11] Others were startled by their alienation from what they later remembered to be a worthy patriotic endeavor. Time and reflection both strengthened and weakened the hold of the "indescribable." "Good wars" appeared and disappeared.

In their accounts, with "the things they carried," soldiers revealed themselves to be the civilians they once were, sons and citizens with ties both mended and torn to a wider community and an earlier life. They killed other civilians, and they died as civilians, elsewhere, scared and brutalized.

A piece of mail is just that: a single fragment of a larger set of correspondence that in sum might reveal shifts over time but rarely exists in its entirety. Working with an unusual collection of more than three hundred letters written by a single soldier over the course of several years, historian Klaus Latzel illuminates how one soldier continually made and remade his history of the war. The correspondent is "Hans Olte," a pseudonym for a private in the 4th Army's signal corps who served from the beginning of Germany's war against the Soviet Union in June 1941 when Hans was twenty years old until he was taken prisoner near Minsk three years later. We can read all his letters because they were written to his parents back home who preserved them as a single bundle.[12]

Hans's letters began in March 1940 with his induction into the Reich Labor Service, a six-month deployment that he shared with all boys his age. It was the first station in his journey to become a citizen-soldier, an adult in the Third Reich. Overall, Olte saw his military duties as a formative stage to complete his education before he would return to civilian life. At the same time, he reported with growing satisfaction on his socialization in uniform: how he fitted into the supportive structure of the group, how he bore up to the sometimes arbitrary rules like "a man," and how he trained his physical body and honed his skills in the crafts of war. With the expansion of Germany's war against France in 1940, he embraced the prospect of fighting as a "real soldier" in "enemy territory" to do his part to bring about a quick and victorious end to the conflict. The Wehrmacht fulfilled Hans's idea of himself as a man; his place at home combined with his longing to be away at war. Home and war were complementary parts of life in the Third Reich. However tough things might get, the young man accepted the premise and the mission of soldiering for Germany.

When Hans crossed into Russia with the 4th Army at Brest-Litovsk on June 22, 1941, everything he saw confirmed the clichés he had assembled in his worldview. His letters flipped through the supremacy of German arms so that at the end of the first day, "we are already a good bit into Russia," and the Red

Army, after the "best troops" had been destroyed, was fighting with "cheap reserves." "It will be all over here" in a few weeks; "that much is pretty obvious."

Hans also looked at the "poor people" whom Communism "enslaved" just as the best-selling Nazi author Edwin Erich Dwinger had in his reportage on the Bolshevik experiment, *And God Is Silent?*: "We had that book at home." "All in all, I am doing very well"; the only thing the confident soldier needed to keep him going was "CIGARETTES."

Even when the Red Army's resistance slowed down the German advance, Hans replenished his experience with Nazi words. He came to see the "very friendly" inhabitants as an almost inhuman "rabble." A few weeks in, they were sufficiently formidable so that their defeat required sweeping destruction: "Better 10 of them than one of us."

Three months into the campaign, however, Hans's vocabulary began to shift, and to slip. For the first time, Hans thought about the end of the war as an undefined, unreachable moment. It was not "all over," but "we trust" that it will "come to an end this year." After remarking on acquaintances, Reimers, and also Behring, who had been killed—"every day I think about it"—Hans added a more general remark about casualties: "Incidentally, you see a lot of soldiers' graves here in the East. But the Russians are suffering significantly greater losses than we are." The injection "incidentally" disrupted what the word "but" was supposed to put back into place. Nazi coordinates had become wobbly.

Hans's letters revealed more and more dissonance. At the end of November, "the boots get stuck with every step," both literally because of the mud and figuratively because explanations no longer worked. The disappointing news that "none of us will go on leave for Christmas" opened up the more corrosive question of "whether we will ever see our homeland again." Instead of the end of the war, there was just another day, "always the same, no diversion, no recreation, nothing." Stuck "here in the East," he had moved much farther away from home than when he was rapidly advancing. "Yes, that is the way it is here," he wrote, summarizing a place that had become strange and wild.

Hans hit the boundaries of his Nazi world in the difficult winter of 1941–1942. "Our Adolf now has the situation in hand," he wrote on February 2, 1942; "you can count on that." The Germans to which he addressed himself and to which he felt he belonged: all this still remained in place. Even so, his letter was filled with details about his exceptional life during "all the days of misery." He itemized, beginning with the cold—minus 61 degrees on January 19—before moving on to postponed leaves and his own homesickness. "I have already cried," he admitted to his parents a few weeks later. This "great homesickness" was unbearable because he considered himself a "man and soldier," yet had only with "every effort suppressed my tears."

Hans Olte returned home three times, and it is clear that he was thinking about leave all the time. Since only victory promised release from the eastern front, Hans continually bolstered his confidence in Germany's military prospects. Yet he also opted out of the war by spending more energy planning his life back in Germany. By his own admission, he reached the point where he could no longer express himself as a "real soldier." He counted up the dead not from the ranks of his unit but from his neighborhood: "Konrad," he asked his mother on May 25, 1944, wasn't he "the bartender from Hotel zur Post?" It was as though the pieces of his envisioned postwar future kept falling away. He added one more question: "When will this murdering finally come to an end?" A little more than a month later, Hans Olte was taken prisoner. He died in a prisoner-of-war camp in Kirow sometime in the winter of 1946–1947.

Two sentences illuminate "the beginning and end of Hans's development," notes Latzel: "Oh, I'd love to be out there with the soldiers" in May 1940, and "When will this murdering finally come to an end?" in May 1944. Was Olte a Nazi? The building blocks of Hans's understanding of the world never came crashing down: the Führer, the national community, and racial judgments on Russians (and, elsewhere in his correspondence, Jews). His growing sense of his own weakness did not make way for a radical reappraisal of the war. Yet he ended up discarding key values of National Socialism, namely, the spirit of self-sacrifice to endure trials even to the point of the hero's death. Latzel appropriately describes Hans Olte as a "fair-weather Nazi," someone who wanted to go along as long as soldiering seemed elevating, but began to look for his own way out when the fascination came to an end.

Hans's correspondence revealed that National Socialism's huge program of socialization from the Reich Labor Service to the Wehrmacht did not overpower "the particulars of individual autobiography." The collective enclosure of "consciousness," of National Socialism, remained tight, yet the experience of the war had made more room for the individual self.

What about Olte's startling statement about murdering? It was one man's rejection of what the Nazis "retailed" as heroic sacrifice. But focused as it was on his murdered friend Konrad, it left broader distinctions between (German) friends and (Russian) foes in place and did not implicate Germans or Olte himself as murderers. "Fair-weather" when it came to Konrad's death or his own homesickness, but still "Nazi" because Olte could not imagine a fundamental alternative to "our" Third Reich.[13]

Hans Olte's correspondence registered his growing unwillingness to sacrifice himself, but that change did not generate more detail of his own involvement in the killing machine. In general, soldiers' letters from the eastern front did not have much to say about the execution of noncombatants and are almost completely silent on the murder of Jews. Yet the fact is that the German military, along with the Japanese army, killed more civilians than soldiers. Where activity in the "death zone" did leave traces was in the pitiless turns of phrase that soldiers used when writing summary accounts and in their eagerness to provide relatives supporting material documenting the mission in the East. There are enough clues about Hans's missing photographs, for example, to suggest that they depicted more barbarism than did his archived letters.

The unrestrained violence of German soldiers on the eastern front showed how the ranks mobilized themselves according to the pitiless norms of National Socialism. Again and again, the struggle against "Judeo-Bolshevism" was described as a "life-or-death" struggle that, as the Wehrmacht penetrated deeper into the Soviet Union, took on the character of an uncompromising race war. The tougher the Russians appeared, the more ready Germans were to mete out preemptive and indiscriminate violence.

In a chain of associations going back to the lost war, the revolution, and Versailles, German warriors reaffirmed the existential stakes of the war. All of this was shorthanded with references to the year 1918, a black-letter date that verified the terrible dangers all around Germany and justified the violence of the invaders. A young tank gunner admonished those at home: "You must always keep in mind what would have happened if these hordes had overrun our Fatherland. The horror of this is unthinkable." "God have mercy on us, had we waited," wrote another soldier. These were testimonials to the cruel melodrama of German history the soldiers had incorporated.[14]

The Nazis' greatest political accomplishment was to have legitimated in the public mind the false recovered memory of German death in 1918. From the premise of defending German life flowed all the preemptive violence at home and abroad in the years that followed. This was so to such an extent that Germany's imagined downfall manifested itself in the soldier's own physical disintegration. On the western front, twenty-five-year-old Heinrich Böll—even during the war, the future novelist was no friend of the Nazis—recounted how "the French have come up with a new dirty trick, which, when I saw it for the first time, hit me like a ton of bricks! Really the effect is amazing. They simply write 1918 on the walls, just this combination of numbers without commentary."[15] The writing of "1918" expressed a totally embattled view of the world in which death threatened to overwhelm collective life in the ongoing struggle for survival.

The melodrama cast a savior. On October 3, 1941, Wilhelm Prüller and his comrades stopped to dig in for the night; "we set up our wireless set as usual." After completing the task, "we nearly fall flat on our faces when we realize that the Führer is about to speak." It was Hitler's first broadcast to the nation since the start of the campaign. Two days earlier Hitler's proclamation had been read to the troops—"Now, my comrades"—in which he announced the beginning of "the last great, decisive battle of this year." Hitler reiterated the battle's "decisive importance for the world." "This enemy is already broken. He will never rise again,"

he assured his German audience. As they listened to Hitler, soldiers took up their places in history. A spike in letters followed
Hitler's speeches as soldiers connected to loved ones whom they
imagined listening to the same broadcast. "You can't fail to
hear," concludes Latzel, "the extent to which soldiers oriented
and pumped themselves up according to Hitler's speeches."
More than just a leader, he served as "their mouthpiece." Hitler's
withdrawal from radio after Stalingrad endangered the power of
this factor and left many soldiers speechless.[16]

After Hitler's October 1941 speech, Albert Neuhaus wrote a
letter to his wife "to provide a bit of insight into our experience"
and affirm the "affection and enthusiasm" with which the troops
took up Hitler's orders. Albert even provided detailed instructions on keeping historical mementos of the war. "Dear Agnes!
I am sending you 6 films to develop. I don't have to tell you how
important these pictures are to me. Let me ask you to develop
these pictures with *total care* in a 6 x 9 format. Preferably, silk
smooth matte finish." Later, he wanted 12 x 18 enlargements to
provide "an ornament for our apartment."[17]

Neuhaus belonged to a vast network of photographers in
Russia, camera stores in Germany, and curious viewers at home.
Already in France, CBS correspondent William Shirer found
it "funny" that almost "every German soldier carries a camera."[18] On the eastern front, Wilhelm Moldenhauer had both a
Leica and a Kodak with him and sent rolls of undeveloped film
(including color film) to his wife, who kept track of expenses
since Moldenhauer sold prints back to his comrades (Bethgre
paid 6.50 marks for thirty-five). He also experimented with
slides in order to assemble a sequential projection of the war in
"good order." Back in the Reich, local photo shops enjoyed "high
season." One owner pointed to a box with eight hundred prints

ready to be picked up. "Our soldiers photograph well and often," she explained. Correspondents on the front expressed concern lest a roll of film got lost in the mail or a picture did not turn out since cameras malfunctioned in the cold or snow reflected too much light. Moldenhauer wanted to make sure: "You did get the pictures of the murdered Ukrainians?" Hans Olte, too, provided captions for prints he sent back home. "The pictures where the house has burned down and the corpses are lying" were taken at "the location partisans attacked on 24. XI."[19]

Photographs of the Holocaust exist for the most part because ordinary German soldiers took them and saw to it that they were developed and archived. In town, the owner of the shop pulled out a "small album" including images of "demolished houses" and "sub-humans" that "rekindled the memories" for our soldiers. "I have seen photographs" of Serbians on the gallows, of "murdered Greek women," and of "a naked girl in the square of a Ukrainian town," confirmed Ilya Ehrenburg, who examined a great deal of the material found on captured or killed German soldiers.[20] Such snapshots were commemorative documents that, once assembled and captioned, constituted pictorial histories of the great war German *Landser* shared with Nazi leaders. The premise of photography at the front was an understanding of the war as camera-ready action ready to be developed as history.

By 1943, however, correspondents stopped worrying about their negatives; perhaps the shops in Germany had closed or lacked supplies, or perhaps the history of the war no longer seemed so memorable. In May, Agnes Neuhaus sent her husband "crackers, soap, razor blades, toothpaste, and pudding mix," but film no longer appeared on the list. In later years, soldiers preferred playing skat to taking snapshots.[21]

There was something "uncanny" about the East, as victories in the summer gave way to a tough slog in the autumn. Summing up the shift in morale in the Sixteenth Army, one chaplain noted how "the incessant threat from all sides, the permanent sense of insecurity, the desolate feel of the country, and the struggle against all the ruses of nature and the enemy" created a heavy "physical and emotional" burden. "Hurrah patriotism back home" was wrong to "present the Russian soldier as an easily vanquished foe." Everything appears "strange and inaccessible."[22]

The reliable coordinates of time and space steadily broke down. These were "bad times" with "heavy losses." "Always the same story," complained one private at the beginning of September. "Only one hundred miles to Moscow and sixty miles to Smolensk," but for "five weeks we have been dug in at the same spot." "Again and again we have been promised that we will be going home," hopes raised "for nothing." On the eastern front, "the war seems endless": the spaces that needed to be secured, the time necessary to destroy the enemy, the losses that would have to be endured before victorious troops could return home. All these imponderables looked bigger after the United States entered the war in December 1941.[23]

Endlessness took measure of the growing sense that soldiers were at the mercy of uncontrollable forces or "ruses." Without signs of progress, Willy Reese, a bewildered twenty-year-old private, compared the war to a "carnival," a world upside down in which nothing could be directed and everything seemed possible. It was the sort of place where the "clown" had become the leader, the "Führer." More to the point, the image of carnival acknowledged the lurid horror, allowing Reese and his fellow soldiers to see themselves as victims of a great diabolical scheme. Whenever soldiers went back or forth to the front, they remarked on the crosses marking "the hasty burial of the thousands of Germans and Russian soldiers who had fallen on this plain." At train stations, they saw hospital trains on the siding and, through the windows, made out "soldiers swathed in bandages." They were "waving to us," almost like in a freak show. After one firefight in late December 1941, Reese did the arithmetic: "Eleven men died or were badly wounded, three more lightly, two went over to the Russians, and one mutilated himself. Of thirty men in all."[24]

Delivered to fate, soldiers sang Lale Andersen's "Everything Passes," a wildly popular song in 1942. The song infiltrated soldiers' letters as no others did, expressing a casual, melancholy, almost defeatist attitude: "This too will pass when all is said and done" / "After every December comes another May." With a direct reference to the longed-for pass for leave to go home, the song calibrated wartime as seasonal and capricious, unrelated to the march step of perseverance and victory. The wounded all sang it "slowly, wistfully."[25]

The sentimental song promised that May would follow December, but on the eastern front soldiers felt permanently extradited with few chances for leave, diminished prospects of victory, and little sign of an ending. The only way to survive was through more violence. Action was the "cure" to avoid "being consumed by this foreign land," reflected Gottlob Bidermann, a lieutenant in the 132nd Infantry Division. Soldiers developed "a remorseless, ever-increasing rage," aiming "to kill the enemy and to destroy." It grew to "suicidal levels."[26]

In a bitter reply to his wife's reproach that he was insufficiently dedicated, Hellmuth Stieff, a senior officer, tried to explain. "We are standing here on the knife's edge. That is also why we feel *so* betrayed" and so abandoned. "We are fighting here for our own naked existence, every day and every hour, against an enemy who, on the ground, is in *every* respect superior to us." "Our 'winter gear' is a *joke*," he wrote on December 7, 1941, so much so that prisoners went barefoot since "*our* people" had stolen their felt boots. "We don't give a damn about *any* crusade." If "little bunny" took issue with his "alleged softness," Stieff assured her that she had no cause for concern: "It has *long since* disappeared! Nowadays I give orders to shoot so and so many commissars or partisans without *even blinking*; it is him or me—it's that damned simple." "Spare me all the pompous words," he went on to admonish his wife—"you don't understand me anyway"—and "the same goes" for "your father," who "doesn't get it." Even if he had the chance, Stieff would have found it difficult to go back home. The world had turned into a cruel place, and the soldier acted out his estrangement. He had become a wolf among patriots.[27]

With orders to shoot Russians and burn their villages, Willy Reese saw himself wandering through "a depopulated, smoking, burning, wreckage-strewn desert." In his burlesque portrait, "prisoners of war dangled off the trees all around." "When we were issued a supply of cigarettes," he noted, "we lit them at the burning houses." Like all soldiers, Willy Reese dreamed of a "better life in peacetime," but, stopping to consider "the moment" when he stood at "the door of my father's house," he had to admit that he "no longer believed such a moment would ever come" because he would be either dead or a stranger.[28] Reese was killed in Russia on June 22, 1944.

The case of Hans Olte is instructive. On the one hand, Olte's tears and his despair about the "murdering" provide a way to approach all the soldiers in the war as fragile, ultimately traumatized human beings. The shock of the war was disillusioning, whatever the source of patriotic conviction. They had all been taken on a carnival ride. On the other hand, German soldiers went into battle with brutal and racial ideas, and when they rearmed themselves they did so according to prevailing Nazi prescriptions. They were not extraneous wild men.

No ARMY SEEMED as ideologically driven as the Japanese, but diaries and even songs amended these convictions. If there was one tenet that characterized the Japanese Imperial Army in the eyes of soldiers serving in its ranks and of Americans who fought it, it was the no-surrender policy. Through 1943, after Guadalcanal, New Guinea, and Tawara, the Allies counted a grand total of 604 captured Japanese soldiers, whereas the Japanese held tens of thousands of British and Americans prisoner. On Guadalcanal, Marine commander Alexander Vandegrift expressed his astonishment at the Japanese soldier's willingness to die: "These people refuse to surrender." Right until the very end of the war, Japan's government considered surrender an unacceptable alternative to honorable death. Even former premier Hideki Tojo attempted suicide at his home in Tokyo when American soldiers came to arrest him on September 11, 1945.

The "idea of sure death," the *Japan Times* commented, distilled "the essence of the Japanese wartime morale": "With a traditional cup of cold water," soldiers pledged each other "to die rather than retreat or fall prisoner. Such a vow is a true manifestation of the supreme virtue of the Japanese race."[29] The other side of no surrender was abuse of prisoners-of-war whose willingness to lay down arms underscored their own weakness and the decadence of the West. By order of the army, images of captive Americans circulated widely to impress on Asians the final outcome of the global struggle between the strong and the weak.

In fact, Japan's "no-surrender" policy in World War II was unprecedented. It had not applied in either the Russo-Japanese War or World War I. It emerged out of interwar debates regarding Geneva conventions that Japan, a growing power increasingly at odds with the West, refused to ratify. Japan's willingness after 1937 to wage a long war in China to achieve its imperial ends popularized "glorious battle deaths" as much as it dehumanized the unyielding enemy. The army's Field Service Code codified "no surrender" as official policy in January 1941. Although the number of soldiers surrendering increased over the course of the war, from less than 1 percent in Tawara in 1943 to around 10 percent in the Philippines in 1945, what stood out were all those who did not. It was with this grim calculus that the US military contemplated the invasion of Japan in the summer of 1945.[30]

Long after the war, Japanese remembered the solemn patriotic march "Umi Yukaba" (If I Go to Sea) with mixed emotions. It had been played during enlistment and farewell ceremonies, sung in unison to begin neighborhood meetings, and broadcast over the air to introduce roll calls of fallen soldiers.[31] "We shall die by the side of our Emperor" went the words that, in the geopolitical context of the 1930s conjured up faraway tropical places: "Across the sea, water-drenched corpses / Across the mountains, grass-covered corpses." The march provided a stunning visual of vast graveyards throughout East Asia.

The extravagant cult of dying required the soldier and his family to honor ritualized obligations. If the thousand-stitch belts that women at home knotted for men in the field brought good luck, then the preaddressed military envelopes that officers distributed before deployments were creepy reminders of soldiers' "sure death" at the end of the march. They dutifully clipped their nails and trimmed their hair to put in the red envelopes that would be sent home in the event of death. Typically, Japanese placed remains of the dead on the family altar in conformity with Buddhist funeral practices to allow the purification of the body so that ancestors could rest in peace. Soldiers sought out buddies whose responsibility it was to make sure that a part of the dead body was recovered and sent home.

The cult of death dramatized the willingness to die. It also revealed unexpected bonds of intimacy among ordinary men who prepared one another to do so. Throughout East Asia, spectators took note of Japanese soldiers marching, victoriously, ceremoniously, holding the carefully folded white bags with the remains of fallen comrades.[32]

The popular school song "War Comrade" upheld the soldier's duty to fight for his country and closed to linger at the scene of death. It created an exorbitant feeling of sadness around the conventional honor of sacrifice. The two comrades first "shook hands" after their ship "left the port last year / and we could no longer see the country." "On the sea," farther away from Japan, "we shared cigarettes" and showed each other letters. Having become buddies, "We used to say to each other that we might die / any day, and that if one of us should die, the / other would take care of his remains."

The war song continued to elaborate obligations to comrades, but not necessarily duties to the nation. When "In battle, my comrade / suddenly fell," "despite myself, I ran up to him" to provide first aid. "Although the military code strictly prohibits / this," the words take note, "how can anybody overlook this?" Relief overrode the code in an act of love. Still, the dying comrade spoke for duty: "With tears in his eyes," he said, "Don't be late. Don't care for me. You have / duties for the country." Yet "When the fighting ended and it became dark," the friend returned to the dead man, to "dig a hole for him under the red evening sun / of Manchuria," and to write a "heartfelt letter" to his parents on which he shed a tear, the sign of individual grief.[33]

Japanese soldiers were frequently close to tears. "As a man I should not cry," "tightly biting lips" in order not to do so, explained the fighter in a song written just after the fall of Singapore. "Carrying My Comrade's Ashes" became a favorite drinking song among Japanese serving overseas. Entering Singapore in the morning, the soldier carries the ashes of his comrade "in my arms." He intends to plant the "flag that is his keepsake" on a mountain in view of the Southern Cross, symbol of the new southern empire. What allows the friend to cry—"I cannot help, but my cheeks get wet"—is the cry of *banzai* that heralds victory in the name of the emperor. These seem to be tears of joy. However, the collective duty of war is subordinated to an implicit "but," which underlines the final thought of the intimate obligation between two men amid the losses of war: "Although," "our assaults will continue," "I will go ahead tenderly carrying your ashes / Watch over me, my comrade."

Writing in his diary on March 2, 1942, Fusayama Takao, a signals officer in Malaya, remembered that "whenever we sang this song, we could not help tears welling up in our eyes." While singing, he recalled his brother-in-law and others who "gave their lives to the fatherland"—Okada and Yoshihashi and Kawabata—and "I could not prevent tears from welling up." Fusayama renewed the general spirit "the night when we reinforced the guard" and the next morning "when we entered

Singapore City," but he retained his own private thoughts. The joyful tears of victory disguised tears of sorrow and anguish.[34]

The rituals of death acted out Japan's collective and sacred mission. However, death in faraway places tested the norms of social discipline that depended on self-abnegation to successfully integrate experience. As soldiers imagined elaborate personal details of fellowship, they confessed their own fears of being abandoned by comrades, their surrogate family.

A Japanese soldier's notes from Guadalcanal revealed the distress of abandonment and, with it, growing cynicism about the imperial way. Officers encouraged soldiers to keep diaries. In the daily work of writing entries, the individual transcribed and internalized social norms and validated his place in society's history. At the same time, however, diaries offered a way to store individual experience, and soldiers often regarded the texts as very personal items, keeping them "close to their actual bodies: inside their helmets, stuffed in their boots, in the breast pocket."[35] On Guadalcanal, Americans came across many diaries on the Japanese dead, giving them insight into the enemy's morale in the fall of 1942. What they found was both transcription and translation, renewed expressions of loyalty as well as cries of despair.

Like many Japanese accounts, Toyoji Hashiba's "record of Pacific War" begins on the troop ship where soldiers had time to talk with one another as they began their journey "across the sea." With "deep emotion filling our hearts," the soldiers anticipated reaching the battlefield "at last," but they also worried, "thinking of their homes and loved ones." It was "a mission for which we were ready to die." As Hashiba and his comrades sang and drank, "we all said that we were doomed to go to the Yasukuni Shrine, which is the most sacred shrine of the souls of dead soldiers." Everyone in the group was happy, yet Hashiba himself wondered "where I would go after my death."[36]

Hashiba's account of action is structured in terms of two failed assaults on Henderson Field and two long retreats back across Guadalcanal. The "Advance" began on September 3 with the determination to finally shove the Marines off the island. However, the assault failed and makes room for Hashiba's excruciating detail of the grueling "Retreat," which completely depleted the fighting force. By September 20, the soldiers had been "marching for 7 days without food and very little water." Along the way, Hashiba's company came across "suffering and dying men" who "had been deserted by their comrades." The soldiers felt "terrible," but "we could do nothing to help them." About halfway up a steep hillside, Hashiba stumbled upon Lance Corporal Sasaki, who came from his hometown. "He was sleeping against a tree with his ammo can at his side. I shouted at him, but he did not respond. I tried to lift him up with the help of the walking stick, but he collapsed."

In the second retreat in October, "a good many men" chose suicide over continued suffering, "blowing themselves up with their own hand grenades" without inflicting any injuries on the Americans. At roll call, Hashiba learned that "Lance Corporal Yokoyama of the signal corps had shot out his brains with his own gun." One by one, the junior officers deserted the companies, leaving behind men without leaders or the ability to fight in a cohesive way.

After "Lance Corporal Takahashi" was hit with shrapnel, "he let out his last breath saying, 'Long live our Emperor! Banzai!'" "A man of true military spirit," Hashiba summed up, yet he admitted to himself that the corporal was "probably one of very few warriors who died on Guadalcanal with the word

Banzai on his lips." Newly arrived reinforcements did not rally Hashiba's spirits. "Just wait and see," he thought. "The time will come when you guys will be just like us," hungry and dispirited.

After the new year, Hashiba was evacuated from Guadalcanal with some ten thousand others; his war was over. But just as many thousands of soldiers died of disease and starvation on what the Japanese called "Starvation Island"—"a wordplay on Ga-to, the abbreviation of the Japanese name for Guadalcanal"—many more than had been killed in combat.

If Hashiba's account is at all representative, any number of soldiers lost the fighting spirit in which they had been trained and socialized. In this regard, Guadalcanal is really the original location for Shohei Ooka's acclaimed 1951 novel, *Fires on the Plain*, which opens with a slap to the face of a soldier who finds himself completely cast off by the army on an island in the Philippines at the end of 1944. As he makes his way down the corpse-strewn valley, the narrator reflects on his status as the selfish survivor he has become after the new draftees like himself had been left to fend for themselves. Without comrades or faith, he is no longer a soldier.

WHETHER WE READ Hans Olte's letters or hear Toyoji Hashiba singing, the war stories were strikingly self-centered. There was little reflection about the soldiers fighting or killed on the other side. Rather than a revelatory experience about war and suffering, a merely personal sense of vulnerability and loss prevails. The individual's dissatisfaction with himself as a weak soldier in fact upholds the ideological scaffolding of the collective military effort. The strong form of ideological mobilization is readily apparent because it mandates social expectation and self-judgment. It ultimately corrals general experience, but the stories often followed private routes to reveal soldiers as disoriented or traumatized victims of war. In the texts, the killing revealed the fragility, not the sturdiness, of the soldier's form, but not the total bankruptcy of ideas. As a result, soldiers' accounts constantly struggled with the recovery and loss of meaning.

In the end, there was remarkable ideological coherence among the huge civilian armies mobilized in World War II, in contrast to the dishevelment of the ranks in the Russian, German, and even French armies at the end of World War I. This consistency existed even at the level of soldiers' assessment of weakness as a personal failure to maintain binding military values. In World War II diaries and memoirs, there were very few scenes such as the subversive one in *All Quiet on the Western Front* where Paul and Gérard find themselves in the same shell hole in no-man's-land and Paul recognizes himself in the dead body of his foe and goes mad. A summary of the fighting would conclude that consciousness determined being, at least more so than the other way around. This is why the soldier's story needs to be studied from the perspective of the belligerent sides, from the "man's-land" on which they fought, rather than only through the disorienting experiences of "no-man's-land."

The uniformed soldiers did not just receive ideas about the war; they reshaped them so that evidence of their falsification proved to be highly disruptive. In other words, stories were surprisingly strong, but not unbreakable.

CHAPTER 11

At Sea

A cross the sea" is the most evocative image to think about the soldiers who left home and had gone away. How many men were on the oceans, which constitute more than 70 percent of the earth's surface area, at any one time? Counting naval personnel and the merchant marine as well as transported troops, certainly more than one million.

Almost all Japanese, American, and British Empire troops who fought in the war were transported overseas; this was not the case for the vast majority of Soviet or German troops. Ships landed nearly one million Allied soldiers in Normandy in 1944; 160,000 on the first day, June 6. Every fighter on Guadalcanal arrived on the island by ship. Moreover, all the belligerents maintained large navies: 3.5 million men served in the US Navy over the course of the war. Another 1.5 million passed through the ranks of the German *Kriegsmarine*. At war's end, the British

Royal Navy counted nearly one million sailors; Japan's navy was nearly 1.6 million men strong in 1945. Between the United States and Great Britain, nearly 500,000 civilian men served on merchant ships. The Japanese merchant marine lost a total of 2,346 vessels, including almost all over 1,000 tons (a standard low-cost Liberty ship weighed about 7,000 tons), most of them torpedoed by US submarines—three times as many as the United States lost, and in terms of tonnage (nine million), one-third of the prewar world total.[1]

It was sea power that transported and supplied troops and ferried raw materials to the belligerent nations and the territories they occupied. Ships transported Japanese armed forces to Malaya, the Philippines, and the Dutch East Indies and American forces to Britain, North Africa, Italy, and France. Japan and Great Britain, both island empires, depended on merchant shipping to deliver necessities such as food, fuel, and war matériel. As a truly global power, the British Empire was centrally involved in the allocation of movements of freight around the world on a finite number of ships. Its role in prioritizing shipping was crucial in calamities such as the Bengal famine in 1943.

Japan was overstretched to adequately protect shipping, but the basic model applied: vital transports were protected by a screen of warships, including aircraft carriers that served as floating bases to provide air support. The same naval forces sought to interdict the transportation routes of the enemy. To maintain or dismantle these security belts around ports and transports, navies fought huge sea battles across hundreds of miles with aircraft carriers and their air forces often playing the lead roles. Both the United States and Japan understood the importance of the aircraft carrier as the key to all long-distance naval operations; the only difference was that the United States had the capacity to build carriers and Japan did not. If the two belligerents were matched in naval power in 1942, that was not the case in 1944.

Like the land- or carrier-based torpedo and dive-bombers, submarines sought to pierce the screens protecting the sea routes. Dependent on diesel engines, submarines generally moved and attacked on the surface (or half-submerged), but, with limited battery power, they could dive to the depths of the ocean if threatened by ships with artillery and depth charges or aircraft with bombs. Despite their reputation for stealth, submarines were not very effective against properly escorted convoys; in World War II as in World War I, the advantages of escort ships designed for antisubmarine warfare far outweighed the disadvantages of bunching up the merchant vessels as easy targets. However, convoys found submarines extremely danger-ous, and there were periods in the first years of the war, particu-larly in the months with less daylight in 1940–1941 and again in 1942–1943, when the losses of supply ships outpaced the ability of either Great Britain or the United States to produce replace-ments, and imports to Great Britain plunged. At times, the majority of convoys crossing the Atlantic came under attack. No wonder anxious crews scanned the ocean where any "crease in the grayish-green cloth of the sea may have a periscope hiding in it."[2] Throughout the war, however, it was Japan that faced dire supply problems, nullifying the promise of a resource-rich East Asian empire.

Shipping always involved sinking and being sunk. Although the vast majority of soldiers died on land, almost as many sol-diers (and prisoners-of-war) died at sea as did sailors. Ship-wrecks and sharks were part of sailing lore. And lifeboats vividly incorporated the dangers and dislocations of the war.

AT THE END of December 1942, Twentieth Century–Fox announced the first of two films that Alfred Hitchcock agreed to direct for the studio. According to Hollywood sources, Hitchcock had "devised the plot" for *Lifeboat*, "a yarn about the survivors of a torpedoed American merchant ship and a Nazi submarine who have to share the same lifeboat." The picture took shape quickly. It opened with the sinking of the ship "(2 minutes)," but, "to capture a feeling of authenticity," the action focused on the occupants in the lifeboat "(90 to 120 minutes)." Standing in front of a "toy model" in "Hitch's' office," which contained "nine little figures"—six men and three women—Jo Swerling, the picture's screenwriter, explained that "the lifeboat is our stage. The wings are the ocean and our players make their entrances by climbing over the side." With the camera serving as a "tenth passenger," the drama revolved around the interactions of the survivors, not the menace of "hunger and thirst."[3]

By producing "the world in microcosm," *Lifeboat* intended to explore the "divergent viewpoints" of "today's varied social and nationalistic classes." In addition to the U-boat commander and the overarching tension his presence introduced, the proposed occupants included a "middle-class English radio operator; a woman writer," serving as the "representative of the American intelligentsia"; a businessman en route "to sell merchandise to General Franco's government; an Englishwoman who had lived through the Coventry bombings; a leftish ship's oiler; a Negro steward; and an ex-jitterbug crew member." The sensations and conflicts of the war would be dramatized by the remnants it had cast adrift.

There were never any German submariners in American or British lifeboats, but the sinking of merchant ships was real enough. A huge increase in U-boat attacks on American shipping along the East Coast followed the German declaration of war in December 1941. Newspapers filled with stories about sunken freighters, the large numbers of crew members who perished, and the survivors' struggle aboard lifeboats. America's "ace of aces," Eddie Rickenbacker, had been rescued from an inflatable raft in the Pacific in November 1942 after having gone missing for three weeks, a suspenseful saga featured on the front pages and meriting editorial commentary in the *New York Times* five times. The news that he was alive "brought spontaneous smiles to the faces of millions of Americans."[4] (The germ of Hitchcock's idea?)

As wartime features, the stories cast Allied civilians as plucky but innocent victims whose lamentable fate recalled the attack on Pearl Harbor. Often enough, submarines surfaced to inspect their handiwork with the result that survivors recounted tense encounters with submarine crews. Since the U-boats themselves were vulnerable to increasingly effective antisubmarine warfare, crew members thought about their own deaths in "iron coffins" or their chances of survival as they observed shipwrecked crew members in peril in the water. In this regard, Hitchcock was right to force a kind of familiarity or intimacy between the two sides that was missing on the battlefield. The real premise of Hitchcock's movie was the salient ways in which the survival stories in 1942 revealed human weakness and the ways in which privilege and race corroded teamwork and social solidarity.

The setting of *Lifeboat* in the midst of the "Battle of the Atlantic" made sense because it embellished a critical chapter in the war that has captured outsize attention. Churchill coined the term "Battle of the Atlantic" in March 1941 to emphasize the stakes of the struggle against German attacks on shipping and the need for the United States to produce merchant ships to maintain the lifeline of supplies to Britain. The "U-boat attack," he wrote, "preys upon us as the greatest danger" to "our Island." It was another one of those "only" things "that ever really frightened me during the war."[5]

For his part, Erich Raeder, commander in chief of the German *Kriegsmarine*, never lost his conviction that submarine warfare had almost knocked Britain out of the war in 1917, and he resolved to do so twenty-five years later; German intentions seemed ominously clear the very first evening of war when the *U-30* sank the British passenger liner *Athenia* off the coast of Ireland on September 3, 1939 (a German submarine had also sunk the previous *Athenia* in 1917). Indeed, Raeder's submarines accounted for more than two-thirds of all Allied shipping losses in World War II. There were times in 1942 when Raeder appeared to have been proven right. His submarines imperiled Allied oil and food supplies, while the number of new replacements still lagged behind the number of lost ships.[6]

For all its importance, the Battle of the Atlantic was never totally joined. The lifeline to Britain was crucial to sustain Britain's fighting capacity around the world, but the determination of military priorities in the global conflict continuously pulled resources away from the Atlantic so that the "battle" stretched into a years-long campaign in which Churchill accepted notable losses of merchant ships. The defense of Britain in the event of a cross-Channel invasion depleted escorts for convoys almost to the end of 1940. Long-range bombers were assigned to Bomber Command's offensive against German cities in 1942, not Coastal Command to defend shipping. Escorts were also pulled away from Atlantic convoys in preparation for the invasion of North Africa in November 1942.

Overall, however, the battle was there for the Allies to win: there were never enough German submarines to imperil the Liberty ships produced by the end of 1942 in assembly-line fashion in US shipyards. In many ways, the Germans lost the Battle of the Atlantic before it began since the *Kriegsmarine* did not have the numbers when in 1940 the British were most stretched. Moreover, the vast space of the Atlantic made finding a strung-out convoy difficult. Submarines wove a net with "hundred-mile mesh." And since submarines "hunted" merchant ships and fired their torpedoes on the surface—"on the march" was the ironic term—they could be spotted by long-range aircraft. It was therefore possible for the Allies to provide planes and escorts along the entire route from Halifax to Liverpool, although "gaps" remained in the mid-Atlantic until 1943. (Submarines or U-boats are boats, not ships, the difference being that ships like freighters can carry other boats such as lifeboats.)[7]

At close distances, Allied ships also learned to track U-boats with radar and sonar. Once the threat was verified, escorts gave chase, often directed by the wake of fired torpedoes, casting off depth charges, and forcing the submarine to take evasive action and abandon the hunting trail. "*Scheissgeräte*," submariners later complained—the "damned devices" had "spoiled the fun" and "wore us out."[8] The picture of "wolf packs" circling helpless prey is mostly myth. All the defensive tactics and hardware never eliminated the threat U-boats posed, but the aim was to manage dangers sufficiently to ensure the "safe and timely" arrival of a continuous sequence of convoys. (Crammed full with up to fifteen thousand men, troopships, "monsters" such as the *Mauretania* and *Aquitania* or the "Queens," the *Queen Elizabeth* and

Queen Mary, were difficult to handle in rough seas but sufficiently fast at thirteen to fourteen knots to sail alone and evade submarines.)

U-boats spent most of the time waiting, as was the case with all things military. Crews spent half of their six-week tours going to and returning from the shipping lanes. Then they searched the seas; the masts of merchant ships and their escorts were visible only at a distance of fifteen miles. Otherwise, only telltale signs of garbage on the surface indicated ships nearby. "Senseless joyriding around in mid-Atlantic," a crew member noted in his "blue exercise book": "No sign of the enemy. Feels as if we're the only ship in existence. Stench of bilge and vomit." In fact, the majority of U-boats never attacked an enemy ship; only a few submarines and captains accounted for most Allied sinkings.[9]

As convoys came into view, they appeared as "dots the size of bugs," moving "along the indistinct moonlit horizon." From time to time, "long rolling waves hid the ghostly parade" until, at closer range, the masts "stuck up along the horizon like a heavy picket fence." From a distance of four or five miles, U-boats could fire their torpedoes, often in a spread of three or four to increase the chances of hitting a vessel. Few crew members ever saw a stricken merchant ship through the boat's periscope, but the rest could imagine the fate of the seamen as they listened to the eerie sounds below the waterline. In his "personal account," Herbert Werner recalled the explosions on a freighter. "It was gruesomely beautiful." "The great broken hull stood out black against the red, yellow and golden flames." Other times the torpedoed ship was "simply gone." As the vessel sank, the submarine crew could hear as it "shrieked in her last convulsive agony." "Crackling and crunching," "horrible noises" as "the frame broke apart," wrote one sailor.[10]

In "iron coffins"—the Allies called them "hearses"—submariners had an alert sense of how easily they could be obliterated in the depths. They were violently rocked about when depth charges exploded near their boats, and they listened for hours to the high-pitched sonar impulses that "struck the boat like a hammer hitting a tuning fork." Given their sense of vulnerability, men on the U-boats easily imagined themselves as the merchantmen they stalked. A reporter who accompanied the crews, Lothar-Günther Buchheim, stepped into his engine room after which "a series of pictures rushes through my mind." How often, he wondered, did merchant seamen "measure the thin plates that divide them from the sea," the "blast of the explosion," the "scream of iron," and the "roaring inrush" of water? The fate of a tanker, he reflected, was much worse since the torpedo switched on "a gigantic torch": "every square foot white hot from bow to stern." Eight hundred feet away, Buchheim watched how "burning oil spreads faster than the men can swim."[11]

After a torpedo attack, U-boat crews could sometimes see men in lifeboats or in the rafts that floated free. "What will become of them?" Buchheim asked himself, knowing that in another situation he himself might be thrashing in the sea. Buchheim played out the thought: "They escaped immediate catastrophe when their ship sank. But is there any hope for them? How cold is the water in December?"

In the bars back in the French ports, in L'Orient or Saint-Nazaire, submariners debated whether to fire on the survivors in the lifeboats—in Hitchcock's *Lifeboat*, Willi is asked why the Germans did so ("captain's orders"). The whole debate turned on whether shipwrecked sailors were to be seen as companions in distress or unforgivable foes. In the "Bar Royal," Böhler broached the "burning topic." "Are we carrying on a war or just a demolition campaign?" he asked, answering the question on whether to fire machine guns. "What good is it if we sink their steamers and then let them fish out the survivors so they can just sign on again?" Thomson admitted his own reluctance to kill "the poor bugger" who is "struggling in the war," though his sensitivity seemed "pretty ridiculous." Perhaps Trumann found the solution to the dilemma. "Don't touch a hair of their heads, but shoot up the lifeboats," he suggested; that way the customary rules of the sea could be respected. It was really like burning down a house without executing the Russian peasant. The arguments often split along generational lines, weary "old men" who saw themselves as survivors against idealistic, aggressive Nazi "schoolboys" so young they could not even grow the submariner's beard while on tour. While Hitler favored firing on survivors, the navy abstained because such a policy hurt morale. It only went so far as to forbid rescue attempts.[12]

The debate in the Bar Royal revealed that when submariners deployed to destroy merchant ships, they "opened the door" to atrocities against survivors. Each of the belligerents fired on unarmed vessels, and each side shot up men in the sea, the Japanese more so, the British and Americans less, although such conduct did not become standard. However, the Allies killed many more stricken people in just a few incidents.[13]

"When Allied reconnaissance aeroplanes flew over the Huon Gulf yesterday," reported the *Manchester Guardian* about a successful bombing run against Japanese transport ships off the coast of Papua New Guinea early in March 1943, the sea was "littered with survivors and debris." Pilots observed "sharks swimming" around those who were on rafts or clinging to pieces of wreckage. After sinking the transports, bombers competed with the sharks. They "expended many tons and thousands of rounds 'strafing' targets in the water." "When we arrived here there were 500 men" in the water, recalled one pilot; "there are now 200." "It is not so much what has been done as what has been shown to be possible that is chiefly remarkable about the Battle of the Bismarck Sea," commented the *Guardian*, a promise made good with the destruction of thousands of civilians in Tokyo and Hiroshima two years later. The "indescribable carnage in Huon Gulf" was "magnificently coordinated," added the *Sydney Morning Herald*; the sublimity of slaughter belonged to the experience of wartime.[14]

Survivors sometimes reached lifeboats, but many more sailors were drowned. And the vast great majority of German submariners died at sea, three out of four, a total of nearly thirty thousand; the five thousand sailors captured by the Allies confirmed the slim chances for survival once submarines had been hit. This "cruel sea" provided the backdrop to Hitchcock's film; "our curtain becomes the surface of the sea," he explained. In *Lifeboat*, it opened onto a debris field: a first-aid kit, golf balls, playing cards, a copy of the *New Yorker*, as well as a German body (in a life vest stenciled *U-78*). Buchheim confirmed the lifeless surface of the black oily waters after a ship had been sunk: "splintered lifeboats, charred remains of rafts, life preservers," and beyond "a whole field of floating corpses, most of them without life jackets, faces submerged."[15]

There were enough shipwrecked sailors that one of them thought it necessary to write the manual *How to Abandon Ship*, which provided information on "swinging out" and lowering the lifeboats, rowing, and "open boat seamanship." Other sections included "Medical" and "Morale," which extolled the "magic in cigarettes" and warned that despondency "proved fatal far more often than the lack of water." With the growing number of survivors, the US merchant marine constituted the "Torpedo Club" and even introduced the "Torpedo Hop," a two-step around "the principal steps" of "sighting the sub" and being sunk.[16]

In the encounters that took place when German submarines surfaced in the vicinity of the lifeboats, all sides of the debate in the Bar Royal were represented. Lifeboats on an empty sea had either been missed by the last ships in the convoy or passed by the escorts whose first priority was to ensure the safety of the convoy, not pick up shipwrecked mariners, or else they came from a stricken ship sailing as an "independent." Submarines sometimes lingered in the area in hopes of using lifeboats as lures to torpedo the rescue ship, the premise of the 1944 movie *Western Approaches*. In one case, a submarine trailed a lifeboat for five days in the Caribbean, venturing close enough for the occupants to hear the captain give orders to the men of the gun crew who were "young, blond and stripped to the waist." Sailors certainly shared rumors of sinister German crew members shooting survivors in lifeboats, but most attacks were on crewmen who remained on the sinking ship and occasionally fired on the U-boat, which is why Willi was shipwrecked in Hitchcock's movie. However, what really threatened survivors were convoy policies making rescue a matter of discretion as well as lack of provisions and supplies in the lifeboats themselves.[17]

The encounters between the U-boat and the lifeboat are fascinating since they are so at odds with the brutality of the battlefield. They revealed a seaman's code in which the predator could recognize himself among the prey. Captains ordered U-boats to surface in order to learn which merchantman they had torpedoed and to provide survivors with bread, water, and cigarettes, even a bottle of rum, and give directions. In one case, a seaman spent four days in a German submarine after he was picked up drifting alone at sea. One of the crewmen "came into the forward compartment one day and snapping his heels said, 'Heil Hitler.'" "The others growled, 'Nix heil,'" and "told him they were fed up with that stuff." Basically, they were "a lot like seamen I've met all over the world." There were still torpedoes on board, which "made the crew unhappy"; they were "ordered to stay out until they had no more 'fish,'" and "they all wanted to go home."[18]

At the same time, survivors detailed the dark side of the German attackers to make the point that shipwreck served as an allegory for the war, teaching the lesson of Allied virtue in the face of Axis villainy. And that was the point of Hitchcock's *Lifeboat* too.

Submariners continued to fight the war in their exchanges with survivors. According to one group in a lifeboat, "the captain of the merchant ship and his chief engineer were taken aboard the submarine to hear an oration" on the theme that "Roosevelt is a dangerous man to have at the head of your country." The "crew stood in the background and joined in the chorus of 'To hell with Roosevelt!' each time the commander came to that part of the speech." In another encounter, "someone in the lifeboat asked for drinking water and cigarettes and a member of the crew started below for some, but he was called back on deck by the captain, who said, 'Let Mr. Roosevelt supply them.'" "We had no one to blame but Mr. Roosevelt" for being torpedoed, the captain added. The sailors argued back to assert the Allies would win the war. Once when "the Nazis photographed us," it was "too good a chance to miss and we all gave our 'victory' sign or 'thumbs up.'"[19]

Stories like these turned the submarine with its "vile method of warfare" into a symbol of death and the lifeboat into one of life. According to the *New York Times*, survivors proved "the one basic truth about democratic peoples in this war: the will to live," while "the Axis drive is a drive toward death," which "the Axis fanatics worship." Shipwrecks around the world represented the very "flesh and blood of the free peoples." Merchant seamen leaned on ideology to will themselves to live, explaining, "I went through '36 and '37, I helped to build the union. I said to myself, 'I'll be Goddamned if I'll let a few Nazi bastards kill me!'" In one case, men kept a log, called "MFOW Men Fight thru After 18 Days Adrift," in which they imagined themselves "fighting the Nazi bastards tooth and nail" in order to win the war. When it was published in the National Maritime Union's weekly, editors spliced in details of the overall "world picture":[20]

Nov. 28—4:50 pm—the SS _____ sunk in the South Atlantic. Number one lifeboat launched.

The world picture: Trap closing around Nazis at Stalingrad . . . CIO-AFL to meet on unity . . . New fight to beat poll tax.

Dec. 3—Everything in good order. . . . [W]e must do all by dead reckoning. Clear hot day. Gentle SE breeze. Slight SE sea.

The world picture: AFL-CIO agree to act on disputes jointly . . . Soviets capture key Stalingrad point . . . World-wide day of mourning and protest by Jewish people, who vow to avenge wholesale murders by Nazis.

Here, lifeboats, Stalingrad, Jews, and Jim Crow were all parts of the same war.

Hitchcock tried to tie up all these strands of solidarity and resistance in order to make *Lifeboat* stand for the drama of the war itself. The film posed the critical question directly at the very end: "What can you do with people like that"—meaning Nazi-grown Germans whom Allied civilians kept encountering in the high seas. The question was apt because the occupants of the lifeboat include Willi, who was later revealed to be the captain of the U-boat. For some reviewers the movie confirmed the basic virtue of the Allies who, represented by the British and American survivors, vote to save Willi when they first encounter him even though they know he is a German. They "share their food and water with the Nazi." They also defer to his authority once the skilled seaman assumes command. The "Allies" band together and throw Willi overboard only when they discover that Willi himself had pushed an injured, delirious sailor into the sea. Not long after Willi's execution, a second German, portrayed as single-minded as the first, appears on the scene, posing the question all over again. He is also rescued by the occupants of the lifeboat because "as humans they cannot murder another defenseless human in cold blood" as Willi had killed Gus.[21]

Many reviewers were not satisfied with the clear moral distinction between killers and rescuers even as they praised the film's technical aspects. They found that the democrat's procedure ended with the Nazi's usurpation. According to the *New York Times*'s Bosley Crowther, *Lifeboat* "sold out the democratic idea and elevated the nazi 'superman.'" Willi was unmistakably the bad guy, tricky and brutal. But he was also "practical, ingenious and basically courageous in his lonely resolve," while the "democratic folks" had neither resources nor pluck to assume command. Divided by class and temperament, they bickered among themselves. "We have the suspicion," Crowther growled, "that the Nazis, with some cutting here and there, would turn

'Lifeboat' into a whiplash against the 'decadent democracies.'"
The film failed to provide a stirring example of democratic unity
and action, like the 1942 hit *Casablanca*, perhaps because such
an appeal required the Allies to take on the "superman" attributes of the enemy and not to fret about having "joined the mob,"
as one character offhandedly described the rush to kill Willi.
The "mob" was what fighting looked like, pointed out another
reviewer, the aim being to beat the "Nazis into pulp." In its ambi-
guity, *Lifeboat* resisted this unconditional surrender to war.[22]

The democratic deliberations on the lifeboat also highlighted the issue of race. Arguing against letting Willi stay in the
boat, Kovac, an ordinary seaman of Czech heritage, pointed out,
"A guy can't help bein' German if he's born a German," just as "a
snake [can't] help being a rattlesnake if he's born a rattlesnake."
This was precisely the biological reasoning used to justify the
mass internment of Japanese Americans. His vote was to get the
German "outta here," but Kovac was a lone voice since his position contravened the precepts of Christianity and the rights of
prisoners-of-war to which the other survivors appealed.

The vote also featured Joe, the Black steward, played by Canada Lee, a figure in the Harlem civil rights movement. In the
film, Joe abstained after pointedly asking, "Do I get to vote too?"
(The disenfranchisement of southern Blacks by the poll tax was
a major political issue in 1942.) With the character of Joe, who
on the merchant ship had been called "Charcoal" but on the lifeboat gets a name, Hitchcock underscored the racial hypocrisy
of democracy in the United States. Later on, Joe is the only one
in the lifeboat who does not join in the violence of the (white)
"mob"; there were well-publicized lynchings in 1942. In fact, in
an earlier treatment of Hitchcock's idea by John Steinbeck, Joe
defied the mob by diving into the sea in an attempt to rescue

Willi. Yet in his published short story, which previewed the movie, Hitchcock had Joe join all in and hit Willi with a "rabbit punch," so the movie actually moved the character back closer to Steinbeck's draft. This confusion about where to put Joe signaled the unsettled place of African Americans in the war. Joe and Willi were the characters by which *Lifeboat* made inquiries into the social and moral state of the war and into the temptation to regroup individual people into "us" and "them."[23]

In different ways, the lifeboat stories of 1942 featured Joe and Charcoal. In Hitchcock's early short story, Kovac, the "oiler," reached the lifeboat completely coated in oil "so that he did not look unlike a Negro." Only later do the rescued occupants see Joe in the water. In blackface, Kovac prepared Joe's arrival to suggest that "we are all in the same boat," in which "Charcoal" could become Joe. But the survivor in "blackface" also indicated that oily shipwrecks came with the discomforting collapse of the distinctions of race and class that the fair-sailing ship of state had upheld literally and figuratively. Yet once the "mask of oil" was identified as nothing more than blackface by the white men in the sea, the color line could be reaffirmed. "I told them they looked like a couple of Al Jolsons," recalled one survivor of *Repulse* off the coast of Malaya, and they replied in jest, "We must be an Al Jolson trio, because you're the same." Stories commented on the startling blackface of the shipwreck, the tempest that threatened to wreck social boundaries.[24]

About 14 percent of "deckhands and sailors" working in the United States in 1910 were African American, a proportion that had dropped by half on the eve of World War II. American crews became more all-white, and more self-consciously so. The British Merchant Navy had long employed seamen from the West Indies and especially "lascars" from Bengal whose pay, terms of service, and rights to shore leave indentured them in ways that unionized white sailors resisted. Even the gripping accounts of survival on lifeboats relegated lascars to a nameless, docile, and even insolent role in the stern. It was the rare "Eurasian" who noted the common disdain "Europeans" had for nonwhites. They were the ones who performed the most menial labor and had never been trained as able seamen, often did not speak English, and did not share the devotion of the British to the cause of the war. Shipboard contempt for "black bastards" reappeared on an American lifeboat after it had been adrift for ten days. And once rescued, "Smith and Williams" were forced to resume their roles as stewards to wait on the rest of the rescued crew on the voyage back home. Both men remembered "most pleasantly their stay on the Isle of Nukunau" (in the Gilbert Islands); "Smith said he would have liked to stay there."[25]

Racism was also contested. The common peril posed by German submarines generated a surge of union activism among lascars beginning in 1939, and, in the United States, the National Maritime Union championed integrated merchant ships, reminding crews and owners that "tin fish don't discriminate." The union's weekly, the *Pilot*, published letter after letter urging "full participation of Negroes for victory"; anything less was a "flagrant violation of our Constitution." "The Nazis want to sink ships so they can conquer and enslave the world," the maritime union editorialized, but it was "Negro seamen" who "have shown themselves to be true defenders of democracy because they know what democracy means" since "it has so long been denied to them."[26]

The National Maritime Union energetically took up the cause of Hugh Mulzac, a "professional sailor" for thirty-five years who held a "master's license" yet had never received a commission. There was "not a single colored officer in the entire American merchant marine." With the war, Mulzac renewed his effort to be appointed captain of his own vessel. When the War Shipping Administration did offer him an "all-colored crew," he refused, explaining that such "*jim crow* ships" were "what we're fighting *against*, and for me to lend my name to such a project would be wrong." Ultimately, Mulzac captained an integrated Liberty ship, the *Booker T. Washington*, which, in his words, "became a kind of miniature United Nations. Two Danes, a Turk, five Filipinos, a British Guianan, a Honduran, two British West Indians, a Norwegian, a Belgian," as well as thirteen Americans.[27]

Upon his return, New York's unions honored Mulzac at a festive dinner at the Commodore Hotel on Forty-Second Street on January 12, 1943. In addition to the tributes of the crew, whose diversity offered a "smashing reply to the race theories of Hitler," Langston Hughes read a poem he composed for the occasion. "There are those who, too, for so long / Could not call their house, their house / Nor their land, their land," he pointed at history. They "stood, individual and alone, / Without power." But, Hughes announced, "They have found their hour." With "a crew of many races" and "many bloods," "Our charts and compass and bell-buoy" will "guide us to the harbor of the new world" with Mulzac's "Booker T" the "flagship / Of a new day." "Victory through the unity of all races and creeds keynoted every speech," the maritime union added.[28]

Langston Hughes had often anticipated the "new day" while always suspecting its postponement. Just as Mulzac failed to find a commission before the war, he was refused one afterward, blackballed by Martin Dies and the House Committee on Un-American Activities and other "Captain Blighs" for being a

Communist fellow traveler, as were many civil rights activists in the late 1940s.

From convoys to civil rights, *Lifeboat* told the story of the Battle of the Atlantic quite well. The U-boat war opened on a German-built stage. Submarines were supposed to be the wonder weapons in attacks on the enemy's supply lines. But it was Allied theater that took up the shipwreck to perform the story of wartime virtue, of democratic pluck and fascist destructiveness. Lifeboat stories recounted terrible suffering as the headlines indicated: "Watched Last 10 Die of Thirst in Lifeboat" or "24 Days of Hunger and Madness."[29] They also told about great resourcefulness as survivors figured out how to catch fish and navigate by the stars. They found faith in daily study of the Bible. What the men and women performed was a demonstration of the innocence and steadfastness of Allied victims who fought for life against the Nazis' judgment of death. The melodramatic script fitted the mood of the year 1942 in which the Allies were on the defensive. However, the stories also announced the importance of the "second front" to the war, not the one in Europe to relieve the Red Army, a land invasion all the maritime unions loudly supported, but the domestic fight for genuine democracy for those who had been denied liberty long before Germans and Japanese began to snatch it away or drown it in the sea.

CHAPTER 12

In the Air

The Allies invested more money in the air forces than in any other branch of the military. The idea was to win the war efficiently without incurring the casualties required by a land invasion of Europe or Japan. In many ways, the bombing campaign was justified by painful recollections of trench warfare in World War I. The years 1914–1918 stood as a bloody monument to what not to do: not to go to war in the first place and, if it was necessary to do so, not to engage in costly frontal attacks against entrenched enemy forces.

Yet the cleaner, more morally satisfying pursuit of war from the air, an end run so to speak, escalated violence against civilians, who, everyone knew, constituted the primary targets of the bomber. The ability of airpower to achieve strategic ends through decisive knockout blows or to spawn internal unrest by bombarding cities proved mistaken. Great numbers of women and children were killed, but never in the numbers predicted or feared.

Only at the very end, in a sinister tribute to scaling up, did the bombing of Tokyo on March 9–10, 1945, the single deadliest day in modern warfare, and Hiroshima on August 6 achieve the desired political end, the capitulation of the enemy. It was a bit like wiping out the village in order to save it. In addition to hundreds of thousands of civilians killed in their homes, air forces suffered staggering losses of their own personnel. It was in 1942, with the onset of massed bomber attacks against German cities, that air war revealed how indecent was the discrepancy between the means and ends of combat. Air war was calamity: in the optimistic scientific calculus, in the expenditure of military resources, in the loss of life.

FEW DEPICTIONS OF bombing are complete without it: the detail of what looked like a dollhouse pried open by detonations. In one of the scenes that "have etched themselves into my memory," a resident of Leningrad looked at a demolished house: "One wall remained, still papered in the favorite cornflower design. There is even a picture hanging on it, as straight as ever." She walked and came upon another bombed apartment. "On the floor," toys were "scattered everywhere as if the children had just finished playing." After years of war, it was the sight of "half demolition" that struck the soldier walking around Cologne after the Americans entered the city in March 1945. "The whole facade of a four-storey tenement had collapsed," but "on the first floor, hanging down pathetically," he spotted "a white cot," its side painted with teddy bears, "their red bow ties" clearly visible.[1]

The teddy bear was always there, seen by both the bombed-out and the bomber's surrogate.

"Half-demolition" was a threshold setting off the wrecked city from its untouched precincts. The details of life such as the cornflowers on the wallpaper and the "red bow ties" decorating the bed reflected at once the interruption of daily life and the will to resume it. The terrible blow cleaved previous existence in two, into sudden death and still alive. Survivors of the bombing stumbled onto this threshold again and again. "Inside a house that stood alone and intact" along a street of rubble in Hamburg at the end of July 1943 a woman was seen "cleaning her windows."[2]

The dollhouse stood as a witness to the fact that air war furrowed domestic life into front lines. The most dangerous place would be the home, predicted novelist Aldous Huxley in 1932. It must be made "unequivocally clear to civilians of every age and sex that the next war is meant for them." "There will be no soldiers to suffer vicariously for them," he explained. "All the bleeding and choking, all the groaning and dying will have to be done personally."[3] What the trenches were to World War I, the bombings were to World War II.

Designers of incendiary bombs paid close attention to the combustibility of the home. Tests determined the flammability of different kinds of German roofs and stairwells. "Standing in front of Building 8100," a facsimile of a Berlin apartment building constructed in the Utah desert, one observer "couldn't help but think: 'This is like bombing Brecht.'" The testers found that "a German house will burn well." They also built Japanese models "fully furnished with *futon*, *zabuton* and everything else one finds usually in a Japanese house. They even had *amado*," the sliding shutters that were tested both in an open and in a closed position.[4]

Bombing was a form of urban warfare. Indeed, bomb-blasted cities had become central features in the way future war was imagined in the 1920s and 1930s. Thrillers such as *Invasion from the Air*, *Bombs on Hamburg*, and *The Gas War of 1940* all "entertained the idea of an apocalypse." Cities became a wartime measure of destruction. Indeed, Nazi leaders spoke openly of their aim to "coventry," or raze, cities. The British standardized the scale of the bombing of German cities into "'1 Coventry,' '2 Coventries,' and so on," with "an attack on the scale of '4 Coventries'" expected to yield 22,515 German deaths.[5] More than anything else, the destruction of cities, the built environment in which people had woven their lives and fashioned their households, heralded the very end of civilization. It was cities, not nations or empires, that inventoried books, pianos, and teddy bears. As the general use of the term "Coventry" suggests, the bombing of cities was a way of making war against oneself.

Yet the destruction was not complete, which made the dollhouse such an arresting image. Living in half-wrecked apartments, with a mix of wonder and relief, survivors of the bombing found renewed strength to make do and carry on. A journalist considered the aerial surveys the British commissioned to assess the damage after a bombing attack: "Occasionally around noon, English airplanes can be spotted over the Rhine." Bomber Command analyzed the photographs to draw "conclusions about the psychological and political impact" of the bomb damage. But the wreckage in these images did not tell the whole story. Across the way, the writer pointed out, the building's roof had caved in, and the third floor had been vacated. "However, white curtains hang in the second floor, and the lights are on. A window has been opened. Still dressed in her civil-defense overalls, a slender blond typist sways in front of the mirror applying red lipstick." At seven o'clock the next morning, church bells rang out the beginning of "the busy, undaunted everyday life of the big city." The scenes disproved theorists of air war who had prophesied that long-range bombers would produce total annihilation. The correspondent made sure to place a teddy bear in a blown-out window. In this case, half-demolition stood for life, for the resilience verified by the sappy household inventory.[6]

Since German cities were attacked multiple times, the undamaged rooms of the dollhouse also indicated the deferral of the destruction still to come. What was portentous about the bombing of Cologne on May 30–31, 1942, was not the achievement itself but the anticipation of "things to come." "Unfortunate people," the newspaper added, "theirs is a grievous fate." For Hans Nossack, who had been bombed out in Hamburg in 1943, such survivors were unfortunate because they "still stand at the edge of the abyss," squeezed between the past they continued to curate and the future that would bring the losses they feared. As a passageway, half-demolition foretold the more comprehensive reckoning that would demolish the rest of the dollhouse.[7]

The dollhouse was never fully demolished, so expectation exceeded experience. Despite the material damage and the growing number of civilian casualties, there was no knockout blow that undermined civilian morale or broke the legitimacy of the regime and its war effort. Londoners could "take it" during the Blitz in 1940, and so could Berliners. Only the atomic bomb proved airpower theorists right in their guiding assertion that technological means could produce political results by forcing surrender and achieving victory. In most ways, however, the opposite was true: civilians under bombardment fastened rather than loosened ties to government. It did not matter whether it was democratic or dictatorial. In some ways, this confirmed the premise that total war had erased fundamental distinctions between civilians and soldiers, which propelled the bombers' attacks on resilience itself. Moreover, fantastic aeronautical advances in the late 1930s in terms of payload, range, and speed strengthened the commitment to urban demolition. The Allied aim was total destruction even if "wings over Germany" fell short of delivering "doom over Germany." "The Reich lies open to the most terrible rain of fire and death of which man can dream," trumpeted the *New York Times*. "There is no place of refuge. There is no sheltering roof."[8]

After more than one hundred attacks in the months-long Blitz on London, the city endured one of its worst bombardments on Sunday, December 29, 1940. Vere Hodgson, who worked in Notting Hill, looked up: "A great red glow filled the sky." With her neighbors, "we went up on the roof to look." Herbert Mason, a photographer for the *Daily Mail*, also rushed to the roof of the newspaper building on Carmelite Street. What he saw was that "the glare of many fires and sweeping clouds of smoke" had partially obscured St. Paul's Cathedral, the distinctive landmark looming over the old city. Suddenly, the "dome and towers stood out like a symbol in the inferno." In that moment, "I released my shutter" to produce the iconic photograph of the Blitz. On its front page, the *Daily Mail* introduced readers to "WAR'S GREATEST PICTURE: St. Paul's Stands Unharmed in the Midst of the Burning City." It was one "all Britain will cherish," showing "the firmness of Right against Wrong."

Berlin's papers published the same photograph, but edited so flames appeared to consume the city and its cathedral. "The City of London Burns!" read the caption. For Londoners, the bombardment was "the Second Great Fire," after the first devastating one in 1666. Depending on presentation, St. Paul's symbolized London's survival or the city's doom.[9]

At the Air Ministry, Charles Portal, chief of the Air Staff, and his deputy, Arthur Harris, who in two months would be appointed commander in chief of Bomber Command, were also on the roof watching "the old city in flames." They too saw the "incredible sight" of "St. Paul's standing out in the midst of an ocean of fire," but it was the fires, not the cathedral, that struck Harris. What he saw was "kaputt," the illustrated German version. "I said out loud as we turned from the scene: 'Well, they are sowing the wind.'" Later on, Harris developed his thought, repeating the reference in the Old Testament in which the prophet tells of God's impending destruction of Israel for its transgressions. Assuming the role of a vengeful God, he explained that "the Nazis entered this war under the rather childish delusion that they were going to bomb everyone else, and nobody was going to bomb them." With Rotterdam, London, and Warsaw, "they put their rather naive theory into operation. They sowed the wind, and now they are going to reap the whirlwind." He acknowledged what Germans had initiated, but he would follow up and teach the Germans a lesson by fully realizing their idea. "If the Germans had gone on using the same force for several nights against London," he admitted, they would have raised a "fire tornado" worse "than anything that happened in Hamburg" in July 1943. "The whole of London would have gone as Hamburg went." "To reap the whirlwind," it was necessary to apply sufficient destructive force for a long-enough period of time. Rotterdam, London, and Warsaw lit up the bombing path to more cities, Cologne, Hamburg, and Berlin. When Harris looked at the "Second Great Fire," he saw many greater fires burning down Germany.[10]

President Roosevelt issued an appeal to potential belligerents on September 1, 1939, the first day of the war, urging them to refrain from "the ruthless bombing from the air" that had "profoundly shocked the conscience of humanity." It was a bit like fumbling for change from a bygone era. The up-to-date idea of total war regarded "social, economic, and political systems" as foundations for the nation's war-making capacity. It was the entire "social body" that went to the war. Effective offensive operations therefore targeted the various parts, "nerve centers," "main arteries," and the "heart and brain." Total war meant going after the enemy's entire productive capacity, which meant civilians in cities as well as armies in the field. In the doctrinal "triumph of the airmen," the long-range bomber provided the means to destroy the machinery of war and the civilian morale necessary to keep it running by laying waste to the homeland.[11]

When British prime minister Stanley Baldwin declared in the House of Commons in 1932 that "no power on earth can protect" the man in the street, "the bomber will always get through," he expressed a modern consensus.[12]

The terrible potential of the long-range bomber provided a sound reason to avoid war; it served as a deterrent just as the second-strike capability does today in scenarios of nuclear war. But in the 1940s, unleashing terror was a great temptation so as to "shock and awe" the enemy in a series of obliterating decisive strikes. "You do your worst," Churchill publicly challenged Hitler in July 1941, and "we will do our best." MOMA's *Road to Victory* promised "Terrible birds of death" and "Tornadoes of hell and ashes." The whirlwind in the sky had the additional great virtue of burying trench warfare forever "in the mud, slush, and war cemeteries of Flanders."[13] The horror of one sort of death authorized another.

There was always something transgressive about dropping bombs to kill ordinary people. Until the end of the war, the Allies tended to describe the bomber's target as "industrial centers" or "marshaling yards," not cities, to be killed. But all the talk about besting the worst suggested that judgments about bombing came down to the idea that "we were all good and the enemy was all bad," "Deep down," the British public knew "what this policy actually meant and were glad of it." What they did not want to do was confront the details; "they shied away from the savage in them. After the war they would try to deny it altogether."[14]

What was not questioned in the debates about where to drop bombs and for what purpose was the accuracy of the bomber, whose calculation both avengers and their critics wildly overestimated.

Moral scruples about bombing cities could be put aside relatively easily, but not operational difficulties. In 1941, the Royal Air Force's Bomber Command suffered staggering losses in nighttime assaults against German cities; manageable losses to antiaircraft fire and German fighters had been put at 6 percent for each mission, yet the figure climbed to well over 10 percent in attacks on the Ruhr and Berlin. On some nights, more British airmen lost their lives than German civilians.[15]

According to a report commissioned by Britain's War Cabinet in the summer of 1941, statistics challenged the very premises of the bombing campaign. Only one in four raiders managed to drop their bombs within five miles of German targets; in attacks on the well-defended Ruhr, it was one in ten. In other words, most bombs hit the German countryside, not German cities. Beyond the assertion that "what merely stiffens our backs flattens a German," there was also no evidence that bombing cracked morale in Germany. In the absence of well-aimed bombs, the entire air offensive appeared to be a wasteful, misguided effort.[16]

However damning the report, it led experts to conclude that the target had to be redefined to encompass a much larger urban area "whose destruction would be useful" so that misses could be counted as hits. Make the problem the solution by missing on purpose; there was a certain logic to this idea. The purpose of bombing was redefined to "dehouse" German workers in order to create millions of refugees on the road as well as thousands of corpses beneath the rubble. If enough long-range bombers were made available in order to hit cities again and again—the magic figure was always four thousand—German morale would break, as Harris believed London's would have if the Luftwaffe had followed up its attack on December 29, 1940.[17]

What flight crews called "area bash" became the aim of Bomber Command under its new commander in chief, Arthur Harris, himself known as "Bomber" Harris for his dedication "to laying Germany absolutely flat." It was a simplified strategy without distractions of "panacea targets" such as oil refineries or ball-bearing factories favored by proponents of precision bombing who aimed at the "choke points" of Germany's war economy. These were taken up by the Americans in a division of labor that suited Harris because it allowed him to concentrate on smashing cities. "The USA by day and the RAF by night," went the 1944 pop song.[18]

Strategic bombing was embraced at the moment of Britain's defeat in Asia. "WE CAN LOSE!" warned the *Daily Mail* on February 13, 1942, just days before the fall of Singapore. It was time for new men to fight a new war to achieve "victory at all costs," "in spite of all terror," as Churchill had put it. Single-minded in his approach to build on the Luftwaffe's assault on London in December 1940, Harris set to devising spectacular missions to produce immediate results.

Harris's big idea was a thousand-bomber raid against a well-known target in which nighttime bombing would be compressed into a few hours so that the intensity of the attack would overwhelm air defenses and emergency services. Clearly demarcated along the Rhine, Cologne, a city of eight hundred thousand, about the size of St. Louis or Boston, was selected. "Operation Millennium" was designed to inaugurate a new approach in which Germany could be defeated by destroying the Reich city by city in a rolling series of massive air raids. This "wholly new operation" was a risky operation because Harris committed "not only the whole of my front-line strength but absolutely all my reserve in a single battle." However, success would breed more success, since it would enable Harris "to press for the aircraft, crews, and equipment we needed." A single crushing blow would hurt Germany as much as it would clinch Air Ministry arguments about the allocation of resources in the War Cabinet.[19]

Saturday, May 30, 1942, marked "the greatest air attack of all time." Taking off from fifty-three airfields, 1,046 bombers were coordinated into four streams each with a specific time slot and height band. To arrange and fly in close formation was dangerous, but it was calculated that only two aircraft would be lost to collision, prompting the airman's snide query: "Have the boffins worked out which two?" The first two groups launched the attack by dropping incendiaries that landed on roofs and crashed into the top stories. Incendiaries started fires along the wood timbering of the roof, in junk in the attic, and in the curtains, bedding, and furniture; it was household inventory that lit up buildings. Two later groups dropped explosives to blast away walls, spreading fire from story to story, building to building, street to street. The point was the combination of incendiaries and explosives in order to set up the kindling, light the flame, spread the fire, and block the street and destroy the water main beneath it. Later on, bombs with delayed action mechanisms terrorized rescuers—"Nice, pleasant, friendly world we live in, eh?" commented Campbell Muirhead, an RAF bomb aimer.[20]

Sirens began to wail seventeen minutes past midnight, the usual time for RAF attacks on cities in west Germany. Twenty minutes later the first wave of bombers, which had taken off two hours earlier, dropped incendiary bombs; by 2:30 in the morning the raid was over. "Raider Every 6 Sec. for 1½ Hours," boasted the headline in the *Daily Telegraph* about "the world's biggest air raid." "The sky over Cologne was as busy as Piccadilly Circus," reported one pilot. "It was almost too gigantic to be real," added another; for all the statistics about the number of raiders, the tonnage of bombs, and the traffic in the sky, the bombardment was an almost cosmic event that the press described with "a sense of awestruck wonder."

In the first moments, "everything stood out clearly, as if you were seeing it on stage, brightly lit." In the light of the full moon, "you could see people running in the streets." Every part of the city burned: "It was strange to see the flames reflected on our aircraft," a pilot remembered; it was "as if we were on fire ourselves with the red glow dancing up and down the wings." In the dawn of the "rising suns" the fires had created, the bombers returned to their bases. When they reached the coast nine minutes later,

Cologne was still visible as the crest of "distant volcanoes" and, farther out, "a huge cigarette-end, in the German blackout."[21]

For residents of Cologne, the bombs had destroyed entire neighborhoods as well as the measures they used to calibrate the raids. Before, the city's chronicler explained, newspaper photographs of the damage provided the kind of detail an insurance adjuster might use. Yet the destruction in this raid did not have a particular address because the "ocean of flames" ravaged "whole streets," not "individual buildings." Witnesses took up the Bible to find the appropriate reference: "the days of Sodom and Gomorrah, when fire and brimstone rained down from the skies."[22]

Cologne had already endured 104 raids, so civil defense was well organized; the loss of life was relatively small, with an estimated 469 dead. In this raid, as in others, analysts tended to overestimate the effects of the demolition and underestimate the efficiency of local efforts to restore city life to normal. Even so, hundreds of fires burned through more than half of the old city; some 1,500 commercial and industrial buildings lay in ruins, 13,000 apartments and houses were destroyed, and 45,000 people were left homeless. Cologne made enough of an impression to secure Bomber Command's future. The deployment of "heavies," the four-engine Lancaster, which carried a much larger bomb load, up to 17,000 pounds, intensified the punishment as the RAF pursued a methodical approach to area bashing in the Battles of the Ruhr, the Battle of Hamburg (a late July assault that killed 40,000 civilians), and the Battle of Berlin in 1943. (More than 4,000 planes were delivered over the years, but, given cumulative operational losses, the fleet's size at any given moment was much smaller.)

Cologne's bombers were "the first blasts of the whirlwind"; Germans "will learn to hear the voice of doom in the thunder of bombs," lectured the London *Times* on the judgment of God. "Cologne was just the beginning." "We harden our hearts" to adjust to the new era, although, with "terror" carried into "the home of German workers," the *Daily Mail* was "sorry for the women and children." At the same time, Londoners opened their hearts to the new superheroes. In "Wings for Victory," more than one million people plastered Trafalgar Square in March 1943 to see the Lancaster bombers on exhibit: it was "the biggest crowd since the coronation," pronounced the *Daily Express*.[23]

The future Harris glimpsed in London on December 29, 1940, had arrived. Once established, the mission to bomb German cities drove an unstoppable machine that claimed an exorbitant proportion of resources and lives of airmen. In a way the *Daily Mail* had it right. "We have spent a tremendous amount of time and effort in building up a force of giant bombers," it noted, so much so that "nothing will stop the development of this attack." After Cologne, it was easy to see how Bomber Command was "gathering speed" like "a lorry without brakes rolling down a hill," an accelerating, expanding force in conditions of total war. A broadcast warned Germans: "We are bombing," and "You cannot stop it and you know it." Bomber Command, writes one historian, "bombed and bombed and bombed as if bombing were simply an industrial process."[24]

However, in 1942 and into 1943, Bomber Command lost hundreds of aircraft and thousands of airmen every month. Despite increased production and delivery of the "heavies," there was no prospect for a swift or powerful blow. The "weapon was not able to pull off six Hamburgs; instead it produced a thousand Gelsenkirchens." It drained resources without breaking

Germany. What Harris ended up fighting was the war of attrition the bomber was supposed to have made unnecessary.[25]

Calculations suggest that just over half of the airmen were killed, and between 24 and 31 percent completed the first tour. One study of 2,051 American airmen flying over Germany with the Eighth Air Force found that just over 25 percent completed a twenty-five-operation tour, while 57 percent were killed. Harris himself admitted that "scarcely one man in three could expect to survive his tour of thirty operations." Of the 18 men who left Australia with Don Charlwood and deployed with Bomber Command in 1941, "five of these had come through, one was a prisoner of war and twelve were dead . . . perhaps a little better than average." German submariners faced worse prospects, but among the Allies no other military service approached these decimating casualties over the course of the war.[26]

Airmen persistently calculated the odds. "Thirty ops? It's a forbidding sort of total," ventured Charlwood. "And yet," replied a flier on the base, "'it's not a cumulative risk. Actually a man runs no more risk on his tenth than he does on his first. In fact, the further he goes the better his chances should become.'" Charlwood contemplated the math: "I could see that this was a theory he had argued often with himself, but it was far from convincing." Crew members were not statisticians, but they could count. "Always was quite good at arithmetic!" noted Campbell Muirhead in his diary. Every week, the new faces in the mess hall were "stark reminders of bleak prospects"; "we seldom learned to know their names." Just "strangers, strangers."[27]

Good-luck charms shortened the odds. One fellow from Newcastle carried "an American machine spanner" in one of his boots, while another from Winchester still put faith in rabbits' feet. There was bad luck too. Twenty years on, a soldier remembered, "The chop-girl on our squadron was reputed to have lost five boy-friends," each one killed on operations. "It was, of course, nothing more than a series of tragic coincidences for the girls involved," but airmen became superstitious of "super-natural influence" and avoided the "pretty cook-house" girl.[28]

If the airman in the Air Ministry translated crew members into nonhuman "flows" and "wastage," airmen on the airfield translated the world around them into good and bad magic. However, magical thinking was adaptive rather than rebel-lious. While individual morale might falter and crews become cynical about numbers in operations, the volunteers continued to support the overall effort. They accepted the premise that "war is war."

Bomber crews felt ambushed when they flew into the patch of sky near the target when all the lights were suddenly switched on by searchlights and flak fire from the ground and flares dropped from fighters up above. Being "coned," or caught by German searchlights, was like "running naked through a busy train station, hoping not to be seen," or "being naked in broad daylight in Piccadilly Circus with everybody shooting at you." Still, as Muirhead recollected impressions of his last run: "You know you've got to fly into it and through it"; "your very last one and where has your effing luck gone?" This was a stoic recapit-ulation since on earlier missions Muirhead had heard his men over the intercom: "'Turn back,' 'Mummy,' 'I don't want to die,'" plus a selection of blasphemies with "every second word being 'fucking.'"[29]

Given these impressions, it does not make sense to think of RAF bombers over Germany as remote technicians who engaged "a faceless enemy from a great distance away." They were forced to think quite directly about death and destruction;

bomber crews could see men from blasted planes tumbling through the sky around them. The very proximity of death also led the airmen "to contemplate the effects of their weapons on other human beings." "I would try to tell myself then that this was a city, a place inhabited by beings such as ourselves," wrote Charlwood, yet the line of thought went nowhere.[30]

The process of rearmorization was quick and thorough in the conditions of total war. One night over Gelsenkirchen, Muirhead felt "a faint niggling at the back of my mind; how many women and children had I killed simply by pressing that little tit" as bomb aimer? There was "no point in deluding oneself over that—one had killed people," since "some of my load must have fallen on houses; maybe even on air raid shelters." He considered them carefully: "men, probably mostly elderly the fit being in the Forces, women maybe some of them factory workers but probably most of them older. And children. Children of all ages. I know the Germans brought it upon themselves," but "God, it's a terrible killing time." Even so, on a second raid on Gelsenkirchen a week later, Muirhead could write: "No faint niggling this time; didn't even give it a thought." "Anyway, the Germans are doing the same thing to us."[31]

Nearly one hundred thousand British and American airmen lost their lives, most of them at the beginning of the bombing campaign, in order to kill some six hundred thousand German civilians, most of them at the end—a poor ratio seen from London or Washington. There was always something that tied these two groups of casualties together: the anxiety the bomber and bombed shared as they scanned the sky. "In bombers named for girls, we burned / The cities we had learned about in school— / Till our lives wore out; our bodies lay among / The people we had killed and never seen," wrote Randall Jarrell in "Losses."

Bombing raised questions about the rationale behind the large casualties on both sides. In the end, however, the logic of war prevailed, "the terrible killing time" in which the destruction of civilian life was acceptable even at great military cost. It always mattered whether dehoused refugees or shipwrecked mariners were "ours" or "theirs." Once again, the war had won.

On October 24, 1942, Matthias Mehs noted local conditions in his town of Wittlich in western Germany. "One hour alarm from 11 o'clock at night on. Rumbling in the distance. Hazy and rain."[32]

Air raids had become the local weather. Indeed, residents learned to look at the moon to reckon the odds of a bomber attack. "Last night we had a full moon," an observer reported— the bomber's moon; "no one expects anything good to come of it." Newspapers stopped reporting weather during the war, but the old rubric included new information: "Black-out period (London): 10:49 pm to 5:24 am" as well as "High water at London Bridge, 9:40 am and 9:53 pm." Later on, firestorms created their own weather as flames consumed the available oxygen. As the air rushed in over the center of the fire, "whole trees were torn from the ground," and "people were blown off their feet and sucked into the flames by the same invisible force."[33]

Just as everybody talked about the weather, everybody talked about air raids. This was no surprise since residents of west German towns had endured dozens of alarms and sleepless nights long before the big attack on Cologne. People learned to go to bed in their street clothes and readied an emergency suitcase containing identification papers, jewelry, linens, and cash as well as "a steel helmet, gas mask, and warm clothes." They prepared themselves as refugees and firefighters. The war with Britain was not even a year old when Paulheinz Wantzen added up the "156 hours and 43 minutes" he had spent in his basement in Münster. Although the hours would increase substantially, his calculations resembled those Muirhead made after he had completed his tour of thirty operations: "Hours flown on Lancs were 187.10," and, once he included flight hours in Wellingtons and Halifaxes, his summary read: "Total flying hours *472.04*."[34]

For Germans, Cologne changed everything. It functioned as a placeholder for the more notable and far deadlier bombing of Hamburg in July 1943. After the news, daily conversations in Munster included rumors that "the English will raid one west German city after another," a fair copy of Churchill's statements after the May 30, 1942, raid. "Not much is missing to make it a real panic," noted Wantzen, a local newspaperman. Even so, he added, the weather is "wonderfully warm and everything is blooming so peacefully that one can scarcely imagine fire and death raining down from the sky at night."[35]

Even before the arrival of evacuees from the burned-out cities, the bombs forced Germans across the country to confront the realities of the strategic air war. They made their own calculations: "Will it be our turn tonight?" Residents believed that longer nights in the fall meant more distant "Berlin and Munich will finally get their turn"; "this feeling of great Schadenfreude is really all over the place," commented Wantzen. Better yet was the ditty police picked up in the Ruhr: "Dear Tommy, fly on past. We're all miners. Fly to Berlin. They're the ones who shouted 'Yes!'"[36]

A few days after the bombing of Cologne, the *New York Times* quoted the city's prominent newspaper to drive home the point that the Rhenish metropole had been "lost." Inhabitants "bade farewell to their Cologne." It basically affirmed Harris's assessment that Cologne had been "virtually destroyed." Actually, the article in the *Kölnische Zeitung* was not titled "Lost" but rather "Steadfast," and while it detailed irreparable damage to the old city, it also highlighted the spirit of cooperation among its residents. The story was basically a study of the bombed-out dollhouse, dividing its labor between examining demolition in some quarters and exploring signs of life in others. If much of Cologne had died, its people were very much alive and spoken for by the newspaper that published without interruption in those days.[37]

When the *Kölnische Zeitung* set out on its "tour of the sights of devastation," it found beloved features of the city "destroyed and gutted." The city's "little gems," including bars and taverns, "are no more." In what appeared to be an obituary, one writer admitted that "Cologne is more like a memory than a city. I get to some spot and recollect that there had been a street there or a cinema that we used to go to, or the Ramke store, or the 'White Stag.'"[38]

Residents confronted the "dead city." Curiously, the disaster of the 6th Army in Stalingrad a few months later did not have the same effect. It did not register the loss of home. The demolition of cities like Cologne had a completely different chain of associations that did not conjure up the nation or even its potential defeat in Hitler's war. The destruction of cities represented the death of communal memory in a way that military losses did not. A sign of this was that survivors usually thought about bombing in calamitous or cosmic terms. They tended to avoid the geopolitical aspect of the war or terms such as "terror" and "murder" to describe air raids. People who had lost their homes did not feel themselves as Germans, but as puny casualties, not of the enemy in particular, but of a supernatural event that threatened civilization itself. "We were completely defenseless"; above in the sky, "wings, quiet, majestic, purposeful"; below in the ground, a "small group of people in this tiny basement."[39]

The *Kölnische Zeitung* took another tour around the city in the days after the bombing. Here the stations were encounters rather than sights: the praiseworthy son who had rescued the belongings of a neighbor, the lady at the office who provided extra ration cards to make up for lost reserves, the man who appeared at local Nazi headquarters to donate a second pair of shoes. The idea was that "the magnitude of misfortune revealed the magnitude of tenacity that had lain dormant in the souls of the people of Cologne." "More powerful than fate is the will to order," concluded the *Kölnische Zeitung.*[40]

Discipline and organization kept casualties in Cologne low. Householders learned to fight incendiary fires with sand and shovel. In addition, residents relied on large public air raid shelters and emergency services in the hospitals. Authorities also arranged for truckloads of supplies to manage the calamity. Within days, Anna Schmitz had received an "extra allotment" that she described to her son stationed in Norway: "all sorts of things"—"1/4 lb meat; 1/4 sausage, 1/4 butter, 1/4 sugar, ½ rice, ½ noodles, ½ vegetables, 1/4 nuts, ½ strawberries," which were in season, as well as 50 grams of oil for cooking and a large loaf of bread. After a week, trucks delivered shoes (30,000 pairs of street shoes, 25,000 pairs of work shoes, and 10,500 pairs of house slippers in complete conformity with the Germans' podiatric division of labor), 61,000 sheets, 700,000 cakes of soap in addition to ten million cigarettes and 650,000 cigars. A "small army" of soldiers and construction workers began the cleanup.[41]

Even so, after large air raids, Nazis made it a point to study the mood in working-class neighborhoods. Nineteen eighteen stood out as a terrible nightmare; everything National Socialists did was undertaken to exorcize the ghost of national disintegration at the end of World War I. Goebbels, whose mother and mother-in-law had been bombed out in Berlin, traveled around the country to pat it down for signs of weakness. After a trip to Duisburg in November 1942, he found that morale held up in exemplary fashion: "This trip has really shown me just how loyal particularly workers are to the regime and to the Führer." Goebbels took a "victory lap" in which Allied bombing served the Nazis as a plebiscite. The "bombed-out" Germans he surveyed had become impoverished, and more patriotic, but not more Bolshevik.[42]

In an essay on "new roofs," Hans Schwarz van Berk, a Nazi correspondent, recounted his own "journey to the bombed cities." "The roofs in the Ruhr and along the Rhine have become more colorful," he cheered; newly replaced tiles "come in different shades. Looking at the new and brightly colored patches, you can see how often the hail of shrapnel pelted down on these towns," necessitating rounds of new repairs.[43]

There was more to the new color coordination than roof tiles. Among "stacks of wood, sand, cement," a "column of prisoners-of-war are unloading bricks," and "Bolsheviks are digging a cable trench." "Really and truly, hundreds of thousands of foreigners are moving around in the middle of the combat zone." What the air raids had done was to pull the satellite camps of the big concentration camps directly into German cities where brigades of uniformed prisoners worked as glaziers, roofers, and laborers to repair bomb damage. The concentration camp at Sachsenhausen provided Düsseldorf with a brigade of six hundred workers, while Buchenwald supplied Cologne with one thousand. The prisoners worked twelve-hour days, seven days a week, and slept in temporary prisons often set up in the middle of residential neighborhoods.[44]

Other colors disappeared: the yellow Jewish stars. As he walked around bombed-out Cologne gathering impressions, the Swiss consul informed himself about new directives regarding Jews. "In order to acquire more free apartments," the consul noted on June 15, 1942, "the transports of Jews to the East are going to be started up again. Last night, a large number of Jews living in Cologne" received the order to assemble the next evening in the convention center. It is worth noting how well informed Franz-Rudolf von Weiss was. Following up on leads, he learned that "SS Obersturmbannführer Eichmann" was in charge of measures against Jews: "He had been in business in Palestine before going bankrupt, which makes him the right man for going after the Jews." "His office is in the Kurfürstenstrasse in Berlin, where there are at present some 60,000 Jews, while in the Reich whole there are still 200,000."[45]

Since Jews were deported from Cologne in the fall of 1941 and again in March, April, and May 1942 (leaving about 6,000 Jews in the city), it is unlikely that the bombings did anything more than accelerate some transports, but Cologne's residents certainly believed that Jewish departures freed up apartments, and many welcomed the deportations for that reason. As "punishment" for the air raid, the Jewish nursing home was vacated on Monday, June 1. The consul also knew that the city's Gauleiter promised a "Jew-free" city by the end of July. After the bombing, transports to Theresienstadt resumed on June 5, the Friday following the Saturday night raid. Subsequent trains were scheduled on June 9, June 13, and June 15, departures that coincided with the arrival of strawberries and slippers for bombing vic-tims; the last large transport, with 1,165 victims, left Cologne on July 27, 1942. Writing about the deportations, the consul com-mented that "we assume that the transport has in the meantime been gassed since no news has been received in Cologne about its whereabouts." The sureness of this conclusion was highly unusual. It tells the truth about the deportations, although Ther-esienstadt itself was a transit, not a death, camp.[46]

The end point for Cologne's deported Jews was Theresien-stadt; for their household goods, it was suburban railway sta-tions such as Köln-Lindenthal or Hamburg-Dammtor that provided storage. Cologne's Gauleiter arranged for barges to deliver to the city the household property of 850 Jewish fami-lies who had been deported from Hilversum in Holland. Regu-larly advertised in the local newspaper, auctions of Jewish goods resumed in Cologne's convention hall on June 5. According to one estimate for Nuremberg, 127 out of 645 families who had been rehoused up to January 1943 had been placed in emptied Jewish apartments.[47]

While Goebbels visited Duisberg on November 18, 1942, Paulheinz Wantzen recorded his own day in Trier: "Today we received a visit from a bombed-out couple (senior state coun-cilor) who are in the process of refurnishing themselves from among the goods of Dutch Jews that are stacked up in a ware-house in the harbor. One has to say for peanuts. A heavy lounge chair: 60 Marks; a walnut wing chair: 30 Marks; an iron table inlaid with 18 old Dutch tiles: 60 Marks; the kind of scale you find in a doctor's office: 10 Marks." "The only scandal," Wantzen went on to write, was "200 complete sets were totally, thought-lessly broken apart." In the case of a double bedroom set, "even the beds and mattresses were sold separately. Apparently, the whole process is easy and completed without paperwork; a man shows you the things, you select what you want and name a ridiculous price—sometimes the man pushes a bit higher, but mostly not—you nod and hand over the money." The purchase is "settled without formality or a receipt." The couple expressed "full satisfaction with their acquisitions."[48]

Price-shopping at auctions for scarce goods indicated that people were not completely without resources and managed to accommodate themselves to the new circumstances. "One of the terrible paradoxes of total war" was "that both the bomber crews and the bombed could be traumatized by their experience," yet both groups managed to reintegrate themselves into the war effort and accepted its premises. To approach the civilians only as traumatized victims or the airmen only as traumatized heroes would be to miss the larger structures of the war. A similar distortion appears in postwar memory in Britain where the Blitz is remembered, but not the bash.[49]

In 1942 the only clear winner of the war was the war itself. There was a huge effort to create dead zones behind the lines of actual fighting by using indiscriminate violence by land, sea, and air. The lifeboat encapsulated the disarray and displacement of the war that had turned civilians out on the road and pitched them into the sea as luckless refugees. Destroying the business of life also came at a huge cost to the attackers, to the companies and battalions fighting in the earth, to the U-boat crews, and to the bombardiers. The closer one got to victory, the more it looked like defeat. In these circumstances, ideological motivations seemed pointless, yet paradoxically they functioned as a prime mechanism in the deadly machinery. All the training to fly the plane and all the civil-defense exercises at home did not create the militant. Air war was the perfect storm in the war.

A FEW MONTHS after the bombing of Cologne, Schwarz van Berk introduced readers to "Frau Schmitz" who had evacuated to her daughter-in-law's house in Silesia with only the clothes she had been able to rescue wrapped up in a woolen blanket. She was not happy with the arrangement because the two women did not get along. She cried when she thought about her wrecked living room and the memories it had held. "If only she knew," commented Schwarz van Berk, "how many people have to wander the earth!" Schmitz was only "a tiny grain of sand in the gigantic dunes" drifting across continents in the "storm" of war. Schmitz and other evacuees like her needed to see their misfortune in a wider, global perspective, which Schwarz van Berk surveyed in a remarkable exposition.[50]

Schmitz was one among a great many passengers in transit. There were repatriated ethnic Germans from Volhynia in western Ukraine who sought a better life in the German Reich. After crossing the border "on the straw sacks of their covered wagons, thousands had to start off in the squalid farms abandoned by Poles with nothing more to set up house than the contents of a chest they had brought along," the remnant, like Schmitz's bundle, of homes left behind. It was not long before German families settled in, releasing their sons to the Wehrmacht or the SS.

Germans made up only a "small chapter" in these "journeys of the war." Schwarz van Berk kept spinning the globe to point out the skilled optician who had left Switzerland to work in the armaments industry in Britain, the diamond cutter from Holland resettled in Palestine, the Communist refugee from Spain who after internment in France was at work building Germany's coastal defenses, the French chemist employed in a Frankfurt factory—altogether there were three million foreign laborers in Germany in 1942. With another spin Schwarz van Berk could see "columns of Africans" forced to abandon cotton fields in Sudan in order to construct airfields for the Allies' east–west route across the continent. He also pointed to the Indian laborers who immigrated to Burma for low wages before fleeing foreign invasion and local anger only to perish in the mountains, "a wartime Passion of 700,000 people." And in the United States, thousands of new migrants pulled up their "trailers" in front of Kaiser's shipyards. They lived in "modern-day gypsy camps," temporary compounds filled with women and children. In the war's industrial plant, a "mysterious sea of humanity" worked in three shifts, shopped in stores open at midnight, and trekked through the dark between gaps of light cast by their trailers.

Schwarz van Beck's journey around the world concluded with the thought: "Even far away from the fire barrages and threatening skies, a great restlessness has swept out the homesteads and erected new wartime barracks, tearing up the rules, flaunting the laws of nature, reversing night and day."

This was quite an unusual review of passages around the world at war (and of issues of *Life* magazine stacked up at the Propaganda Ministry on Wilhelmstrasse in Berlin).

Despite a reference to predator capitalists in the United States, and to Germany's "attractive future" and "modern lifestyle," Schwarz van Beck did not divide the world into ideological camps. There were no haves and have-nots in his write-up. Lining Frau Schmitz up with so many others, he created functional equivalencies that denied Germany or Nazism any particular pride of place. The common denominator was worldwide mobility, whether it was coerced or not.

The war was the main culprit, and it had become a promiscuous actor on the global stage. Schwarz van Beck described the relentless machinery of severance, segmentation, redistribution, and collision. Ethnicity or religion played a subordinate role: "German," "American," "Japanese," and "Ukrainian" were identification tags for ingredients in the larger churn. He did not even mention Jewish malefactors. Only in one context did Schwarz van Berk refer to Jews, comparing the hostility between Jews and Arabs to the hostility between Indians and Burmese, a conflict in which he cast the Indians as Christ-like figures in the "Passion"—were they not the overseas "Jews" of the British Empire? And there was also the Dutch jeweler in Palestine, a Jewish settler who stood in the same line behind Frau Schmitz. In other words, Schwarz van Berk completely displaced the prominent Jewish element in ideas in the Third Reich in order to emphasize the vast machinery of displacement.

Silesia, Sudan, Burma, Palestine, California—Schwarz van Berk's perspective was completely global. The war was much more than a "world journey German-style" but a planetary conflagration characterized by the movements of civilians rather than armies; it was Schmitz in Cologne and not her son in Norway who was really on the front lines. The field campaigns of the Napoleonic era and trench warfare in World War I no longer captured the essence of military conflict. "The war," Schwarz van Berk explained, "has become a real people tractor and people plow turning over the ground of layered history." (*Volkstraktor* is not the "people's tractor" but a "people mover" for "ethnic cleansing.")

War had shaken down the whole world, uprooting historical anchors, opening up spaces for newcomers, and necessitating extreme vigilance, effective organization, and mass militarization. By acknowledging the disasters, Schwarz van Berk refined a kind of Nazi way of life based on the management of the emergencies that came with the struggle for existence. National

Socialists prospered by claiming to contain the catastrophes they themselves had imagined and created. The state of permanent emergency was the premise of authoritarian rule. With his panoramic survey of the world, Schwarz van Berk implied that Nazism's accomplishment had been to recognize the tough nature of the new world. And by learning the "melody of hard facts," contemporaries could flourish. They had to become survivalists. However, the dominant idea in Schwarz van Berk's travelogue was simply subordination to the powerfully imagined motions of disassembly and reassembly. It was a very modern view: homelessness as the general condition. It also completely ignored the political muscle behind conscription, deportation, and murder.

Criminal behavior like murdering civilians was not so much passed over as deliberately evaded by sneaking soldiers in with civilians so that everyone, including the Nazi and the Jew, was tossed about in the same storm of the war. Metaphors about the war like the wind, the inferno, or the beasts and machines work in a similar way by making the different groups war acts upon essentially equivalent. The images are evocative because they capture the extensiveness of war as well as its violent energy, but they are morally dubious, emphasizing verbs at the expense of their subjects and effects rather than causes. Schwarz van Berk's travel to war evacuated the Nazis right along with Frau Schmitz.

PART IV

PUSH DOWN THE ROAD

CHAPTER 13

Transit

The "winds of war," the title of Herman Wouk's best-selling novel, is a commonplace recital of war: how winds drove soldiers such as Charles Teed across land and sea and how they tossed civilians including Frau Schmitz from their homes. Books in the Bible summoned up the winds to denote adversity but also the specific fierceness of war in which storms reached into crannies and crevices. The winds are also capricious since there are "four winds." The conventional recital makes sense because so many people felt the calamitous weather of the war, separating them from old lives, acting with great destructive force, evicting them to somewhere else. "Winds" counted the rucksacks, suitcases, and bundles by the road.

Gusts of refugees were signs of war in the twentieth century. Fear of aerial bombardment during the Czechoslovak crisis in September 1938 emptied cities in France. A year later, thousands of Polish civilians crowded roads to flee German armies on the first weekend of the war. Japan's rapid advance in Burma pushed waves of refugees into the hills. Everywhere declarations of war came with the internment of resident aliens: Germans in England, Japanese in the Philippines, English in China. There were many more civilians who evacuated homes than soldiers who marched into battle. Even for people who at first did not leave places, wartime regimes brought terrible times: food shortages, forced labor, military retaliation, and wholesale murder.

"Winds of war" identified the turbulence of war, but the agitation was not whimsical or erratic. As potential fifth columnists, as laborers in war industry, as bearers of national morale, civilians were treated and mistreated as deliberately as were soldiers. The difference was the uniform. Even children appeared as foes because they were future avengers who threatened the future of the children and grandchildren of friends. Civilians suffered for being considered both indispensable and disposable.

As a phrase, the "winds of war" obscured the politics of war that were neither nature's doing nor God's. It was an image without a body. It conjured up a vast collective misfortune of people caught up in the war without differentiation, eliding distinctions between victims and perpetrators and between the powerless and the powerful. Yet Jews were not just tossed about; Hitler sorted them into the sinister category of "international finance Jewry" that he claimed to be the original cause of the war. For all its rhetorical power, the "winds of war" is an exceedingly passive portrayal of the war. It reveals the startling fact that mostly civilians died, but does not indicate how or why.

In her novel *Transit* (1944), Anna Seghers, a refugee from Hitler's Germany, explored the new state of itinerancy during the war. However, the book fell through the cracks because the

existential displacement Seghers considered the primary tragedy of the war, readers often saw as incidental damage in a basically heroic, uncompromising struggle. Readers did what they
do today: they exiled the exiles.

Like "remnants of crushed armies" and "escaped slaves,"
like hordes "who had been chased from all the countries of the
earth" in ancient times, Jews, Communists, and other refugees
crowded Marseille after the fall of France in June 1940. But
before reaching the shore to board ships, they were dispersed
into the alleyways of the old port where they became stuck
as they tried to procure the visas, transit visas, and exit visas
necessary to depart Europe. Along the Canabière, refugees sat
in cafés trading "age-old harbor gossip" about favorable trade
winds and pliable consular officials. They conversed "in many
languages about ships that would never leave, ships that had
arrived at their destinations, and others that had run aground,
been sunk or seized." Indeed, the novel opens with news of the
sinking of *The Montreal* on which Marie had secured a place.
"Forever running from one death toward another," the refugees
described "perpetual circular motion."[1]

Reviewers criticized the inert "futility and despair" of
Seghers's novel. With this sort of "mainspring," the novel,
a contrast to the hero's escape from a concentration camp in
her previous book, *The Seventh Cross* (1942), "will simply not
tick"—it was "too corrosive" to stir readers. The problem was
that the refugee was "already dead."[2]

Transit did not reflect martial virtue or fit into the militancy
that reviewers saw advancing the Allied cause. Neither did the
deportation train, the camp, or the ghetto. Paradoxically, war
burnished the idea of freedom—of action to overturn and overrun. What Seghers tried to point out in her fiction was that

heroes who beat the odds to fight for the Allies had become hard to see. The Nazis were such "a terrible, cruel enemy" because of the "mysterious evil of the rumors, bribery and lies" they spread in their wake. She made the case for the four winds of war that continued to disassemble the wished-for partisans into bunches of unwelcome refugees. What doesn't tick? The futility and despair, its representation in fiction or history, or its elision of heroes? Transit reveals a lot of different routes but not clear or satisfying choices. That too was the state of war.

"The typical Soviet subject between 1937 and 1949 was a displaced person," writes one historian. With a population of 194 million at the time of the German invasion in June 1941, the Soviet Union included major additions in 1939 and 1940: more than one-third of the old prewar Polish population as well as the inhabitants of the former Baltic states and Bessarabia, a total of nearly twenty-two million people. Then the German invasion left one of every three Soviet citizens under foreign occupation for at least some time, sixty-five million in all, including most of those who had been recently patriated. More than twenty million Soviets fled the Germans or were evacuated by state authorities. They moved east. A total of thirty-six million soldiers mobilized to fight. They mostly went west.

For a time in 1941, it looked like the pieces of Soviet society could all be found lying "on the miserable floor of the train station": "peasant men and women, whole families, middle-class people, workers, intellectuals"—"all of Russia was on the move," wrote Polish writer Aleksander Wat. "Everyone gazes from some foreign window," added Anna Akhmatova, who had been evacuated to Tashkent in Uzbekistan.[3]

In the German-occupied zone, from Leningrad in the North to Crimea in the South, the Wehrmacht captured more than five million Red Army soldiers, and administrators deported several million civilians as forced laborers to Germany; by 1945, an additional two million Soviet citizens evacuated westward with the retreating Germans. As long as it was in their hands, the conquered territory formed the foundation for the Germans' new empire, a grandly scaled racial order in the East. Imperial construction work was preceded by demolition: updated several times in 1941 and 1942, the "hunger plan" calculated the rapid death of millions of Slavic people with a remnant toiling as slaves in planned German colonies. The first step to the purification of the land was the complete eradication of Jewish life. The majority of Jews, those not able to flee the invaders, were murdered almost immediately after the Germans arrived, more than one million souls in all. Soviet authorities themselves deported more than three million non-Russian people, Poles mostly, but also Ukrainians and Balts, some to be murdered, many to die of neglect. Without the war, the population of the Soviet Union would have approached 224 million; with the war, it decreased to 170 million.[4]

One way to consider the convulsive displacement in the Soviet Union is to compare it to the sixty-two million moves in Great Britain, a country of thirty-nine million; this large figure was tabulated from change-of-address forms departing or newly arriving residents handed over to the post office.[5]

The winds of war deflected the politics of the war by not making distinctions, but the destitution and the difficulty of holding on to names and identities, and the capriciousness of finding recognition, were also part of the calamity of the world war. The pervasive wartime distinction between "us" and "them," between friends and foes, pushed out of sight people who were lifted up in one story and forgotten in another. The violence of dividing up humanity between "us" and "them" was terrific, but so was holding on to a heroic partisanship that overlooked the refugees who found the war unfathomable, uncountable, and therefore unaccountable. The "winds of war" remains an apt description precisely because it muddies the moral clarity of fighting and sacrifice.

ONE OF THE most famous photographs of World War II depicts a burned baby abandoned on a platform in Shanghai's South Station after the Japanese air raid on "Bloody Saturday," August 28, 1937. Earlier that month, widely circulated newsreels captured the chaos following attacks that destroyed the Cathay Hotel and Sincere Department Store in the city's foreign settlement. Iconic representations of the war often featured violence against civilians: to be sure, there is Joe Rosenthal's photograph of the flag raising at Iwo Jima and Yevgeny Khaldei's at the Reichstag, but consider St. Paul's Cathedral during the Blitz, the ruins of Dresden from the Frauenkirche, the little boy in the Warsaw Ghetto. Without showing the attackers, the photographs document the terror pressed into civilian lives. In the case of H. S. "Newsreel" Wong's photograph of Shanghai, the image, along with reports of the atrocities in Nanjing, the Chinese capital, in November, galvanized worldwide opinion against Japan's war in China. When *Life* magazine published the full-page photograph on October 4, 1937, editors emphasized "the Chinese baby's potential audience": twenty-five million readers of the Hearst newspapers who employed Wong, twenty-five million more readers through international distribution, and as many as eighty million moviegoers around the world who saw "News of the Day" and Movietone newsreels.[6]

About two hundred commuters were killed in Shanghai's South Station on "Bloody Saturday," but there are no vivid photographs of more turbulent scenes in the war. The deliberate flooding of the Yellow River in June 1938 drowned at least one hundred thousand villagers in a desperate attempt by the Chinese military to slow the Japanese advance. Hundreds of thousands of farmers were displaced by the flood. Millions of people starved to death during the subsequent famine in Henan in 1942. Yet these slow-motion blows did not evoke the melodrama of battle or the spectacle of aggressive raiders. They were muted by war and its imagined partisans.

Engineers succeeded in breaching the dikes at Huayuankou in Henan, thirty miles west of the Japanese advance guard on June 9, 1938. It was only on the third attempt that the great stone and dirt ramparts channeling the flow of the river gave way to the detonations. "The river pounded, swirled and bubbled against the broken dikes." "Finally with a terrible roar," the river turned south to "bend itself to the Chinese plan." In "sodden, mucky, yellow columns, the river swarmed down on the Japanese," drowning many soldiers, miring their tanks and guns, and "throwing an impassable wall of water" between the main Japanese army and the upriver city of Zhengzhou. The threat to Wuhan, the new capital after Nanjing had been abandoned in November 1937, had been lifted. "China had been saved."[7]

The waters advanced south and west about ten miles a day, eventually flooding an area of twenty-one thousand square miles (about the size of Croatia), two to three feet deep. "The ground became a lake and the villages became a part of the river," a survivor recalled.[8]

The breaching of the dykes "has given the world a new term," Jack Belden noted. It stamped the Chinese word *jiāotǔ*, or "scorched earth," into the vocabulary of war. The phrase militarized suffering. By burning crops, devastating cities, and flooding fields, the retreating Nationalist armies hoped to use earth (and water) as a substitute for soldiers to check the enemy. As the Japanese advanced up the valleys of the Yellow and Yangtze Rivers, they encountered the essential geography of China. In the interior, "the battlefield is either mountainous or covered in water," wrote Chiang Kai-shek, chairman of the national government and generalissimo of the National Revolutionary Army. These features negate "the advantages of the enemy's weaponry." "The longer our enemy struggles," he concluded, "the more he involves himself in difficulties," while "the longer we struggle the stronger and more determined we become."[9]

Prone to flooding, the Yellow River was known for centuries as "China's sorrow." It was "'Japan's sorrow' now." "From the humanitarian point of view," wrote Harrison Forman, correspondent for the *Times* of London, the "price paid by the Chinese was stupendous," yet as a piece of strategy, the destruction of the dikes stood out as "a brilliant achievement." In Shanghai, the floods earned general applause. One reporter had "yet to find a single Chinese who is perturbed over the prospect of the widespread suffering and death over the North China plain." The *New York Times* was not so sure. "The Yellow River rises," the editors wrote, while people in the North "are thrice scourged, by flood and epidemic on top of unprovoked war." Even so, the flood remained "sacred" in accounts of the resistance.[10]

The refugees in Henan fled west, upriver, into China's interior, not downriver, toward the towns and the coast—and the Japanese. They joined the national movement of resistance to the Japanese invasion. Destitute villagers crowded roads along with urban folk from Beijing, Shanghai, and Nanjing. In place after place, Japanese troops had murdered civilians in the areas they overran, sometimes a few dozen, often hundreds and thousands, each slaughter a terrifying rehearsal of the "Rape of Nanjing." In fact, Chinese came to see Japanese as "devils," a completely unreckonable affliction. Across the countryside they emptied, Japanese soldiers could see the slogans written in white chalk on the walls, expressions of unprecedented national defiance: "Good Men For Soldiers," "To Bear Arms Is An Honor," "Drive Out The Japanese." According to the prominent republican newspaper *Dagongbao*, this was "the first war of the entire nation in Chinese history."[11] Maybe the entire nation, because so many millions of people experienced the war on the road.

China had bought time, but what sort of time? "There is always still time to die," remarked Belden about the flooding and fleeing.

As the waters spread, they displaced many more people than had the Japanese; in Henan, 2.3 million households against 1.4 million. Breaching the dikes was "perhaps the most environmentally damaging act of warfare in world history," concludes one historian. Seen another way, drowning the earth and its people was "one of the first mass killings" in World War II. Even after the waters subsided, millions of tons of silt had been left behind. One refugee had summed it up: "Run far away from that damn place and never come back."[12]

In the end, the advantages the Chinese won were slight: Wuhan was taken in October 1938, and the capital moved even farther up the Yangtze to Chongqing. And the political disadvantages were great. To leave villagers to "scatter like rats, to survive or die," reflected one Nationalist general after the Communist victory in 1949, was "the beginning of us losing the trust of the people." The failures of the "scorched-earth policy" ultimately induced Wang Jingwei, the republican hero in 1911, to collaborate with Japan to seek peace in 1940. The initial exuberance of the national front to resist the enemy and revive the unified country gave way to a sense that one calamity followed another, blocking out the future almost completely so that the war was just one part of a gross defeat.[13]

As observers had gloomily predicted, "the greatest flood in the history of China" set the scene for "the most appalling famine."[14] In the spring of 1942, hot weather and lack of rain caused the disastrous failure of the winter wheat harvest in Henan on which peasants relied to pay land taxes to the government. Summer crops of sorghum, millet, black beans, and sweet potatoes were also poor. Yields decreased by as much as 40 percent. In addition, thousands of acres of arable land and the laborers to work them had disappeared in the crises of the previous years. And then came the locusts.

Most tenant farmers subsisted from harvest to harvest with little reserve. Now they had less than a little. Bicycling into the countryside from Luoyang, Graham Peck, a junior diplomat stationed at the US embassy in Chongqing, reckoned that in a time when taxes and other requisitions had become "so heavy, the average farmer knew that if the weather should get a little worse, or if this plow would break, this ox should die, he would be in serious trouble." What was inalterable were confiscations of grain. A disproportionately large number of soldiers, nearly one million men, were garrisoned in Henan, and their "voracious appetite for energy" in the form of calories, labor, and conscripts could be supplied only by the province. Even if the government provided more relief, the standing army it supported made the choice it faced very clear: "either starve the troops or starve the peasants."[15]

Inspecting villages around Zhengzhou, Edwin Ashcraft, a long-serving Methodist missionary, came across people "whose lives were ebbing out, due to starvation." "Going past the front doors of these homes were carts loaded with grain for military use," he added. The seizure of grain effectively "drained the pond to get the fish." The armies had become "military macro-parasites" that threatened to kill their host. Soldiers in the "locust armies" ate and pillaged their way through the villages; whether the locusts were Japanese or Chinese did not matter to the inhabitants.[16]

It was villagers themselves who supplied the conscripts who became their predators. Taxes, rent, conscripts—everything was borne by the farmers. Albert Wedemeyer, the American chief of staff to Chiang Kai-shek in 1944, understood the local burden well enough: "You are working in a field looking after your rice," and there come "a number of uniformed men who tie your hands behind your back and take you with them." While "hoe and plough rust in the field" and "the wife runs to the magistrate to cry and beg for her husband, the children starve." Unfortunate conscripts were in fact sometimes roped together so they would not desert. All in all, more than 40 percent of the 1,167,000 men conscripted in 1943 either died of hunger and disease or deserted before reaching their assigned units in the field. Year after year, half the army simply vanished.[17]

Utterly destitute, farmers took the last desperate step of abandoning their villages and the graves of their ancestors. As in famine areas in the Soviet Union and India, some of the most horrendous scenes took place in dilapidated train stations where refugees gathered. "I went to Luoyang," wrote one witness, and "all around the station there were refugees, groaning and crying—hearing them was unbearable. If a train came, they would fight to get on it, hanging from the roof." Carriages were "encrusted with humanity." And "because the people on the roof were piled up," when trains entered a tunnel "countless numbers of them were crushed" or swept away. Those who could not get on a train often "sold their children—no matter what the price, they just handed them over," an observation that suggests that parents abandoned children to save them, not to buy food for themselves.[18]

Most refugees did not make it to train stations or onto trains. They traveled on foot or by cart. Theodore White, a correspondent for *Time*, recalled how "the endless procession rose beyond the horizon, wound across the paths between the fields, passed silently into the grayness behind." Roads in Henan "were jammed with blue-clad humanity pushing wheel-barrows which were piled high with the most precious belongings: bundles and babies in baskets were slung from the ends of bamboo shoulder-poles, while women with bound feet and staves in their hands trudged painfully along ankle-deep in the yellow dust."[19]

Left behind were abandoned villages: "The silence was frightening," remembered White. "People fled the impersonal cruelty of hunger as if a barbarian army were upon them. The villages echoed with emptiness; streets were deserted," the "doors and windows boarded up." In one village, he saw "two women shrieking at each other with no one else in sight, where normally there would be a crowd to watch them scold." In a famine, old lines remembered, the "dogs do not bite, chickens do not call, wells dry up, rivers run dry," the "trees drop their leaves, weeds and crops wither, the sky is cloudless, the yellow wind blows." A few people still lived in the towns with children "crying *k'o lien, k'o lien* (mercy, mercy)."[20]

The silence of the towns enveloped the refugee crisis. There was little attention to their plight in Chongqing, and newcomers from Henan were not welcome when they arrived in Shaanxi. County governments urged local residents not to exploit them: "Do not bully refugees!" "Do not wantonly impress refugees for military service!" and "Relieving refugees is a benevolent act!" read the slogans on the leaflets.[21]

Theodore White's spare, powerful account of the famine, "Until the Harvest Is Reaped," appeared in *Time* in March 1943 just as Madame Chiang Kai-shek arrived in the United States to galvanize support for the Kuomintang government. She was infuriated by the "unreal" scenes White had witnessed: "dogs eating human bodies by the roads, peasants seeking dead human flesh under the cover of darkness . . . beggars swarming at every city gate, babies abandoned to cry and die on every highway." "Most terrible of all," White added, "is the knowledge that the famine might have been averted." His final paragraph indicted the government for its neglect: "Before we left Chengchow [Zhengzhou] the officials gave us a banquet. We had two soups. We had spiced lotus, peppered chicken, beef and water chestnut. We had spring rolls, hot wheat buns, rice, bean-curd, chicken and fish. We had three cakes with sugar frosting."[22]

While officials in Chongqing praised the nobility of the taxpayers' sacrifice, villagers themselves attacked and killed as many as 50,000 of their own soldiers after the republican army retreated into Henan during Japan's 1944 Ichigo offensive. No historian fails to note how the famine wrecked the legitimacy of the Nationalist government and prepared the way for the Communists.[23]

Nearly one in four people on planet Earth lived in China, a total of 455 million, about half of whom lived under Japanese occupation. During the Sino-Japanese War from 1937 to 1945, an estimated sixty to ninety-five million people lived as refugees at some point. During the famine of 1942–1943, three million fled Henan, and many of these were impoverished famers who had been displaced by the flooding of the Yellow River. "Migrate and 'go west!'" was the cheerful watchword in the stricken region. In Henan alone, two to three million villagers succumbed to hunger and disease during the famine. In World War II only people in the Soviet Union paid a ghastlier price; in China, some three million military deaths were overshadowed by fifteen million, perhaps as many as twenty million civilian ones, the vast majority of whom were villagers who lost their lives well outside the combat zone as they struggled to find sustenance and safety. The detonation of the dikes proved far more perilous to human survival than the bombs on Shanghai or the massacres in Nanjing.[24]

"When fleeing disaster, there was no one to carry the baggage. When begging, there was no one to beat away the dogs." With this summary a widow described her solitary fate after her husband had died. She recounted the perils of the road that had stolen family and security. When Jack Belden surveyed the waters of the Yellow River, he saw that it had "broken China irrevocably in half—north and south, occupied and free, Japanese and Chinese"; he might have added that the waters had broken the villages and the families who lived in them. The great shoving of war, observed acclaimed journalist Edgar Snow, had "more profoundly shaken the Chinese family-clan system than any previous catastrophe." Flight from home meant abandoning family, friends, and neighbors. By the time refugees were counted, they lived in "broken families," often single women with children in the absence of husbands who had died or disappeared or been conscripted. Children lost their parents, husbands abandoned wives, and mothers did not know if missing children were dead or alive. All "these personal griefs and uncertainties" added up to "a mighty and unrecorded drama of sorrow." Survivors groped "for ways to live on amid the desolation," to swim "in a sea of bitterness."[25]

Early in the war, writer Ba Jin moved from Shanghai to Guangzhou, near Hong Kong, to Wuhan, then to Guangzhou again, to Guilin, in south-central China, back to Shanghai, and on to Kunming in the southwest, to Chongqing, and finally to Chengdu. It was a journey that for most Chinese readers traced the fractures that had completely undermined the sheltered universe of Jin's *The Village* (1933), a popular book in which the patriarchal grandfather, Master Gao, steadied duty under the pressures of progress. These villages disappeared because they had been abandoned by so many of their guardians. Ba Jin followed up the village story with *Cold Nights* (1947), in which Leo Wang, a government clerk, shivered as sickness and death crept around him. In his mind's eye, he saw that his wife had "thrown him aside," and his mother had "died somewhere or other"; thinking only of himself, he clung to life: "I'll just never get anywhere," "I haven't any ideals left," "I am alone." And alone on Victory Day, after Japan surrendered, Wang "breathed his last" to the "deafening noise" of firecrackers.[26]

Ba Jin wrote about the lonesome struggle for life once the supportive village structure had dissolved. The trials on the road added up mostly to disappointment and failure. In literature as in life, the characters self-destructed, adding to the sense of general collapse. The breakdown of the individual was a kind of prelude to the breakup of society in the civil war that followed the war. All this terrible clearance of the historical and familial foundations of China may have finally lent legitimacy to the efforts to build the new nation under Communism. (Ba Jin died at the age of one hundred in 2005.) South Station is the enduring image of the war in China, but the flood, destroying villages in order to save them, was what remained.

CHAPTER 14

So Many Hungers

"People first began to beg. Then who could give alms? The people began to starve. Then they began to fall victims to diseases. They sold their cattle; they sold their implements of agriculture; they devoured their seed grain; they sold their houses and land. They began to sell their daughters, next sons and after that wives. Then who would buy girls, boys and women? Every one wanted to sell and none to purchase. For want of food they eat the leaves of trees and the grass of the field as also weeds. . . . Many helpless people left their villages. Those who left died of starvation in strange places. . . . Pestilence broke out—fever, cholera and small-pox. . . . In every house people began to succumb. Who would tend the sick and touch them? No one was attended to—no one was looked after, and no one removed the corpses. Beautiful men and women died in the houses and their bodies were left to rot."

To get to the heart of the calamity, the narrator of this har-
rowing account of famine in Bengal journeys from the outside
to the inside, walking first along the roads lined with beggars
to reach the market in the town and enter the houses where so
many family members starve that there is no one anymore to
provide care. The sick waste away alone, untouched. And when
they die, their bodies fester, left behind. The individual is hungry, but the social body collapses as well.

The famine is tied to social relations. The shared practices of
caring for the sick and burying the dead cannot be carried out.
At the same time, the larger nexus of economic power and property rights compounds the distress. The poor are forced to sell
their assets cheaply, losing any hold on the future, enabling the
rich to get richer. What distinguishes the famine are not simply
the bodies left to rot, but distortions in the ability to buy and sell
tools, land, even children.

The reader is left to imagine the play of economic power: the
legal obligations of tenant farmers and the rights of property
owners. Famine says more about political economy than about
seasonal weather or natural disasters. According to Amartya
Sen, famine is generally not the "characteristic of there not being
enough to eat" but of "some people not having enough food to
eat" because of distribution, legal obligations such as taxes and
rent, and access to emergency relief.[1]

The backstory or social and political history of famine is
the reason this account of the Great Famine of 1770 that enveloped Bengal after the British defeat of the Mughals circulated
so widely. Written by Bankim Chandra Chattopadhyay for the
opening of his 1882 novel, *Anandamath* (The Sacred Brotherhood), a foundational text of Bengal's national literature, it was
quoted frequently during the Bengal Famine of 1943, which

occurred as India mobilized in Britain's war with Japan. Chatto-padhyay's text was taken up by a new generation of writers who explored the famine and the imperial society it set in relief in wartime India.

By the fall of 1943, famine killed an estimated 1.5 million people in Bengal, a province with a population of 60 million, as many later died of disease. Surveyors found corpses in homes, in the fields, along the roads (which desperate victims traveled after they had abandoned the villages), and on the pavements of Calcutta. Beyond Calcutta was the war. Bengal shared a border with Japanese-occupied Burma; refugees streamed into the province in 1942 just as Allied soldiers reported to newly established bases and airfields carved out of the countryside. Military traffic rumbled through Calcutta. The famine cannot be separated from new patterns of "distribution" and "obligation" imposed by the war, which completely distorted the mechanisms of the market and reassigned emergency relief efforts. The war with Japan in 1942 set the stage for the famine in Bengal in 1943.

Calcutta was India's real wartime capital. All the traffic in and out of the city, India's largest, made New Delhi, the imperial capital since 1911, and the seat of Britain's viceroy, seem "almost Edwardian" and "out of date."[2]

India's defenses had always faced northwest, toward Afghanistan and Russia, but after Pearl Harbor and the Japanese invasion of Burma, Calcutta in the northeast was suddenly transformed into a major military base busied by British and American troops mobilized against Burma. Across the street, you could see the Auxiliary Fire Service training in blue uniforms; on the main road, military police kept "long rows of military lorries" moving between the suburban traffic of trams and double-decker buses; long queues assembled in front of "Control" shops for rations; airplanes continuously buzzed up in the sky.[3] In addition to the foreign soldiers, workers from across the subcontinent streamed into the city to work in war industries. Refugees crowded in as well.

The war shook the economic foundations of Calcutta and the state of Bengal. The fall of Burma meant two things: it added at least a half-million refugees to the districts, an addition equivalent to India's monthly population increase. For weeks on end, evacuation trains, carrying soldiers and civilians from Burma, passed through Calcutta before dispersing the travelers across the rest of India. The Japanese occupation also put an end to Burma's rice exports that had flowed mostly to Bengal, a "food-deficit" region that produced only 85 percent of its annual requirements. What is more, Bengal was suddenly called on to export grain to meet the empire's uncovered needs in Ceylon and Mauritius, a small island but important military base that experienced terrible shortfalls of food during the war.

Aggravating the dire situation of more people and less rice was the government's panicky decision in May 1942 to confiscate fishing boats and bicycles in the war zone. As news stories had reported, the crafty Japanese had used both boats and bikes to infiltrate Malaya; the authorities were determined to deny these to potential invaders of Bengal. For fishermen and peasants in the Ganges delta, who relied on boats for transportation, the so-called policy of Denial was a disaster. To seize the river craft, a "bullock cart, motor truck, goods train" all in one, was like "cutting off a vital limb," observed Gandhi. Hundreds of bicycles were still stacked in the old fort in Midnapore at the end of 1943.[4]

By itself, the wartime policy of Denial did not create the food crisis. It added costs to the production and distribution of goods. But the real calamity was how Denial set the stage for hoarding and speculation that officials compounded by attempting to guarantee at any price the allocation of rice. Normally, government purchases of rice would have served as a reserve in the event of regional food deficits. In wartime, however, food grains were redirected to cities such as Calcutta (places of potential unrest among workers who were designated "priority classes"), to critical colonies (the only large rubber plantations the British had left after Japan's advance were in Ceylon), and to the metropole itself (the biggest hoarder, Britain, which was not to be starved by German submarines). These were man-made priorities in distribution and obligation. Stocks of rice in the entrepôt made Calcutta a powerful magnet, which, by the time rice could not be found in the countryside in summer 1943, added to the influx of people into the city.

Amid all the comings and goings of the war, observers kept a sharp eye on the price of rice. More than any other official signal, Denial prompted hoarding in anticipation of rising prices as the government scrambled to secure enough rice for vital workers in the defense industry. "Do you know the price of rice today?" the enterprising trader asked. "It's fourteen rupees. Well, tomorrow, it'll go up to perhaps sixteen." "If you buy a good stock today," he explained, "and sell it off tomorrow, you make a clear profit of two rupees on every maund." Let's see: "If you buy and sell fifty maunds every day, you make a hundred, that means three thousand a month, thirty-six thousand a year. . . . It's not so bad!"[5]

By September 1942, there was so little rice on the open market that the price surged to eighteen rupees per maund, up from four rupees a year earlier, though well below the thirty-five, fifty, even eighty rupees per maund at the height of the famine in August 1943 (a maund weighs approximately eighty pounds, with a rupee priced at thirty American cents). The inflation was a disaster for tenants and agricultural laborers as well as fishermen and artisans who had to purchase food and other necessities once they had settled rent and taxes.

What did it take for farmers to leave their land and crowd the streets of Calcutta, with its reputed stockpiles and wealth?

"Rice was one seer for a rupee" before "rice became three quarters of a seer for a rupee. Then half a seer. A quarter seer. And then rice—just vanished!" At the end of this arithmetic there was no rice at all, just a rupee. (Forty seers made a maund.)[6] Families suffered in private, reducing the number of meals and selling off reserves—jewelry, cattle, tools. But for most tenant farmers, there were few reserves. When there was not enough money to buy smaller and smaller amounts of food, family members stopped living.[7] In 1943, it was just as Chattopadhyay had written about 1770.

At the point when rice vanished, deaths dispersed the family or the family split up—widows were often thrown out of the house. Most of the destitutes in Calcutta were single mothers with children (40 percent) or single men and women (20 percent). "There was no end to the tales of miseries which our informants repeated about the break-up of family life," reported anthropologist Tarakchandra Das. "Those who could never dream of crossing the threshold of their house traveled hundreds of miles": "Husbands had forsaken wives and wives had deserted ailing husbands at home. Parents stealthily left immature children to their fate and drifted away to seek for food." Children quit home in the same manner.[8]

Signs of a serious food crisis could be glimpsed across India in 1942. On leave in Bombay over the holidays in 1942, Clive Branson, a thirty-five-year-old "British soldier" in the "other ranks," booked into a hotel. "Breakfast, lunch and dinner are all five-course meals." He browsed shops for something to read. The apparent bestseller: Hitler's *Mein Kampf*, "on sale prominently at *every* bookstall," followed by cheap fiction and "a mass of religious-fanatical literature." Walking the streets of Bombay, Branson also noticed the city's workers standing in "queues for eight hours a day" to receive rations of food. The English newspapers had it all wrong: "You know that Calcutta is being bombed," he raged, "but do you know that an acute food crisis is raging throughout Bengal?"[9]

A few independent newspapers raised alarms about the long food lines. In prior famines in British India, trouble in one year pointed to serious deficits in the next. Given the dislocations of the war in 1942, 1943 looked treacherous. Observers confirmed the shortage of one million tons of grain at the end of 1942 given the "heavy demands of the Army." In December 1942, the *Statesman* called for the central government to organize supplies depleted by hoarders and the "mysterious Black Market." By the following spring, people began to die for lack of food. First it was "a mere beggar" who "stumbled, fell, and never rose again," but then "other men sank down and died." "Then women. Finally, children." It was only in August 1943 that "the avalanche" "moved fast" through the rural districts and "crashed down upon Calcutta."[10]

In October 1943, Branson was transferred to Bengal where he arrived by train. "The endless view of plains, crops, and small stations, turned almost suddenly into one long trail of starving people" when he entered the province. "Men, women, children, babies, looked up into the passing carriage in their last hope for food. These people were not just hungry—this was *famine*. When we stopped, children swarmed round the carriage windows, repeating, hopelessly, 'Bukshish, sahib'—with the monotony of a damaged gramophone. Others sat on the ground, just waiting." As the train pulled into Calcutta, "for *miles*, little children naked, with inflated bellies stuck on stick-like legs, held up empty tins towards us."[11]

Once in Calcutta, "it was quite a job to walk along the pavement." There were "rows of destitutes squatting on the ground, their number increasing from day to day, watching with dull, dispirited eyes" and "setting up here and there a kind of family life, picking lice out of each other's hair, dirtied by days on the road." The "destitutes," as they were called by observers, could be seen "almost at every street-corner," but "a large number found refuge under the Railway Sheds at the suburban Railway Stations. Both ends of the abandoned Howrah Bridge were occupied," and "by the side of the Lower Circular Road, between Dhurramtolla Street and Sealdah Station, many families were found bivouacking day and night." In literary accounts of famine, destitutes hovered around the hotels, by Firpo's restaurant, and anywhere else the contrast between satisfied well-to-do and hungry poor could be made.[12]

As early as July 27, 1943, fifty-five dead bodies were picked up from Calcutta's streets; in the weeks that followed, the daily number rose into the hundreds. There were so many corpses in the streets in August and September that no attempt was made to identify the bodies or count them, though, once in possession of the dead, authorities took care to distinguish between Muslims, who were buried, and Hindus, who were cremated. One newspaper photograph showed heaps of decomposing bodies at Nimtala Ghat, the crematorium on Beadon Street. "Hari, the stoker of funeral pyres, was reported to be unable 'to cope with his harvest of dead.'"[13]

Later regarded by Bengali readers as a "singular act of courage," the *Statesman* published photographs of the destitute at the end of August 1943, hoping to rouse authorities in Calcutta, New Delhi, and London to act. The publicity added force to arguments for political independence and social reform. But daily encounters with beggars became difficult for Calcutta's residents. "You heard it day in, day out, every hour, every minute, at your own house-door and your neighbors," until, novelist Bhabani Bhattacharya admitted, "the cry stunned the pain and pity it had first started"—"the ceaseless whining, the long hollow wail," "*Ma! Ma-go-ma!*" The destitutes were "the befouled ones." To many residents, they "became a race apart," "sub-human."[14]

Storytelling was a way to introduce particular individuals out of the indistinct mass of scavengers who themselves insisted on who they had been before they became destitute: "We are farmers, not beggars," and "we left the village because of the bad times." Yet the stories often undermined the human qualities the telling was intended to highlight. Many accounts turned women, who, on the road or in the streets, were often raped or driven into prostitution, into monsters. Reporters told about mothers selling their children for a few rupees or devouring food at the free kitchens while the child they were holding died of hunger—"a monster that ate its birth child" was Bhattacharya's example of people who "slid in spirit to the level of animals." Or else it was women who died with children still feeding at their breasts. It was *her* motherhood, *her* soul, that had been crushed. These stories had a kind of poignancy, yet they forced the female characters to bear the shame and anguish of India. Or China. Or Russia.[15]

Observers were astonished by the passivity of victims, which made them so strange, at odds with Bengal's rebellious traditions. "There was no shouting, no violence, no looting of shops," observed Ian Stephens, the editor of the *Statesman*. "If any nation deserves the Nobel Peace Prize, it is the Indian"—this was the opinion of one character in Krishan Chandar's 1943 "story of Bengal." "They starve and die in their millions without a word of protest." Indeed, intellectuals found it a curse to be forced to witness the helplessness of the hungry on Calcutta's streets. The very existence of destitution seemed to sap the energy of the Quit India movement and resistance to the British.[16]

Stephens tried to explain the indifference of the public in the face of the famine. "Death by famine lacks drama," he pointed out. "Bloody death, the deaths of many by slaughter as in riots or bombings is in itself blood-bestirring; it excites you, prints indelible images on the mind. But death by famine, a vast slow dispirited noiseless apathy, offers none of that. Horrid though it may be to say, multitudinous death from this cause . . . is very dull." This insight pertains to the sparse coverage of the famine but also to other civilian catastrophes during the war. In these transits, there were no clear sides, no battles to hang in the balance, no victors. The famine was not a conventional war story, so it was ignored; it was anything but a war story, so it was cursed.[17]

For decades, imperial authorities had made provisions for the event of famine when stockpiled supplies would be released from across other regions in India. But during the war, state governments held grain back in order to guarantee supplies to "priority" classes such as urban workers. The War Cabinet in London also refused to divert shipments from Britain, which was to be continually replenished with sufficient food, or to reroute shipping away from the military fronts. Arguments about global shipping capacity continued well into 1944 without any appreciable increase in emergency shipments to India, which had factored in war plans as an exporter. As a result, Britain's role in the famine is to be judged not so much by the critical role it had as a cause as by the attitude of indifference it showed when the effects were self-evident.

The struggles of "our small Nation" remained paramount: the imagery spoke for itself, although the official line of explanation was that "all parts of the British Empire" should "feel the pinch in the same way as the Mother Country has done." In Churchill's view, the empire had favored India by steering it clear of civil wars, revolutions, and other calamities in the modern era. He considered Indians profoundly ungrateful and thus undeserving of more charity.[18] Churchill's real failure during the famine was lack of empathy, which is the reason his offhand remarks about Indians "breeding like rabbits," and eating away at food stores, or his apocryphal (but completely in character) response trivializing the scarcity during one of Gandhi's fasts— "Then why isn't Gandhi dead yet?"—continue to resonate. In the view of Indians, with the famine, the colonialists themselves had become caricatures or stick figures.

The symbolic value of the destitutes remained ambiguous, as figures of India's agony but also its passivity. Most observers believed the famine proved the illegitimacy of British colonial rule: imperial dependence was a death watch, independence a matter of urgency to restore life. The Nazis certainly held Britain responsible for the tragedy in India. German readers knew more about Calcutta, the "city of lingering death" at the mercy of "the colonial politics of hunger," than did British or American ones.[19] But in India itself the debate on the famine indicted local colonial elites more than it did British rulers. Indian novelists revealed the famine to be a family affair.

Writers in India endeavored to extract the famine from its setting as a timeless biblical story "deep in the valley of the shadow" in order to report on those fronts World War II reporting had ignored.[20] They filled in the tragedy with contemporary features to connect the famine to the war. Along the roads, "telegraph wires ran overhead." The "wind strummed the wires and spoke: *zmmm!*" "The sound of word passing, she knew," but "no word, ever of the great hunger of the peasants and their helpless trek."[21]

But novelists such as Tarasankara Bandyopadhyaya (*Epoch's End*, 1944) and Bhabani Bhattacharya (with his classic 1947 account, *So Many Hungers!*) went much further, shoving war leaders into the background to pull grain profiteers and even the ringleaders and clients of prostitution who preyed on famine victims into the circle of the families they depicted. These provocative plots implied that India's independence was insufficient without radical social and economic reform. *So Many Hungers!* is really about mutually corrosive rather than mutually supporting desires—ambition, fame, money, collective freedom, individual autonomy, food—all of which the war intensified. As the novel opens, on September 3, 1939, the day war was declared, it is the freedom fighter's father who calculates wartime profits: SELL! "Sell, cash in your profit. Peace round the corner," or else BUY! "Buy Steels, War eats steel"—"a ton of steel mangles a brigade. A hundred thousand tons mangle a city. A hundred million tons mangle the earth." Far away from the stock market, the housewife hedges bets, recalling the last war, buying up supplies of "rice and mustard oil."[22] By associating nationalists with profiteering, the writers argued that independence alone would not bring unfreedom to an end.

The broken worlds in Bhattacharya and Bandyopadhyaya are basically Hindu. The communal violence that led to partition is not in view in these novels. Indeed, on the streets of Calcutta most of the hungry set aside caste rules regulating the preparation of food and the acceptance of alms. Statistics confirmed the anthropologist's conclusion: "The destitutes of Calcutta belonged to one caste and that was the caste of the 'have-nots.'" "Hindus received cooked food from Muhammadan houses and Muhammadans reciprocated." At the same time, informants confirmed that "when the famine would pass away they would again observe the usual caste-rules."[23]

The famine was a series of encounters between country and city and rich and poor. With the destitute crowding train stations and city pavements, the disaster had a pronounced physical aspect. Throughout the famine, people approached each other with a sense of abhorrence about touching or mingling in their heads—beggars tugged at the sleeve—and, after the worst of the crisis was over, the famine was debated across communal divisions that had not figured in initial reporting: Hadn't Hindus been in charge of the "Control" shops on the street? Hadn't a Muslim been responsible for government purchases in the ministry? Although the Muslim leader Muhammad Jinnah did not have the famine in mind when he insisted "we are utterly different" from Hindus, he suggested its imagery: "A Hindu would not take water from my hand" or felt defiled "if my shadow falls across him."[24] In this regard, the bodily horror of the famine served to intensify communal mistrust.

Like so many deadly catastrophes in the war, the catastrophe did not fit into the patriotic picture of the war in which the defense required sacrifice or of India's struggle for freedom in which people broke the chains shackling them. Famine weakened rather than strengthened the collective body, including the "Quit India" movement. On a country road or the city's pavement, the hungry did not really care about the Japanese or Cripps or Gandhi. Moreover, many impoverished Indians experienced the crisis in neocolonial rather than colonial terms. It set the stage for the turbulent postindependence future by exposing the profiteering of Indian elites and by widening the economic and religious divisions that empowered them. Famine hastened the defeat of the British Empire, which came to be associated with death, but hardly contributed to the victory of the Indian nation, which remained hungry.

CHAPTER 15

Warsaw's Four Sons

The miserable images couple themselves into a long train. The refugees in Luoyang, climbing onto the trains and waiting around the tracks for the next one. Starving children along tracks converging on Calcutta's railway stations. Around the same time, in a small item published in the *New York Times* at the end of October 1941, the reporter watched from a distance of two hundred yards as "truckers and railroad men assembled the human cargo of probably 1,000 Jews caught up in the mass exodus" at a freight yard in Berlin. "Similar trainloads" departed "almost daily." These were the first of more than two thousand trains specially engaged by the regime to deport German Jews from their homes. There were many more trains in use to transport soldiers to the front and wounded combatants to hospitals in the rear. At any given time, more than a quarter-million

German men in uniform were in transit. Along the dense rail-way networks of Europe, millions of prisoners-of-war and forced laborers, mostly Polish and Ukrainian but also French and Dutch, were pushed onto trains heading into the German Reich. In Germany itself, evacuees like Schmitz traveled by train from bombed-out cities to seek refuge in the countryside. About one thousand passengers made up a normal train. This was a continent in transit.[1]

The Jewish transports were often described as headed to unknown destinations "in the East." Some people committed suicide before the journey; others packed up useful wares to settle in a hard place. Likewise, refugees in China or India took "a blind leap onto a steep slide," the end point of which they could not see.[2] They became the dust of the road. But trains from Luoyang or to Calcutta were filled with the sum of people making their own pressed decision. The difference in Berlin was the operative word "cargo." The German Reich registered, assembled, and commandeered Jews onto trains. They did not come from scattered places to converge at the station to take the train or disperse in all directions once they reached their destination. In most cases, the destination was a killing site.

The departure and arrival of the trains filled with evacuated or homeless people or conscripted laborers were a familiar sight during the war. In Germany, however, the railroad also functioned in a killing machine that the state deliberately assembled in 1942 and maintained over the war years to murder Jews.

A few years before the war, Julian Tuwim published "The Locomotive," a poem much beloved by children in Poland. "A big locomotive has pulled into town," it begins. You could count the "numerous wagons she tugs down the track":

The first carries cattle, then horses not few;
The third car with corpulent people is filled,
Eating fat frankfurters all freshly grilled.
The fourth car is packed to the hilt with bananas,
The fifth has a cargo of six grand pi-an-as.
The sixth wagon carries a cannon of steel,
With heavy iron girders beneath every wheel.
The seventh has tables, oak cupboards with plates,
While an elephant, bear, two giraffes fill the eighth.
The ninth contains nothing but well-fattened swine,
In the tenth: bags and boxes, now isn't that fine?

There must be at least forty cars in a row,
And what they all carry—I simply don't know.

It was hard to imagine how the locomotive could manage such a load.

She chugs and she tugs at her wagons with strain,
As wheel after wheel slowly turns on the train.
She doubles her effort and quickens her pace,
And rambles and scrambles to keep up the race.

"First a toot! / Then a hoot!" Finally, the "steam is churning" and the "wheels are turning!"

The wheels start a rattlin', clatterin', chatterin'
Chug along, tug along, chug along, tug along!

It was a great locomotive, strong yet lighthearted, bringing life and wonder into the town.

In 1942, in the Kraków ghetto, an eleven-year-old boy, Jerzy Ogórek, contemplated his own locomotive that only sort of looked like Tuwim's:

And every wagon is full of Häftlings
The Germans do load them up like horses.
And there are maybe forty such wagons
and each contains sixty such Häftlings.
In each there are children, at least a few
They're tiny and skinny
It will make you feel blue.
They're sitting so still
Like nothing's amiss
And suddenly,
A loud toot,
Suddenly, a hoot,
The steam is churning,
The wheels are turning.

"Where does it go?" "Across the fields / Across the woods / To Auschwitz."[3] The big locomotive had become a *Sonderzug*.

In fact, there was a schedule to the trains deporting Jews, one that bore a perverse resemblance to an ordinary railroad plan. A detailed report exists on the deportation of Jews from Düsseldorf in western Germany to Riga in Latvia over the days December 11–14, 1941. Stops were scheduled along the way not to pick up more passengers but for the Red Cross to deliver food to the police who accompanied the prisoners; train personnel occasionally provided Jews in the locked third-class passenger cars with water. The 1,007 Jews the police and security forces had rounded up in Düsseldorf left the freight depot after delays in loading at 10:30 a.m. on December 11. The German State Railway had pushed for an on-time departure of 9:30. The train reached Hanover-Linden at 6:00 p.m. and Berlin-Lichterfelde at 3:30 a.m. the following morning. At this point, the transport was 155 minutes late.

At Konitz, in the western part of Poland annexed by Germany, the policeman in charge of the transport encountered an uncooperative stationmaster whom he regarded as one of those people who referred to "poor Jews," a group of unfortunate individuals, instead of understanding the concept of "the Jew," a collective and lethal threat to the German people that provided the grounds for the deportation. The train left Konitz just after noon on December 12 and arrived at the Latvian border at 5:30 a.m. on December 13. More than sixteen hours later, the train reached Riga, although Jews were only taken out of the unheated cars and hauled into the ghetto the next morning. A few people on the transport survived the ordeal of the war. After a day of sightseeing in Riga, the police company returned to Düsseldorf on regular passenger trains filled with soldiers on leave for Christmas.[4]

The deportation transport (and the official report) was part of a systematic state effort to rid Germany of Jews. Between the fall of 1941 and the spring of 1945, thousands of trains deported Jews from across Europe to death camps; in the beginning, trains such as the one from Düsseldorf in December 1941 transported German Jews to ghettos in German-occupied territories. About half of the murdered Jews traveled to their deaths by train, and half were shot and killed in Poland and the Soviet Union by special SS death squads, usually in the shadow of their homes. In pursuit of the "Final Solution," the Nazis got rid of three-quarters of all Jews in the European territories they occupied, about six million people in all.

The freight yard in Berlin-Grunewald was a small model of Europe as a whole, which became a "switching yard for entire nations and ethnic groups."[5] Germans from the Soviet Union, Romania, and the Baltic states were repatriated to the Reich, most languishing in holding camps before receiving homes taken from Poles. Poles in the territories Germany had annexed were faced with evacuation to the General Government, the rump of Poland administered by the Nazi Party, but hundreds of thousands were also shipped as forced laborers to Germany. Railroad schedulers made note of all this as they tried to fill up trains both ways, east and west. New German colonies in the General Government required the transport of pioneers as well as the deportation of resident Poles. As the war ground on, racial experts trawled Slavic populations for German stock that could be fished out to be educated or retrained under German auspices. Only "poor Jews" remained fixed as "the Jew" to be transported and exterminated.

The attempt to murder every single Jew in Europe has no equivalent in Henan or Bengal. Wartime assumptions about sacrifice, expendability, and priority contributed to the deaths of millions of people but do not compare to the mass murder that German authorities planned and directed. Images like the winds of war or the dust of refugees cannot conjure up Germany's drive to build a new racial order in its empire. Readers of these terrible histories sometimes wonder why the Third Reich put so much effort into killing civilians only to lose the war in battle. Yet the Nazis waged war first and foremost against "races" in the name of the German people.

Varian Fry, who had worked hard in Marseille to save Jews with the Emergency Rescue Committee, admitted that "one reason the Western world had failed to rouse itself more promptly to the Nazi menace" was the "tendency to dismiss as impossible fantasy the many warnings the Nazis themselves gave us."[6]

The Nazis' deliberate policy of murder was envisioned along a timeline, which made 1942 a year of unprecedented mass murder. In 1939, in a speech on the sixth anniversary of the Nazi seizure of power on January 30, Hitler delivered his famous prophecy that in the event of a "world war," the result would not be "the Bolshevization of the earth" but "the annihilation of the Jewish race in Europe." With Japan's attack on Pearl Harbor on December 7, 1941, and Germany's declaration of war against the United States on December 11, Hitler's prediction had come to pass, namely, in Göring's words, "a world war in the true sense of the word." The conspicuous word "true" was certainly used to verify something outstanding, the prophesied time of the annihilation of the Jews.[7] The world war set off a sequence of events that built the systematic framework for the destruction of Jewish people throughout Europe.

What followed the declaration of war was an energetic international effort in which Germany extended killing operations across the continent to procure and kill every Jew. Once the infrastructure of the death camps was completed along existing rail lines, at Belzec, Sobibor, and Treblinka in the General Government, and at the Birkenau complex in Auschwitz in annexed Poland, the scheduling, systematic deportation, and murder of Jews began in March 1942. At the end of the month, Goebbels confided to his diary that something dramatic had come to pass: "Jews are now being deported to the east from the territory ruled by the General-Government, starting with Lublin."

"A fairly barbarous method" will be used, and he added: "Not much will remain of the Jews."[8] On July 19, Himmler, the head of the SS, ordered "the resettlement of the entire Jewish population of the General Government be carried out and completed by 31 December 1942." Three days later, the SS commenced *Grossaktion Warschau*; in less than two months, nearly three hundred thousand residents of the ghetto had been transported to Treblinka and murdered. This network was expanded to French, Dutch, and other European Jews throughout July 1942. In Amsterdam, Anne Frank's family went into hiding on July 6, a day after Anne's older sister, Margot, received a notice to report to a German labor camp. In the spring and summer of 1942, murder became a central program.

Once up and running, the death camps accelerated the timing and expanded the scope of deportation and murder that continued for many months: first, the inmates of ghettos in Lublin (in March), Lwów (April), and Warsaw (July), then, beginning in July 1942, Jews from Germany, France, Holland, Belgium, and later Greece and Italy. The camps, the railways, and the railway schedules functioned as a huge apparatus of death. With the murder of three-quarters of the Jews in German-occupied territory, the start-up of the "Final Solution" in 1942 very nearly realized Hitler's prophecy in 1939.

In his address to officers of the Wehrmacht on May 26, 1944, Hitler spoke about actions against the Jews one more time—in the past tense. Even to this select audience, he was not direct and referred to extermination as something that would happen to the German people only in the event of defeat. Nazi media often brought up features of the Holocaust (selections, deportations, children, murder) to describe a fate to befall Germans. However, Hitler made it clear that the "removal" of Jewry, a "foreign element in the national body," had been accomplished. His speech only hinted at the murderous form that removal took.

"Not everyone understands why in this respect I acted so brutally and so ruthlessly," he admitted. "Of course, one could say to me: 'Could you have dealt with this more simply,'" that is, "more humanely?" To this rhetorical question Hitler gave an answer cast in typically existential terms: "My dear officers," he addressed the very elites who might have doubts, "we stand here in a fight for life or death. If our enemies triumph in this battle, the German people will be exterminated." "I acted here," Hitler explained, "exactly as is the case in nature, not with brutality, but rationally, in order to preserve what is better." In the context of Jews, the words "I acted so brutally" conjured up one thing only: the task of murdering the Jews had very nearly been completed. "Here as elsewhere," Hitler added, "'humanity' would be the greatest possible betrayal of my own people." A betrayal because the Nazis did not believe the concept existed in a social or scientific sense; only races did. Appeals to human feelings only undermined Germany's racial sensibilities.[9]

It was the "huge pulse" of killing in 1942 that allowed the Allied governments to ascertain the systematic nature of Nazi efforts to exterminate the Jewish population of the European territory under German control.[10] By November, an understanding of the Holocaust had emerged and was reported in the press in a more or less clear way. Jews were always more alert to the mass murder in Europe, but, whether in ghettos or towns in Europe or overseas, they also only comprehended the systematic nature of Germany's "Final Solution" in 1942.

Nineteen forty-two came with other terrible revelations: the large role of blackmailers, opportunists, and killers among the local population so that it was not only Germans who bore the "sign of Cain."[11] Even Jews in the ghettos played sordid roles in the roundups. Germans themselves felt increasingly implicated in the murder of Jews when the year 1942 gave them good reasons to imagine the defeat of the Third Reich. For the public in the United States and Great Britain, this knowledge of complicity remained murky because the war was regarded in such black-and-white terms that only the depredations of the Nazis really counted. American newspapers tended to link the German escalation of violence in 1942 with growing resistance against German occupiers. Hostage executions, deportations, and massacres all registered the revival of European life in the face of German-sponsored death. The prominence of the prisoner's resistance to the jailer's brutality spotlighted an ongoing battle while obscuring German intentions to establish a new racial order in Europe and to wipe out entire populations.

If Americans often saw the sunny side of the conflict, stressing the heroism of occupied people, Jewish victims saw the dark night, extinguishing help and solidarity. There was "earthrise" heralded by leaders such as Wendell Willkie, who, in the name of subjugated people all over the world, regarded the war as a struggle "for the freedom of all mankind" in order to "establish peace by abolishing tyranny." These ideas were held in common by "millions and millions of men," almost "as much as if they lived in the same town." Jews lived in the same town. What they saw was how they had been forsaken or betrayed by their neighbors. For them, the earth had not risen. Surveying the scene, one ghetto inmate described 1942 as "that accursed year in the history of the world, one that cancelled the cultural achievements of all mankind."[12]

It would seem obvious that the enormous effort to transport millions of Jews must have hurt the war effort and, in particular, reduced the Wehrmacht's ability to supply troops on the eastern front. While the destruction of Jews was a key part of German war aims, the "administrative" priorities in the rear had little effect on military operations. Every day, about twenty-five thousand trains moved across the German empire; the average number of *Sonderzüge* was two a day, and even ten trains or one hundred trains would not have made a difference to logistics. Since the locomotives and wagons used to transport Jews were old and could not be switched out to carry personnel or tanks, their deployment aroused no special concerns among quartermasters in the Wehrmacht. The equipment was so decrepit that Jewish prisoners sometimes broke "large holes" in the worn-out planking in order to escape.[13]

However, railway traffic did highlight the international scope of the "Final Solution" and the role played by more personnel of different kinds in all European countries. The operation depended on guards, shooters, and police, but also trainmen, secretaries, and managerial specialists as well as ministry officials and Red Cross teams. From France to Poland, German authorities relied on their foreign counterparts. If the number of Jews who died was greater than the number of administrators required to murder them, the latter group nonetheless included many hundreds of thousands of people—the ratio approached 1:10. Alone this wide net of collaboration made operations well-known to Europeans in the zones of occupation. A lively fascist press in France argued the merits of the deportation of Jews, including children: "It is necessary to free ourselves of the Jews in block and not keep the little ones," argued Robert

Brasillach in *Je suis partout* in September 1942. In Poland, neighbors could see what was happening in the market squares of their own towns.[14]

Zygmunt Klukowski, a physician in the small town of Szczebrzeszyn near Zamość in the General Government, simply looked out of his window to see the horror. "Now," on March 25, 1942, Klukowski reported on a larger operation underway, more systematic than the individual cruelties he had witnessed in the years since 1939. "The Germans are transporting entire trainloads, mostly Jews, but we do not know where, maybe closer to the front for hard labor." The next day he had more information: "Entire railroad trains loaded with Jews from Czechoslovakia, Germany, and, lately, Belgium passed through, possibly to Belzec, where a new large camp was just organized." Obviously, bystanders had asked questions, and passengers answered them. What became apparent were the new parameters of geography (Belgium) and administration (special camps). "The Jews are very disturbed about the forced movement of their population," Klukowski added.[15]

Suddenly, "around 1 am" on August 8, 1942, "I was awakened by unusually loud noises on the street" of Szczebrzeszyn itself; "I heard shouting in German, Polish and Yiddish." Later in the morning, "the mayor informed me the 2000 Jews will be deported east to the Ukraine. Railroad workers said that a large train with fifty-five cars is ready at the station." Such a deportation required considerable organization and the cooperation of local personnel. "Throughout the entire day, patrols of gestapo, gendarmes, *Sonderdienst*, 'blue police,'" along with "the so-called Jewish militia, patrolled the city." They searched houses, moved Jews to the marketplace, and stacked their belongings onto "horsedrawn wagons." At dusk, "several hundred Jews were taken to the railroad station." "No one believes that the Jews will be moved to the Ukraine," Klukowski concluded. "They will all be killed."[16]

"A terrifying day," October 21, 1942. The events left Klukowski "completely broken"; "I cannot describe everything that took place." "From early morning until late at night we witnessed" how nearly one thousand Jewish residents were taken away. In fact, the "hunt for Jews" lasted for several days since many had gone into hiding. There was the "barbarism of the Germans" but also the "very active" part of Polish gendarmes "in the killing of the Jews." Klukowski named names. A city janitor, "Skorzak had no gun, only an ax, and with the ax he killed several Jews." Townspeople stood around, "laughing and even beating the Jews"; others stole Jewish goods. Klukowski was irked by the degradation of neighbors. "People walking on the street are so used to seeing corpses on the sidewalks that they pass by without any emotion." "On all sidewalks there are numerous blood stains," he added. After the Germans arrived, and neighbors pitched in, Jews often spoke about the "different road," the "Jewish road," the "blood-red Highways"—"All the highways are stained, like Jewish history."[17]

The crowd scenes in Szczebrzeszyn between March 25 and October 21, 1942, the period of the most intense murder, involved Germans, Jews, and Poles. Streets bustled with activity. During the deportation of Jews in Otwock in August 1942, Calel Perechodnik could see that "a part of the ghetto was already inhabited by Poles. Women were straightening out the apartments," and others sat outside "peeling potatoes." One day he caught sight of a girl pushing a baby carriage; "my legs buckled under me. I recognized my daughter's stroller."[18]

Perechodnik was tormented by the last thoughts of his wife, Anka, and his daughter, Aluśko. He dared to imagine their train journey to Treblinka: "You have just passed by Swider, Josefow. . . . You are already in Falenica. The train stands at the station a long time. . . . The train goes farther. It is already in Warsaw. The last time you were in Warsaw was in January 1940. You traveled to the bank to pay off the old debt on the movie house." Many Jews on the transports were familiar with the routes. Some had taken long train journeys on summer holidays before the war. And in every group of travelers there was the oddball who, like Tarrou's father in Albert Camus's *The Plague*, took up the pastime of mastering the big railway directories: "He was a walking timetable; he could tell you the exact times of departure and arrival of the Paris–Berlin expresses; how to get from Lyon to Warsaw."[19]

Perechodnik imagined his daughter on the train: "Aluśko, Aluśko, are you still alive? Have you not yet suffocated? Anka, do you still have a little water?" The trains were frightful. According to one report, in a transport carrying about nine thousand victims, two thousand had died by the time the train arrived in Belzec.

Kurt Gerstein, an Obersturmführer in the SS and a willing informant when interrogated in Paris in May 1945, was an eyewitness to the arrival of one transport in Belzec on August 17, 1942. His detailed report, given originally in French and identified as "Document No. PS-1553" in the Nuremberg trials, began with events in the morning "before 7am," when Gerstein was awakened with the news that "the first transport will arrive in ten minutes!" It ended a few hours later when a "Jewess about forty years old . . . disappears into the chamber." Many people prayed, Gerstein wrote, and "I pray with them" and "yell out to my and their God."[20]

In Britain and the United States there was no lack of concrete intelligence—it is astonishing how much of the "Final Solution" could be pieced together by the end of 1942. Even in Germany soldiers on leave, travelers on trains, and talk among relatives passed along news about the killing of Jews. What was not well-known were the numbers and the cooperation of local people in the roundups and details about the death camps.

In the Warsaw Ghetto, Wladyslaw Szlengel composed a poem in which he tried to convey the scope of the "national trag-edy" of the Jews. In "Four Sons," he scattered his Jews around the world: One son fought for the Red Army, probably a conscript from the Polish territories the Soviets annexed in 1939; another was on the "Aryan Side of Warsaw," terrified by the prospect of being fingered by blackmailers. Germans had thrown a third son into a concentration camp. And the fourth son lived in New York City where Szlengel imagined him listening to a radio broadcast about persecuted Jews in Europe that was interrupted by "Firm X"'s promotion of holiday candles, a commercial break indicating the inattentiveness of American Jews.[21]

Like the four sons, each with a different perspective, Ger-mans in the Reich, Jews in the ghetto, and Americans all contemplated the murder of Jews in 1942.

"WE DIDN'T KNOW about that" is what Germans often assured Americans who occupied their country after 1945. The three key words are "we," "know," and "that." "We" made a claim about Germans' general state of knowledge, not about individuals' reflection or investigation. The idea was that the regime had duped the public so that the German people were stupid but not criminally complicit. Moreover, many people suspected crimes or heard rumors even if they did not receive confirmation so as to "know." And "that" presumably referred to Auschwitz and gas chambers, yet ignorance about Auschwitz did not exclude information gleaned from conversations with friends and neighbors about deportations, auctions of Jewish goods, or massacres of civilians "in the East." The commonplace declaration left room for precisely what it intended to deny.[22]

Diaries and letters indicate that rumors about the massacres of civilians in the conquered Soviet territories swept across Germany in the fall of 1941. They came in three parts. First, the inclusion of women and children among the victims. Second, the fact that victims were made to undress and go to their deaths naked or partly naked. Third, the idea that SS shooters sometimes went mad. Composed in this way, rumors passed on information that was regarded as extremely disturbing. Civilians back home did not justify the killings by referring to threats posed to their soldiers at the front by partisans, nor did they explain them away by lamenting the general horror of war. However, the shock receded as the wartime troubles of Germans mounted; many people let themselves be bombed out of a guilty conscience.[23]

Goebbels and others attempted to manage public unease about Germany's military conduct as they put the "Final Solution" into operation in the spring of 1942. This was the very period of time that the better part of the Wehrmacht returned home on leave for the first (and last) time since the invasion of the Soviet Union. Goebbels anticipated difficult encounters as families asked soldiers about the rumors they had heard.

In "Conversations with Front Soldiers," a piece he published in *Das Reich* in July 1942, he addressed mothers and wives at home. Goebbels admitted that relatives would regard returning soldiers as strangers. This was so because combatants were participating "in a gigantic struggle of world views." Without mentioning specific violence, Goebbels thought it "understandable" that "uncompromising thinking about the war, and its causes, consequences, and aims," would produce "points of friction" with "life at home." Therefore, it was necessary for families to "live up" to the (brutal) "face of the war."[24]

As it was, there was sometimes friction at home. The transcript of one conversation after Walter Kessler returned from the front for a few weeks in June 1942 confirms that soldiers repeated the same standard phrases when asked about atrocities. "We can be happy that we are not Jews," Walter said in a summary of more detailed information about what had been seen or heard (all the information was secondhand in that informants were never anything other than spectators). What followed was the resolve to fight until victory lest Germans be held accountable for their crimes: "Certainly it has gone so far that they will do to us as it was done to them, if we should lose the war."[25] It was a common calculation. Only a few soldiers expressed total dismay about whether Germany lost the war. Looking at the destroyed ghetto in Warsaw in June 1943, Captain Wilhelm Hosenfeld knew that "we have brought irredeemable shame, a permanent curse upon us."[26] (Such a judgment made it imperative for others to assert later on, "We didn't know about that.") But having absorbed high casualties, air raids, and Stalingrad, most Germans who lived through the Third Reich seemed to think that the moral balance was about even.

IN SOME WAYS, Jews wanted to even the moral balance sheet if that meant that others would recognize their predicament and see their suffering aligned with everybody else's. Today, we take care to set apart the terrible tragedy of Jews under the Nazis, but most Jews at the time did not want to be set aside because that meant being forgotten or overlooked. The encompassing idea of "mankind" or humanity, as hope and betrayal, structured Jewish responses to the slaughter.

At the end of 1938, Chagall painted *White Crucifixion*, depicting a Jewish Jesus on the cross surrounded by the mayhem of Jewish suffering. Instead of a loincloth, Jesus wears a prayer shawl; Chagall has replaced the crown of thorns with a white headcloth. Jewish patriarchs have taken the place of the angels who customarily surround the crucified figure. At first glance, the painting bears a resemblance to the cluttered topsy-turviness of Chagall's previous work. But a sinister prewar has extinguished postwar whimsy. Littered around the cross is the devastation of a pogrom: a burning synagogue, a ravaged village. A dead body lies on the ground. While Jewish residents scatter in all directions, soldiers converge from the sides: Communists with their red flags on the left and a militiaman beneath the Lithuanian flag on the right. They appear as rivals so that the Communists might be saviors of the Jews, but the groups can also be regarded as multiple threats to the Jews. The refugees themselves, and a lifeboat of escapees with only one oar, flounder along the edges of the painting without clear direction or destination. Enemies from all sides of the painting and all political positions scatter the Jews in all directions.

The painting of the crucified figure emphasizes the lonely suffering of Jews. The cross stands as a scathing, ironic statement about Christian persecution of Jews. *White Crucifixion* asks the viewer to see Jews empathetically as fellow sufferers *and* to see Christians critically as complicit militiamen. More than that, the persecuted have nowhere to go. The patriarchs are powerless and the survivors helpless in flight. The condemnation of hatred works in two ways, as an appeal to the world and as an indictment of the complicity nullifying appeals to the world. The viewer faces voice and silence.

The insertion of contemporary history into the allegorical portrait of a Jew on the cross integrated the present into the long record of Jewish suffering. But the painting is more immediate. The Jews are about to be wiped out; they no longer find refuge. Only a comprehension of the unprecedented all-sided nature of the calamity could generate an adequate response from Jews and Christians that would begin by seeing the different scale of events in 1942.

Was there a calamity at all? And wasn't part of the calamity the inability of the rest of the world to recognize the moral disaster by which the Nazis could act with impunity because they had helpers while the Jews had none? And was there a calamity if, after the Jews were destroyed, the words of protest they left behind made no sense or aroused no particular interest?

Since there was a long-written history to the Jews, many Jews took refuge in precedent that recorded many instances of suffering but confirmed the perseverance of Jewish life and Jews' covenant with God. Or else the modern age, these civilized times, it was thought, made a repeat of ancient or medieval catastrophes unthinkable, canceling out precedents altogether.

The baker in Dubno, a mostly Jewish town in the part of Poland annexed by the Soviet Union in 1939, had his answers ready. He replied, "My grandfather used to tell me stories about pogroms by Kosaks. . . . In the last war, 1915–1918, we lived

three years under the Germans. It was never good, but somehow we survived. I sold bread to the Germans; we baked for
them from their flour. We Jews are an eternal people, we cannot be destroyed." He added: "I grant you some Jews will suffer
under Hitler, but this is the lot of the Jews, to suffer and to wait."
To wait for the Messiah. This was the familiar argument Raphael
Lemkin heard when he stayed overnight with the baker as he
fled across the border at the end of 1939 to escape the Nazis.
Lemkin, a lawyer from Warsaw, tried to explain to his host that
"this is a different war." "It is not a war to grab territory so much
as to destroy whole peoples and replace them with Germans."
"Many generations spoke through this man," Lemkin commented when the baker continued to object. Hitlers came and
went, and the baker's fellows would survive. This amounted to
his private "covenant with God."[27]

The baker and the lawyer debated a topic that would be
argued over countless times in the next years: the question of
precedence and whether the Nazis represented something completely new. Was it even possible to destroy millions of Jews if
this was Hitler's intention? Later, Lemkin would systematize
his insights with the concept of genocide, a combination of the
Greek word for "race" or "kind" (*genos*) and the Latin-derived
suffix "-cide" for killing. In 1945, he learned of the "mass execution" of Dubno's Jews on November 5, 1942.

One of Szlengel's sons was in the United States, another in
the Soviet Union. Jews in Dubno experienced the world differently from those in Warsaw. It was hard to imagine that suddenly Jews all over Europe confronted the same lethal fate. Even
in the places taken over by Nazis, Jews still reproached pessimists like Lemkin: "*Ich habe nie etwas Unrechtes getain. Was
können sie mir tuen?*"[28]

On the first day of spring in 1942, Chaim Kaplan, a well-respected educator in the Warsaw Ghetto, which the Germans had sealed in November 1940, noted down "horrible" rumors that circulated. They were so dreadful, "people are whispering." "First news item": "Lublin has been evacuated. About 100,000 Jews were herded into railroad cars and transported." "Where?" Kaplan asked himself. "No one knows." In fact, the organized deportations to the death camps had begun. He debated with himself. Weren't Lublin's Jews treated "so much more cruelly" because of the community's "spiritual" and religious ties? If so, it did not necessarily follow that Warsaw would be next. On the other hand, Kaplan recognized that since Lublin, "not a day passes without some Jewish settlement being completely wiped off the face of the earth. Take Wlodawa!" he pointed: "Take Tluszcz! Both of them were emptied of Jews." From town to town, this chain of activity added up to something more than pogroms.[29]

Kaplan wrote the "scroll of agony," as he referred to his wartime diary, so that he would "remember the past in the future." Without documents, he feared, the resolutions of life tended to level out earlier hardships. By 1942, however, Kaplan doubted that he himself would ever look back on his time in the ghetto or use the diary to remember for himself its agony. Instead, the diary took on a life of its own that he served by continuing to write for the sake of "future generations." If it was true that "not a single deportee will be able to hold out to the end of the war," he would make the effort to ensure that reports would survive. The reason he continued to write was not to remember later, but that he knew he was going to die before. All the record keepers in the Warsaw Ghetto, especially Emanuel Ringelblum who curated the Oyneg Shabes Archive, continued the work of documentation because their greatest fear was that Jews, their suffering, and their deaths would vanish into the oblivion.[30]

The difference for Europe's Jews was that they might just disappear in the war. "For us," noted Jan Karski, the courier of information about Poland's Jews, "it was war and occupation" and eventual liberation for Poles or the French; "for them, it was the end of the world."[31] The end of the world was more than the death of the Jews with whom Karski talked. It was the end of any sort of remembrance of Jewish life.

When the Allies referred to the murder of Jews, they regarded the fallen heroically, as resistance fighters who had been killed in the struggle against the Germans. This sort of memorialization also wiped out the Jews who were slaughtered en masse not because they were fighters but because they were Jews. Jewish death was a "garbage death," in Szlengel's words, without decorations or communiqués or memories.

The furious onslaught targeting Jews for deportation to unknown destinations, the effort to snatch all residents including women and children from their hiding places, and the collaboration of police and neighbors left Jews feeling completely cut off from community, from humanity, even from God. The degrading conditions in the ghettos magnified the isolation. News could be transmitted into the ghetto, but did not report on Jewish conditions. Marked by the stages of dying, not living, without connections on which to hang meaning, life in the ghetto produced waste. "Dogs are barking, horses neighing, birds twittering, *slaves are toiling*, but we," wrote Oskar Rosenfeld from Lodz, "we here in the ghetto are vegetating . . . our lives have lost all purpose." It was "cursed, shaming time." Worse than death was the absence of a grave.[32]

Rosenfeld composed lines in his notebooks, although writers suspected that keeping a record was a fool's errand. Jewish historian Isaac Schiper confided his fears about the forces shaping postwar history to a fellow inmate in the Majdanek concentration camp, where he later perished. "History is usually written by the victor," he explained. "What we know about murdered peoples is only what their murderers vaingloriously cared to say about them. Should our murderers be victorious, should <u>they</u> write the history of this war, our destruction will be presented as one of the most beautiful pages of world history." If they did not write their own Jewish history, the Germans "may wipe out our memory altogether, as if we had never existed, as if there had never been a Polish Jewry, a ghetto in Warsaw, a Majdanek."[33]

"Unbelievable" indicated the incredulity of readers who came across the "scroll of agony"; "indescribable" suggested the inadequacy of the words sought by writers to augment the scroll. It might not be possible for someone in the future to understand the self-absorbed turmoil of Jews without dismissing the responses as foolish and naive—the reproaches, the declarations, the faith, the hope, the denial. What sort of words might ghetto occupants think would not be comprehended by "future generations"?

"It has fallen to us to be victims, because the time of the Messiah is approaching."

"Lovely stories: they say that the Germans are burying us alive or exterminating us with gas. But what is the point of repeating such things, even if they are true?"

"I still believe, in spite of everything, that people are truly good at heart."

The last quote continued: "This cruelty too shall end."[34]

Szlengel tried to capture the dilemma about recollecting turmoil after death in his poem "Monument": "Was she good? Not really— / she often quarrelled after all, / slammed the door, scolded . . . / but she was." Any attempt to comprehend Jewish life and death must take up desperate, even seemingly frivolous, responses; to put aside phrases as too formulaic or too brave or insufficiently astute or helpless would alter the scroll of agony.

In "The Last Stage of Resettlement Is Death," which was written from September 1942, at the end of the "Great Action," to January 1943, the start of Jewish resistance in the Warsaw Ghetto, Gustawa Jarecka could not get past her "repugnance of words." "We hate words," she explained, "because they too often have served as a cover for emptiness or meanness. We despise them for they pale in comparison with the emotion tormenting us." In the ghetto, words no longer fitted what was seen and experienced. "The word—well, you know," mused Paul Celan after the war—"corpses. Let us wash them, / Let us comb their hair, / Let us turn their eye / to the heavens."[35]

Waste paper. *The Chronicle of the Lodz Ghetto* observed in June 1942 that "the price of waste paper is reaching unprecedented heights in the ghetto." Even in the "Last Stage of Resettlement," Jarecka admitted that ghetto inmates had a great and urgent "desire to write." It is astonishing how many people from all walks of life took up diaries and wrote chronicles. The pages of diaries outnumbered survivors. "Everyone wrote," remarked Ringelblum, "journalists, writers, social workers, teachers, young people and even children." Diarists themselves commented on the tendency to write diaries in the ghetto.[36]

Jarecka tacked back and forth, but she would not completely give up the hope that as "in the past," when "the word meant human dignity and was man's best possession—an instrument of communication between people"—that the cries of the ghetto would eventually "produce an echo." In some ways, writes one scholar, "the confession that 'no words are able to express it' is a sign of a stubborn struggle with the resistant material of language, and not a testimony to giving up on words." "The record must be hurled like a stone under history's wheel in order to stop it," Jarecka added. Record keepers in the ghetto struggled to get their hands on paper, to stay awake to write, and to preserve their testimonies.[37]

Diarists such as Anne Frank in Amsterdam and Chaim Kaplan in Warsaw wrote on the assumption that postwar readers would share the moral values of the diarists themselves. When Kaplan realized he would be taken away, his thoughts turned to the diary: "My utmost concern is for hiding my diary so that it will be preserved for future generations," he wrote on July 31, 1942, on the tenth day of the Great Action. If it was lost, "all my efforts will be wasted." (He paid 2,000 zlotys, about $400, or $9,000 today, to get the diary smuggled to someone on the outside.) In the midst of the depredations, Jews wrote notes for a common history of humanity in which they could not be an extraneous part.[38]

Writers compared themselves to trapped miners or shipwrecked sailors, acknowledging that their physical connection to the rest of the world had become broken, but affirming their existential connection to readers who would pore over their last words. "The scenes of panic" will "vanish with the sinking ship, or with a burning house from which nobody manages to escape, or from a coal pit at the time of an explosion, when the bodies of the miners are buried alive," wrote Rachel Auerbach, but "our descriptions may remain as our witness." Stuck in the Warsaw Ghetto, Szlengel also thought about trapped sailors in a submarine accident that had been the subject of a prewar Soviet film. He believed that the future would be enriched "through my poems, sketches, and writings: "On the wall of my submarine I scrawl my poem-documents . . . I, a poet of AD 1943." The conventional nature of the disaster scenes hardly squares with the unique destitution of the ghetto, but these references to melodramatic plots reported in prewar newspapers offered a way for Jewish writers to affirm their parts in the outside world. It is an important point when considering questions about the comparability of the Holocaust. The rescue efforts failed, but victims, like shipwrecked sailors, who threw bottles with messages into the sea, would be remembered.[39]

There is a concern today that the assimilation of horrific events into regular narratives strips them of terror and of the unsettled responses they might generate in subsequent generations of readers. But part of the disquiet must be the recognition of the desire to create recognizable stories. There is what one scholar refers to as a "double paradox." On the one hand, ghetto chroniclers repeatedly insisted that words were not adequate to the demands of the terror, even as they continued to search for suitable forms. It was as if they were saying to imagined readers, "You must understand, but at the same time you cannot." On the other hand, historians sometimes take the key to present-day understanding to be what was not comprehensible at the time and remains so. In the ghetto, narrators worried constantly about the relationship between form and content, words and experience, an anxiety that added to the instability of narration. But the overriding fear of Jews was that they would be excluded from history. Writing meant the struggle to be included in remembrance, and not to be forgotten.[40]

WHAT ABOUT THE fourth son in New York City whom Szlengel imagined estimating the price of candles while listening to the radio?

What Americans or Britons learned about the murder of the Jews in German-occupied Europe was often "buried by the *Times*" and other news outlets. Careful readers of prominent newspapers would have had a good idea of the "Final Solution," but editors did not draw it to the attention of casual readers. "In all parts of Europe the Germans are calling meetings or issuing orders to bring about what they call 'the final solution of the Jewish problem,'" the London *Times* wrote in "Terror Against Jews" on December 7, 1942. Crucial information was not lacking. There were 139 stories about what was happening to Jews in Europe in the *New York Times* in 1942 (down from 207 in 1941 and 240 in 1940). The stories sometimes left a strong impression. For Swedish readers, the biggest story of 1942 was the "transportation of about 1,500 Jews from Norway to Poland," bigger even than Stalingrad by a margin of 2 to 1.[41]

Overall, however, the difficulty to appreciate the entire sweep of the "Final Solution" led to a failure to understand both the singular nature of Nazi racial policy toward Jews and the totality of their destruction. The persecution registered, and so did incidents of murder, but the deliberate extermination of Jews did not.

European Jews were not so much overlooked as recast so that they were counted alongside all the victims of German oppression in the occupied countries. Jews got lost in romantic, even militarized notions of combat that emphasized the fighting spirit of freedom-loving peoples. Specific features of Jewish suffering dissolved into larger statements of Nazi brutality that, in turn, upheld the righteousness of the Allied cause. One recurring word that was particularly misleading was *Herrenvolk*. That the Nazis saw themselves as superior masters, lording their dominion over the occupied nations, hindered a close analysis of the concept of race by which Jews across Europe were systematically deported and murdered and Slavs in Poland, Belarus, and Ukraine enslaved and discarded. Most of the civilian dead that German occupants left behind were Slavs; the people who suffered the most grievous losses were Jews. The problem of perception might be summarized as follows: Lidice (the Czech village "murdered" for the assassination of a leading Nazi) overshadowed Auschwitz (the systematic extermination of Jews), and Auschwitz overshadowed Zamość (the capture, resettlement, and murder of Poles). The drama of occupation and resistance in western Europe largely determined the apprehension of the quite different sequence of enslavement and murder in eastern Europe.

A vintage example of the burial of the Holocaust was a news report in the London *Times* on December 4, 1942, under the rubric "Diplomatic News" since the primary source was the Polish government-in-exile. The unruffled format, a single column on the left-hand side of the third page, contrasted with the content, perfectly encapsulated by the leader, "Nazi War on Jews," followed by the unambiguous subheading "Deliberate Plan for Extermination." Sentences of elaboration hung on words such as

"Jew free," "liquidation," and "cattle trucks." The fate of the Jews during the critical year 1942 occasionally reached the front page of the *New York Times* and other big newspapers but without the orientation of the large headlines merited by ongoing military events in Stalingrad or the Solomon Islands. Even so, the stories provided sufficient detail to open doors to the chambers of horrors.

The "laid-back" layout of the *Times* and other broadsides was not entirely representative. A tabloid such as New York's *PM*, a new left-wing addition to the newsstands, grabbed readers with full-page headlines and, turning the front page, galleries of pictures, guaranteeing that passersby got the message: "How Hitler's Mass Murders Are Germanizing Europe" or "The Verified Record of Hitler's Massacre of the Jews as Told to FDR." A front-page teaser promised "5 Pages of Cold Facts of History's Greatest Crime." "Pages 4–8" provided broad context to the shocking news with a textbook layout of chapters ("Hitler's Extermination Order," "Caravans of Death") and accompanying maps and tables and a reference to "Ozwiencim."[42]

Whether appearing in the *New York Times* or *PM*, stories on the Nazis' implementation of the "Final Solution" were technocratic in spirit. They were written from the perspective of the high command implementing orders that resulted in the disappearance and death of millions of people. The "Final Solution" elicited few editorials and no feature stories to relay "human interest" angles. Simply, the *New York Times*'s headlines on the execution of hostages in reprisal for the assassination of German military personnel in France conveyed more drama. Alternating between the front page and page 5 or 6, the news items suggested what Parisians might have seen and felt: "45 French Face Death in Hostage"; "116 Are Executed in Paris by Nazis";

"Hostages in Paris Receive Reprieves"; "Victims Rode Own Coffins."[43] Reports from France were easier to file since a mutilated public sphere remained in place. Readers learned details regarding hostages' last letters, the honor they received from French guards, and the impromptu memorials set up at their execution sites, all of which shaped a storyline of how outrage laid foundations for resistance. *Life* titled its reportage "They Die for France." But for whom or what did Jews die?[44]

It was difficult to know precisely what was happening in eastern Europe. German propagandists provided the only first-hand accounts. But that did not keep Allied newspapers from imagining the destruction of the Czech village of Lidice in June 1942. Readers were asked to take "the highroad leading westward from Prague" to get to the ruins of Lidice that had been blotted out. "Where its hundred-odd small houses—mostly stone and slate-shingled—had stood were nothing but blackened ruins." Earning "their bread, for the most part in near-by mines, in the fields, in the small brick factory, in the town's flour mill," the inhabitants had been dispersed or killed. There was no similar effort of imagination when it came to the destroyed homes of persecuted Jews or the "new life" of the ghettos themselves.[45]

"This Was Lidice." The story was not reported by correspondents stationed in Czechoslovakia, yet Lidice became the outstanding "symbol of Nazi evil around the world." In reprisal for the assassination of Reinhold Heydrich, Himmler's deputy in the SS who administered the "Final Solution" and, at the same time, governed the German Protectorate of Bohemia and Moravia, "Nazis blot out Czech village." Why they chose Lidice is not clear, but on June 10 the Germans executed all 173 men and deported 307 women and children mostly to concentration camps, although a few children were selected for "Germanization" and adopted by German families. In the months that followed, hundreds more civilians in the area were executed. Before razing the village, the occupiers carted away agricultural implements, sewing machines, bicycles, and baby carriages.[46] There were debates about the wisdom of the assassination of the guilty given the inevitability of the slaughter of the innocent in reprisals, just as there were arguments about the use of anti-German "terror" in occupied France. However, these played no role in the energetic Allied effort to honor Lidice, to expose the brutality of German overlords, and to reveal the heroism of Czechs living under their yoke.[47]

Lidice became notorious the instant the Germans broadcast details over the radio. Intended as a maximal deterrent in the Axis-occupied zone, the destruction of the village circulated as a terrific scandal in the Allied sphere. Commenting the next day, the *Los Angeles Times* considered the massacre to be "the most savage single act of repression in the history of German occupation of Continental Europe." Cold in a way that "the rape of Nanjing" was hot, according to *Time*, Lidice stood out as "the worst atrocity committed by a civilized nation in modern times." A few days later, the secretary of the navy of the United States, Frank Knox, remarked that "if future generations ask us what we were fighting for in this war, we shall tell them the story of Lidice."[48]

The public's identification with Lidice as anybody's village was immediate and emotionally packed. Whereas Jews were always grouped as Jews in the reporting, or "men, women, and children," it was "coal-miners and woodworkers" who lived in the Czech village. The people of Lidice "were people like other people," people like *us*. "We fight for little towns at home as well as little towns far away," the *New York Times* pledged.[49]

"What happened there will never be forgiven, never forgotten," the editors promised. "We need tanks, planes, and guns," but "we need symbols too," the editorial reflected on the same day in which the newspaper reported that "12,232 persons died in the Warsaw ghetto from hunger, disease and other causes between April and June." Lidice had a mainspring; Warsaw did not.[50]

Allied observers had little trouble recognizing that a great crime against Jews had taken place. They understood that horrific atrocities were committed against unarmed civilians. Yet commentators tended to expand the particular crimes of the Nazis against Jews to encompass all the captive populations in Europe, thereby leveling away what made the murderous assault on every Jew different. (The Soviets went the furthest here, hiding Jewish dead in the collective description of victims as "citizens of the Soviet Union.")

Even when some commentators recognized that the ongoing war against the Jews might not leave Jews in eastern Europe alive at all, and the word "extinction" was used, Jews were repeatedly reinserted as the first in a longer European line of victims. In an editorial, "The First to Suffer," the *New York Times* explained the "martyrdom" of Jews as a result of their "minority" status: "Nazism needed a scapegoat." That was why the Jews pulled the "first number," but "people of other faiths and of many races— Czechs, Poles, Norwegians, Netherlanders, Belgians, French"— were also under threat, and the punishment would continue until "there is not God but Hitler and that there shall be no masters on this earth but the Germans." In another formulation the editorial stated that the suffering of Jews "would be reserved for all who dare . . . to be different from Hitler's Herrenvolk." Here Jews were cast as political resisters, basically similar to other victims because the *Herrenvolk* was at work stamping out non-conformists. Jews certainly did resist, but they were not killed because they had. They were murdered because they were Jews, not because they were rebellious Czechs or Poles.[51]

Moreover, most portrayals of Lidice enlisted the dead in the larger struggle of Czech and European resistance. Lidice was militarized, its inhabitants enrolled in "the fighting spirit of all those who live and hope for freedom." In *Silent Village*, a stunning 1943 propaganda short, the murder of the town is preceded by local resistance to the German occupiers, and the film ends by recalling other miners in nearby towns who presumably continued the underground struggle in the same spirit of self-defense. In similar fashion, *The Dead Look On*, an "instant" novel about Lidice appearing less than one year after the massacre, concluded with the assassination by a passing motorcyclist of SS Obergruppenführer Horner, who had organized the reprisals to avenge the assassination of SS Obergruppenführer von Bertsch in the first place. In this logic, the massacre was necessary to ignite resistance that in turn led to more reprisals, more fighting, and more terror and counterterror. This valiant "never-say-die" dynamic does not really describe the ghettoization and murder of Jews. All the victims of the Nazis were romanced, sacrificed even, because Allied observers kept seeing the villagers of Lidice. They did not see Lublin, Auschwitz, or Zamość, the site of the deportation of Poles and resettlement of Germans. As a result, the entire design of the German racial order got lost from view.

Shaping all accounts of the Nazis' war against the Jews was disbelief. It was shared in different forms by Germans, Jews, and Americans. An inability to understand the "Jewish road" the Nazis had paved was one of the reasons that the extermination of the Jews slipped so easily into conventional narratives about resistance. It was difficult to understand that administrators of the "Final Solution" had implemented a plan in which Jews from across Europe were shipped in freight cars to killing camps. After he read news about gas, electric current, and air bubbles injected into the veins of children, about special installations constructed in Poland, and about two million murdered Jews— the account published in the *Times* on December 4, 1942—the archbishop of Canterbury wrote a letter in which he confessed both despair and failure: "It is a horror beyond what imagination can grasp."[52]

In October 1942, the Polish underground sneaked Jan Karski into the Warsaw Ghetto where he disguised himself as a Jew; to make himself "look very small and thin," he wore "an old, shabby suit and a cap." When Karski arrived in the United States to report on what he had personally seen in Warsaw as well as in a transit camp near Belzec (where he had disguised himself as an Estonian guard), Felix Frankfurter, the Supreme Court justice, responded by simply saying: "I do not believe you." Poland's ambassador to the United States, who was present at the meeting, interrupted: "What are you talking about? He is not lying!" "I did not say that he is lying," Frankfurter tried to explain. "I said that I don't believe him." He could not accept what Karski was reporting. Frankfurter's comment in the summer of 1943 suggests how many contemporaries read the news, taking it apart and putting it into more familiar shape. In its wild form, Karski's "report to the world" required a revision of what it meant to be human. Yet the first impulse was to domesticate the horror in order to be able to align it with experience. Digested in this way, knowledge was not comprehension, and more information did not lead to greater understanding of the difference between Lidice and Lublin. Felix Frankfurter repeated himself: "I cannot accept it. No. No. No."[53]

THE DISPERSED, BEATEN civilian victims of the war were forgotten or simply recounted and remembered as freedom fighters for the national cause. Again and again, the civilian dead were posthumously recruited as prisoners or soldiers. This was the case with peasants in Henan whose public-spirited sacrifices saved the nation, with destitutes in Bengal who provided dying emblems of the injustices of British colonialism, and even with Jews whose suffering at the hands of German invaders indexed the general discontent that would overthrow the barbarians. In this sense, there was "one world, one war." Remaining almost invisible were the actual refugees who were unwanted and largely expendable. They had no clear destinations either on the road or in the story.

The loathing of Jews, the collaboration of neighbors, and the quarrels among the destitute themselves did not provide the mainspring to make the narrative of the war tick. The strong form of the patriotic storyline rendered millions of civilian victims invisible. The narratives of history did not speak for all victims and could not cope with their plight. History was both curse because it silenced and an anticipated salvation providing voice and recognition, yet the great audience of humanity, with novels and romances, remained highly selective in the approach to the victims of war. Edward Said saw the twentieth century as "the age of the refugee, the displaced person, mass immigration," and the world war certainly created millions of these outcasts. But precisely because there were so many black roads and Jewish roads, some people traveled better than others. The literature of the war itself hardly recognized what it meant to an outsider or a migrant, who wandered between the fronts, who were exiled in exile. The romance of war drew emotional fuel from the victims of the treacherous foe, but, lifting the down-trodden up into the great battle against the enemy, stories did not really see the general condition of dispossession in the war. Nineteen forty-two was the year of the refugee, but she did not make the cover.[54]

PART V

PULL UP THE ROAD

CHAPTER 16

Richmond, California

Kraków's main train station was the site the guardians selected to celebrate the New German Order on March 13, 1943. The occasion was the departure of the Polish worker who rounded out the total of one million recruits who had purportedly shown goodwill to cooperate with German occupiers by volunteering to work in the Reich. Hans Frank, the governor-general, presided over the farcical scene, presenting the lucky worker with a gold watch and best wishes for a "happy and fresh return" at the end of his sojourn. More than eight million foreigner laborers toiled in Germany, the vast majority forcibly conscripted. Indeed, there was no greater scandal in German-occupied Europe than labor impressment. It aroused more fury among local people than the deportation of Jewish children. From France to Ukraine, the prospect of forced labor in Germany, more than any other factor, propelled young men and women to join the partisans.

At the very beginning of the war, a smattering of workers voluntarily left for Germany in search of secure employment and better pay. In 1940, cities in the Greater Reich seemed like the prosperous metropoles of a new European future. But supply never met German demand, and workers quickly found conditions atrocious, more like those endured by prisoners-of-war the Germans released when collaborating French authorities filled quotas with sufficient substitute laborers. A French worker conceded in a November 1942 letter to his mother that "we can't complain," but it was because "we're the ones who've got the most respect in this whole thing." Other deported laborers were treated far worse and kept under close guard in the racial regime. "The Russian prisoners are the most unfortunate of all. The poor devils get nothing to eat."[1]

Germans approached the foreign workers all around them with a mixture of pity and fear. "Frenchmen, Poles, Ukrainians, girls too, heaped together in front of the main train station," where they milled about on Sundays, their day off: "Dirty, shivering, most without coats, the girls in summer dresses and headscarves," wrote Lisa de Boor on a visit to Frankfurt in January 1943. "An unending sense of gloom hangs about these people so far away from home."[2]

To an astonishing degree, wartime needs were filled according to well-worn colonial schemes of forced labor. In East Asia, Japanese occupiers drafted workers and established labor camps that recalled the most cruel operations of the white imperialists from whom they claimed to have liberated colonial people. When it came to finding workers to build bridges or grade roads, Japan revealed a "rabid master-race mentality" that dissolved initial enthusiasm for its liberation of Asians after the fall of Singapore.[3] Millions of forced laborers drowned on the torpedoed Japanese merchant ships or died of disease and neglect in the field. The Allies themselves revived labor conscription in their colonies to extract badly needed commodities or build transportation routes. Across Africa, closed labor encampments recalled nothing more than "the time of rubber" in the Belgian Congo at the end of the nineteenth century, prompting once again the "mass exodus of the people to the bush" to avoid service. Hence the new life to King "Leopold's Ghost."[4]

Bad old times coexisted with better new times since boomtowns across Africa and the rest of the Allied sphere depended on unprecedented amounts of free labor in factories, mines, and railways. The "mass exodus" to the bush also occurred in reverse as migrants left tribal villages to become "new men" in the new cities.

Workers were expelled from their homes and pushed on the road as in Kraków, but millions of others clambered onto the trains to "travel north and travel south" around places like Nigeria because they were pulled in by wartime opportunities. It was in bursting urban locations—such as Lagos, Nigeria; Johannesburg, South Africa; Richmond, California; and Detroit, Michigan—that labor migrants opened up a second front, demanding shelter and rights so that the issues of freedom posed by the global war found local addresses across the world. Unlike the forced conscripts, free workingmen and -women announced themselves insistently in voices and songs.[5] They sounded out in the cacophony of the war.

THE BARTENDER ON Third Avenue in New York City hated the song. "'The prairie sky is wide and high,' and then the goddamn four claps." "Or is it three claps"—"only they are not clapping together. How can they, some giving three claps and some giving four?" It was number 15 on the jukebox: "Deep in the Heart of Texas" (with four claps). One customer paid for his ten-cent beer with a dollar bill and asked for change in nickels; "he put in eighteen nickels, one after another."[6]

The jukebox likely played Perry Como's big-band cover with trombones sounding out the claps. Five versions of "Deep in the Heart of Texas," written by June Hershey with music composed by Don Swander, reached the billboard charts in 1942. Hard and fast, with the boisterous clapping, "Deep in the Heart of Texas" instantly became part of the soundtrack of America's war. A crowd favorite, it even made it into the Hollywood Canteen, the famous servicemen's club. "Deep in the Heart of Texas" played so often the BBC banished the song from the airwaves during work hours because people would drop their tools to clap their hands.

"Deep in the Heart of Texas" became a wartime staple on jukeboxes around the country. That was the sign it had arrived; no longer confined to radio programs such as *Grand Ole Opry* broadcast by Nashville's WSM, country had become city music. It crossed into the currents right alongside swing, which it took up with "western swing." With customers punching in number 15 on the jukebox, the popularity of "Deep in the Heart of Texas" took measure of how many Texans and other southerners had fanned out around the country, migrating to cities or to California to take up well-paying jobs in the burgeoning defense industries. Roy Acuff attracted more than eleven thousand fans in Venice Beach after "Los Angeles County Barn Dance" opened on the pier in June 1942.[7]

Promoted by hearsay, advertisements, and paid recruiters, the pull of work in war industries was so strong that one in five people in the United States moved; from 1940 to 1947 an estimated twenty-five million migrated across state or county lines. One million Blacks, one in ten, left the South for cities of the North and West. Statisticians in the Census Bureau believed that "never before in the history of the United States has there been internal population movement of such magnitude." By 1945, the country had become an urban society, not primarily a quilt of rural places. The population of California increased by 1.6 million, or 20 percent. Securing 12 percent of all government war orders, particularly to manufacture ships and aircraft, the state experienced, the *San Francisco Chronicle* announced in April 1943, its "second gold rush." Kaiser eventually built four shipyards in Richmond on the San Francisco Bay, causing an "avalanche" that utterly transformed the plain refinery town of 23,000 inhabitants. It was a messy wartime boomtown of more than 100,000 that built one-fifth of all Liberty merchant ships.[8]

Added to "the sound of ten thousand workmen building ships" was the sound of country music, a repertoire spotlighted by "Deep in the Heart of Texas." "Decked out in the rough and ready style of the old west," members dressed as farmhands, cowboys, and cowgirls to attend the monthly barn dance of Richmond's Townsend Club, a group advocating federal retirement pensions, on March 21, 1942. In summertime, bands such as Dude Martin and His Roundup Gang played at Eastshore Park from 9:00 p.m. until 1:00 in the morning with a live broadcast on KYA at 10 p.m. "Gentlemen" paid 75 cents, "ladies" 55. (The park also sponsored plenty of swing; back by popular demand, "Paul Basham and his ten piece orchestra" played in August.) Richmond's own Sammy Lico entertained "ladies in gingham and men in bright shirts and blue denims of the '49ers" at the Richmond Gold Club. Until long after the war, Lico, who worked as an auditor at Kaiser's Shipyard No. 2, played at McCracken's Ballroom in Richmond or dinner dances at the Fratellanza Club.[9] Radio programs such as "Eddie the Hired Hand's Hillbilly Hit Parade" (KLS-Oakland), "Foreman Bill's Rhythm Rodeo" (KYA-San Francisco), and "Long Horn Joe's Cowboy Hit Parade" (KROW-Oakland) catered to the newcomers, blaring country music throughout the Bay Area.[10]

Fully half of Kaiser's workers were "Okies" or "Arkies" or Texans, and Black migrants, most of them from the South as well, made up an additional 20 percent of the labor force. By a small margin, more women than men migrated into the Bay Area. All the newcomers were attracted by wages that at Kaiser started at $1.05 an hour at a time when the minimum wage was 30 cents. (Multiply by twenty for today's equivalent.) As a result of the war, California towns became southern migrant communities. In its spread on Richmond, *Fortune* introduced readers to a couple who had been sharecroppers in Arkansas. "They paid $100 down on the land now occupied by a $15 trailer." They planned to send for their four children once they had built "a house out of the pile of second-hand boards" in their yard. High turnover rates in all the new industries indicated that migrants remained on the move, but they did not move back. *Fortune*'s captions read: "Arkansas Sharecropper Here to Stay" and "Nothing in Iowa to Go Back To."[11]

Alone among the belligerent nations, the United States experienced the war as a time of affluence. Wages went up more than taxes and inflation. After the Depression, no one knew if bad times would not return; this was a big worry reported by national polls. For the time being, however, there were more money and more laughing and dancing. In Richmond, during the Christmas season at the end of 1942, a year after Pearl Harbor, "shoppers literally could not get into the stores. They lined up on the sidewalk outside, and were let in a few at a time."[12]

Newcomers first lined up at bus stations in small towns to catch a ride out. Writer John Dos Passos got on: "The bus rumbles down the sunny empty highway through the rusty valleys and the bare rainwashed fields and the scraggly woods and the hills the color of oakleaves that are the landscape of winter in the southeast states. Inside, the air is dense with packed bodies and stale cigarette smoke." "Behind me," he noted, "two men are talking about jobs in singsong voices pitched deep in their chests." They traded information: "What's it like down there?" "Aint too bad if you kin stand that bunch of loudmouthed foremen." "Well, I've worked in about all of 'em."

"I been on this bus a thousand times"—all America seemed to be on the move, with "whole sections of the country being loaded into cars and trucks and trailers, buses, and trains and moving off the land and into the towns and cities where there were jobs to do and money to make." Even with gas rationing and tire shortages, most people moved from city to city by private car, but bus travel increased from 9.5 billion miles to 27 billion, and so did train travel, from 24 to 98 billion, a fourfold rise in public ridership. Even at the national wartime speed limit of thirty-five miles an hour, buses, with the destination serving as an exit sign, were popular because they served small towns. Westbound traffic flowed on Highway 41 or 66 to California; white migrants complained about the "cattle cars" on Southern Pacific trains, but Blacks in transit sometimes thought of them as "liberty trains."[13]

When travelers got where they were going, they found themselves in "a milling crowd": "Every other man seems to be in work clothes." "In twos and threes" girls wore "slacks and overalls" as well. At the light, a young man "dangling a welder's helmet on a strap from the crook of his arm" turned to laugh: "I jes' got tired an' quit." Additional lights had become necessary because shifts pumped so many more automobiles through the streets. Traffic never seemed to come to a stop. "There were no more weekends or nights," recalled an old-timer. "It was just twenty-four hours a day, seven days a week."[14]

Along with its *New War Map* of the Pacific war theater, Richmond's *Independent* published a full-page advertisement on December 19, 1942, listing which drugstores and food markets remained open until 10:00 p.m. Guides to the growing town needed to be regularly updated. New grocery stores stretched out along MacDonald Avenue: Quality Market, United Grocers' Richmond Market on MacDonald and Barrett, Buy-Rite at Eighth, and Shurfine on Eighth and Barrett. They were popular because customers could serve themselves from among the "over 20,000 commodities on display." With self-service refrigerated cheese and dairy counters and "drive-in" parking, the markets tailored themselves to the wartime boomtown. When Lucky, one of the "finest" supermarkets, opened on Nevin Avenue, thousands of customers arrived on opening day, meriting a page full of photographs in the *Independent*. During the war the number of supermarkets in the United States increased from under five thousand to more than sixteen thousand.[15]

Movie theaters sprang up faster than shipyards. Built in just ninety-seven days, the Grand on Twenty-Third opened on February 5, 1942, while the article "Fox Reveals Plans for New Theater" advertised seating for a thousand customers. Robert Lippert, who owned the Grand, also opened a "showhouse" on MacDonald: "The Studio Theater will open each day, except Sunday at 10 am and will operate until 5 am," business hours that became standard. Even more grand was Lippert's third theater, the "V" for "victory" that reported "New 4 Star R.C.A. Sound," "New Motiograph Projection Equipment," and a "New Plastic Screen"—"A Real Treat for Your Eyes."[16] Richmond's *Independent* also showed readers the way to the new Sears Roebuck (on MacDonald at Twelfth), Richmond's "Newest and Biggest Liquor Store," and the "New" Marlene's Apparel Shop featuring "discriminating styles" in spacious "fluorescently lighted" rooms.[17]

For newcomers as much as for old-timers, Richmond suddenly became a startling place. Sidewalks were "blocked by gaping strangers in cowboy boots, blue jeans, and sombreros"; women in "slacks and leather jackets and shiny scalers' helmets wait in long lines." Even a visitor could see that "nobody knows anybody," whereas before "everyone knew everybody else." One native felt completely menaced: "I don't like to be tramped on by dirty cowboy boots when I go into a store," she complained. Along MacDonald, which connected to the shipyards, traffic snarled; "no car in Richmond had four good fenders," remarked one resident. In the evening, "wow-boys" used the avenue as a speedway. "Broken glass, abandoned cars, and garbage" soon cluttered Lower MacDonald where bars, juke joints, and pool halls grabbed workers leaving their shifts. "Every hour for three years," the place looked like "carnival night." Whereas before the war residents enjoyed strolling down MacDonald, chatting and bumping into friends while out shopping, with shifts drifting workers through town, they stayed away.[18]

For newcomers the first order of business after arriving was finding housing. From April to September 1942, the vacancy rate in nearby Oakland collapsed from 0.81 to 0.06 percent, which meant six units available for every ten thousand that were occupied. Municipal authorities relaxed rules on hotels and boardinghouses that offered "hot beds" rented out "by the shift on a round-the-clock basis." When the *Independent* published photographs of trailers, "tin houses," and "cardboard shacks" on the north side of Richmond, the incredulous caption read: "It can't happen here. But it has." The ramshackle covered the flat-lands of the East Bay.[19]

Schools hardly kept up with the expansion of movie-theater capacity. Enrollment in elementary schools rocketed from 2,987 to 13,112 from 1941 to 1944, forcing children into two half-day shifts in classrooms each with as many as seventy pupils. When Dorothea Lange photographed a group of local schoolchildren, most of them raised their hands when she asked, "How many of you were *not* born in California?" However, the number of high school students initially dropped because of the lure of avail-able work. About one thousand children were completely unac-counted for, reported Richmond's superintendent of schools in April 1943; police picked up about twenty-five at the movies on any given day.[20]

With more parents working and teenagers taking advantage of easy money in town, juvenile delinquency for boys and girls shot up. They also had migrated—from playgrounds to streets. The moral panic of delinquency vexed Richmond, as it did other places around the country. Newspapermen invited read-ers to "take a walk down Macdonald Avenue between First and Seventh streets": "You will see children in their teens drinking out of bottles while standing on the sidewalk"; "you will hear cuss words that you probably never have heard in a blue moon." Police also spotted "Seagulls" and "B-girls" (bar girls or bad girls) as they kept track of the growth of prostitution. "Teen-ager," "latchkey kids," and "juvenile delinquency" were the new words entering American vocabularies during the war.[21]

Divorce and marriage rates hit record highs among new-comers in search of hookups and whirlwind romances like the one that brought together Judy Garland and Robert Walker in the 1945 movie *The Clock*, which counted down the forty-eight hours before the end of the soldier's leave. When a "sailor's lonely wife asks if it is wrong to date," saying she would go "crazy" "being alone all the time," the advice columnist made it plain that such behavior was inexcusable. Yet "Dear Miss Alden" also counseled against quick wartime marriages in the first place since there was so much going on: "You would be horribly lonely," she informed the twenty-year-old correspondent who "dearly" loved her twenty-three-year-old boyfriend in the service. "There would be no dancing," and "in a few months you would be very tired of such a daily life." Popular songs even promoted sentiments behind a quick fling: "You can't say no to a soldier"; the idea was that "if he's going to fight, he's got a right to romance." "Fortyeight hours left in the world" became a standard pickup line, but the girl John Dos Passos observed in San Francisco blushed. "'Let's just stay on the ferry and feed the gulls,' she said." Love itself was part of the fugitive sense of life.[22]

Historian Kevin Starr had it right about the "swing shift": "California would never be the same" after having pulled in so many migrants from across the country and settled them in the cities to work around the clock.[23]

"Wherever you go in the Bay Area," wrote a local writer, "the yards are present, twenty-four hours a day, seven days a week. They are present in the lunch-pail and hard-hat parade of the workers" and in "the gleam of lights on the night horizon."[24] Americans might have known little about Richmond, but they had heard plenty about Kaiser, the shipyards, and Liberty ships. When the SS *Robert E. Peary* was launched at Richmond's Yard

No. 2, at 3:26 p.m., four minutes ahead of schedule, on Thursday, November 12, 1942, the event made headlines around the country. From laying the keel to the launching, it had taken "4 days, 15 hours, and 25 minutes" to build the ship, a record that stood for the rest of the war. It was another three days before the *Peary* was delivered to the US Maritime Commission: in the outfitting basin, the ship had to be wired, pipes laid, and machinery installed. In the meantime, the keel of the next ship was laid on the shipway. The prefabrication of large sections made it possible to reduce time on the shipway to the length of time it took riggers to haul and hoist the big pieces and welders to fasten the seams. All the parts were manufactured elsewhere and assembled in huge sheds that fanned out behind the shoreline.[25]

In the sheds, 250,000 separate pieces were built into the units, and on the shipway, the completed units—the deck and hull plates, the bulkheads, the bow, the stern, which could weigh as much as 200 tons—were hoisted into place. Welders secured the big pieces along 194,000 feet of seams. Welding saved an enormous amount of time since rivets needed to be heated, hammered, caulked, and chiseled: 55,000 rivets held together a Liberty ship as opposed to the 900,000 required by its World War I equivalent. What really saved time was the prefabrication of a small number of ever-larger units. "We are not only building ships," the chairman of the Maritime Commission told Congress; "we are assembling ships." Kaiser compared the process to completing a "gigantic jigsaw puzzle." Rationalization made speed in the process of assembly possible, but only huge orders, the Department of War's program for twenty-three million new tons of shipping for 1942 and 1943, made prefabrication economical. An estimated 1.8 million Americans played some small part in "Kaiser's circus" to cast, build, and assemble the parts of a Liberty ship.[26]

It took only days to learn the single skill sets into which the skilled trades of master shipbuilders had been broken down. Shipyards were "ravenous for men" and "absorbed them all." There were only 6,000 shipyard workers in the Bay Area in 1939, but the unrelenting appetite for wartime labor drove the numbers to 240,000; demand was so great that by 1942 the yards dropped conventions, hiring first women, then African Americans. Kaiser made a virtue out of necessity in its advertising materials: "We are of every color—black and white, yellow and red—and of every faith—Catholic and Protestant, Jewish and Mohammedan. . . . But whatever we are or were, we get along fine, working side by side. Americans all, we know it takes all kinds of people to build ships." "Farmers, housewives, salesmen and schoolgirls have learned how to assemble a ship," marveled one writer transplanted from Hitler's Europe, "Sandy, Chuck, Jason, Albi, Lovella"—and Dimples.[27]

When a Berkeley graduate student, Katherine Archibald, resolved to study social life in the new shipyards, she expected to find a facsimile of Kaiser's brochure; in time of war, American workers pulled together. Just as volunteers streamed into military recruitment offices after Pearl Harbor, war workers shipped themselves across the country to work in war industries. Slipping into the role of a unionized war worker for two years, Archibald produced an arresting study of Moore Dry Dock Company's "Wartime Shipyard" in Oakland, California.[28]

Archibald was dismayed by what she observed on the shoreline. Three times a day, "the inward flow coming on shift spilled into the yard reservoir, and filled it," and three times a day, "the homegoing surge poured forth," spreading out over "the wide plain of the surrounding community." Inside the yard, however, she found a highly agitated workforce. There was no sense of unity among shipyard workers, as she had expected. The "social abysses" were so "deep" that there was little possibility of spanning them. Even "slight linguistic and cultural differences" appeared to have brought "the ghosts of feudal snobbery" to life again. The liberal contrived her "dream of equalitarianism," but the sociologist she had become discovered "the weaker suppressed by the less weak." At Moore, Kaiser's claim of "Americans all" proved false.

Three overlapping groups were the focus of antagonisms measuring the "social abysses" in the shipyard. Like "soldiers infiltrating enemy lines," women found a workplace that was both hostile and hyperattentive. "These women worked!" Archibald asserted, but neither this evidence nor the "bombardment" of the workforce with "Rosie the Riveter" imagery broke down conventional prejudice. "The pleasures or the problems of sex" occupied "the largest part of shipyard conversation." Some women took advantage of the highly eroticized environment, yet the majority felt it to be oppressive. Most of the female workforce regarded employment as a temporary interlude before returning to the home.[29]

Favorite targets of ridicule, the "Okies" from the South and Southwest were in fact most assimilable. They constituted the majority of Moore's wartime labor force. During the years of the Great Depression, they had been resented as unwelcome intruders and even racialized as a lesser, more stupid people. The whole issue of "Okies" revealed the breadth of racial hatred in California, although Japanese and African Americans suffered the dire consequences of its depth. Indeed, Okies mostly shared ideas about white supremacy. As the personnel office at Kaiser summarized, "the men from the South complain" about the fact that "they must mingle with all races, creeds, and colors."[30]

In Archibald's "immediate circle" at work, Beulah was "abnormally sensitive" to ridicule. One morning she was especially put out. Jostled in the streetcar, a stranger had turned around and remarked that if "shipyard Okies such as she so plainly was" would "go back where they came from," then "there might be room for the people who belonged in California to ride to work in comfort." Archibald saw the occasion to "pronounce the obvious moral lesson." Beulah was "surely as American and surely as privileged to ride on streetcars as anyone else." "Prejudice is always unfair," Archibald chimed in, whether "prejudice against the Okie or the man whose skin is black." Beulah "fairly shrieked": "But I'm no nigger! I'm not black!" Beulah stood "at the bottom of a thousand higher steps," but she looked down at those she put below her. For Archibald, the "sudden storm" shaped "an experience sufficient for a lifetime."[31]

Archibald ended her study with the depressing insight that "shipyard generosity never crossed the barrier between black and white." "Hatred of the Negro" not only made it nearly impossible to bridge social chasms but also supported a fatalistic sense of living in a cruel, unequal, and unchanging world. "It's dog eat dog, and the strongest gets the most in this man's world," one worker told her; "it's always been that way, and that's the way, I guess, it's always bound to be." Archibald assumed that wartime exigencies made the situation worse, so she hoped attitudes might soften. However, the conflicts described by Archibald over streetcars, housing, and other spaces anticipated the white working-class backlash against New Deal liberalism; ethnic groups did not see themselves as parts of a multicultural whole.

For Kevin Starr, the "people's" historian of California, World War II simply compounded the state's history of racism; residents had waged war against Japanese and Chinese immigrants, against Okie farmers, against African American "intruders." "The United States," he concluded, "was at war with itself as well as with the Axis powers."[32]

"LIKE ALL PECKERWOODS," they "couldn't stand being around colored people. They would do anything to mess you up!"

"A Jap is a Jap, whether he was born in California or Timbuctoo"; "I know there's not one of the yellowbellies you can trust."

"Back where I come from we've got a right and proper kind of home law, and if one of them black fellows even so much as talks smart to a white gal, we hang him dead."

In the shipyards, race talked loud and race talked back.[33]

"The white folks had sure brought their white to work with them that morning," remarked the shipyard worker in Chester Himes's Los Angeles novel *If He Hollers Let Him Go* (1945). And Bo Jones brought his Black to work too. He jockeyed for advantage like everyone else in the early-morning "scramble" on a "thirty-mile highway." "But for me," Bo admitted, "it was racial": "Time and again, I cut in front of some fast-moving car, making rubber burn and brakes scream and drivers curse." At intersections, he started "playing a game." "Whenever I saw some white people crossing the street in front of me I stepped on the gas and blew. If they jumped they could make it; if they didn't I'd run 'em down. All of 'em jumped." "All I wanted in the world was to push my Buick Roadmaster over some peckerwood's face." "I didn't give a damn whether they jumped or not."[34]

The highways promoted fantasies of freedom, and payback for all the racial affronts in the shipyards where Bo worked, but, in his travels on the streetcars of Los Angeles, Himes himself saw how white people staked out space. "Three drunken white sailors...on a Red car coming from Watts," were boasting "how they had whipped the Japs": "Ah'm tellin' yuh, Ah fought lak a white man!" When a pretty Mexican girl got on, the sailor upped his ante in a "loud, whiskey-thickened voice": "Boy, did those native gals go fuh us. Boy, uh white man can git any gal he wants." Himes recalled the incident as he reflected on Los Angeles's "zoot suit riots" when in June 1943 servicemen pulled "dark-skinned people who wore zoot-suits" ("or what might have been taken for zoot-suits") out of streetcars or movie theaters and beat them up on the streets. Whether it was whites in general or servicemen, who, in uniform, were known to display a "belligerent, virile masculinity," rioters "proved beyond all doubt" that "Los Angeles was at last being made safe for white people—to do as they damned well pleased."[35]

You could get on a bus or streetcar in any wartime boomtown and experience the same scramble for space and shove of bravado.

The procession of "creeping, congested" streetcars moving along the streets of Detroit carried all sorts of "impatient, tired" commuters. According to Cyril H. Crane, the British consul-general in America's fourth-largest city, the crowding "on the street, in transport, in parks, lifts, shops and places of amusement" was "very obnoxious to everyone." Crane provided a telling list: "You are jostled by negroes, fat women," and "fall over children." On Woodward Avenue, the main thoroughfare, passengers were sometimes packed sixty or seventy in a single car, "jammed to the doors with people." Some of the crowd-ing was due to shifts that interrupted normal traffic patterns. Weary workers complained about the "horde of silly high school girls who bum around the stores after school and fill seats." But when "for me it was racial," it became so for others as mass tran-sit dramatized the anger Blacks had after being denied public services and the resentment of whites who believed their places at work or in neighborhoods were being invaded.[36]

Crowds started to pile up in the spring of 1942. At the same time, labor shortages compelled Detroit's Department of Street Railways to hire Black motormen, conductors, and "conduc-toresses," this in contrast to transit systems in Washington, DC, and Los Angeles, where unions and companies refused to allow Black workers to occupy "platform" jobs. About a quar-ter of "DSR" jobs were held by African Americans, which vastly expanded the play of feelings of entitlement and resentment. Incidents occurred every day, and letters to the DSR fattened the files. Passengers used the jerks of the streetcar to step out of place or feel aggrieved that someone else had. Whites con-tended that Blacks didn't move when asked, or move fast enough or far enough. For Blacks, the streetcar ride was a kind of the-ater, much as Himes described, in which the commotion made it possible to challenge standards of deference and comportment.

Paranoia about physical contact charged rumors about orga-nized all-Black "Bump Clubs" or "Push Clubs." Complaints about a so-called Push Day imagined Black commuters not only getting together to push whites on streetcars but planning to push them out of their neighborhoods as well by moving in. For their part, Black motormen found that white passengers used the hasty forth-and-back of paying fares or showing trans-fers to take offense with a barrage of insults at once self-righteous and crude.[37] Wartime gasoline rationing aroused as much opposition as it did because Detroiters wanted to get back into their own cars to commute to work. In the meantime, ride sharing to avoid streetcars proved popular. After the war, white Detroiters would use the highways that state and federal authorities constructed to move out of the city altogether.

In the South, whites also stood alert to infractions of Jim Crow, the laws and standards of behavior that kept Blacks segregated from whites and in their "place." White men's stories about "uppity" Blacks often started on the bus. Speaking for "white majorities in the South," John Temple Graves, a Birmingham newspaper columnist, gathered up evidence: "There seems to be a disposition on the part of many Negroes to disregard and resist the Jim Crow Law" so "that in many instances it has been necessary to stop and hold buses and street cars until officers could be summoned to make unruly Negroes occupy the part of the car reserved for them or remove them because they refused to do so." A "long list of 'atrocities'" followed: uniformed Black soldiers in transit had blown kisses and otherwise "insulted" a "number of young ladies," or a "black soldier sat down beside a white woman, threw his arm around her, and told her what he would do to her 'after all the white men are gone.'" Pointing to "a group of Negroes," a bus driver in Birmingham confided: "Right there, mister, is where our next war will break out, and it may start before this one is over."[38]

These outlandish stories had their roots in the fright of slave insurrections. But the rumors also told the truth about changing Black attitudes in the 1940s, a time of war, migration, and political literacy that multiplied the impact of Black newspapers. "In thousands of subtle and dramatic ways, black people stopped playing their parts in the public theater of segregation," writes one historian; "they refused to tip their hats to whites, make room for white pedestrians on jammed sidewalks, or give up their seats on crowded buses." Whites correctly perceived that Blacks resisted more tenaciously Jim Crow's possession of their bodies.[39] However, they persistently misunderstood Blacks who they believed wanted to replace whites by "taking over" the order, rather than destroying the regime itself.

Whites were convinced that the war had created a kind of prerevolutionary situation in which militant Black agitators, northern liberals, and especially the federal government's enforcement of fair-employment practices threatened to upend the "status quo" of Jim Crow. For sociologist Howard Odum, the war had put "two great regional folk cultures," one Black and one white, "in the midst of transition between the powerful heritage of the past and the mighty pull of the future." The defense of Jim Crow was perhaps the "least right" of the positions, yet rumors about Blacks defying whites swept the South after the United States mobilized for war like "flood waters suddenly released by a bomber's blast," the measure of "extraordinary crisis."[40]

The Great Migration, the largest movement of people in the United States, larger even than the arrival of Irish or Poles or Jews, saw the establishment of African American communities across the entire continent. Whereas in 1910 the majority of Blacks lived in the rural South, two generations later, in 1970, just under half lived in the urban North and West. The migration came in two parts, both centered on the world wars. If the first part created the infrastructure of Black communities in big cities such as New York, Detroit, and Chicago, the second part brought the larger numbers. Pushed out by oppressive conditions in the South and pulled in by economic opportunities in the North, an estimated one million Blacks migrated in the World War II years. Yet they discovered the promise of a "new Canaan" torn and tattered. Many of the customs if not the laws of Jim Crow followed them north, where African Americans found restricted employment, segregated housing, and white resentment. The migration of whites from the economically depressed southern regions, which ran parallel to the movement of Blacks from the same places, compounded racial discrimination in what many came to see as the "upper South." Portland, Oregon, for example, was known as a "northern city with a southern exposure."[41]

"I pick up my life / And take it on the train," wrote Langston Hughes in his poem "One-Way Ticket" (1949)—"And I put it down in / Chicago, Detroit, / Buffalo, Scranton, / Any place that is North and East—And not Dixie." "Gone up North," but was it, as "they say," the "kinder mistress"? he asked in his poem "The South" (1926).

The war compressed and hardened existing social patterns even as it popularized and amplified democratic messages.

Never before had the African American press spoken with such clarity and influence. With a combined circulation of 1.3 million in 1940, Black newspapers were purchased by more than one-third of all Black families in the United States and reached many more in barbershops, stores, and lodges. Almost every Black person in the city talked about news the *Chicago Defender* had published.[42] Journalists trumpeted race "progress," but also measured the great extent to which America's ideals fell short. Increasingly, the front-page story in the *Defender* covered the shortfall rather than the long promise. This shift in emphasis accompanied the prominence of the "new Negro," whose growing reluctance to compromise reflected a militance of sorts.

At the same time, the war in Europe after 1939 made more voluble rhetoric about the defense of democratic rights. Rights talk opened ways to advance racial justice, but that struggle made sense only if the talk was walked and manifested in policy and action. For all the boom in the wartime economy after 1940, many signs had simply been switched from "No Help Wanted" to "Help Wanted, White." In California, as late as 1941, "Douglas Aircraft Corporation employed only 10 African Americans out of more than 30,000 employees." North American Aviation's 12,500 workers included no more than 8 African Americans. Employers were begging for applicants, but when Blacks, many of them graduates of vocational training courses, applied for jobs at defense factories, they were informed that "the Negro will be considered only as janitors and in other similar capacities."[43] With *American Gothic, Washington D.C.*, Gordon Parks provided the appropriate photograph for the year 1942: Ella Watson, a cleaning woman in a federal building, held a broom in one hand, a mop in the other.

Black leaders threatened direct action, instead of public appeals and private lobbying. They scheduled a march on Washington for July 1, 1941; newspapers spoke of 10,000 on Pennsylvania Avenue, or 50,000, then 100,000. The pressure was sufficient for President Roosevelt to sign Executive Order 8802 on June 25. It prohibited racial discrimination in industries under federal contract, a big step forward, although the Fair Employment Practice Committee remained underresourced, forcing it to make do simply documenting how reality lagged behind promise. Not surprisingly, "Negro morale" remained a touchy topic throughout the war. Black soldiers took to saying, "Here lies a black man killed fighting a yellow man for the glory of a white man."

The *Pittsburgh Courier*'s famous 1942 "Double-V" campaign for "democracy," a "double victory" to be achieved "at home—abroad," put a lively banner on the Black community's refusal to go along with the obvious contradiction between the aspiration for freedom around the world and the lack of freedom in the United States. Instead of passivity or spite, Double-V sought action on both the domestic and foreign fronts to achieve "victory over aggression, slavery and tyranny." The fight was concurrent, just like the victory sign made with both fingers at once, not one after the other. Black leaders were quite consistent on this issue: there would be no repeat of World War I in which the victorious fight for liberty in Europe never came with the dividend of liberty at home. The Double-V campaign also reflected the global dimension of the war that was about universal rights, not particular violations. Local issues gained salience because the global conflict rejected contained, limited, or conditional war aims in the overall fight against militarism and fascism. As a result, the global public in World War II quickly took up questions about India's independence and African American equality.

Double-V was about the "billion of colored peoples to be freed by war" that included "colored peoples" in the United States. With regard to the status quo, there was nothing that could "put Humpty-Dumpty together again, even if we wished." "We are fighting a war of liberation for a self-possessed world," concluded the *Courier*.[44]

The initial impetus for a campaign against "Axis forces and ugly prejudices on the home front" came in a letter the *Courier* published on January 31, 1942. It posed the question "Should I sacrifice my life to live half American?" James Thompson, later identified as a cafeteria worker at an aircraft plant in Wichita,

Kansas, pointed out the obvious fact that "Colored Americans suffer still the indignities that have been heaped upon them in the past."[45]

Wichita was no Utopia, reminded George Schuyler, the *Courier*'s editor who flew out for a visit in April. "Its 6,000 Negroes are largely employed as laborers, messengers and domestics," and "out of the thousands of workers hired by the four aircraft plants in the city, only about 150 are colored," including the cafeteria worker. Moreover, "Negroes are not served at downtown restaurants or hotels. Barred from some theaters, they are sent to the balconies of others." "The YMCA and YWCA are segregated as usual, despite the 'Christian.'"[46] Since the United States was not a "true and pure democracy," concluded Thompson, it was threatened as much by prejudice at home as Axis forces abroad. Any defense of the United States required a two-front war, and any victory needed to be a double one.

The Double-V campaign "against our enslavers at home and those abroad who would enslave us" promoted the idea that Black Americans had "a stake in this fight." It caught the imagination of Black Americans. More than 200,000 joined Double-V clubs; civic and youth groups, high schools, business associations, and NAACP branches signed on as "affiliate members of 'VV' Clubs of America." There were Double-V dances with Double-V hairdos. The whole effort gave an exuberant, patriotic look to the demands for complete enfranchisement in American life. Eventually, the hoopla receded, but the idea that the global conflict legitimated local struggles against inequality remained a basic premise for African American thought and action. "This is our war," insisted the *Michigan Chronicle*.[47]

The wartime interplay between the local and the global became clear in the violent confrontation at the Sojourner Truth public housing project in Detroit in the winter of 1942. With the influx of five thousand new immigrants a month, mostly from the South and about one in every six newcomers African American, wartime Detroit encountered a severe housing crisis. Local and federal efforts to construct public housing never came close to meeting demand in Detroit or anywhere else. Since the Sojourner Truth project was built with the assumption that it would accommodate either Black families or white ones, but not both, the issues became communal.

Built in a mixed-use checkerboard neighborhood of all-Black and all-white blocks, Sojourner Truth did not fundamentally change the neighborhood or its schools. Yet at Fenelon and Nevada, the homes were located immediately adjacent to all-white blocks whose residents mounted furious opposition once it became clear that Black families would be the occupants. "We Demand Our Rights to Protest, Restrict, and Improve Our Neighborhood," leaflets read. Others objected to the "guinea pig experiment" that defied "racial differences" while penalizing white homeowners.[48] Protests at city hall moved to the neighborhood's streets where white activists set up pickets that, on move-in day, February 28, 1942, obstructed incoming traffic. For several hours police lost control of the situation, unable to disperse either the blockaders or the Blacks who attempted to charge the lines and allow moving vans through. Order was restored only when Michigan's governor called in the National Guard, which oversaw the peaceful move of Black families six weeks later.

The war charged the situation in dramatic ways. The federal government had the final say, yet exacerbated tensions by vacillating. And although liberals and other civic organizations and, tepidly, the mayor's office supported the Black community, the melee revealed a city that in the busy shifts of wartime work seemed to divide again and again into Black and white. Known as the "Arsenal of Democracy" thanks to one of Roosevelt's fireside chats, praised by the *New York Times* as the "Forge of Vulcan" that cast "engines of death," "Detroit the Dynamic" now bore the warning affixed by *Life* magazine in August 1942: "Detroit Is Dynamite." New jobs were going for $1.85 an hour. But with the "lusty" United Automobile Workers and its wildcat strikes, with "200,000 Polish Catholics" who populated a kind of "Polish island inside Detroit" (Hamtramck), and with "200,000 Southern whites who have migrated to Detroit with the barbecue stands and tent shouting evangelists" as well as "150,000 Negroes," along with groups of "Communists, Fascists, Ku-Kluxers," "Detroit seethes with racial, religious, political and economic unrest." The city "can either blow up Hitler or it can blow up the U.S."[49]

Black readers of *Life* would have read the "or" about Hitler or the United States a bit differently. Many justified Black militancy as helping the war effort, not hurting it, as unsympathetic commentators charged—John Temple Graves regarded African Americans' wartime pursuit of minority interests a form of extortion. Black Detroiters aligned the foreign force of Hitler *and* the domestic force of white reaction. Following the Sojourner Truth riots, many felt that "if we're going to die for democracy, we might just as well die here." Young people championed the "jitterbug" street fighters, while church elders found them misbehaved and aggressive. (It turned out that most of those arrested were Black, and most of those Black men were married, employed, and somewhat older—around thirty years old, the very people who had a stake in fair housing practices.)[50]

The global war was used to explain the willingness to pick the local fight. As the *Michigan Chronicle* saw it, "Nazis Capture

Detroit." "Negro-hating police, enemy aliens, Nazi Catholics, Ku Kluxers," it contended, had "declared open war upon democracy and the rights of the Negro people in Detroit." In the weeks after the riot, the talk became increasingly strident; editorials refused any maneuver to "appease the enemy forces here any more than we can appease the enemy forces abroad." Black leaders insisted on the necessity of waging "total war" without which "there can be no victory for democracy or a lasting peace in the world." "We have taken the announced war aims very seriously," the *Michigan Chronicle* explained to readers.[51]

Was it white reaction or Black resistance? Was it the Nazis or the jitterbug? Was it local rights or global charters? The Detroit chapter of the National Association for the Advancement of Colored People grew into one of the association's most active; over the course of the war, the NAACP emerged as a real power in American life, expanding from 350 branches and 50,000 members in 1940 to nearly 1,000 branches and 450,000 members five years later. Conscious of themselves as a proud, if wronged, minority, African Americans argued and organized to make plain the case for democracy. "There must be no blackout of this effort until full FREEDOM exists for ALL," insisted the *Pittsburgh Courier*. In the global context, "the black American understands the meaning of true democracy as few whites do," Edgar Rouzeau, a prominent journalist, pointed out.[52]

In Detroit as elsewhere, the fight for fair housing, with the aim to abolish covenants and redlines, to attain eligibility for federally financed mortgages, and to build up family wealth in home equity, continued for decades, and the effects of losing that fight lasted even longer. After World War II, the automobile permitted the growth of middle-class white suburbs outside Detroit's city limits, leaving mostly Black residents to languish on eroded tax foundations. In California, Richmond never recovered from the economic bust that followed the wartime boom. Step by step, the struggle over the common wealth lost potential when the commons diminished in size or the wealth moved somewhere else.

"THE NEWS DISPATCH follows the well-grooved pattern of lynching stories," *PM* explained. The particular case always distracted from recognizing the fact that white men routinely took the law into their own hands to enforce local codes of racial justice. Indeed, the omnipresent threat to resort to lynching was repeatedly invoked in stories people told about their hometowns— "Back where I come," whites in the Oakland shipyard would say about the "proper kind of home law." Lynching was one of the ways everybody knew a small town did things.[53]

After a lynching, white residents closed ranks in silence and complicity. Local newspapermen in the 1930s and 1940s chose to believe that "anything you say" about a lynching "will do more harm than good," as one concluded in Lillian Smith's 1944 best-selling novel, *Strange Fruit*; it would just "stir up a mare's nest." The actual circumstances involved two young Black boys and a white girl passing each other in Shubuta, a small lumber town of several hundred people in Clarke County, Mississippi. Ernest Green, fourteen years old, and Charlie Lang, a year older, were arrested for aggressive behavior and hauled to jail before a group of white men stole the accused boys from the county's jail and strung them from Shubuta's "hanging bridge" on October 12, 1942. The old railroad bridge was a well-known landmark because four Blacks, two men and two women, had been lynched there in December 1918.[54]

After the lynching in Shubuta, Langston Hughes wrote "Bitter River," in which the steel bars of the "hanging bridge" reflected on the surface of the water it crossed. "There is a bitter river / Dark with filth and mud . . . Too long has the taste of its water / Been in my mouth." The bitter river, Hughes continued, "That strangled my dream: / The book studied—but useless, / Tool handled—but unused, / Knowledge acquired but thrown away, / Ambition battered and bruised." What "it gives back" is "only the glint of steel bars": "The voteless share-cropper behind steel bars, / The labor leader behind steel bars, / The soldier thrown from a Jim Crow bus behind steel bars," and "my grandfather's back with its ladder of scars." "I did not ask for this river / Nor the taste of its bitter brew," Hughes reminded white readers: "I was given its water / As a gift from you." "'Wait, be patient,' you say / 'Your folks will have a better day,'" but, he replied, "the swirl of the bitter river / Takes your words away." "Tired now of the bitter river," Hughes wrote in the last stanza; "Tired now of the steel bars / Because my face is black."

At a dinner party in Harlem, guests talked and cried. They cursed the "kid-lynchers." "'It makes you wonder why the hell you should fight for a country that does that,' the doctor fumed. A 'pretty browned-skinned woman' spoke up next. 'When I think of my husband breaking up his career, leaving me and our little girl, going off to fight in some jungle to save this country so those so-and-so in Mississippi can lynch children,' she sighed, 'I just HATE white people.'" Another New Yorker, preacher Adam Clayton Powell, felt "the hour has arrived for Mississippi to secede from the Union" and be counted among the Axis powers. The reports from Clarke County and a photograph of the two children lying in the bed of a truck, hands tied behind their backs, nooses around their necks, enraged the Black community.

With that sort of war news, "the average Negro would rather give $5 to bomb a mob of Mississippi lynchers than to donate 5 cents to bomb a regiment of Japs or Germans," asserted one NAACP leader in Illinois. It was an appealing fantasy. When Canada Lee, who later starred in Hitchcock's *Lifeboat*, performed a skit about bringing the war home to "crackers down South" at a civil rights rally in Madison Square Garden in July 1942, he brought down the house.[55]

The coverage in the *New York Times* calibrated to wartime. It accepted the authorities' summary that the girl had been "waylaid" even as it condemned the lynching itself. The real issue was that "lynching is the best grist for the Nazi propaganda mill." "Why should our Negro people want to fight for the United States?" was a legitimate question, yet the *Times* drew up a "Negro Balance Sheet" to demonstrate the decline in lynching over the decades (sixty in the war years 1917–1919; four in recent years): "Such, then, is part of the answer to the Negro bill of grievances." This sort of detached response to a case of kidnapping and murder rankled staffers at *PM*, the upstart competitor to the *New York Times*. Victor Bernstein, a native New Yorker who in the 1930s had been the Berlin bureau chief for the Jewish Telegraphic Agency, might well have felt the *Times* missed the story.[56]

Bernstein had already gone south to "hang around awhile" in the summer of 1942. "Asking questions and drinking beer and cokes with new-found friends, you get the uneasy feeling that the war the South is fighting isn't the same war that the rest of the country is fighting." Bernstein heard people talk about "damyankees," which he learned was one word down south, and "uppity niggers." His friends told about "Negroes attacking white women" and "throwing white men off buses" and "strutting around in Uncle Sam's uniform 'as if they owned the world.'" Bernstein interviewed the secretary of Birmingham's Chamber of Commerce, "a very fat fellow," and "not very jolly." "'There's one thing you can put in your pipe and smoke,' Foster said to me. 'There's no white man down here goin' to let his daughter sleep with a nigger, or sit at the same table with a nigger, or go walkin' with a nigger.'" In fact, "the war can go to hell, the world can go to hell," but the white man "ain't goin' to do it." The demand for "the Negro's right to sleep with a white woman" was "the artificially contrived bugaboo of almost every Southerner," observed Bernstein. "You talk to him about giving the Negro a fair break with a job," and "somehow the argument winds up with threatened rape."[57] (Langston Hughes took up everybody's question, "Would you want your daughter to marry a Negro?" on a national radio broadcast in 1944. He remarked on the fact that "that Negro might not want to marry his daughter never seems to occur to the questioner." And "suppose the Negro did, all the daughter has to say is, 'No.'")[58]

In October, Bernstein returned to the South, this time to Clarke County. He talked to the governor who had referred to lynching as murder, but the governor did not want to talk about his "courageous stand," only the deeper reasons behind the killing. "You know we have certain prejudices down here," he explained to the reporter. "Down here" there was not a single white person who "would sit down with a Negro and eat with him at the same table. You know we'd rather die first, don't you?" Bernstein spoke to the "responsible businessman," who agreed that the lynching was an "outrage," but believed that Black people had to be kept in their place. "You mean hanging from a bridge?" Bernstein asked. "'No,' he said hastily. 'Not that.'" But "you Northerners get our backs up with all your shouting and hullabaloo. Why don't you leave us alone? We could settle our problems fine if you'd leave us alone." And "'How would you settle this one?' I asked. He didn't know."[59]

The voices of Black residents were harder to hear. "You must keep quiet to LIVE here," "colored people" across the county said to a reporter for Baltimore's *Afro-American* "in trembling and whispering voices." A Black person could get lynched for anything, remembered Charles Yates, who grew up in Shubuta—for "using the front door instead of the back door" or not moving off the sidewalk for "Miss Ann or Mr. Charles." "If you were Black in Mississippi," he wrote, "lightning would surely strike home sooner or later." Not talking, but walking: since the last war, the Black population of Clarke County had declined by 30 percent.[60]

Bernstein was not the only reporter to travel to Clarke County, but the overall pattern of conversation was the same. Any compromise on inequality would unravel all of Jim Crow. Whether the issue was employment, housing, or the ballot box, the whole question of rights always ended up in the bedroom with the sanctity of white womanhood standing for white supremacy. Social responsibility was one thing, laudable for Blacks to achieve, but "social equality" was unacceptable (a mix-up of the two phrases provides the comic opening to Ralph Ellison's *Invisible Man*).

White liberals minced no words explaining that southerners would never agree to any revision of segregation. In time of war, they used robust battlefield imagery to make their point. According to Virginius Dabney, the "liberal" editor of Richmond's *Times Dispatch*, "if an attempt is made forcibly to abolish segregation throughout the South, violence and bloodshed will result." As a member of the Fair Employment Practice Committee, Mark Etheridge, the "liberal" editor of the *Louisville*

Courier-Journal, hoped to set the record straight for northern liberals and southern Blacks who needed to "recognize that there is no power in the world—not even in all the mechanized armies of the earth, Allied and Axis—which could now force the Southern white people to the abandonment of the principle of social segregation."[61] No liberal voice or reporter's notebook or poll revealed anything but unanimity on segregation; it was not a complex issue for southern whites, and no single part of social life, not eating, or working, or soldiering, could be pried from the whole. Even common courtesy was viewed with suspicion. Rumors passed on the effrontery that domestics wished to "be called 'Miss' and 'Mrs.' and not just their first names." This was a time when southern newspapers refrained from using courtesy titles such as "Mr." or "Mrs." when referring to Blacks.[62]

Genuinely alarming to white southerners was the reassertion of the idea that universal suffrage should apply across all the United States; it made sense since the country was fighting the war to defend democracy. The Congress's effort to end the poll tax that disenfranchised about three-quarters of all adults in the South passed the House of Representatives by a vote of 252–84 the day after the Shubuta lynchings; a filibuster led by southern senators in November 1942 repulsed the effort to intervene in state elections. (The poll tax aimed to deny Blacks the right to vote, but with the result that most of the people barred from voting were in fact white.) "In making this fight against the unconstitutional anti–poll tax bill," explained Mississippi's senator Theodore Bilbo, "I feel that I am as much a soldier in the preservation of the American way and American scheme of Government as the boys who are fighting and dying on Guadalcanal." When whites complained about "damyankees" sticking their nose in the business of the South, they were thinking first about the poll tax, the cornerstone to all-white Democratic Party primaries and states' rights. After Shubuta, one Mississippi newspaper noted self-righteously: "Washington is sowing tragic seed. We must harvest bitter fruit."[63]

The untouchability of segregation created the illusion that it upheld a stable, well-suited southern way of life, with "magnolia blossoms and mint julep colonels." Sociologists even spoke of the "realistic folkways of the South" as if they constituted an organic order, characterized by a particular mode of production. Yet this "racial dream world" rested on constant violence. Predictions of "race war" confirmed the wobbliness of race relations. Lynchings themselves testified to the fact that "the Negro in his place" was not settled. Indeed, the issue of being soft on race proved decisive in primary elections.[64] The subordination of all economic and social issues to race created a society highly mobilized to defend its "way of life," the "solid South" that emerged in the 1930s and 1940s. Below the Mason-Dixon Line, mass politics revolved around race.

The white South mounted its own Double-V campaign, victory abroad and victory at home, which was defined as the entrenchment of white supremacy based on states' rights. The South's "Double Victory" was also regarded in global terms as a struggle against totalitarianism, since both fascism and Communism threatened indigenous liberties. According to Graves, the United States was not fighting "for democracy"; it was fighting for "states rights, for the right of individual lands not to be invaded by outsiders, not to be dictated to or aggressed against." In this view, southern vigilantes were not the ones who helped Hitler, but the northern agitators who provoked them and had their own "(Axis?) axe to grind."[65]

In the global fight against totalitarianism, the South identified its enemies but not its friends, except to point out that northern whites were "no different." It is true that polls showed broad support for segregation among whites in the North, as their own behavior so often attested. But support varied, with differently sized pluralities lining up for segregation at the workplace, in the military, in restaurants, in neighborhoods, and in marriage, whereas southern majorities were nearly unanimous on every single issue.[66] In 1942, there was no awareness in the South of efforts of whites in South Africa to advance segregation.

"Highly motivated for self-defense," believing its own homeland to be a theater of operations in the greater war, the South militarized the advocacy of its way of life. The end of segregation could be conceived only as a complete military defeat for a home army of true believers. Segregation was generally not regarded as a problem, something southerners needed to figure out on their own, but as the core to white (and patriarchal) identity. Jim Crow was defeated in the 1950s and 1960s by internal Black revolt (and exit) and external federal pressure against the almost unanimous will of white southerners. It left behind all the soldiers who had failed to safeguard the double victory. This defeat allowed ghosts of white supremacy and states' rights to return in many shifting forms right up to the present day, moving around as the living dead long after the establishment of fair-employment practices, the abolition of the poll tax, and the Supreme Court's finding for the unconstitutionality of prohibitions against interracial sex and marriage.

CHAPTER 17

Johannesburg, South Africa

Daisy invited Dick to a *marabi* dance in Malay Camp, an African settlement on the outskirts of Johannesburg. Three shillings for them both, and five more for a bottle of wine. Dick could see that "nearly all the men wore suits and nearly all the women had long dresses." "A man sat pounding out a savagely monotonous rhythm on the piano," while "couples clung to each other," moving slowly. Their bodies swayed "from side to side like mealie stalks," which provided the daily cornmeal, or like "train coaches sway between the stations of Langlaagte and Croesus" on the railway journey to the big city and back.[1] Daisy and Dick danced to the wildly popular music called *marabi*, or township jazz, played by small combos with a piano and guitar and a tin can filled with stones for rhythm at countless house parties. Johannesburg's Jazz Maniacs and the Merry Blackbirds made a name for themselves performing *marabi* in African dance halls like the Bantu Men's Social Centre downtown. It was Johannesburg's Solomon Linda and His Evening Birds who "combined *marabi* with Zulu choral harmonies" in the 1939 hit "Mbube," which was later covered by the Tokens in "The Lion Sleeps Tonight," South Africa's most famous song.[2]

With an "endlessly repeated chord sequence," *marabi* performed "rhythmically propulsive dance music." Partygoers danced away Saturday nights in the tumbledown townships in which Africans made their homes after moving to the city. The dances, and the drinking in shebeens, the private houses that sold illegal home-brewed beer, were weekend attractions for the miners who walked over from the men's hostels around the pits or domestics who had a night out from life in the white suburbs, Park Lane or the Hill. After a week of work, they dressed up and met up, walked over to the townships like Malay Camp, and danced "to make life sweet and brilliant," Johannesburg's African newspaper *Bantu World* explained.[3]

Marabi was more than "hot, highly rhythmic" dance tunes; it was "the name of an epoch." Its material was the "drama, tragedy, and comedy in the life of a people" who had been "rendered landless and homeless and exploited by an alien race in the land of their birth." The African population of Johannesburg increased from 229,000 in 1936 to 384,000 in 1946. The majority of white South Africans had long lived in the cities, but during World War II most city residents had become Africans. By 1942, Africans could no longer be regarded as "temporary sojourners" on leave from the tribal reserves that the "natives" had been allotted in the countryside.[4]

Young Africans had become city people, and they created a modern, jazz-inflected music for the new conglomeration of migrants to dance to on weekends. *Marabi* was stamped out of urban experience that inside a generation had formed the Bantu, the people, in the rhythms of work and play.

THE STORY OF twentieth-century South Africa is one of the steady imposition of a strict regime of legal apartheid to insulate the minority of white settlers who controlled the economic enterprise and political fate of the country and to manage the unwelcome masses of black Africans whose presence in the cities had become an established fact alongside that enterprise. English colonists imagined that with "civilization," more residents would eventually obtain political rights, a prospect incorporated in Cape Town's qualified franchise in which, until its abolition in 1937, small numbers of black Africans and "coloured" or "mixed race" remained on voters' rolls. But the segregationist views of the larger community of Afrikaans-speaking Dutch prevailed in practice. For the most part, Dutch South Africans or Afrikaners regarded themselves as constituents of a pure, select, and separate republic of God in which Africans performed their appointed task as "hewers of wood and drawers of water." While African labor followed white enterprise into the mines and cities, the idea was that "natives" were "permitted within municipal areas in so far and for so long as their presence is demanded by the wants of the white population." According to 1920s legislation, they were to "depart therefrom when they cease to minister to the needs of the white man."[5] The places "natives" belonged were the rural reserves that, by the twentieth century, amounted to very small and poor parcels of land; if men sojourned to the cities, they also returned home to their tribes and families, a "rural world of chiefly governance and customary law" that kept Africans outside the political and social order of the modern state.[6]

The racial scheme based on temporary needs foundered on industry's demand for unskilled and semiskilled labor, which pulled both poor whites and blacks from the impoverished countryside into the cities. It collapsed completely in the war that strengthened the industrial economy.

With urban settlement came the unquenchable demand for domestics whose numbers provided the final confirmation that black men and women played a permanent (if totally unequal) part in city life. "One had to be a very poor white not to have employed a servant"—a nanny, a gardener, a cook. The Communist newspaper the *Guardian* poked fun at the entitlement in a "Sunday Drive" in 1942. "We went to Orlando location," looking for a cook:[7]

> We want a girl who can cook.
> Who will tidy the flat.
> Who will wash, darn and iron.
> Who will put out the cat.
> Who will get £3 a month
> For doing all that

In a population of about twelve million people at the end of the war, there were more than 550,000 black domestic servants. The ratio of African men to women in the cities declined from 3:1 in 1921 to 1.8:1 in 1946.[8]

The war endangered the idea of a white-only South Africa, but it also enforced apartheid. As Africans pointed out, non-Europeans around the world were on the march against European rule, the Japanese most obviously, but also colonial subjects who demanded the rights and liberties outlined in the Atlantic Charter. "Today, up North," in Egypt with the British Eighth Army, African "boys are shedding blood in defense of South Africa and the Democratic World." "They cannot, when they come back," the *Bantu World* insisted, "be expected to live under conditions that are incompatible with the principles of democratic life," the lack of basic social services, the denial of political representation, and restrictions on free movement. Even government ministers referred to the "New March of Liberalism" that would loosen segregation. In the world war, "we see before us a world—the new world," proclaimed an editorial in the *Bantu World* in 1942.[9]

The war shook up whites in South Africa. As in the United States, war in the city broke out at the front door by intensifying struggles of belonging and contests over space. The hustle and bustle in Johannesburg made interactions among different kinds of city people more common but also more racially charged. The war vastly increased the demand for unskilled and semiskilled work in the mines and in expanded and more mechanized manufacturing shops. However, craft-based labor unions resisted advancing Africans who would scramble the equation of race with skill, agreeing instead to the recruitment of as many temporary white women as possible. Even so, white residents had the impression that public spaces had become "infested with natives," with "their bundles of blankets and mealie meal and other paraphernalia." Municipal authorities moved to banish Black entrepreneurs from downtown areas by clearing out "cafés de move-on," the street vendors on whom African commuters depended.[10]

In the suburbs, residents looked out to see Africans "prowling" the streets. These were their servants. In between the headlines about Stalingrad and advertisements for the patriotic movie about the Blitz *Mrs. Miniver,* more popular even than *Gone with the Wind,* readers posted angry letters about their own "state of siege" in which "every window is screwed down, doors are locked and bolted, and a loaded revolver and a torch are kept handy." In order to keep Johannesburg "white at night," authorities were urged to "first win the war, then clear the slums" by moving all of the city's African residents in Sophiatown and other freehold neighborhoods to "locations" such as Malay Camp or the Southwestern Townships (Soweto) outside the city.[11]

The proposals of the 1940s had all come to pass by the late 1950s when urban blacks of all income classes lived in standardized (and substandard) housing in controlled locations.

While criminals did in fact menace both whites and blacks in 1942, it was white nationalists who bombed government buildings to protest the war and its British-style reforms. They wrecked the offices of the *Bantu World* and assaulted Africans in the streets.

"A huge bony Afrikaner prodded me in the ribs," recalled novelist E'skia Mphahlele, who had been watching a parade downtown: "Step out, Kaffir! This is no monkey show." Another man "slapped me a few times on the cheek." Each insult "came back, fresh and poisonous, to plague my sleepless hours." Wherever he went, "I was 'Jimmed' and 'boy-ed' and 'John-ed' by whites." Whites in turn expected to be called "baas," or boss. "Beware of the white man, he's very, very strong," Mphahlele remembered his mother saying.[12]

In the city, the "black man" saw his shadow grow longer, and blacker.

THIS WAS THE busy city of collision and trespass that Dick first saw when he climbed to the top of a hill right after his arrival. From farm to dorp to city, from road to railroad, people made for the city. "All roads lead to Johannesburg" was the refrain of Alan Paton's classic novel about South Africa *Cry, the Beloved Country* (1948). And the roads filled up during the war. Before him, Dick saw a vast sea of twinkling lights. After a while, the stars arranged themselves into different social constellations: "Slum is darkness. Dark folk live in darkness. Beyond Malay Camp, a little to the left again, was white Fordsburg. White: lights. Black: darkness." "To the right of me, beyond the heart of the city, lights moved away in waves." Each place told its own tales of "laughter and tears; of loves and hates; of death and of life."[13] "The song of the city."

"This is the city, and I am one of the citizens"—Abrahams's epigram comes from Walt Whitman—but in Johannesburg every move collided with race. The song of the city, the beat of *marabi*, was "like a stream through which flowed the pent-up emotions of a repressed people," wrote Peter Abrahams, a coloured novelist. His character Dick was engulfed by the "mass rhythm," but "like a stream the two-point rhythm washed away" all the troubles "so that on the morrow the houseboy would be a good and humble house-boy! And the kitchen-maid too. And the mine-boy. And the riksha-boy." And then it was *marabi* again, "and again peace and good work and again the Maraba. So the circle went round." The "song of the city" went around as well: a voice "took up the song and told of the odyssey of a young man who had come to the big city and had been arrested and imprisoned for seven years." Then "the song was picked up" by other voices. Echoing the hum of the work stations, with chords of travail today and hope tomorrow, "it is the song of the big city," explained Daisy. "Tomorrow you will add something on to it, and then someone else, and after yet another person."

Marabi constituted a counterpublic, a swing alternative to the Christian assimilationism and church chorals of middle-class Africans and to the color bars imposed by Europeans. You didn't stay in your place at the dance: Daisy had invited Dick, and couples walked to the shebeen and swayed on the dance floor. *Marabi* beat out the anticipation of the newcomer who arrived by train. In Joshua Mohapeloa's charming "Chuchumakhela," a female vocalist fronting a male choir sang about the "choo-choo train" winding its way from Maseru to Johannesburg accompanied by the *"Oi-oi-i-I* of the siren and the *chu-chu, chu-chu* puff." The Merry Blackbirds performed the song about a police raid on the illegal beer-brewing that replenished the dance parties. *Marabi* protested the ubiquitous pass laws that controlled the movement of Africans in the city: "I can hear the big curfew-bell at the police-station peal 'ten to ten, ten to ten, ten to ten' for the Black man to be out of the streets to be at home to be out of the policeman's reach." "It was always like this," recounted Mphahlele: "Saturday night and torchlights; Saturday night and police whistles; Saturday night and screams"; Saturday night and white man's "cursing and swearing."[14]

The next day, "the yard was as muddy as a cattle kraal, and the smell of beer, thrown out by the police on their raids," combined with "the stench of the lavatories." Mofele Yard was also home to twenty people, overcrowded in rooms without electricity under tin roofs that burned red-hot in summer and left occupants blue with cold in winter.[15]

The budget of unskilled workers who lived in the segregated yards was very skinny. According to a 1942 government survey—and these were the changing war times when government surveyed social conditions—it was "more remarkable for what it omits than what it includes." It did not allow "a penny for amusements, for sport, for medicine, for education, for savings," not a penny "for holidays, for odd bus rides, for newspapers, stationery, tobacco, sweets, hobbies, gifts," or comforts of any kind. The wage was insufficient for a "'human' standard of living."[16]

Race defined work as well as housing. "Poor whites" identified more as white than as poor. Already in 1922 a general strike against the use of the cheaper unskilled African labor had been waged under the banner "Workers of the World Unite and Fight for a White South Africa!" and they subsequently became beneficiaries of a "civilized labor" policy that applied the color bar to semiskilled work and raised wages; otherwise, "the white man becomes a white kaffir," explained Prime Minister J. B. M. Hertzog. In the railways, for example, the number of unskilled white workers rose from 9.5 to 39 percent between 1924 and 1933, while the proportion of blacks fell from 75 to 49 percent.[17] South Africa's Labor Party and even its Communist Party had a hard time thinking of workers as anything but white. As a result of the color bar, the ratio of unskilled to skilled wage rates was one of the worst in the world: 1:6 in 1938 as opposed to 1:1.3 in Britain and the United States.

What most angered Africans was the pass system that kept them in a perpetual state of confinement. Abrahams, who as a "coloured" man was exempt from the controls, had the system explained to him: When "Jim" decided to leave his village in the northern Transvaal, "he had to go to the nearest police station" to get a Trek Pass. "This permitted him to make the journey to Johannesburg. On reaching the city he got an *Identification Pass* and a *Six-Day Special Pass*. He paid two shillings each month for the Identification Pass. The Six-Day Special was his protection while he looked for work." Once he found a job, he got a *Monthly Pass*. "Like all house-boys," he wanted "to visit places like Vrededorp and Malay Camp, to drink a little, find a woman if he was lucky, and get to know the life of the city. But these places were outside the district in which he was registered. To go there without fear of being picked up, he got a *Travelling Pass*. When he got to know black people of the city and wanted to visit them on his Sunday off, he got a *Day Special Pass* from his employer, made the journey, and got a *Location Visitor's Pass* from the superintendent of the location where his friends lived. Armed with these two, he could enter the location freely." And "to talk without fear after nine at night he had to have a *Night Special Pass*."[18]

The result of the pass system was to criminalize the city's African population, the majority of whom had violated pass laws at one point in their lives. Most people in South Africa's jails were blacks convicted of pass offenses even after the laws were relaxed for a short time during the war. Of course, Africans had elaborate methods of "escaping, hoodwinking and baffling the law" so that the outlaw earned his place in popular culture.[19]

The definition of race, the codification of behavior, and the control of movement completely disfigured everyday life. In more liberal Cape Town, amenities such as parks, museums, and libraries were open to all because laws did not require separate lavatories. However, swimming pools were segregated, and white-owned businesses, including restaurants and cafés, did not serve Africans or "coloured." Given the unfolding legal landscapes, coloured, who were the progeny of early Dutch settlers and "native" women, had trouble proving they were not African. Yet coloured people often preferred Johannesburg to Cape Town because it was easier to pass as non-African. Ralph Bunche, a professor of political science at Howard University, found that the people he met on a 1937 visit were surprised that he identified as African when he could have passed as coloured. Peter Abrahams also contended with fellow coloured, who, he discovered, opposed on principle marriage to an African. "Would you approve if she were your sister?" Abrahams was asked since, whatever the African's education, "he's still Black!" "It's the same thing!" Abrahams objected: the Afrikaner "says it of all the non-Whites and you say it of the Blacks." "You're either for or against the colour bar," he insisted, and "if you're against it you're against it all the way." It was a position that earned him a rebuke: "So you don't really care about your own people, Mr. Abrahams."[20]

For their part, Africans mocked coloureds who had neither kings nor history before the white man. In other words, they did not belong by right or might. Africans themselves divided according to tribe and language. The Zulus may have had kings, but were disparaged for being "Uncle Toms" by serving as "native" policemen.

"South Africa is an *entire* country ridden by race prejudice," concluded Bunche; paper passes and color bars meant that "there is absolutely no escape at all for these black and coloured people."[21]

Marabi was one way to unspool a new kind of history beyond the shadows cast by whites. So was the Bantu Men's Social Centre on Eloff Street on the southern edge of Johannesburg's downtown. (*Bantu* refers to "people" as opposed to nation or tribe.) Abrahams described his first visit there in the 1930s:

"Black men appeared from everywhere"; "the men about me, their faces, their bearing, carried all the proof. That was a black man! The voice of a black man!"—they all spoke English at the center, a language Afrikaans-speaking Abrahams would adopt as his own. At one end of the room, across from the billiard table, was a shelf of books. "I reached up and took out a fat black book. *The Souls of Black Folk*, by W. E. B. Du Bois. I turned the pages. It spoke about a people in a valley. And they were black and dispossessed, and denied. I skimmed though the pages"—"The Negro is not free." Abrahams wondered why he had not thought it through before. What did come to mind was a walk that he, not restricted by a pass, had taken around Johannesburg. Abrahams recalled that when he wanted a cup of tea, he saw a sign, "Reserved for Europeans Only"; when he sought a bench to rest, "Reserved for Europeans Only"; and when he needed to "piddle," the sign on the lavatories read "Reserved for Europeans Only." "Now," however, "having read the words, I knew that I had known" the part about not being free "all along. But until now I had had no words to voice that knowledge." For Abrahams, Du Bois's words lit up a road: "The problem of the Twentieth Century is the problem of the color-line—the relation of the darker to the lighter races of men in Asia and Africa, in America and the islands of the sea."[22]

The Bantu Men's Social Centre featured a whole shelf of books by African Americans.

Eloff Street was the hub of African culture, sport, and politics in Johannesburg. The social center hosted *marabi* parties in its large hall. On a Friday night in October 1942, "the Merry Blackbirds Band assembled on the stage and itching feet itched more. They played, presenting a girl trumpeter, Sarah Monkoe," as well as young trombonist Abel P. Matante, to a "fair" house of "Bantu, Coloureds, and Europeans." There were also cinema and theater. Poking around the center, Abrahams met amateur boxers who championed American prizefighter Joe Louis. He enrolled himself in "an Atlas body-building course to be a man." As a result of his visits, Abrahams became "a color nationalist," and nationalists like him certainly met up with regulars such as Nelson Mandela (a swing dancer himself) and Walter Sisulu, who founded the African National Congress's Youth League on the premises on Easter Sunday in 1944. (Sisulu and his wife, Albertine, held their wedding reception at the center later in July.) The league resolved to press the "African claims" against tyranny that the African Nationalist Congress, the oldest and most important black freedom movement in South Africa, believed the Atlantic Charter had legitimated. The ANC opened the fight for the "common people" who belonged to the "new world" opened by the "people's war."[23]

The work to build democracy in wartime South Africa was hard. There were bus boycotts against higher fares to the locations, but African trade unionists had a difficult time since they were not recognized by the all-white federation with which the government and employers negotiated. A wartime petition against pass laws fell well short of the one million signatures organizers had hoped to collect. In any case, the gentle breeze of reform championed by white liberals died down in the dusk of 1942, when at year's end South Africa no longer seemed threatened by Germans "up North" or Japanese in the Indian Ocean. By contrast, white nationalists were much more able to overturn the "café de move-on" and lay foundations for their apartheid regime. After the National Party's victory in the 1948 elections, national laws made the cities "white at night," eventually forcing Johannesburg's Bantu Men's Social Centre to close in 1971. (Abrahams died in Jamaica in 2017.)

ON AUGUST 8, 1938, two ox wagons, or *ossewa*, pulled to the base of Table Mountain in Cape Town. The occupants dressed up in pioneer costumes, the men in corduroys and women in long dresses and *kappies*, or sunbonnets. They were participating in a reenactment of the Great Trek in which, beginning for several decades after 1838, descendants of the original Dutch settlers in Cape Colony, since the end of the Napoleonic era a British possession, had reestablished independent settlements in the South African hinterland. Prompted by the British Empire's abolition of slavery in 1834, the treks populated two Dutch republics, Transvaal (with its capital in Pretoria) and Orange Free State (Bloemfontein). Proposed by the "Afrikaans Language and Cultural Union," an association of white workers in the South African Railways, the reenactment was supposed to deepen a sense of Afrikaner identity among the impoverished white migrants who had made the second great trek into the cities. After thousands of well-wishers gathered in Cape Town to see the wagons off, journalists and broadcasters scrambled to accompany the entire trek, which they covered with daily updates along the way. The wagons were scheduled to arrive at Monument Hill outside Pretoria on December 16, Dingaan's Day, a holiday marking the centenary of the defeat of the Zulu king and his armies by outnumbered voortrekkers in the Battle of Blood River. In this spot about halfway between Durban and Pretoria, Afrikaners recognized God's covenant with their people.

The crowds grew larger and more fiery in every town along the journey. According to radio reporter Gideon Roos, "The spirit of the Trek had really fired the imagination of the entire nation": "Every night stop of the waggons became the occasion, not only for celebration, but for the re-enactment of incidents from local history." It was a real "jamboree," wrote a reporter for the *Sunday Express*, complete with bands and campfires and people grilling *boerewors*, or sausages, pioneer style on *braaivleis*, or rustic barbecues. The voortrekker trousers, the beards, and the *braavileis* all became fashions of the day. "Even the hard-bitten representatives of press and radio were imbued with the same spirit," recalled Roos, "and soon they were all clad in the voortrekker costumes and cultivating beards."[24]

No words were sung with greater gusto than the verse "We will live, we will die, we for thee South-Africa," from "Die Stem van Suid-Afrika," the new national anthem that was paired up with "God Save the King." Gradually, "we" evolved from the Europeans, who, in Roos's telling, had advanced the "epoch-making" triumph of "civilization over barbarism," to the Afrikaners themselves. Across South Africa, voortrekkers collected funds to aid "poor whites" in the cities in "The Act of Rescue" and spread the spirit of Afrikaner independence that had been defeated in the Boer Wars that had led to the establishment in 1910 of the Union of South Africa, an enlarged British colony. Like all good nationalists, the trekkers stopped at the graveside—first, as planned, at places commemorating the massacres of Afrikaner pioneers by Zulu tribesmen, then, as enthusiasm grew, at sites where Afrikaner patriots had been executed by British soldiers. The young writer Alan Paton arrived at Monument Hill in Pretoria having "trekked from Johannesburg by ox-wagon 'flying the Vierkleur flag of the defeated Transvaal

Republic.'" All around him Afrikaners saluted themselves: "Now we're going to knock hell out of the English." By the time the trek arrived in Pretoria, the very idea of playing "God Save the King" alongside "Die Stem" seemed to "defile" rebel pride. As a result, Prime Minister Hertzog and other officials stayed home.[25]

Dingaan's Day belonged to Daniel François Malan, the leader of the opposition Purified National Party, an Afrikaner contingent that had refused to join the merger, in 1934, of Hertzog's National Party and Jan Smuts's more empire-friendly South Africa Party with the mutual goal of securing Dominion status, that is, de facto independence from Britain, and building a modern country. (Held in May 1938, South Africa's whites-only national elections had returned 27 members to Malan's opposition, up from the 20 who had originally broken away; the United Party retained 111 of 150 seats.) Malan was an Afrikaner nationalist, an ardent republican who disdained the equal standing of the English language (and "God Save the King") and mistrusted the imperial affiliations of Smuts and English-speaking South Africans whom he believed opened doors to racial equality and sullied God's covenant with the "People" saved at Blood River. He admired the anti-British thrust of Hitler's Germany, a country Malan believed to have been wronged at Versailles, as Afrikaners had been in the Boer War, but he rejected a one-party state, or *Führerstaat*.

One in 10 Afrikaners, 100,000 in all, gathered at Monument Hill. They camped out to listen to Malan declare that "the battleground has been moved, and the task to keep South Africa a white man's land, which has become ten times heavier than before, rests on the shoulders of those who are the least able to bear it." White Afrikaners had left the farms and settled in the cities, the new frontier for black Africans as well. "One hundred years ago," Malan explained, "the circle of white-tented wagons protected the laager"; however, "today black and white jostle in the same labor market." Therefore, "Our Blood River lies in the city and our Voortrekkers are our poor who, in the most difficult circumstances, have to take up the cudgels for our nation against the swelling dark tidal wave."[26]

The reenactment of the past was a declaration of independence in the present: a white South Africa based on the exclusion of Africans to re-create the Dutch republics and restore God's covenant with the Afrikaners. In one hundred years' time, "the generation of 2038" would "judge the generation of 1938 on whether or not it had succeeded in preserving the Afrikaner nation and keeping South Africa a white man's country." (Today Dingaan's Day is celebrated in South Africa as the "Day of Reconciliation," which commemorates the start of armed struggle against apartheid by the African National Congress on December 16, 1961, as well as the Battle of Blood River on the same day in 1838.)[27]

The voortrekkers built on the idea of *apartheid*, or separateness, a term that gained currency during the war. Apartheid combined two related meanings, one very clear and the other somewhat obfuscatory. First, it rested on the consolidation of racial segregation to establish white dominion in which Africans had no civic place. Second, it projected separate paths of development for Africa's white and black "tribes" while preserving South Africa as a "white man's land." In the view of Afrikaner nationalists, the British Empire beckoned a common future based on universal values, while apartheid ensured separateness.[28]

The struggle to realize the Afrikaners' tribal vision was realized after the war: the parliamentary victory of Malan's party in

1948, the creation of a national apartheid regime, and the severance of the remaining imperial ties to Britain with the founding of the Republic of South Africa in 1961.

THE CENTENARY OF the Great Trek in 1938 provided Afrikaner nationalists a fair guide to the rapid-fire developments brought on by the war. The war put focus on relations between Afrikaners and the English, the place of South Africa in a world divided by Axis ideology, and the role of the majority black population in the country's future among the Allied nations. The immediate effect of the war was an acceleration of long-term trends: the expansion of South Africa's manufacturing base and with it the continued migration of Africans into the cities. But war insistently raised the question of who exactly "will live" and "will die" for "thee South-Africa." In the first place, South Africa's participation in the war was hotly contested—only 7 votes in a chamber of 153 (3 seats held by whites to represent "Natives" had been added) decided the declaration of war on September 4, 1939. Given these divisions, the war itself left unresolved whether South Africa's future lay existing apart as a white republic, the vision of those who voted against the war and eventually followed Malan, or whether the future would be claimed by joining South Africa with the commonwealth of nations in a liberal global order, the premise of those who followed Jan Smuts, the new prime minister, and voted for the war.

A spirit of reform followed the declaration of war and especially its expansion in 1942. In the end, however, neither the emergency of war nor liberal alignment with the democratic aims of the Allies overcame the racial fears that united whites more than reform divided them. The liberal or imperial alternative to Afrikaner nationalism was not coherent because enough whites in South Africa shared the existential fear of black majority rule. To this day, debates about the alternatives opened up in the 1940s revolve around the plausibility of a third way between both Afrikaner and African nationalism, between apartheid and majority rule as championed by the African National Congress, the main liberation movement in South Africa.[29] Put like this, the third way sets up a false equivalence that recalls the basic weakness of reformers during the war.

Like white southerners in the United States, many Afrikaners rejected the democratic claims of the world war. The difference was that Afrikaners opposed the war on these grounds, while southerners reconfigured the defense of states' rights as a democratic war aim. Both, however, made an exclusive historical claim on their lands, and both correctly estimated the dangers to white rule posed by the universal ideas animating the global war. And both shared an illogic: that their own acute awareness of the perils of enfranchisement served as an adequate defense against it. Yet in the short term, Afrikaners and southerners thought they won the war. Apartheid was put on firm foundations in South Africa until the early 1990s, while white supremacy remained in place in the US South at least through the mid-1960s.

Most of white South Africa probably stood behind Smuts and the declaration of war, but the opposition was large and vocal. Some, including Smuts, found Nazism's racialism abhorrent, more corrosive to the idea of common Christian civilization than even Bolshevism.[30] Afrikaners, on the other hand, wished the Third Reich well. It was an ideological confederate and a military force strong enough to break up Britain's empire. In this regard, Afrikaners never displayed the "cognitive dissonance" of white southerners who eagerly fought Adolf Hitler while anxiously defending Jim Crow.[31]

Across the Union of South Africa, everyday scenes reproduced the irrevocable split of the United Party, one part of which remained with Smuts, while the other amalgamated with Malan in 1940 to form the Reunified National Party (the "Reunified" was dropped after the party's election victory in 1948). Most pedestrians stood still during the two minutes of silence that followed the firing of the noonday gun from Signal Hill in Cape Town, but there were those who went ostentatiously about their business. Cinema audiences took up the duels of the two national anthems, hooting and hollering during newsreels. Street-corner fights broke out on Saturday nights as both sides recruited foot soldiers—the Afrikaner nationalist organization Ossewabrandwag, the ox-wagon guardians or sentinels that had formed after the reenactment of the trek, boasted some 340,000 followers by 1941. This was a very large group, about equal to the number enlisted in the Union Defence Forces, in a white South African population of two million. The sentinels beat up soldiers marked with the red blazes (*rooi lussies*—some called them *rooi luises*, or red lice) that indicated their willingness to fight anywhere on the continent, while Allied sailors in port went after bearded men. So many rocks were thrown at Malan's home in Cape Town that he moved to Stellenbosch.[32]

The Ossewabrandwag represented a genuine fifth-column threat that receded only after the government prohibited civil servants from membership and after Allied victories demoralized the secret army. Throughout the first half of 1942, in step with the Japanese and German offensives, saboteurs cut telephone wires and bombed department stores, post offices, and other buildings across South Africa. At the end of May, a bomb destroyed the Danish Pavilion on the grounds of Johannesburg's Liberty Cavalcade, a fund-raising exhibition at the zoo. (The entertainment the next evening featured a civil-defense exercise with sirens and searchlights in which "planes will 'bomb' Cavalcade.") In South Africa, the front lines of the colonial war that cut across the geopolitical one were plain to see.[33]

The union's defense forces fought and died in the world war, but no other country in the Allied sphere expressed conflicts about the new global order as starkly as did South Africa.

The Afrikaner opposition imagined itself as protagonists in a sacred salvation history in which they were besieged by "cycles of suffering and death," the Great Trek, Blood River, the Boer War. What was not for Afrikaners was alien and, on a basic level, inadmissible. By contrast, Smuts inserted South Africa into the wider world. He was intellectually open, insofar as he was a structural thinker in which parts found places in larger wholes. But he was limited by believing that stable structures repelled the radical or qualitative change that created new compositions. In practice, he sought to adjust, not alter, South Africa.

Tellingly, Smuts was an amateur botanist rather than an amateur zoologist who would have required more fluency in evolutionary biology. He was fascinated by the paleoanthropological evidence of the African origins of humanity, which Louis Leakey would later make renowned. For Smuts, however, these discoveries did not confirm the sameness of human beings but rather validated the antiquity of their differences.

In Smuts's view, the British Empire was evolving into a commonwealth of regionally important dominions, each with autonomous character and separate responsibilities but connected to the whole. The future of South Africa lay in assuming the leadership of southern Africa. For that reason, he was able to regard

Johannesburg as a powerful economic and financial hub, connected to London, the European capitals, and the United States and drawing in migrants from across southern Africa. Precisely the functional importance of the parts kept him from accepting the prospect of their dissolution in the undifferentiated whole of majority rule.[34]

The world war confirmed Smuts's way of thinking. The Italian invasion of British Somaliland in August 1940 posed a regional threat to South Africa and provided practical justification for the deployment of South African troops in North Africa. South Africa also assumed geopolitical importance as Japan advanced in the Indian Ocean. Durban became a major port along supply lines from the Atlantic Ocean to the Middle East and East Asia. Smuts himself was deeply involved in the planning of the preemptive Allied invasion of Madagascar in May 1942. Malan, by contrast, dismissed Japan as an "imaginary threat," since its deterrence would require adopting an internationalist outlook.[35]

The world war also warranted Smuts's descriptions of South Africa and of relations between blacks and whites in a field of wider forces. South Africa's part in the global whole Smuts outlined in an important speech at the Institute for Race Relations in Johannesburg on January 21, 1942. He put a good face on "the best of feeling between white and black up in the new big army we have in the north." South Africa was part of a greater African mobilization, which he championed. What Smuts did not say was that the experience of South Africa's unarmed black soldiers in North Africa "made the social structures at home seem both mean and petty."[36]

The war made it easier for Smuts to concede the inevitability of African migration into South Africa's cities and the "intermixture of the various Native tribes and races." "How could it be otherwise?" he asked. What Smuts focused on was social development promoted by intergroup communication and "interstate trade." Isolation has "gone for good" in South Africa, he argued. This was the social science language of globalism. It was at odds with Malan's moral attachment to the white tribe and also with Africans' constitutional demands for the right of every citizen to vote and determine the future. Smuts depicted a common future among groups, not equal rights for all people.

Smuts was proud to recognize South Africa as a society of more than ten million people. "When people ask 'What is the population of South Africa?'" he explained, "I never say 'Two million.' I think it is an outrage to say two million. It is an insult." With ten million in mind, Smuts believed that "segregation has fallen on evil days, too." What did he propose for the ten million inhabitants who were in the same place but without the same rights?

Speaking at the Institute for Race Relations in January 1942, Smuts heralded a policy of trusteeship that imposed duties on the guardian to "benefit the ward" in accordance with the ward's human rights, while anchoring the guardian's political responsibility in the different abilities of the white race. The European, Smuts asserted, could not continue to "look away from the helpless person on the doorstep." Since Africans were "on the doorstep" by living in the suburbs of the city, the good of the whole required government action to improve material conditions. When Smuts referred to "human rights," he meant basic levels of care in health, education, and social security. However, Smuts left the person to be helped "on the doorstep," barred from entering the house with equal social and political rights.

Ideas to expand "Native" representation remained moribund, while existing segregationist legislation with which the "old" Smuts was identified remained in place. Reform efforts lost their urgency once the Allies seemed to turn the tide of war at the end of 1942. In any case, there could be no "people's war," since the "people" as a single political unit had no practical or rhetorical legitimacy in South Africa. Even liberals anxious to push along Smuts could not bring themselves, when they formed a separate party in 1953, to endorse universal suffrage; for years they remained wedded to some sort of term-limited trusteeship.[37]

Malan and Afrikaner nationalists had it easier because they rejected cooperation and common history. Malan distinguished between *die volk*, the white people who constituted the nation, and *die bevolking*, the total population. Nationalists mistrusted the empire precisely because it promoted intertribal ideas of the commons of ten million people.

For all the sympathy Smuts mustered on the international stage, his ideas failed to mobilize either Europeans or Africans for reform while confirming the fears of both. According to one poll of white South African soldiers taken during the war, about half favored "more chances" for "Natives" (only 5 percent endorsed the need for the "same chances"), but almost as many wanted to leave conditions "as things are now."[38]

Close as it was, the Nationalist Party's electoral victory in 1948 was built on this "as things are now." It was a mandate strong enough for apartheid. "Today South Africa belongs to us once more," exclaimed the new prime minister, Daniel Malan; a confederate put it more bluntly, "From now on a kaffir is a kaffir again." The "once more" measured the political threat that Smuts's reformism had posed as well as the constant vigilance and violence necessary to impose the white sovereignty of the *volk* on a black majority *bevolking*.[39]

Smuts aimed to head off black demands for political rights by recognizing Africans' place in the commerce and cities of South Africa. Yet halfhearted concessions that provided just a little bit of dignity did not add up to dignity and simply increased frustration and anger.

Since "all races were irretrievably dependent upon each other in one developing economy," and since Africans themselves constituted the great majority of "society's workers, producers, and consumers," South Africa was manifestly not "a white man's country." As the *Bantu World* pointed out, Orlando was not a reserve or a location, but a suburb of Johannesburg. This was not a political demand, but a sociological fact.[40]

"Give the people the tools," declared A. P. Mda, the cofounder of the African National Congress Youth League in 1944, "and a new great South Africa will be built up in a few decades." Political development in the twentieth century had shown that social and economic advance should be measured in years, not centuries—here the Soviet Union was the model example. In its 1943 manifesto, *African Claims*, the African National Congress looked out at the lights in the city of Johannesburg as Dick had when he first arrived. It demanded "full participation of the African in the Government of South Africa" and "freedom of the African people from all discriminatory laws."[41] It would take another fifty years before the politics of South Africa recognized the society of South Africa.

Smuts's outlook remained paternalistic and segregationist. He looked at structures and their parts, but did not estimate political or social change. Without a single African he could call a friend, Smuts did not hear the beat of *marabi* or feel the sway of the "choo-choo" train. The great image of movement in the world war was "marching," and the destination of the marchers was a "new world" that would leave "things as they are now" behind. "Behold men and women on the march not in one place but everywhere," commented the *New York Times*.[42]

They marched, but this forward movement brings to mind soldiers. People also made their way into the cities as workers looking for new opportunities. They took the bus and boarded the train. Once in the city, they swayed, torn between one job and another, between old affiliations and new—which is what all the marrying and divorcing during wartime was about. They kept up with the war news, and they made the war for themselves with sharper expectations, demands, and anxieties about its aims and consequences. They fought for freedom but not all in the same row or column.

Township jazz, railroad songs, football games, "industrial men" in the cities, demands for trade unions and for the vote—all this was evident in the other cities of British Africa, particularly in Lagos, the capital of Nigeria, with twenty million inhabitants the most populous African colony. Everything was sharper and louder and brighter in Lagos in contrast to Johannesburg because only a minuscule European population obtained privileges without asserting control over the movements of urban residents. The city itself and not the white man in the capital featured in the songs and tales of the new world. "Person who's not careful, the city will eat him!" was the warning given to Amusa Sango, the twenty-six-year-old newcomer at 20 Molomo Street.[43] In Nigeria, the new world was not a rebuke, but a near goal to be achieved by mass demonstrations and strikes and by marching. Decolonization was strong in its "dread of imperialism" and in the struggle to defeat it "everywhere." It was also divisive and violent. What did not disappear in the new world claimed by Africans, or disappear anywhere else, were the loyalties to group, language, and religion that had immobilized Smuts's thinking. White republicanism in South Africa provided the most perverse confirmation of the wartime ideal of home rule.

The war pulled millions of migrants down the road into cities all over the world.

In many ways, the culture of the urban settlers mirrored and deepened the democratic spirit of the global war. They fought local struggles with global slogans. The power of the Allies looked robust amid the bustle and noise of the cities, a more direct "road to victory."

But new settlers also divided along lines of race and ethnicity, which extended the conflicts of the war onto the homeland. Whites and blacks fought over space and invoked their liberties and rights, in Johannesburg as well as Detroit. Sometimes they lined up with the war aims of the Allies, sometimes they contorted them, or fought as a "fifth column" against the general enfranchisement in wartime.

The great road trip of the war mobilized people. It transformed them into industrial men and women, fluent in ideas of self-government and military sacrifice and happy to leave behind many traditional customs, but not necessarily willing to jettison parochial or exclusive conceptions of belonging. The very motions of the war raised rather than settled conceptions of who belonged where.

PART VI

OCCUPATION

CHAPTER 18

"Quit India"

War was fought to occupy space. Even workers who moved into Richmond or Johannesburg bumped and pushed against the regulation of movement as local people brought their "white to work" or local police put "white to work" in Jim Crow and passed laws. Moving around pressed questions about who belonged in what places and who constituted the public according to rights that were themselves redefined by the war. War entrenched the contests over space, displacing some groups and resettling others. In Detroit, the daily contest over room occurred on a narrow, confined stage. Foreign enemies claimed territory on a much grander and more sinister scale. Everywhere occupation extended the war by deepening divisions between rulers and ruled and resetting ethnic or religious conflicts. People fought over place in the final push to compel the British to "Quit India," to assemble the "People's Army Against Japan" in the Philippines, and to create "Jew-free" communities in Ukraine. Raids and reprisals furrowed the land so deeply that civilians found almost no place to shelter.

All over the world, people were "on the march." Everywhere the same "dread of imperialism." From all corners, the question "What about India?" As Britain's largest colony, and one of the oldest, India had become the "symbol" for fidelity to the Atlantic Charter, which had promised people the right to determine their own future. Wendell Willkie repeated the question when reporting on his "one world" voyage in fall 1942. He confirmed how the global war seeped into local struggles for the freedom that remained "priceless" only for "the white man," for the Pole or the Frenchman. Had he traveled to Detroit or Johannesburg, Willkie would have heard the same question. So "What about India?"[1]

"Freedom-loving Gandhi of India is holding his umpteenth fast." With these words, Anne Frank surveyed the news as she saw it from her hiding place in Amsterdam on February 27, 1943. Other items included her father's pronouncement on an Allied invasion ("any day") and a report on Churchill's pneumonia ("getting better"). A week later, she updated: "Gandhi is eating again." From the confines of the Lodz Ghetto, eighteen-year-old David Sierakowiak commented on India as well: "A national Congress that wants independence has assembled. Gandhi is its chairman." What excited Sierakowiak were the "colossal changes" "taking place all around the world." Yet "we are rotting here in the ghetto." Jews in German-occupied Europe identified with Gandhi's fight for freedom. Above all, they envied the sheer freedom of action his fight represented. There is no figure in World War II who received the close and sympathetic coverage in all belligerent countries as did Gandhi. German newspapers also provided extensive commentary on the situation in India.

Like Anne Frank, they tracked Gandhi's fast—"Gandhi Ends Fast," Cologne's newspaper noted on March 4, 1943. On the occasion of Gandhi's seventy-third birthday, the *Manila Tribune* honored "the Greatest Man of the Age," publishing a poem, "To Gandhi." *Time* magazine referred to "Saint Gandhi."[2]

From the Cripps Mission, dispatched in March 1942 to negotiate the road to India's self-rule, to the Quit India uprising in the summer of 1942 and Gandhi's fast of twenty-one days— his longest ever—the next winter, events in India constituted one of the great dramas of the war.

More than any other political issue, India also divided Great Britain and the United States. It exposed the different claims about the legacy of empire and the broader democratic aims of the Allies in 1942. There was not a collision of points of view since the British recognized limits to imperial rule and the Americans compromised on principle in order to achieve postwar security. Nonetheless, the debate over India sharpened arguments about freedom and empire. It inserted the German invasion of Poland into a more global frame.

The fall of Singapore in February 1942 raised the general alarm. It made clear that "We Can Lose," as the *Daily Mail* put it. In addition, Singapore cast doubt on the ability of empire to provide security while denying freedom. The slogan "This is our war too" drove home the point that the mobilization of broad popular support rested on realizing the hopes of colonial subjects and oppressed people. Singapore turned unfreedom in India into a global cause in a way that Germany's invasion of Poland had not.

In an "open letter," *Life* magazine hoped to straighten out "the People of England," whom editors addressed as "members of our own family." What "We Americans" were "*not* fighting for," they asserted in October 1942, "is to hold the British Empire together." To "cling to the Empire" was to "lose the war." India provided the illustrative example just when the Quit India protests against British rule enveloped the subcontinent: "In the light of what you are doing in India, how do you expect us to talk about 'principles'" or "look our soldiers in the eye?" According to *Life*, the war was a single global effort requiring worldwide reciprocation. "Our own freedom" means "learning that others must have freedom." It followed that "the only kind of war that will win a real victory" was the one "to establish freedom" over "a wider area, on this earth." With reference to problems at home as well as challenges overseas, the letter urged the English people to see that "our Side is as big as all outdoors," from "the muddy banks of the Mississippi" to the "steppes of Asia" and "deserts of Africa."[3]

The great outdoors was a spectacular image because it led in so many directions, inviting free association and showing common ground. It urged the British to leave behind the enclosures of empire, "the club, the mess, the bungalow," and "the English flowers in the garden" in order to play with everyone in the commons outside.[4] It recognized the marching of all sorts of aggrieved people. Expansiveness is what made the war "our war." The Black man's fight in the war, wrote Langston Hughes, "will eventually shake the British Empire to the dust," and "will shake Dixie's teeth loose too, and crack the joints of Jim Crow South Africa." "Our war too" realized "one world, one war."[5]

The survey of the commons did not go uncontested. The great outdoors was a typically American place, "an immoderate form." Winston Churchill did not want critics such as Willkie anywhere indoors in the empire. The American "reminded him of a Newfoundland dog in a small parlour, which had wiped its paws on a young lady's blouse and swept off the teacups with its tail."[6]

If Willkie knocked on doors to canvass for the Atlantic Charter, Churchill firmly shut his. "In case there should be any mistake about it," he asserted in a notorious November 1942 speech, "I have not become the King's First Minister in order to preside over the liquidation of the British Empire." For Churchill and conservatives, freedom was defined in terms of empire. After becoming prime minister with nothing to offer but "blood, toil, tears and sweat," Churchill stood before the House of Commons on May 13, 1940, to declare the ultimate aim of war as the victory without which there could be "no survival for the British Empire." A month later, on June 18, the anniversary of the Battle of Waterloo, he stood again to give his "finest hour" speech: "the Battle for France is over," he acknowledged; "the Battle for Britain is about to begin" to defend "our own British life, and the long continuity of our institutions and our Empire." Churchill (and his ministers) repeatedly invoked the words he first uttered in the run-up to the Great War: "We have to hold what we have won."

"Winston's refusal to accept things as they are and not as they were in 1895" merited criticism by his closest associates; as one put it, the prime minister had "never got beyond the early Kipling stage." Colonial authorities reckoned with the end of empire, but they spoke about a sequence of stages that postponed it into an indefinite, unknown future. In 1942, the secretary of state for the colonies admitted, "We all know in our heart that most Colonies, especially in Africa, will probably not be fit for complete independence for centuries." Maybe it was only "a good many years." The temporizing was why Willkie insisted on the need for "firm timetables" and "ironclad agreements." Yet even the most shameless equivocation legitimized pertinent questions about the how and when of the end of empire.[7]

Across the world, people regarded how Britain and its sub-jects staged the question of empire, examining the empire's resilience or erosion, judging its principles and hypocrisies, wondering about its willingness and capacity to adapt. In other words, they watched India.

SIR STAFFORD CRIPPS's mission to secure the cooperation of India's political parties in the war effort by outlining the path to self-determination in early 1942, after the Japanese occupied Malaya and Burma, turned India into the dramatic stage on which the future of the British Empire played itself out. It was a "world sensation," noted Goebbels in his diary on March 13.[8]

From the arrival of Cripps's plane in Delhi on March 23, 1942, until his departure three weeks later, Cripps and his negotiating partners, including Gandhi and Jawaharlal Nehru of the Indian National Congress and Muhammad Ali Jinnah of the Muslim League, were the focus of intense press scrutiny. A week into the negotiations, Cripps stepped in front of journalists, who numbered around two hundred. Dressed in a white suit, Cripps had "the snap and sparkle of an auctioneer selling a particular good lot to an eager market. For 20 minutes he wisecracked at the rate of about ten wisecracks a minute, squeezing in here and there a gobbet of hard, vital fact." Alan Moorehead, the *Daily Express* correspondent, added: "I never saw a press conference conducted so well as this, despite the laughter and noise." Newspapers kept close tabs on the talks: "NEHRU MAY DECIDE IT," read one *Express* headline. These were "fearfully decisive days." "Every word from India," wrote the *New York Times*, "is like news from a mighty battlefront in which the fortunes of war go now one way, now the other." In fact, it was a journalist who added "drawn on a failed bank" to Gandhi's dismissal of the final offer as a "post-dated cheque" to complete the memorable phrase so that it referred to the collapse of British rule before promises could be cashed in after the war.[9]

Once Japanese attacks brought the United States into the war, India had become central to the Allies' global war effort; Cripps's mission was a response to the immediate military threat the Japanese posed, but also an effort to allay American concerns about the steadiness of British rule. After Malaya and Burma, military planners braced for a Japanese incursion in the northeast against Bengal as well as attacks on Madras in the south. They drew a line around the "bastion" of Calcutta. Already in March, General Archibald Wavell, commander in chief of the British Indian Army, estimated "present resources" to be "utterly inadequate" for the defense of India. His pessimism was shared in London, where Alan Brooke, chief of the Imperial General Staff, considered prospects "gloomy" for "saving India from the Japs."[10]

It was not far-fetched to imagine the British on the verge of a historic defeat. From exile in Germany, Subhas Chandra Bose made the first broadcast under his own name on February 19, 1942, to announce that "the fall of Singapore means the collapse of the British Empire." "Now the hour has struck." Gandhi himself came to believe that the British were about to lose the war. So did the many Indians who when they purchased radios, the "big dealers in Bombay" reported, asked the "usual question": "Can I hear Germany and Japan on this?"[11]

"R is for rumor" went the ditty; "someone told me at noon / that a Japanese army has invaded the moon." "The crisis of early 1942" was a clear "turning point in the history of the Raj," affirms one historian, a period when "millions of Indians became vividly aware of British weakness and failure."[12]

India was so important to the empire that Britain was willing first with Cripps to offer a plan leading to independence after the war but then, after the Indian National Congress rejected Cripps's offer and launched the Quit India movement, to reassert "old-style colonial repression."[13] The British rocked back and forth between conciliating Indian opinion and disavowing it altogether. In the end, the confrontation between Great Britain and the Indian National Congress in 1942 severely damaged the ability of both to achieve the goal of India's self-determination on the terms each party had envisioned. Independence on August 15, 1947, took the form of violent partition that was hardly foreseeable in 1939. It was the intervening events in 1942, Japan's war against Britain and the general roiling of imperial waters, that made the sudden scene changes possible.

Shortly after Britain's declaration of war on September 3, 1939, following the German invasion of Poland, the viceroy unilaterally announced India's. Lord Linlithgow did so in the name of "principles of international justice and international morality" without which "the law of the jungle" would prevail. He was sure Indians would commit themselves to "the side of human freedom as against the rule of force." It was a grave misstep, ignoring provincial assemblies elected in 1937 as instruments of self-government in accordance with the Government of India Act of 1935. Linlithgow also restored wartime emergency powers. In matters of war and peace, the imperial ruler retained the first and last word. The Indian National Congress, the main independence party that had taken power in seven of the ten provinces, did not oppose the war on principle but demanded a clear statement of how its aims pertained to India "in regard to democracy and imperialism." India could be at war only as a "free and independent nation," maintained Gandhi, the spiritual leader of Congress.[14]

Linlithgow provided an answer that was little different from Britain's unkept promise in World War I. Dominion status would follow after the war, he stated, without clarifying how the dominion would be constituted out of the provinces and "princely states" or how India's political representatives would be involved in central governance during and after the war. As a result, Congress pursued a policy of noncooperation and, in a dramatic gesture, resigned its ministries on October 22, 1939. Further discussions did not resolve the deadlock.

Perfectly content not to adjudicate Congress's demands for power or determine the role of the Muslim minority or the states in a power-sharing agreement, the viceroy decided to "lie back for the present." Since Congress refrained from launching a public campaign of disobedience as it had in the past, he considered its opposition a mere "nuisance factor."[15] With the expansion of India's industry and army, which by the end of 1941 had tripled in size to 820,000 men to constitute the world's largest volunteer force, signals confirmed Linlithgow's confidence in the overall loyalty of the Indian population. What completely undermined the government's equanimity was Japan's war.

While Congress was the most powerful force in Indian politics, its claims to represent the nation as a whole, with support from Muslims as well as Hindus of all castes, were disputed by Jinnah's Muslim League. The league had performed poorly in elections in Muslim-majority provinces (Punjab, Bengal), and so Congress discounted it as a political force. Yet it gained support in Muslim-minority areas where Muslim voters shared its contention that Congress served primarily Hindu interests. Jinnah positioned himself as the leader of the entire Muslim minority, which he believed constituted a separate nation, one on par with what he regarded as the Hindu nation and, as such, entitled to political parity its numbers alone (about 24 percent) could not achieve. For the league, the Congress resignations were an unexpected turn of fortune. It gained influence as a cooperative partner in war and in negotiations over the postwar settlement.

Despite the league's limited parliamentary clout, Jinnah went on the offensive, calling on Muslims to celebrate December 22, 1939, as a "Day of Deliverance" from Congress. Across India, the league used prayers of thanksgiving to organize Muslims, most of whom had previously voted for regional parties. It was in the war years that the league emerged as a mass political party able to mobilize exuberant supporters across India. Although Jinnah had once been a strong adherent of Muslim-Hindu unity, his claim to be the "sole spokesman" culminated in the Lahore Resolution adopted by the league's working committee on March 23, 1940. On the basis of the "two-nations" idea, the league rejected federal frameworks for Indian independence to endorse "autonomous and sovereign" Muslim states—the first definition of Pakistan, "land of the pure."[16] (After Lahore, Pakistan Day was celebrated on March 23; at a meeting in Lahore in 1929, Congress had called for India's complete independence and declared January 26 Independence Day—now Republic Day.)

Japan's offensive in Asia hurried along ideas about Indian independence. But Jinnah saw "a great danger in the British Government being stampeded under pressure" to make a declaration "to give India a constitution as a single unit on the basis of a united and democratic India." At home or abroad, when people "talk of the freedom of India," they "entirely ignore the hundred million Muslims in the country." Since majority rule in a "single unit" meant Hindu rule, Jinnah's idea of the Muslim nation, whether defined as a sovereign state or not, gained resonance among Muslims. Both Muslims and Hindus lived in a country where citizens divided themselves according to religion even when they moved into cities and enjoyed modern pleasures such as playing cricket or going to the movies. "There is no such thing as an Indian nation," Jinnah asserted in a key statement at the end of 1941; "India is a constellation of nations and the two major nations are the Hindus and Muslims."[17] That Britain's rulers dramatized religious differences, dividing in order to rule, should not obscure the importance those differences assumed in the age of mass politics. Questions remained, however: Jinnah offered partition, but how many Muslims agreed? Could there be a Muslim nation without a Muslim state, particularly since other "nations" in the "constellation" would remain in India? And by what provincial and national mechanisms would voters decide the issue?

After Pearl Harbor, talk about the freedom and independence of India grew more insistent—the expanded war was not Jinnah's dream scenario. The so-called Cripps Mission in March 1942, led by Sir Stafford Cripps, Britain's former ambassador to the Soviet Union who was seen as able to work well with adversaries, was designed to offer concrete proposals on these issues to cement wartime partnership with Indian political groups, precisely what the British had been unable or unwilling to achieve in 1939. If wartime events in 1942 compelled the British to act rather than postpone, they convinced Congress that British rule had run its course and required the fullest assertion of Indian sovereignty, precisely the unmediated empowerment of the majority the Muslim League feared most. Both Japan's aggression and Cripps's mission forced the issue of India as a "single unit."

Cripps's offer promised India dominion status after the war, but not independence. The one did not block the achievement of the other, but the offer fell short of Congress's demand and, for the duration of the war, kept the apparatus of British colonial rule in place. More vexing were the mechanisms proposed to constitute the dominion; members of the envisioned constitutional assembly were to be nominated by the elected governments of the provinces and by the "princely states," which empowered the princes rather than their people. (There were twenty-one proper princely state governments, including Hyderabad and Kashmir but also Benares and Bhutan; they covered 40 percent of India's landmass and contained 23 percent of its population.) The question of representation was especially relevant since any one of the constituent units in the assembly, the provinces or the states, could opt out of the new union to establish its own future. The "Pakistan cuckoo's egg," Leo Amery, the secretary of state for India, explained, was included in order to allow Jinnah to accept the proposals (and perhaps force Gandhi to refuse them). The opt-out provision for Muslims also raised the possibility of other "Princes' 'Stan[s].'"[18]

In many ways, Cripps's proposals paved the constitutional road to partition—"vivisection" is how Gandhi described the British approach after "centuries of work."[19] (For someone such as Gandhi who denied himself food to protest injustice, the bodily integrity of India was a domineering image: "Denial" policy severed limbs; foreign rule suggested rape.) Even if Jinnah had compromised on a federal solution short of partition, the centralized state Congress assumed it stood entitled to inherit seemed unattainable. The devolution of central Indian power was also incorporated in the maintenance in the interim of the viceroy's veto and his retention of the defense portfolio.

After three weeks of discussion, the Indian parties rejected the plan, Congress because it compromised all-India sovereignty, the Muslim League because the mechanism of representation that permitted the creation of two nations was not premised on their prior existence, and the others because it gave either too much or too little power to the Hindu majority. The argument, put forward by many moderate Congressmen, to accept the principle of Pakistan in order to fund the goodwill necessary to avoid its realization, was not followed up. If Cripps was disappointed, Churchill and Linlithgow were not. They found that the onus of failure was on India, not Britain, and this view was accepted by the all-important American press. As a result, the British had a clear conscience as they responded with force when Congress launched the Quit India uprising to throw the colonials out of the colony all at once in the summer of 1942.

Regarding this anxious spring—the loss of Singapore, the collapse in Burma, the threat to India itself—Indivar Kamtekar refers not to "shivers," a series of discrete shocks, but to "the shiver of 1942," a prolonged physical reaction to the decline of British authority. It expressed itself in the sudden change in Gandhi's rhetoric. Congressmen found him in a "uniquely militant mood." This was quite a contrast to Gandhi's graduated approach in 1939, when he counseled Congress to go "so far and no further."[20]

Japan's war of aggression widened Gandhi's horizon while shortening his timeline. He drew attention to "powerful elements of Fascism" in both Great Britain and America, where "the position of the Negro" made the defense of freedom an "utter lie."

British rule was not only hypocritical but also brutal so as to justify immediate resistance. Gandhi compared the situation in India to the assault on a woman or, as he explained in his speech in Bombay on August 8, 1942, to the man who "holds me by the neck and wants to drown me." "May I not struggle to free myself directly?" Gandhi asked, sanctioning violence in the moment of great danger.[21] Gandhi spoke up as the victim of attack: "Do or die."

Meeting at Gandhi's ashram in Wardha, the working or executive committee of Congress crafted its official response to the failure of Cripps's mission. Over the opposition of Nehru and Maulana Azad, the Muslim president of Congress, Gandhi's position prevailed. Given "India's inalienable right to freedom and independence," the committee agreed on July 6, 1942, to demand an immediate end to British rule. A week later, the committee sanctioned "mass struggle" to force the British to quit India. The country would "utilize all the non-violent strength it has gathered during the last 22 years of peaceful struggle." The "Wardha Resolution" did not plan to ratchet up the struggle for independence, which had seen pauses in the past. Quit India was the final exertion to achieve freedom in a few weeks. None of this—the working committee's resolution or its adoption by the All-India Congress Committee on August 8—was part of a calculated plan to strengthen Congress's negotiating position. An existential decision to "do or die" had been made in a cracked-open world to immediately grab and take control of the country.

Sympathetic observers did not understand Gandhi's "bloody mindedness." It was as if "the only way left of demonstrating one's right to ownership" was to "pull the house down." Suddenly, Gandhi and his compatriots in Congress seemed ready to "take risks beyond the wildest dreams of gamblers," although "no straight fight with Britain is possible."[22] But in the scenario of the rapist at the door (like the Germans in Poland's corridor), such a "straight fight" appeared viable because necessary. Interestingly, the scenario more or less evenly matched the victim and her assailant, imagining an almost complete reversal of fortune in which the violated rights of the victim would be restored. In such danger there could no longer be any interval of time.

The All-India Congress Committee gathered in Bombay on August 7, 1942, to adopt the Wardha Resolution, demanding Britain quit India by packing up and leaving now. *Time* seemed to quote from Congress's playbook: "Inside their huge *Pandal*," or assembly hall, "electric fans hummed. They had the unprecedented extravagance to provide chairs for everyone. They opened their meeting with terrific trumpet blasts. A band played *Marching Through Georgia*." An Indian commemorative stamp quotes Gandhi's declaration on August 8: "The mantra is 'do or die.' We shall either free India or die in the attempt." With other Congress leaders, Gandhi was arrested at dawn the next day and imprisoned for nearly three years until the end of the war. He had "a copy of the Bhagavad-Gita, the Koran and an Urdu primer under his arm, a garland of flowers around his wizened neck."[23]

In the morning, "the small boy in a tattered dhoti idly dawdled toe marks in the deep dust. Monsoon skies were slate-grey overhead. The oppressive heat gave added pungency to the smell of human filth in the Girgaun district of Bombay's slums. Shopkeepers moved listlessly; talk dribbled in the bazaars." Then "suddenly everything changed." As "word sputtered from mouth to mouth that the British Raj had jailed Mahatma Gandhi," Hindus "ran riot. Four double-decker busses were wrecked."

Throughout the city, "traffic snarled. Foreigners were stoned. So were police who answered with tear gas fired directly into the crowds." The insurgency had begun; "the small boy ran from one trouble spot to another."

The revolt blazed quickly, burned hot, and spread far. Although the British regained control, the arrests of Gandhi and thousands of others and the "drastic punishment" police and soldiers meted out ensured that the restoration of colonial order remained brittle and provisional.

As soon as news of the arrest of Congress leaders reached the Hindu city of Ahmedabad, the largest city in Gujarat, workers walked out of factories, merchants shuttered shops, and students quit schools to demonstrate in the streets. Crowds roughed up policemen and chased away pedestrians in European business attire—shirts tucked into a pair of trousers. They also set fire to the police station. After pursuing the attackers, the police were able to disperse the crowds with tear gas, and several demonstrators were shot and killed. Although armed guards were posted around Ahmedabad, thousands of people congregated the next day. For two weeks, business came to a halt as police and students fought running battles in the streets.[24]

In one city after another, Bombay, Ahmedabad, and Calcutta, protesters attempted to dismantle the colonial state by breaking the infrastructure of law and order. "A peculiar feature of the disturbances has been hostility to post offices and pillar boxes," noted the *Statesman*; other posts of the colonial state such as railway stations were also mobbed. The idea was to "pull the chain" of the emergency brake and stop the colonial-era train.[25]

On August 15, thousands of demonstrators armed with spears, stones, sticks, and even bows and arrows completely outnumbered police, who tried to hold their compound in

Madhuban in the Azamgarh district in northern India. Robert Niblett, an Anglo-Indian district magistrate, described the scene: "A market is usually held here on Saturday afternoon, but not a soul was in sight"; the "gaunt and lonely appearance of the *thana* and the sentries on the roofs reminded me of tales of the Foreign Legion." At about two in the afternoon, protesters approached from two directions. From a distance the demonstrators "with their *lathis* and spears looked like a *sarpat* jungle on the move." Niblett and his men withstood a two-hour attack, in which a number of attackers, shouting out Gandhi's miracle rendering "all fire harmless," were killed. But once assailants had injured sufficient numbers of the defenders and scaled the walls—here elephants were useful for their height—there was little the police could do but flee. What is striking is how tenacious both sides were; Indian police defended beleaguered posts without prospect of reinforcements, while crowds regrouped even after demonstrators had been shot.[26]

The rural aspect of the rebellion is crucial as villages, one by one, ousted the small contingent of colonial administrators, thereby establishing self-rule and reclaiming India. Delhi had been prepared to punish protesters in urban areas, but was surprised by the speed of events and the number of villages the rebellion occupied. After three weeks, the viceroy admitted that the violence constituted "by far the most serious rebellion since that of 1857, the gravity and extent of which we have so far concealed from the world for reasons of military security." Public acknowledgment of outbreaks fueled general combustibility.[27]

For participants, "do or die" represented the "final struggle" in a national revolution. Insurrectionists described themselves in the present tense. Pamphlets propagated "the news": "India is free." "I have thrown off the shackles of slavery from my heart,"

439

and "I have decided that nobody can prevent me from proceeding along the path of freedom." Even if individuals were killed, the nation would live: "The task of bringing Government rule to a standstill will be completed within four weeks from this day," insurgents promised. It was imperative to "take direct action." In support of the revolutionary time frame, Congress issued assurances that there would be no pauses or postponements. "Acts of violence even of the type of Chauri Chaura," where Gandhi had dismayed supporters by halting the disobedience campaign in 1922 after policemen had burned to death in an attack on their station, "will not stop the movement."[28]

The present tense was immensely powerful but demanded immediate success. After just about four weeks, the insurrection lost energy and the government regained control thanks to 55 Indian army battalions outfitted with mortars and machine guns and supported by airpower. In the fight against the British, 208 police outposts, 332 railway stations, and 945 post offices had been destroyed and more than one thousand protesters killed. Taking place in the absence of the directives of leaders, the uprising revealed the depth and breadth of anti-British feeling. At the same time, the uprising revealed limits. Its base was mostly restricted to the Hindu middle classes in cities or better-off peasants in the countryside. Labor support was intermittent and divided in its loyalties given the antifascist popular front strategy of trade unionists and Communists. Even in Calcutta, students did not demonstrate unanimously behind Congress, which some patriots suspected of aiding the Japanese enemy.

There were also few desertions by civil servants, police, or enlisted men in the army, something Congress had counted on. It took 55 battalions to restore order, but these battalions were composed almost entirely of Indian troops who remained loyal.

India's Muslims were not involved either as targets of violence or as protagonists. Their "complete aloofness" served to confirm Jinnah's assertions about India. "This movement," wrote "Sha-hed" in the *Statesman*, "has more completely than ever before divided the peoples of India into two distinct nations."[29] For all the strength and spirit of Quit India, the movement did not display the national unity earlier Congress campaigns of civil disobedience had in 1920 and 1930. As a Hindu insurrection, however, Quit India was the largest civil uprising in World War II, more popular than most resistance movements in Europe but equally violent. It cut deeper than the Boer rebellion in South Africa.

Counting up "the 90,000,000 Muslims," the "50,000,000 Depressed Classes, or Untouchables," and "the 95,000,000 sub-jects of the Princes of India," Churchill boasted to the House of Commons on September 10, 1942, that "the Indian Congress party does not represent all India. It does not represent the majority of the people of India. It does not even represent the Hindu masses." The apparent failure of the Quit India movement to dislodge the British gave Churchill the confidence to take up Nehru's challenge, expressed after Britain's military defeat at Tobruk, to commence the "complete liquidation" of the empire, by refusing, after the victory at El Alamein, to "preside over" just such a liquidation.[30]

Despite Churchill's satisfaction, the suppression of Quit India cost the British because it revealed once more the violence on which imperial rule rested. The detention of more than one hundred thousand people, the floggings, and the collective fines imposed on villages, which were also subject to police may-hem, advertised the scandal of empire. An Anglo-Indian, Nib-lett himself was removed as magistrate for his opposition to the "official hysteria" and *"terreur blanche"* of government reprisals in Azamgarh.[31]

If Quit India in 1942 revived "old-style colonial repression," in which Britain's subjects were treated as traitors, the Bengal famine in 1943 exposed old-style colonial neglect. Famine dramatized the agony of India and made more irrefutable the right of Indians to rule themselves. The British never recovered from the war the authorities in Delhi had joined in an elementary act of imperial allegiance.

India had changed a great deal by the time the Congress leaders were released from prison in May and June 1945. A look at 1945 helps clarify the global moment in 1942. Most notably, the Muslim League had grown into a powerful mass movement. Its prominence scrambled Congress's hopes to lead a united India, but hardly buttressed British authority that was contested at every point. Britain had defeated the Japanese in Burma in 1945 only to find the colonial people it had "liberated" determined to build on the empire's initial defeat in 1942. Japanese aggression had the effect of disqualifying any sort of foreign domination.

In this context, the Indian National Army (INA), which emerged from the fields of South Asia in disarray, won recognition in the months after the war for defying the British, as had Quit India insurgents—each group embellished its own historical legacy by saluting the other. As the British discovered when they tried three officers of the Indian National Army (a Hindu, a Muslim, and a Sikh) for treason in November 1945, the fundamental differences among the Indian parties and even the loyalty shown by the Indian army throughout the war did not prevent resentment over London's claim to distinguish between traitors and freedom fighters. With Bose's death in an airplane crash in Taipei in August 1945, his "pact with the devil" (Hitler) slipped

into history. The public enrolled the INA in the liberation struggle, in which its valor for enduring "hunger, thirst, privation"
on the march to Delhi shined. Bose's soldiers became heroes,
compelling Claude Auchinleck, the commander in chief of the
Indian army, to release the defendants after they had been found
guilty. "Jai Hind," Victory to India, the slogan first formulated
in Germany in 1942, was taken up throughout India, and the
INA's national anthem, "Jana Gana Mana," adopted from Tagore's
song, became India's. The military rebel "has cast its spell on us,"
observed Gandhi.[32]

The trial of the three INA officers put a sharp light on the fall
of Singapore and the cause of "our war." Lawyers for the defense
argued that the defenseless position in which Britain had left
the troops in Malaya in 1942 "forfeited its claim on their allegiance." Moreover, they described Bose's army as the legitimate
armed force of an independent nation that exercised sovereignty
(over the Andaman Islands) and enjoyed international (Axis)
recognition. And for the first time, the Indian public learned
that tens of thousands of Indians, commanded by Indian officers, had fought for India's independence in a series of "victories
and defeats" under fire in Burma. In a few weeks, the trial transformed a "ghost army" into "the real thing." Nehru, who had
once vowed to fight Bose as well as the Japanese, recognized that
"those three officers" had become "symbols of India fighting for
her independence." The issue was not whether Bose's provisional
government constituted a sovereign state. It was whether war by
a "subject race" for the purpose of "liberating oneself from foreign yoke" was justified by international law and international
public opinion. If an Indian soldier could fight for the freedom
of England against Germany, he could fight for the freedom of
India against England.[33]

The right to wage war was uppermost in the mind of the dissenting judge, the Indian jurist Radhabinod Pal, in the International Military Tribunal for the Far East, the Tokyo warcrimes trial established in 1946 shortly after the conclusion of the INA trial in Delhi. In light of Europe's wars of imperial aggression, Pal disputed the formal or categorical differentness of Japan's. What the Japanese had disrupted was the status quo, not the law that had frozen in place the outcome of Europe's predatory conquests in the last century through the legal protection of much later international agreements codifying good behavior, namely, the 1928 Kellogg-Briand Pact renouncing the use of war. This freezing was illegitimate since it singled out Japan as a pariah for its aggression in the twentieth century. And it criminalized armed anticolonial resistance to the domination foreigners had achieved in the past. In Pal's argument, Japan's wars were not unlawful, while anticolonial wars were not illegitimate. "Dominated nations of the present day *status quo*," Pal summed up, "cannot be made to submit to eternal domination only in the name of peace."[34]

There were deficiencies in Pal's argument. His formal arguments tended to emphasize the equivalency of all imperialism, smothering the brutality of Japan's occupation. Nor could the immorality of colonialism in the past exonerate wars of aggression in the present. Nonetheless, Pal's dissent in the court of law justified what Japan's conquest of Singapore had made clear to much of the world in 1942: the bankruptcy of Western colonial rule in Asia and the legitimacy of the struggle for national self-determination by subjugated peoples around the globe— whether or not they had been invaded by the Nazis in 1939.

CHAPTER 19

The People's War
in the Philippines

The fall of Singapore on February 15, 1942, validated the global idea of the "people's war." Originally a designation for the virtuous antifascism at the core of the struggle against Hitler, as opposed to the common waste of war in 1914–1918, later a recognition of the parts regular folks played in the defense of Britain in 1940, the "people's war" came to express the urgency of extending freedom everywhere. It sought to secure the liberties of all subject people. The idea confronted directly the hypocrisy of the Allies who fought a war for democracy in Europe while denying liberties to people in the United States or across the British Empire. Opening up a second front to combat racial injustice, champions of the "people's war" linked together histories of slavery and daily experiences imposed by the color bar. Its iconic figure was not the plainspoken housewife during the Blitz but the cleaning woman with her mop or the prisoner in the township pickup van.

When the lawyer appealed to international law to defend officers of the Indian National Army, he invoked the legacy of the "people's war." It was untenable to recognize the warrior for freedom in Poland but not the warrior for freedom in India. His argument served as the premise for the American "Double Victory" campaign against Adolf Hitler abroad and "Jim Crow" at home. With the conquest of Singapore in 1942, Japan energized "revolt against the West" in "the ruins of empire."[1]

"One thing this war has done has been to awaken the one billion peoples of Asia," reflected Victor Buencamino, a pro-American civil servant in the Philippines, three days before the fall of Singapore. "The fire and iron and steel" of the war "have entered their hearts" so that the billion "have become strong." The defeat of Britain in Malaya and Burma and the United States in the Philippines portended the political rise of Asia (and Africa) and a global war for racial justice. "Singapore may in the future be recaptured by the British," acknowledged Buencamino, but even if the rebuilt fortress was "ten times more formidable," the "myth of the White Man's superiority, the aura of his invincibility, has forever been crushed." Therefore, he considered Singapore to be "a turning point in the history of mankind." (Buencamino wrote this at the very time when he looked down the street and noted "another naked woman tied to a post," a "mestiza" assaulted by the Japanese.)[2]

There was a great deal of satisfaction to be had when, in the words of the apocryphal (Black) taxi driver, the Japanese "knocked out a lot of the white man's conceit."[3] Japan tried to make the most of this knockout, screening films of its attack on

Pearl Harbor, depicting images of Percival's surrender in Singapore, putting American and British prisoners-of-war on display to demonstrate that the once victorious had forever been vanquished. These images centered on the fall of old empires, a poor justification for the rise of a new Japanese one. Asians were most interested in free and independent nations, which is why they consumed so much news about Gandhi and India's fight for independence. Japan was more popular when it assembled the representatives of East Asian nations in Tokyo in November 1943 when it was losing the war than after it captured Singapore while it was winning.

Leocadio De Asis was a Filipino veteran recruited into the occupation's constabulary and sent for training to Japan, where he was swept up in celebrations of Philippine Independence Day on October 14, 1943. He was "greatly impressed" by President Jose P. Laurel who in his radio broadcast during the Tokyo conference spoke about "the sad plight of the still oppressed people of India, Indo-China, Java, Sumatra and Malaya"—"Java" and "Sumatra" were the only permissible references to "Indonesia," a word the Japanese had banned and a cause they had put aside. When De Asis later toured Radio Tokyo, he "entered the special studio where Great East Asia leaders" such as Laurel, Ba Maw, and Bose broadcast their messages; "we actually sat on the chair where East Asia's 'big 'uns' once sat." It was at this point in his sojourn in Japan that De Asis began to buy Japanese grammars and dictionaries as though recognizing the empire's key role in creating "Asia for Asians" once forms of national independence had taken shape.[4]

If the capture of Singapore represented "a turning point in the history of mankind," as Buencamino remarked, the postcolonial future rested on accepting Japanese tutelage. As steward of the new era, Japan's East Asia Co-Prosperity Sphere sought to promote social development of peoples "according to their talents and faculties." Rights would be apportioned through the fulfillment of duties in which each part assumed its "proper place" in the whole. Independence itself was not the liberal right of self-determination but constituted a more senior status earned by service and loyalty to the Japanese empire. In order to "realize the eternal developments" of the future, the Japanese army played the commanding role first of all to "sweep" the British and Americans out of Asia and then to heal "the wounds" Britain's "bloody squeeze" had inflicted. Japan cast itself as the savior of a grievously injured hemisphere.[5]

Just as Japan intended to "sweep out" the British and Americans, East Asians needed to purge themselves of the decadent attributes of Anglo-American culture. By looking East rather than West, they would attain Asian values of service, solidarity, and industry. A whole series of flaws summed up the contemptuous Japanese estimation of the mongrel Western identities Malayans, Indonesians, and Filipinos had taken on in the colonial period: "unnatural" habits of "frivolity," "idleness," and "excessive love of ease and pleasure." Such a depraved state required a long period of "spiritual reformation" to inculcate virtues of "simplicity," "manliness," sacrifice, and, above all, industry.[6]

Contemporaries sometimes remembered the lessons in virtue with appreciation. In the new schools, "we studied and we sang," and "we were filled with this new spirit of endurance and self-sacrifice. This spirit of absolute dedication," which later served the struggle for independence. Yet even sympathetic accounts of the occupation dramatized the moment when violence intruded. The "inevitable slap" in the face recalled old colonial practices, cutting back on Japan's promise to uphold a new postcolonial stature.[7] Indeed, few traces of Japan's occupation remain except for the words recalling its brutality: *kempeitai* (military police), *rōmusha* (forced laborer), *binta* (slap in the face). However, Bose and Burma's Ba Maw are still remembered today.[8]

As the only Catholic country in Asia, the Philippines was an obvious example of the great diversity of East Asia that Japanese descriptions of the region's cultural and racial unity tended to ignore. Like Burma, it had advanced far along the road to independence with self-government. Given its strong ties to the United States, it was not the model territory envisioned by Japan's occupation authorities who had to contend with all sorts of stateside manners. At the same time, the archipelago was geographically close to Japan, more so than Malaya or the Dutch East Indies. It also boasted the largest Japanese diaspora in South Asia; with nearly 20,000 Japanese residents, Davao on Mindanao was known as "Davaokuo," a Manchukuo in the making. Manila itself was more like Tokyo than Singapore and its largely Chinese population and certainly more so than Rangoon or Batavia (Jakarta). In 1940, with a population of 625,000, it was "the richest and most cosmopolitan city in Southeast Asia,"[9] More American, the Philippines was also more Japanese, socially complex and technologically advanced. With a large resistance movement and a powerful cast of collaborators pulling at two ends, the Philippines offers an excellent point of entry into Japanese occupation.

"OUR TIMES ARE abnormal," observed Juan Labrador, rector of the Colegio de San Juan de Letran, the oldest Catholic school in the Philippines, about the time of the Japanese occupation.

"Events are happening as they never did before, and even nature is taking a direction outside its normal course." Things were quite out of whack: "I have lost count of the number of days it has been raining." As in most belligerent countries during the war, newspapers discontinued weather reports. There were no announcements about "the coming and departure of typhoons." Filipinos had to rely on intuition to forecast wind and rain. The basic coordinates of life were no longer verifiable.[10]

Douglas MacArthur, commander of the United States Army Forces in the Far East, had promised to reconquer the Philippines when he arrived in Australia after leaving the island of Corregidor in Manila Bay in March 1942: "I came through and I shall return." Filipinos quickly minted the words, although their defeat had been quick and bloody with American forces fighting brave rearguard battles on Bataan, the peninsula enclosing Manila Bay, before making a desperate last stand on the nearby fortified island of Corregidor. It was an ignominious exit. Pacita Pestano-Jacinto, a journalist, listened to the "secret radio" and confirmed what everybody was talking about. "I shall return"—three words, but "so full of promise," she confided to her diary. "On these three words will the hope of a whole country rest."[11]

But other than MacArthur's departure, there was no timetable. At the start of the Japanese invasion in December 1941, Filipinos had expected the arrival of US reinforcements at any time, "this week," or "by the end of the month." Others did not have much faith in the Americans: "Hell, it'll take ten years!" "There will always be dreamers and defeatists," summed up Victor Buencamino, but neither the one nor the other group served as a reliable weathervane. Buencamino made do with the idea that "the course of history is a cycle. The present becomes past and the past returns to the present." As for the future, it was "something forever to be hoped for," its form unclear. Two years into the war, in December 1943, everything appeared to be speeding up without advancing toward an end: "How short the time seems to be when one looks back! And how long and interminable when one looks forward!" thought Labrador.[12]

With time unpredictable, distance seemed insurmountable. Fernando Manalac remembered two big maps of the Pacific the Japanese had set up, one at Heacock's Department Store on the Escolta, the other by Santa Cruz Bridge. Little flags on the map marked the areas Japan dominated; so did imperial soldiers loitering in Manila's streets. A huge expanse of ocean showed how far away the Americans were: it would take MacArthur "forever to even knock at the gates of the southern Philippine Islands."[13]

Other signals were crossed. News on the radio was broadcast in Japanese (new), Tagalog (more), and English (still). Ceremonies opened with "Banzai!" while streets blasted boogie-woogie. There was a great deal of discussion about Philippine independence, a very desirable prospect that Tokyo dangled in January 1942, but many people soon considered it "an issue that has become a wet rag from too much handling." It was considered *vals wals*, a contraction of Tagalog for "worth nothing."[14] Filipinos lived two lives, the time of Japanese occupation and the time before the war from which they imagined the future after liberation, but they were not sure which was more real or enduring. When Mr. Toyama, "a very nice, educated Japanese," offered to teach Buencamino's son Japanese, Vic refused—"It'll be a dead language, after this war." The younger Buencamino discounted Japan time as a completely unproductive interlude.[15]

The occupation of Manila came all at once early in January 1942. "The Imperial Army has posted sentries at every conceivable corner on the main thoroughfares," noted Pestano-Jacinto.

"Everyone, young and old, man and woman must stop in front of a sentry when he passes by and make a bow from the waist down. Failure to comply with such a command is punishable by one or two slaps on the face, depending on the sentry's mood." The conclusion was inescapable: "Total submission is a principle we must learn from now on." In fact, across Southeast Asia, contemporaries came to comment on the slap to the face, *binta*, that Japanese subordinates endured as well. Whereas for Japanese the physical act was humiliating but less so than demotion in rank or loss of pay, locals considered slapping deeply offensive, a blow to men and women created in God's image. "You just cannot understand," wrote one Filipino, "the depth of the resentment it causes, the amount of pain it gives."[16]

After a few weeks, enough people had been slapped for jokes about the short Japanese and the tall Filipino to circulate. Later on, Buencamino recounted a conversation with someone he had not seen "for ages": "What do you do these days?" "I'm cooperating with the co-prosperity sphere," he replied and explained how he had given the Japanese "my house and my car and even my face—both cheeks." "You also? Why, what happened?" asked Buencamino. "I forgot to bow," and his friend added in parting: "Well, see you soon . . . when the sun sets. It's cooler then." For the time being, however, the weather got warmer and the imperial sun did not set, even if "the sun is sure to set."[17]

Stories about slapping spawned stories about arrests and detentions at Fort Santiago, the old symbol of Spanish tyranny built in 1565. "Everybody in the office is in a state of high nervous tension," wrote Buencamino, vice president of the National Rice and Corn Corporation, after one of the clerks had been taken to the fort in February 1942. "Why was he taken?" colleagues asked. "What will they do to him?" "Nobody dares ask.

Who will be next?" Buencamino learned that pro-American "sympathizers should beware." "Shall I help Unson? Shall I appeal for him?" he wondered and thought better of it: "What can I do, anyway? I might even be suspected." Given the conflicting pressures, Buencamino appeared to be either a collaborator or a rebel, and both to himself.

Another colleague, Ferrer, left a note on Buencamino's desk before he was arrested. It provided detail about adjustments people made to appease the new occupiers: "My dear Doctor," it read, "I am going to Fort Santiago this morning, as per Mr. Nakashima's instructions yesterday, with a clear conscience, as I know that I have not done anything inimical to the interest of the Army of Occupation. In fact, I have done my bit in suppressing" anti-Japanese talk, and "not only among my fellow-employees but among my friends outside." Ferrer quickly added a qualification lest he be misunderstood: "This is not to say that there has been much talk against the Japanese in our office; far from it." Even so, "I have tried to help guard against any undesirable rumors of whatever nature." A point in his defense was that "some even insinuated that I am pro-Japan." The note showed the possible precautions people took to protect themselves: silence, shushing, appeals, denunciation.[18]

"Employees want to quit," Buencamino reported, and he knew that "some have fled to the mountains" to avoid being arrested like Unson or compromising themselves like Ferrer.[19] A grim tide of suspicion swelled around the movements of people throughout the Japanese empire just as it had in German-occupied Europe.

Fort Santiago quickly earned a notorious reputation among Manila's residents. "Stories have crept out of Fort Santiago," noted Buencamino. "Men are being tortured . . . blows, lashings, chains, hysterical screams." He compared the "reign of terror" to the Inquisition and the purges of leftists and Communists; for the Catholic Juan Labrador, the "reign of fear" was like "Madrid under the Red Terror." For one, the Japanese were fascists, for the other, Bolsheviks, a menace in any case to ordinary people.[20]

It seemed that almost everyone in Manila knew someone who had been arrested and sent to Fort Santiago or someone who had fled to the hills to join the guerrillas. Others were forced into the local constabulary mobilized to fight the rebels. The rest apparently had a son or a brother in the army, soldiers whose fate after Japan's victories was not known; perhaps they languished as prisoners-of-war in terrible conditions at Camp O'Donnell, or they had been forced on the "death march" in Bataan that was quickly talked about as an example of Japanese cruelty. There is no equivalent to the dense ties binding the population of eighteen million to so many soldiers, guerrillas, and prisoners. In the circumstances, Filipinos took on different roles, defeatist and dreamer, collaborator and rebel.

Not long after the victory parade on May 7, 1942, to celebrate the fall of Bataan and Corregidor, the Japanese marched Filipino and American captives through the city on the way to prison camps. Along Quezon Boulevard, people crowded the route anxious to get a glimpse of a son or brother. Fernando Manalac's mother caught sight of his brother, Alfredo, looking "gaunt and famished." It was a "sad procession" with the "walking wounded" followed by "US Army and Navy ambulances and trucks overloaded with the sick and severely disabled." Most were transferred to Camp O'Donnell, a former army camp about one hundred miles north of Manila, close enough for reports on the conditions in the "hell hole" to filter back to the city. O'Donnell was like "a graveyard. Only there are no tombs and mausoleums and headstones," just "thousands of walking corpses, breathing skeletons, lying, sitting, crawling, shuffling aimlessly in a bare, treeless, sun-scorched, desert-like area."[21]

Over the summer, the Filipino prisoners were gradually released. Authorities admonished them to "collaborate with the new regime." The further release of prisoners, the Japanese High Command added, would "depend on the attitude of those released earlier." Many veterans were forcibly enlisted into the constabulary. In extended Filipino families, a cousin might be a constable, another a guerrilla, and a third wandered the streets in a tattered uniform. Each of the cousins recalled the tragedy of the surrender.

The Japanese put up notices giving Filipino soldiers until the end of June 1942 to surrender. In turn, guerrillas "posted bills all over downtown Manila exhorting the Japanese to surrender to them." It was a standoff with the Japanese setting up provisional administrations in the towns while rebels controlled much of the countryside. At the National Rice and Corn Corporation, Mr. Takizawa even found a "guerrilla pass" on his desk: "You are a good Japanese. So use this pass to save your life when the time comes." The make-do mailbox filled up; a poem was left for Buencamino at the end of July 1942; "perhaps there are guerilleros in the office," he thought, in addition to spies. In any case, he transcribed the poem into his diary: "Someday, someday, I'll live again, / I'll sing again." However, "now I must fight, / For country and right." The poet exhorted readers to "come and tramp with me," to "camp with me / Up to the hills" to strike "a blow for liberty."[22]

The desire for liberty was also the basis for collaboration. "The same cooperation and loyalty" the political elite had shown the United States, "Japan now expects from us," explained Benigno Aquino, a member of the Philippine Executive

Committee, which had been established at the outbreak of the war to protect "public order" and ensure "respect for property." After newspapers delivered the announcement "Japan Promises P.I. Independence," the committee urged "full collaboration." "What reasons can we possibly have," it asked, "to change our norm of conduct, especially now that a powerful Oriental nation offers to convert into reality that promise of independence which Americans gave us?" "Let independence come in any form!" declared Jorge Vargas, the committee's presiding officer; "we will cooperate!"[23]

There was substantial self-interest in the decision to cooperate since the landowning elite had learned from its own twentieth-century history to take seriously the threat of peasant revolt. The guerrillas were never simply anti-Japanese patriots but a mix of Communists and bandits who threatened the estates and settled old scores. Both the rich and the Japanese avoided the hills, and the Japanese in 1942 as much as the Americans in 1945 received credit for their anti-Communist sweeps in the countryside.

The Philippines was not Japan's strongest support in East Asia. Too many Filipinos remained emotionally attached to the old government for which their army had continued to fight alongside Americans well into 1942. Yet thousands of Japanese arrived to administer the occupation and give shape to the new "Oriental" family. Members of the Philippine Executive Committee echoed the exhortations: East not West, calisthenics instead of swing, community over individual, the Philippines as part of a new racial and cultural union under Japanese leadership.

To acquire Oriental character meant learning Japanese, "Nippon-go," and here the basic conversational études stressing courtesy were helpful. As schools slowly reopened in 1942, children received about ten hours a week of Japanese-language instruction. However, a shortage of teachers and lack of interest limited the number of older students—only about two thousand adults in Manila, mostly civil servants, were studying Japanese in November 1942. One phrase that everyone learned was "Nippon-go, America—come." It was easier to change the names of the streets—Heiwa for Dewey, Daitoa for Taft, Banzai for Jones.[24]

Filipinization was an appealing way to counter Anglo-Saxon influence and promote indigenous culture. Tagalog was already an official language in the Philippines, and the Japanese rummaged around to showcase authentic "classics," which appeared in the *Manila Tribune* or on KZRH radio. Tagalog fables such as "The Clever Monkey" and "How the Crow Became Black" appeared in the newspaper's Sunday magazine on October 25, 1942. They were certainly more edifying than the feature in the *Shōnan Times*, "Drums," which opened with the lines "Rub-a-dub-dub, Rub-a-dub-dub" to evoke the "mystic charm" of Malaya. Given the pervasiveness of American culture, Filipinos appreciated the new cultural spaces that opened up for Tagalog. Politicians took it up in speeches. Theater revues presented *kundiman,* or Tagalog love serenades, that José Rizal had introduced in his great patriotic novel *Noli Me Tangere* (1887).[25]

To consecrate the new era of the Philippines, the Japanese organized a calendar of celebrations. The first of these holidays was held on Monday, May 18, 1942, two weeks after the fall of Corregidor. Posters, banners, and flags filled "every conceivable" space to mark the surrender of Japan's enemies. With schools and offices closed, and cinemas and public transportation free, people jammed the downtown and, paper flags in hand, lined the parade route.[26]

Detailed instructions indicated the premium the Japanese put on the coordination of the body. In addition to publishing the parade route and a map of where participants were to stand in the Luneta, the large park by the harbor, the *Manila Tribune* went through the correct procedure of bowing, saluting, and hailing "Banzai!" "Every person is supposed to stand at attention, head uncovered when the 'Kimigayo,' the Japanese national anthem, is played and the one minute prayer for the war dead is ordered." A salute to the commander of the Japanese Imperial Army followed. After the order *"Keirei"* was given, "every participant shall remain at attention, head uncovered, hands at the sides, and shall bow 20 to 30 degrees from the waist. The command *Naore!* shall be given after the salute, to resume the original position." This was the "civic body organized."[27]

Throughout East Asia, commemorative documents featured "workers marching in step," rows of schoolchildren reciting Japanese, and "huge crowds doing gymnastics." As people fell into lines they seemed to confirm how regenerate societies took shape. Made more and less voluntarily, these collective efforts helped bring the new society into being. "All Together Now— *Ichi, Ni, San.*"[28]

As the promised date of independence approached, enthusiasm for the new era grew. If the United States was the only Western power to put a colony on the path to independence (scheduled for July 4, 1946) with the Philippine Independence Act of 1934, Japan was the first imperial power to grant formal independence, first to Burma on August 1, 1943, then to the Philippines on October 14. Even with strings attached, independence acquired symbolic value. In the end, it failed to provide the Japanese the help they needed in the short run, but it strengthened the will to national self-determination throughout East Asia.

Contemporaries followed events around Independence Day closely. Noting that the new constitution made no reference to Japan, Labrador admitted that "the Philippines would indeed be the master of its destiny." However, the president enjoyed "unlimited powers"; "the Constitution is Republican in form, but dictatorial in substance," he concluded. Even so, Labrador noted a "greater degree of spontaneity and enthusiasm" among the well-wishers on October 14 than "there had been in other celebrations in the past." Many in the "gigantic crowd" came on their own—estimates ranged up to an unlikely five hundred thousand, but wholesalers had distributed a half-million paper flags. "The truly moving act," even for "the skeptical and the non-conformists," Labrador added, was the raising of the Philippine flag.[29] Many Filipinos took what they could get with independence, the outcome, "here at last," of "the painful struggle started by our forebears in 1571," without dimming hopes for Japan's defeat.[30]

Signs of the times were difficult to read. In a single lifetime, Filipinos had lived under the Spanish, Americans, and Japanese—when asked which regime he preferred, the old man replied: "The best regime is our own regime. A Filipino regime!"[31] The question was whether genuine sovereignty would come with East Asian Co-Prosperity, or after an eventual American victory, or through the self-help of local guerrillas. In any event, in 1943, Japan had not suffered any serious setback in East Asia; the pins on the map stayed in place. Although every Filipino knew that MacArthur promised to return, he had already left.

The people of the Philippines lived in two worlds during the war, Filipino Japanese and Fil-American. The degree to which you had a foot in one world and a foot in the other depended on where you saw beginnings and endings. On how you counted time. Some counted out *Ichi, Ni, San* as they improved themselves on the exercise field. Others tapped their feet to the tune of "Chattanooga Choo-Choo":[32]

Pardon me boys,
Do you believe the Yanks are coming.
I certainly do
I see the red, white and blue
    Do you suppose
There's gonna be a lot of shooting
Certainly not
It needn't be quite so hot
    I know that all of you have really got
Just one big desire
And that's to see the Tokyo paper
Houses on fire
Bombs will soon be falling
Cannons will be roaring
Till all those doggoned Japanese have
Perished forever
    When you hear the siren whistle
Eight to the bar
Then you know that Uncle Sam is not very far
Jump into your dugouts
Don't be too impatient
'Cause Uncle Sam is gonna keep his date

There was a third timeline, the struggle of armed resistance that was intertwined with peasant rebellions against the landed estates and Emilio Aguinaldo's storied fight at the turn of the century against both the Spaniards and the Americans. (Aguinaldo, who sided with the Japanese in 1942, saw it all, dying at the age of ninety-four in 1964.) Not everyone in the hills was a social revolutionary. The rebel units had been seeded and armed by Philippine soldiers and officers, including those Americans who refused to follow General Wainwright's call to surrender after the fall of Corregidor. But the broad rural infrastructure of support in the islands and the leadership of socialist Luis Taruc made the Huk (or Hukbalahap, the "People's Army Against Japan") resistance similar to other insurgencies in Southeast Asia: the Burmese Independence Army, which switched its allegiances to the British in 1945 after supporting the Japanese in 1942; the largely ethnic Chinese Communist-led Malayan People's Anti-Japanese Army; and the Vietminh, a popular front organized by the Communist Party to fight the Japanese in Indochina. In these cases the timeline of liberation was older and longer, and popular anti-imperial struggles stretched well into the postwar period.

As Buencamino's account confirms, Filipinos' everyday interactions with the Japanese were laced with fear. They were accompanied by slaps, arrests, and executions. The Japanese "treat the Filipinos as 'conquered' people, not as 'liberated brothers,'" was Buencamino's summary. Collaborators themselves admitted that most Filipinos never warmed to the occupiers.[33]

However, estrangement from the Japanese did not necessarily mean fighting against them. After the first guerrilla bands emerged, Filipinos were not sure whether these were bandits, or Communist-led peasants, or patriotic militias led by regular army recruits. Catholic rector Juan Labrador always referred to them as "so-called guerrillas," taking note, like other conservatives, of the general threat they posed to law and order.

Even when Filipinos considered the guerillas outlaws, the assaults of the Japanese reached a tipping point so that more individuals felt compelled to seek revenge. "News of each insult, slap, atrocity and destruction inflicted on any Filipino radiated across kinship networks," writes one historian. In T. D. Agcaoili's short story "Tenderness" (1949), the sixteen-year-old boy knifed two Japanese who had raped his sister; now "'I am a guerrilla,' he whispered," having fled the scene. ("Stepped in so far," Macbeth acknowledged, "I am in blood.") As recounted in Stevan Javellana's novel, *Without Seeing the Dawn* (1947), villagers had endured calamities before the war—devastating floods or evictions from the land they leased—but the contrast between hard times in the first part of Javellana's novel and the extraordinary violence of the war in the second is stark. Japanese attacks affected everybody in the village: The whole "cycle of work—plowing, sowing, harvesting"—was disrupted. "Houses are burned down and villages destroyed. People are forced to evacuate." "Death touches the young and the old, the men and the women. One by one, the villagers die from a bullet, a bayonet, a sword." Over months and years, kinship forged a new identification with the Philippine armed resistance. Relays provided information and supplies, allowing guerrillas to operate as a hidden army in the hills.[34]

When the Japanese announced their resolve to "wage a war of extermination against the guerrillas," Filipinos became aware of the extent of the "disorders." Insurgents had "gained the upper hand" in Cebu, Panay, Negros, and other islands, while the Japanese, in reprisal, "burned several towns and gunned down thousands of civilians," noted Labrador about the escalation of

violence at the end of 1942.[35] The aim of insurgency and coun-
terinsurgency was to use terror to force civilians to take sides,
which heightened their vulnerability. As the number of guerrillas operating across the archipelago increased to two hundred
thousand by the end of the war, violence infiltrated into everyday life. At least one-half million Filipino civilians died during
the war—many times the total number of military deaths. Right
through to the end of the war, the partner nations of the East
Asia Co-Prosperity Sphere suffered proportionally more civilian casualties than bombed-up Japan.

During the occupation, the entire nation found itself on the
front lines, and, after the war, the guerrilla movement stood
out as a great romantic theme in Philippine history.[36] What is
striking in accounts of the war of resistance, however, are the
descriptions of unbounded violence. This was certainly so on
the part of the Japanese; one veteran testified at the Tokyo War
Crimes Trial of how he killed more than one hundred civilians:
"Now I am a hardened killer and my sword is always stained
with blood." In despair, the penitent turned to his ancestors:
"May God forgive me! May my mother forgive me!" In the
bloody onslaught against guerrillas, Japanese soldiers themselves
felt besieged and exposed; one former soldier titled his memoir
Jungle of No Mercy.[37] The brutality also stained villagers, whose
clan solidarities splintered as young men were enlisted either in
the constabulary or with the guerrillas.

In Javellana's novel, Carding's guerrillas reflect on killing
Polo, a cousin in the constabulary. Carding tried to end the conversation: "We have our orders," he said quietly. But the others
"would not be silent. 'It is a funny war, this,'" one of the comrades sighed, "where one fights against his brother." "I wish
this war were over"—he spoke for many others. The villagers

eventually banished Carding precisely because he had become a killer with "the sharp taste of blood . . . on his tongue." Villagers feared the terrific Japanese reprisals that guerrilla actions such as Carding's brought down on them, and they feared Carding. They were caught in the spiral of violence. A suspected informer summarized the new law of the hills: the "soldier is the plaintiff, sheriff, judge, and executioner all in one during these days and a bullet costs only eight centavos, they say."[38] "They say" stood in for all the rumors and verbal threats that surrounded the guerrillas and their violence.

Punctuating Filipino accounts of the war was the crime of rape. The role of the Imperial Japanese Army in the rape of thousands of women and the forced prostitution into which the military forced thousands more across East Asia was first documented in the Tokyo trials. Brutalities against civilians were so widespread that it was said that "the Spaniards had built churches in the Philippines, the Americans had built schools, and the Japanese had built brothels." More than a Japanese atrocity since the guerrillas also assaulted hostages and other civilians, rape was a generalized way of thinking about the war and its aftermath. In perhaps his most famous remark, President Quezon, holed up in Corregidor in January 1942, lashed out at the "shameless" Americans who supplied Britain, but not the Philippines, as promised. "How typically American to writhe in anguish at the fate of a distant cousin while a daughter is being raped in a back room!" In this case, the atrocity served to accuse the defender of the home, not the assailant who had invaded. Rape was an assault, but revealed domestic betrayal.[39]

As Javellana tells it, the same soldier who defended the home by joining the guerrillas to take revenge also abandoned his wife, the victim of rape, and attempted to murder her baby. The avenger became a demon in the view of villagers whose lives had been violently seized as much by the guerrillas as by the Japanese. Rape forged the first link in a chain of violence and corruption in Frankie José's classic postwar novel of the Philippines, *Ermita* (1988). After the initial assault, which takes place in Manila in 1945, the highborn victim kills the Japanese assailant only to later abandon the baby in order to protect the family's reputation. As she grows up, Ermita discovers her patrician origins and exacts revenge. She does so by corrupting herself as a high-class prostitute, which allows her to strike back at her family through various means that are facilitated by the courtesan's connections to the political elite that is selling out the country. The story of one rape revealed many more so that José leaves Filipino society ravaged, victimized, and vindictive.[40]

The Philippine story José tells is one in which collaborators have taken the place of false revolutionaries. Even the scrupulous history professor on whom the tell-all account relies ends up in public relations and kills himself in despair. The initial rape by the Japanese soldier gets mislaid because it serves as a catalyst for the politically charged collaborations and betrayals or rapes to come. Since Japan's invasion is simply a proxy for the aggression of post-1945 Philippine society itself, José claims there could not have been a good war.

The violence of the postwar years after Japan's surrender in Asia needs to stay in view: the civil wars in China and Indonesia, the ethnic cleansing of minorities in Burma, and the costs of liberation in Vietnam as well as collaboration in the Philippines and elsewhere. But the view cannot conceal in so many successive postwar links the wartime depredations of Japanese occupiers, whose brutal colonial regime compressed untold violence into very few years. Nor should it conceal the violence of the prewar colonial world of race and place that the Japanese war destroyed. All the scenes of empire, occupation, and liberation played out in the Philippines in a dispiriting twilight. Already in 1942, both collaboration and resistance marked out common ground characterized by often unbearable choices that each side forced onto people in the war.

CHAPTER 20

The "Old Town" in Ukraine

Heroes or cowards? Historians echo the Soviet line about the stark choice that confronted the people of the Soviet Union after the German invasion. It was the premise of Stalin's "No Retreat" order in July 1942: there was no room for further retreat; there was no eastern shore to the Volga River. Red Army soldiers spoke up to endorse the brutal ultimatum as the necessary means for toughening the fighting spirit. By the time historians arrived in Stalingrad even before the final victory had been achieved, they found the fighting men had "fully incorporated Soviet notions of heroism and cowardice" and understood "the battle's political and historical significance." The manifestation of the "Russian 'soul' or 'spirit'" mattered to ordinary people and, by motivating them, made a material difference. This was twentieth-century war—ideological affiliations were critical to bonding the ranks.[1]

"Heroes or cowards" is not wrong or tendentious, but the formula is incomplete in understanding the fate of Soviet citizens fighting the German armies or surviving under their occupation. On June 22, 1941, the morning of the invasion, as residents in Leningrad gathered to listen to the news, tongues loosened. Sitting on a trunk in the hallway, "smiling sarcastically," "our former landlady" made "no attempt to hide her hatred of the Soviet government." She "sees in this war and eventual German victory our only possible salvation." That was one side of the conversation. Another recognized the "clash between two antagonistic forces—socialism and fascism!"—on which "the well-being of mankind" depended. Others took the invasion as an attack on Russia itself. In an extraordinary burst of energy on that first day, more than one hundred thousand citizens showed up to volunteer to defend Leningrad, an example of courage repeated across the Soviet Union.[2]

When it became clear that the Soviet Union would not collapse like a "house of cards" as Hitler had predicted, commitment stiffened. Comments such as "See, today it is already over three weeks and they still hold on!" indicated that the Soviet Union might not go under as had Poland and France. By August, German generals began to calculate the resistance of the Red Army they had not counted on. Moltke talked about the attackers having touched "something terrible" that would cause their own destruction. Whole factories were dismantled and districts evacuated in synchrony with Soviet commands. Every month in the summer and fall of 1941, more than one million people moved to the rear; travelers later encountered these evacuees from Leningrad and Kiev wherever they went.[3]

There was also a feeling that the war had opened to a new, morally purified world in which to build the future. At the sight of the militant virtue of the ordinary Russian at Stalingrad, novelist Vasily Grossman believed that the war was "washing away all the Stalinist filth from the face of Russia." "The holy blood of this war would cleanse us from the blood stains" of the purges of the 1930s. People came together feeling the thrill of a just cause, the fight against fascism, even as the ex-prisoner took note after his early release, "I realized that long before you did."[4] For anti-Bolsheviks, the depredations of the German occupiers forced many to embrace the cause they once despised. Soon enough, the old woman who waited for the Germans with quiet hope, "We've seen what's been, we'll see what comes," was countermanded by the one who realized: "Oh this Hitler, he's a real Satan! And we used to say that the Communists were Satans." As one Polish soldier in the Home Army described his choice: "We await you, red plague / To deliver us from the black death."[5]

However, the landlady's sarcastic smile never faded away completely. Hatred for the Soviet system was anchored in the utter disruption of rural life after the forced collectivization of agriculture in the 1930s and the starvation and deportation accompanying it. Collectivization was experienced as death. Until the very end, Soviet citizens, many but not all of them from the newly annexed western borderlands of Ukraine and Belarus, threw their lot in with the Germans. It was their tragedy, observes Timothy Snyder, that they were forced to compare two bloody systems, the Soviet and the Nazi, and to decide whether to stay or to flee, a more apt alternative than to be a hero or a coward.[6] As it was, the Germans quickly dashed hopes Ukrainians or Russians had for some sort of autonomous existence in the German empire, one that would break up the collective farms, clear out the Soviet bosses, and offer peasants a better life.

For all the patronizing talk about gifting "Ukrainians with scarves, glass beads and everything that colonial peoples like," Hitler resisted any effort to enact reforms or engage the Slavic population, or to recognize Ukraine as a cultural or political entity. The most basic step to graft Ukrainian allegiances, the end of collectivization, was not contemplated. As a result, for Soviet citizens the German future looked bleak. Generalplan Ost outlined the goal of starving the "subhuman" Slavic mass beyond an enslaved remnant. When Hitler compared the Volga to the Mississippi, he had in mind the compression of the long process of usurpation, depopulation, and murder in North America into a few short years by means of deliberately genocidal policies that would eliminate Jews and Slavs to create German space out of ethnic lands. Of course, there was a great gap between what Germans planned and what they were able to achieve, yet this was measured not by restraint or neglect but by the escalation of violence rooted in the fantastical racial ideas of the German conquerors.

From the beginning, the occupation regime was cruel and arbitrary, touching every corner of life. Streets emptied out; corpses were left lying about, an everyday sight throughout occupied eastern Europe. Almost every town in Ukraine had a gallows erected on the public square. Since residents were abused for even the slightest infractions such as an improper greeting, the Germans' threat of punishment or death loomed over everyone. Even more shocking was the sight of columns of prisoners-of-war, whose pitiful march was punctuated by gunfire. Rumors about the vicious conditions in the prisoner camps, where more than two million Soviet men died of hunger and disease before the end of the first year, spread quickly, confirming the systematic nature of the Wehrmacht's murderous policies.

On any given day in the fall of 1941 more Soviet captives died than did British or American prisoners-of-war over the course of the entire war.[7]

Although many householders tended private gardens, starvation was commonplace in the cities. Germans walked around "full and content," but "we all move about like shadows," "buying food by the cup," boiling watery soup without the bread. "There is total famine," confirmed one diarist; "those who have nothing swell up from hunger, they are already dying. Many people have typhus." Since "obviously it is inconvenient to shoot everybody," she noted in April 1942, the Germans simply condemned the population to a "slow death."[8] "They are already dying" described the general condition of all those still alive.

The most "spectacular" assault on daily life in occupied Ukraine and Belarus was the forced deportations of laborers to Germany. If, at the very beginning, there was some interest in opportunities to work in the Reich, the brutality of the roundups to fill quotas as well as the trickle of news from *Ostarbeiter* already there turned deportation into a fate equated with death itself. In just a few months, the German authorities demanded fifty thousand recruits a month; by the beginning of 1943, they were trying to round up three thousand or four thousand people a day. Tatiana Fesenko described one such "action" in a Kiev market in May 1942. When the German authorities showed up with local policemen and dogs, the place broke into chaos: passersby "rushed about with eyes wide with horror, overturning baskets and stands, but the German policemen implacably shoved the screaming women and pale men into the large cargo vans." There was a time when relatives were still notified to bring the prisoners underwear, a coat, and shoes before their transport to Germany. Later on, people just disappeared on an errand in town. After roundups, which netted hundreds of people in an afternoon, residents fell into a state of shock, "moving about like dummies"; otherwise, "the streets are dead, even the children are in hiding." In Ukraine, as in the rest of occupied Europe, nothing stoked hatred for the Germans as did the deportations, the single most critical factor in the calculated decision of young men and women to flee into the countryside and join the partisans.[9]

As a journalist for the Red Army, Vasily Grossman tried to write the collective diary of Ukrainians under German rule that amounted to a lengthy record of "colossal injustice." He tried to tabulate the crimes: "forced labour and secret beatings, children deported to Germany, burnt houses and looted warehouses . . . pits where those suspected of having sympathy for or connections with the partisans were shot," in addition to the everyday "humiliations and mockery, vulgar cursing and bribes, drunken and erratic behavior, and the bestial depravity of reckless, criminal people in whose hands rested" the life and fate of millions of Ukrainians. "There is no home in a single Ukrainian town or village where you will not hear bitter and evil words about the Germans, no home where tears have not flowed," and "no home without an orphan or a widow. These tears and curses flow like streams to an immense river of collective grief and fury."[10]

After the occupation, no more than one hundred thousand residents remained in Kiev; four-fifths of the population had been starved, deported, or murdered. It was "a stunning picture": "There are no children," only "old women and disabled people."[11]

At the same time, growing numbers of partisans stalked the forests. They certainly loomed in the imagination of Wehrmacht soldiers who went on patrol to clear the countryside. One infantryman described how the "path led through swamps" and "endless forests—we are seriously threatened by the partisans who are very numerous and very clever; entire columns are attacked in broad daylight and they even come upon us in German uniforms and speaking perfect German in order to fool us." When hunting partisans, the Wehrmacht killed the innocent, bagging more bodies than weapons. The diary of an "unknown soldier" records highlights of daily life in one unit in January and early February 1942:

> Jan. 14, 1942: Went to church in the morning. Services were going on. Put 50 pfennig into the box.
> Jan. 21, 1942: At 8 o'clock we shot 4 men and 1 woman.
> Jan. 23, 1942: In the evening received mail from my wife and relatives . . .
> Jan. 25, 1942: 15 Russians shot in the afternoon . . .
> Jan. 27, 1942: In the morning 5 were shot.
> Feb. 2, 1942: Shot 6. Roasted a goose; very tasty.

Another soldier in the unit had a "terrible dream" about "the thirty youngsters that I had to kill." However, no one in the Wehrmacht doubted the necessity of eradicating partisans.[12]

The Soviet victory at Stalingrad dramatically increased the number of partisans and the armed attacks they were able to mount. By the beginning of 1943, the Wehrmacht found it difficult to control the countryside outside fortified towns in Ukraine. As a result, the peasants whose villages dotted the fields and forests of the occupied territories felt increasingly closed in as much by the threat posed by anti-German insurgents as by German counterinsurgents. To switch the metaphor, wartime society came to resemble "a raft carried along further and further by a raging river." "The power of the waters was so strong," writes one historian, "that none of the occupants could reach the safety of shore. Rudderless, the raft lurched over rapids and in the falls disintegrated piece-by-piece. Every cataract brought the people closer to their destruction. Everyone on the raft tried to improve their chances of survival. Some desperately tried to lash themselves to logs. Others jumped into the roaring current" to make it to shore or attacked their fellows in misery to throw them overboard in order to reduce the weight of the raft. Hemmed in by threats or pushed into rough waters, society broke apart.[13]

For many Ukrainians, the death and destruction of collectivization in the years before the war had been accompanied by the premonition of a violent reckoning in which the Soviets would be swept away. With the German invasion the day of judgment was suddenly at hand. Hope for a good harvest, the protection of kin and kith in time of war, and the expectation of the restoration of old property made willing collaborators out of Ukrainian peasants. A broad stratum of mayors and village elders stood ready to do their part to fulfill Ukrainian longings for political autonomy in accord with overall German authority. Mayors grew powerful as they imposed and distributed the burdens demanded by the new rulers, the grain deliveries, taxes, and labor recruits, and as they tried to protect the community by denouncing Communists, expelling Red Army stragglers and other outsiders, and collaborating with the Wehrmacht and SS when they came to round up and murder local Jews.

However, the urge to defend the hometown created the practices that cannibalized it. Since denunciations were fueled by long-standing grudges and resentments, social relations were slashed by fear and suspicion. As people looked out for their own, village ties dissolved. The Nazis' resolve to wipe out

Jewish communities was both deeply disruptive and unexpectedly opportune for local residents. Mayors and policemen more or less willingly joined SS efforts to round up Jews, who were often notionally identified with the old Communist authority and visibly degraded by the new German one. Motivated by greed, envy, and fear, and by virulent anti-Semitism, neighbors looted so much Jewish property they bickered about the division of the spoils. One district officer described locals as "mad" about "old Jewish stuff"; news of Jewish shootings in larger towns attracted "caravans of eager buyers" from the surrounding countryside. "Every local massacre," writes one historian, was followed by "an 'epidemic of denunciations' of remaining Jews and of anybody from 'mixed' marriages," which further eroded communal obligations. A "world without Jews" did not restore order for non-Jews.[14]

Since there were always more burdens than available resources and less treasure than prospectors, mayors found themselves in a tightening vise. As they desperately attempted to comply with German demands for grain and labor, they revealed their own powerlessness, which left them more vulnerable but also more violent. On the one hand, mayors were held responsible for security threats posed by partisans, while on the other hand, they pleaded with the increasingly beleaguered Germans to provide them more effective protection against external attacks. With partisan warfare, the logic of enemy lines crisscrossed villages without the front being clearly visible; pacification could take the form of total annihilation. In one instance, a peasant made the decision to join the partisans, who suspected his motives and shot him as a German spy. When security forces learned of his fate, they executed the peasant's wife and five young children as a "partisan family."[15]

Under these circumstances, rewards and punishments could no longer be calculated since the sums seemed completely arbitrary. Ethnic identity made it easier to designate alleged criminals, but like the massacre of Jews, the murder of ethnic Poles or Ukrainians did not restore security to the community.

If Jews had a clear reason to be on one side and not the other, they did not survive the equally clear resolve with which Nazis, abetted by the anti-Semitism of local people, pursued them. For the rest of the non-Jewish population, it was much more a matter of chance if one fought for or was killed by one side or another, a question of "who was in the village when the Soviet partisans or the Germans appeared on their recruiting missions."[16] Larger kinds of orientation, such as ideology or loyalty to the Soviets or hope for a better life under the German overlords, mattered less as time went on and the scale of violence expanded. People did not die as partisans or soldiers or even collaborators, but luckless, as victims. There was often little connection between the story of the war, its presentation, and the way it destroyed lives, its production. Victims could not be assembled as heroes or as cowards, and their deaths were too numerous and too arbitrary to be portrayed as redemptive. "Everything seemed to have become worthless," wrote Grossman about the German occupation.[17]

"TEARS AND CURSES" streamed across Ukraine and other parts of the German-occupied Soviet Union, but they did not flow unimpeded down the hollows into "an immense river of collective grief and fury," as Vasily Grossman contended in 1943. Hitler caused tears and tears, and he was twice, and thrice, cursed, but as he reported from Stalingrad and Ukraine, Grossman came to understand that the people themselves had also been cursed. Their fury was directed against the Germans, but also against Communists and Jews. It was like the plague. As he explored fate in war, he found life to be more and more treacherous. In his stories about the war, Grossman saw cruelty not as a river flowing in bloody streams, but as a vast toxic sea lapping and corroding every shore. Taken as a whole, his work ended up renouncing the epic, heroic features of the battle at Stalingrad he had first depicted. Grossman was not alone in this: the closer victory approached, the more it appeared as defeat on all sides.

When we get to the conclusion, it begins to tremble.

The German occupation of Ukraine served Grossman as a powerful model for the way fascism worked. In his initial accounts of German power, he depicted a confrontation "of good struggling to overcome evil." For all the difficulties of the struggle in conditions wearied by vanity and weakness, Grossman identified two clear figures, the flawed, bleeding defenders and the malevolent intruders, in the battle between the Red Army and the Wehrmacht. This schema structures his first two novels, *The People Immortal* (1943), on the first stages of the German invasion in 1941, and *For a Just Cause* (1952), expanded from notes and translated into English as *Stalingrad* (2019). After Stalingrad, Grossman also explored how Ukrainians themselves became corrupted by fascism, which allowed the German invaders to grip the foreign territory they had conquered. This corruption of the "town" is portrayed in the short story "The Old Teacher" (1943) and provides a miniature template of the destruction of human beings by powerful state regimes. These broad ideas were followed up in Grossman's wide-ranging novel *Life and Fate* (first published in English in 1980 but completed in 1960). Written as a twentieth-century version of

Tolstoy's *War and Peace*, it takes as its subject the "great evil" of both Nazism and Stalinism as each crushed humanity but for the "small kernel of human kindness."[18] Underneath his reporting on war was the half-hidden drama of Grossman's Jewish family. The German invasion on June 22, 1941, posed an immediate threat to Berdichev, the Ukrainian hometown where his mother, a retired French teacher, still lived and where he had sent his daughter for the summer. Efforts to retrieve them failed, although Katya turned up safe in a summer camp. Grossman lost contact with his mother after the Germans overran Berdichev on July 7. Persistent rumors about anti-Jewish actions proved to be true, as Grossman finally learned in 1944: Berdichev's Jews were herded into a ghetto on August 26, 1941, and murdered on September 15, the day after the date Grossman provided for the mother's last letter in *Life and Fate*. Throughout the war, the son tries to find information about Yekaterina Savelievna, all the time nursing a sense of guilt that he has not been able to bring her to Moscow or override his wife's objections—apparently neither Grossman's mother nor her daughter-in-law liked each other, and the issue pops up in his novels. A feeling of reproach shadowed the marriage for the rest of his life.[19] With his mother lost, Grossman honed a new mindfulness about Jews in Europe combined with a new sensitivity to the unmindfulness of others. The fate of Jews both tested and revised the place of evil in Grossman's political thinking.

In both the melodramatic conception of "Good and Evil" and the more tragic rewriting of "senseless kindness" imperiled by greater evil, the existence of the first forbids the total victory of the second, but the outcome is not certain. It is an unequal, unresolved struggle that fuels the energy of *Life and Fate*. There is resilience in the small matter of the "kernel" of kindness that is explored in the "Last Letter" that the mother writes the son from inside the ghetto, the counterpart to the "Old Town" in "The Old Teacher." Twentieth-century history and particularly World War II compose the big parts, the acts, of Grossman's two Stalingrad novels, *Stalingrad* itself and *Life and Fate*, but it is Grossman's more personal engagement with Ukrainian places under German occupation, the "Old Town" and the ghetto, that provides the material for his shift in focus from inhuman fascism to dehumanizing state power in which fascism and Stalinism amount to the same thing. Grossman's wartime judgment on the twentieth century starts in Stalingrad and ends in Berdichev, the town where he was born and where his mother was murdered as a Jew in September 1941.

Grossman introduces fascism in war as almost insurmountable German-made machinery. "All over occupied Europe the long drive belt of the 'new order' was spinning the wheels of hundreds of thousands of smaller businesses of every kind," he writes. It encompassed "French steelworks," "Belgian coal mines," "Dutch precision mechanics," the "Skoda arms manufacturer in Czechoslovakia," "the Romanian oil industry," as well as "textile factories of Lodz." Driven to conquer, it rolled over life that had been so vibrant on "the last night of peace": "the whole of the vast young country" recognizable in the sounds of the accordion "in little city gardens, on dance floors, in village streets," and "in meadows, beside streams." The invaders had violently "opened every door in Russia" to drive "people out of their warm homes and onto black autumn roads." "Is fascism really so very powerful?" The fallen cities on the map, Kiev, then Kharkov and Sevastopol, seemed to provide the answer to the question.[20]

There was something new to fascism, more than its industrial power. Its "terrible mechanics" operated "only with vast aggregates," defeating the idea of individuality. Burning villages, building death camps, perpetrating the "massacres of peaceful civilians we haven't seen since the dawn of history," fascism had "arrived at the idea of the liquidation of entire strata of the population, of entire nations and races." Its victory meant that "man will cease to exist." A single unassailable or unblemished form was not human, which can only be portrayed with the textures and colors the fascists despised.[21]

It was the people who had been driven from their homes who hurled themselves against the Germans. Grossman heard a faint roar from the area of the factories, a cry almost drowned by shell bursts and gunfire: "'A-a-a-a-a-h!' There was something terrible, but also something sad and melancholy" in the long cry uttered by Russian infantry as they staged an attack. "As it crossed the cold water" of the Volga River, to the far bank where the writer was standing, he could "hear the sadness of a soul parting with everything that it loved, calling on the nearest and dearest to wake up, to lift their heads from their pillows and hear for the last time the voice of a father, a husband, a son, or a brother" and to join the battle themselves. At the front, Grossman observed, "there is patience and resignation, submission to unthinkable hardships." This was the patience of a "strong people" who fought the war for life as well as survival. "The front," Grossman concluded, represented "the holiness of Russian death," whereas the rear represented "the sin of Russian life." It was this spirit visible in death and victorious at Stalingrad that Grossman believed could restore society in the rear and revive the ideals of the revolution. Among the fighting men, Stalin's order "Not One Step Back" echoed "sorrow and anger" about dereliction of duty, and also "faith in victory," a victory that would decide "the fate of a great people" and the whole map of the world. He described a mutilated but recognizable heroism.[22]

When Grossman left the victory grounds of Stalingrad to arrive in the first places liberated in Ukraine, he was at once confronted with the evidence of the mass murder of civilians and the almost complete annihilation of Jews. The scale of death stood out. Grossman added more parts to his depiction of the "terrible mechanics" of fascism. One of the reasons the machine kept functioning was that it was able to replace "equality among nations" with a workable racial hierarchy with the "master German race" at the top and Jews at the bottom. Fascism, he explained in his 1943 essay "Ukraine Without Jews," "resolved to poison each nation against all others: to place the Dutch and Danes on the highest rungs of the ladder of punishment," to poison the French with petty privileges denied the Czechs, "to place the Serbs further down, and appease them with the fact that Ukrainians and Belorussians stand below them on the bottom rungs." The fascists could steady this "whole ladder of oppression" with "the horrible abyss of non-existence it had prepared for the Jewish people" who were to blame for the misfortune of all. It was the winning principle of "divide and conquer."[23]

However, Jewish death was different not simply because Jews occupied the lowest rung. When fascists executed Dutch, French, Serbian, or Ukrainian people, it was for "violating fascist rules and laws," however arbitrary they seemed, "but the Germans execute the Jews only because of the fact that they are Jews." This lack of distinction explained why the majority of those killed were "old women, the elderly, sick people, and children." As such, the crime was entirely without precedent in the "history of humanity." By raising the difference between

Ukrainian death and Jewish death, Grossman contravened the basic antifascist principle of not dividing the Soviet dead.[24]

In "Ukraine Without Jews," Grossman tried to remain faithful to the principle of brotherhood by insisting on the grief of Ukrainians: in towns and villages, "people speak with profound empathy for the victims, and with repulsive hatred for the butchers." Yet a "dreadful silence" prevailed throughout the land. This total silence, this complete absence, vexed Grossman, who returned to the unequal fate of the Jews: "If the murdered people could be revived for an instant," he wrote, "the Universe would shudder" to hear the "penetrating cry" from "hundreds of thousands of lips covered in soil." Something did not add up. In the lee of the people's grief, he admitted that local police forces had cooperated to execute Jews and that "policemen, members of their families, and the mistresses of German soldiers rushed to loot the vacated apartments."[25]

Writing about the military fight against the Germans, Grossman had already stumbled on unheroic parts to Russia's deaths. Unlike the Wehrmacht, the Red Army did not dispatch burial teams; "thousands of soldiers, to whom Russia owed its salvation, were left unburied" in "the fields and forest where they fell." That the defenders were expendable was evident in all aspects of "Not One Step Back": the brutality of military justice, the frequent frontal attacks on German lines (thus the forlorn cry "A-a-a-a-a-h!"), and the fact that the heroes of Stalingrad on the Volga were used as bait for the larger Uranus operation around the Don. In his story "The Old Teacher," Grossman went further, working to pry open the group of Ukrainian policemen and mistresses who had swum so conspicuously against the current of grief and fury.[26]

Instead of small numbers of traitors, Grossman found the Old Town filled with complicit residents. He followed long chains of resentment, greed, and fear across the community rather than stepping down the rungs of the German-made "ladder of oppression." And he discovered a ready-made vocabulary of censure that townspeople put into an active grammar of collaboration, exploitation, and murder.

Readers are quickly introduced to a courtyard of characters whose actions, as the "old teacher" explains, historians and philosophers have "celebrated, justified, blamed, and cursed." The courtyard does not divide simply into Good and Evil, sunshine and rain. Among the people "on this splendid earth" are Old Mikhailyuchka and her son, Yashka, a deserter from the Red Army, who has been hiding. A neighbor remarks: "The Germans have arrived—you're going to be quite somebody now! A deserter for a son and a husband in a labor camp for anti-Soviet agitation. . . . [T]he Germans will be putting you in charge of the whole town!" "Our day's dawned at last!" Mikhailyuchka agrees. Yashka himself appears as if it were Easter Sunday the day German soldiers arrive; "he had shaved and put on an embroidered shirt."[27]

Residents in the courtyard also included Voronenko, a hero who had returned from the front with an amputated leg. Now that the Germans are in town, however, Dasha, his wife, appeals to the emboldened Yashka, a former suitor she had spurned years ago, not to denounce her husband since he had been conscripted "the same as everyone else." Unlike everyone else, however, Voronenko had also previously denounced neighbors to the Soviet authorities for being counterrevolutionary "kulaks," as Old Mikhailyuchka reminded Dasha. In a different kind of move, Koryako, the agronomist who had prepared the district's collectivization plan, saves his own skin by switching sides and offering his services to the new German commandant who makes him a block warden; Yashka also joins the police. The poison of collaboration is not just a fascist potion; it is also Ukrainian and Soviet, although the Germans determined how it could be used in 1941.

The town undergoes a rapid transformation. A German cinema opens—and a brothel. Women are marched to the outskirts to build an aerodrome while prisoners-of-war, "ragged, staggering with hunger," are herded through the streets. Language also changes. Words of German begin to appear in Koryako's speech: "I'm on my way to *nach Hause* or for to *spazier.*" On his walks, he apparently wondered about "our Jews": "I haven't glimpsed a Jew all day," he noted; "it's as if they'd never existed. And only yesterday they were all coming back from the market with twelve-kilo baskets!" Jewish space has been constricted in part because Yashka, in an attempt to gain more "living space," has evicted the Weissman family, a Jewish war widow and her daughter, from their rooms.

Grossman makes it difficult for readers to parse the resilience of the town. Modeled in part on Grossman's Jewish mother, the "old teacher," who had asked the unwilling doctor for a vial of poison, decides to live because he has become an optimist. "The Fascists miscalculated," he contends; "they meant to unleash hatred, but what has been born is compassion." The "fate of the Jews has evoked only grief and compassion." It is the Jewish doctor who ends up committing suicide in despair about the lack of compassion. Jews also debate the brutal intentions of the Germans. "How can they kill a man who makes shoes like I do?" asked Old Borukh. "'The Germans are capable of anything,' said Mendel, the stove maker. 'Anything at all.'" Yet Grossman tips the hand of the optimists. Weissman's little girl covers the teacher's eyes with her hand so the old man will not be frightened as both step toward the edge of the execution ditch and wait for the moment of death. And after the massacre, a partisan attack keeps the German commandant from being able to "breathe freely" in a town without Jews. The fire the partisans ignited is Grossman's final, somewhat contrived image in the story: "It seemed to the people standing outside in their yards that the dark smoky flames were burning away everything bad, everything impure and evil with which the Germans had tried to poison the human soul." The optimists win, but pessimists were right in their suspicions about how deep the poison had seeped into the community.

The "Old Teacher" moves directly from the corralling of Jews to their massacre, but the experience of the ghetto in the interim period was documented at length by Grossman in *Life and Fate* in the form of a last letter that Anna Semyonovna wrote to her son, Viktor Shtrum, Grossman's alter ego. The information in the letter was based on Grossman's interviews with neighbors in Berdichev, where he arrived after its liberation in January 1944, and on communication about his mother he received from a surviving cousin of one of her French pupils in the doomed ghetto in 1946. It is the novel *Stalingrad* that provides the backstory to the letter, detailing the circuitous route it took before Viktor opened it, a series of delays and interruptions that indicates how information from the side regarding the destruction of the Jews became central to the main character only in an improbable or roundabout way. It is a relay that simulates the hesitant, misleading reflections on the Holocaust in the Soviet Union. The sum of Grossman's publications suggests this: what compounded the zealous German effort to kill the Jewish people was the townspeople's effort to steal their livelihoods before their deaths and the Soviet effort to extinguish the memory of the totality of their disappearance afterward.[28]

If *Stalingrad* quickly summarizes the contents of the letter as "his mother's record of her last days—from the beginning of the war until the eve of her inevitable death behind the barbed wire of the Jewish ghetto," *Life and Fate* transcribes the entire letter in a separate chapter in which Anna's Jewish voice is brought to life. The later novel probes the letter's powerful transformative impact on Shtrum, who resembles Grossman and shares his family's calamity.[29]

Like Shtrum, and Grossman himself, Anna never really considered her Jewishness until the German invasion. In the ghetto, however, her heart "filled with a maternal tenderness towards the Jewish people," a love she compares to her love for her "dearest son." A sense of Jewishness is fortified through the exclusion Anna experiences in the occupied Old Town where she encounters "gloating spite" or else the kind of pity reserved for "a mangy, half-dead cat." She realizes that "there are people whose souls have just withered, people who are ready to go along with anything evil—anything so as not to be suspected of disagreeing with whoever's in power." This harsh social fact is what the Old Town reveals. Anna therefore finds the ghetto a relief because "everyone around me shares my fate." In *Life and Fate*, the ghetto stands as the defining contrast to the Ukrainian Old Town. Anna's Jewishness is also fortified by the bright life she sees in the ghetto even though it "will disappear for ever under this earth." She warmed to "this whole noisy world of bearded, anxious fathers and querulous grandmothers who bake honey-cakes and goose-necks—this whole world of marriage customs, proverbial sayings and Sabbaths." It is a world in which many Jews nurse hope and continue to live for others. Anna gives French lessons; artisans work their trades.[30]

The Germans destroyed this vital life. At once "some terrible breath has passed over people's faces and everyone knows that the end is approaching." Anna also seems to anticipate the postwar extinction of memory itself. Jews are "digging deep ditches four versts from the town," she takes care to write her son, "near the airfield, on the road to Romanovka. Remember that name," she urges him—"that's where you'll find the mass grave where your mother is buried." Viktor's mother concludes her letter with the last words she will write, "Live, live, live for ever." (In another publication on the murders, Grossman explicitly added words of parting to the death scene: "'Good-bye! Good-bye! We'll soon meet again,' people shouted. . . . 'Farewell' answered those who were already standing at the edge of the pit.")[31]

The strength that Anna describes in the "cattle-pen" of the ghetto is the "small kernel of kindness" that is shadowed by the "great evil," which encompasses the occupied Ukrainians as much as the German invaders. The ghetto's strength is also the mother's strength, on which Shtrum and therefore Grossman come to rely in the face of their own weakness, which is later revealed as the willingness to sign a petition against Jewish doctors in the so-called plot against Stalin after the war. The evil of Stalinism is thus aligned with the evil of fascism and really with all the poisons that allow what is stronger in a political system to prevail against what is weaker. After their "mean, cowardly act," Shtrum—and Grossman—must struggle "every hour, every day, year in, year out" to follow the example of their mothers, to be a man, and to "struggle for his right to be pure and kind." And "if it came to it, he mustn't be afraid even of death; even then he must remain a man."[32] In other words, whether in Stalingrad or Berdichev, you should not give up your humanity in order to save your life.

The outstanding political drama in Grossman's journey to Stalingrad and then to Berdichev and in the succession of a still-mythic early novel, *Stalingrad*, to the harsh honesty of the last, *Life and Fate*, is the melding of "the greatness of Stalin" with the "terrible power of Hitler," the doubt cast on any sort of titanic collective struggle between Good and Evil. There was a "small kernel" of kindness to be found in the town and especially in the ghetto (or the labor camp), but the vocabulary and impetus of "great evil" appeared in those places as well so that the kindness Grossman identified was nothing more than "senseless," power-less, but still the only stuff, the "human in human beings," able to prevent evil's total conquest. Grossman knew that the Old Town lived on without Jews. His depiction of Ukraine without heroics pertains to occupation, resistance, and self-rule else-where in Europe and in Asia. Yet Grossman wrote on so that the last letter would be the last word of the dead.[33]

CONCLUSION

World War III prevents us from seeing World War II. The end of the world has obscured the roads of war.

The greater part of the world caught fire in 1942, the first year of the global war. But catastrophic, pulverizing scenarios of World War III generally ignore the adversity millions of people faced when they were expelled onto the road, the remorseless violence dividing up neighbors in the courtyard, the second fronts opened up by conflicts between imperial rulers and their subjects and among ethnic and racial groups in the towns, and the constant contest between haves and have-nots—the crisscrossing fights that disfigured neat distinctions between military opponents. The vision of the world's end has the effect of flattening out the world before so that it loses much of the leavening of desire, anger, and resentment. The coming war is imagined simply, as fantastic annihilation triggered by conventional global rivalries in which the United States and the Soviet Union have taken the place of the Allies and the Axis.

For those who endured World War II, whose bodies rocked and swayed and were battered, and who trembled, the disaster was not the end of the world, as postwar predictions of nuclear war conceived it, but the continuation of war. It was the war without end, and a world that became more decomposed and protean, the world war as it appeared in 1942.

It was the very end of the war in 1945, when an American B-29 dropped the atomic bomb on the Japanese city of Hiroshima on August 6, 1945, and effectively ended World War II, that launched all the doomsday scenarios of World War III. The bomb that was built overshadowed the Allies' victory and the defeat of Nazi Germany and Imperial Japan in the future-oriented sense that a bigger and better bomb the next time would deny any sort of victory by destroying all sides. After the explosion and the fallout in 1945, "the idea of apocalyptic power cropped up everywhere at once, like dormant seeds sprouting under a sudden rain," writes one scientist. Soon nearly 98 percent of all Americans had heard of "the Bomb," with the words often capitalized to designate a terrific creature in a personalized nightmare. "When will I be blown up?" was everybody's question, admitted William Faulkner, who tried to make the case for the study of literature in spite of all the self-absorbed brooding of the atomic age. There were very good reasons to think about the destruction of "mother Earth." Hamburg and Tokyo had been "near misses." Hiroshima obliterated everyone and everything.[1]

Hiroshima serves as a vanishing point, blinding the eye to earlier tragedies and tempests. To take Hiroshima out of the picture, to withhold the world's catastrophic end, right away reveals multitudes of dangers and dilemmas. Nineteen forty-two tells us about the days left over, not any last doomsday. Yet it has been extremely difficult to remove Hiroshima, with its imaging of brilliant all-enveloping horror, from ideas about what comes next, about the state of conflict in the future. This is what makes 1942 important and pertinent: it is not the ending that it anticipates in 1945 so much as the endlessness of adversity and improvisation that it reveals. The tragedy of 1942 is the constancy of adjustment and adaptation in a state of permanent war. Human beings remain alive, but social life becomes more disfigured, or reconfigured. The disaster is not death, but the unceasing resumption of life. What if the future will look more like 1942, not 1945?

World War III was envisioned even before the end of World War II. Already in 1942, labels such as World War I and World War II invited ideas about World War III. At first, a new war seemed possible in the event Nazi Germany suspended its assault on the Soviet Union, a plausible scenario given the exhaustion of the Wehrmacht at the close of 1941. Observers warned that anything other than the decisive defeat of the Third Reich would leave its expansive, potent militarism in place. There was also fear of a new war if Western leaders gave in to the temptation to "double-cross" the Soviet Union, taking up the anti-Communism that had motivated Axis aggression in the first place.[2] Only the single-minded pursuit of the unconditional surrender of Germany and Japan in World War II guarded against the renewal of conflict in World War III.

After 1945, and the collapse of the Third Reich, it was not tireless or subterranean Nazis but a new kind of superpower that dominated thinking about World War III. The overall risk of geopolitical conflict between the newly established hegemons in the Soviet East and American West was multiplied by the immense destructive power of the atomic bomb—introduced by the United States at the end of World War II and acquired by the Soviet Union four years later in 1949. Predictions about World War III remain transfixed by the irrational technological escalation of geopolitical rivalries among the former Allies of

World War II—the United States, the Soviet Union, and China. Ukraine and Taiwan are regarded as possible starting points today, but the scenario for the outbreak of a new world war has not basically changed over the last eighty years. With a global battlefield configured by superpowers and superweapons, the end of World War II presided over the idea of World War III.

In what the editors pronounced to be "the most important single issue that any magazine has ever published," *Collier's* provided the first popular script for World War III in "Preview of the War We Do Not Want," published on October 27, 1951, with contributions by acclaimed literary figures from World War II such as Arthur Koestler, Edward R. Murrow, J. B. Priestley, and cartoonist Bill Mauldin. It established the genre, imagining in careful detail the origins of the conflict (in the Balkans), visualizing in broad strokes the overall destruction (through intercontinental air strikes), and ending with a satisfactory conclusion to portray the new turn of events, in this case "Russia's Defeat and Occupation, 1952–1960," the scenario's precondition to permanent global security.

In later prognostications there would be no aftermath except for total destruction, or its equivalent, the end, not the resumption, of civilization. The whole point of popular scenarios of nuclear war was to avoid doomsday, which usually meant refusing to contemplate winning or surviving.

Collier's wanted it both ways: to put forward an urgent appeal to prevent catastrophic war and to provide the reassurance that such war was winnable, was even virtuous, because alone tyranny lacks "physical and moral strength." Even so, *Collier's* modeling of the "next war" next year was scary: a disaster in which "millions of innocent people met violent deaths" in "atomized ruins of Washington, Chicago, Philadelphia, Detroit, New York, London, and eventually Moscow."

Like almost all other projections of World War III, *Collier's* "War We Do Not Want" took up familiar rivalries among powerful states in order to cast them into the unprecedented risk conditions made possible by the atomic bomb. (*Collier's* atomic bombs were already two and a half times more powerful than the American one dropped on Hiroshima; today they are three thousand times more powerful.)

The feature story quickly came under attack for its own belligerent stance. Critics pointed out that it depicted "Stalin's regime" as an unyielding aggressor that, the editors had warned, "will disappear from the face of the earth." "The free world will fight" if the Soviet government did not "change its outlook and its policies." At the same time, the righteousness of the free world was scored by its uncommon strategic restraint, something not very apparent in World War II; Moscow was "A-bombed" only after cities in the United States had been scorched, but otherwise American operations confined themselves to military targets and avoided a direct land invasion of the Soviet Union. The scenario was incredibly controlled in other ways, with only two state actors, one hyperfunctional, the other barely so; deadly assaults on the United States produced little more than the "by-product" of "terrified animals" from Chicago's stockyards that "broke loose, hampering civil defense work," while precise attacks on the Soviet Union caused military and civic authority to disintegrate—in contrast to the verified stability of Nazi Germany throughout World War II.

It was too easy to present civil society in the free world as a self-evidently desirable and durable export to post-Communist

Russia where the new dawn was heralded by the production of *Guys and Dolls*, the "fashion-starved" women "jammed" into Moscow's "huge Dynamo Stadium for their first style show," and the best-selling "Russian translation of the Sears, Roebuck catalogue (complete and unabridged) with explanatory footnotes."

In the *Collier's* scenario there were no aggrieved citizens or persecuted minorities, nor were there any perplexing second fronts or civil wars. Displaced people get hustled offstage because "miserable masses of refugees" were massacred during the war or simply returned home afterward. Yet, as one critic noted, given the fact that "we got Communism" out of the "chaos" of the previous world wars, in Russia, the world's largest country in 1917, and then in China, the world's most populous in 1949, the smooth transition to the American way of life all over the world seemed implausible. So did the unruffled response of Europeans to the third world war on their territories in fewer than forty years. According to D. F. Fleming, writing in the *Nation*, it was "tempting to believe that just one more epoch of bombing would really settle everything." Yet, in his view, the third world war envisioned by *Collier's* would more likely advance the "tide of witch-hunting, purges and thought control" than safeguard democracy and capitalism. The danger was the policed state of Nazi-era Germans, not the superweapons of Nazi Germany.[3]

Collier's "unabridged" catalog was silly in many ways, but it was also symptomatic of postwar thinking that made the unearned assumption that goodwill thrived while ugly things shriveled. Precisely because they were nestled in the very shadow of the prospect of being "A-bombed," the global villages constituted harmonious wholes. Society was either fully functional in the normal conditions of the free world or yearning to be so as it survived the perverse circumstances of tyranny. (In a nutshell, this is the whole problem with the slogan rebranded during the Cold War, "Live Free or Die.") It was as if World War II had not taken place, its convulsions and conflicts deleted by Allied victory in 1945 that, but for "Stalin's regime," had basically settled everything in good order.

The actually terrifying thing about the attempt to comprehend World War III was the anodyne way projections approached social and political conflict. Visions of World War III ignored the conflicts at the heart of World War II. In other words, doomsday rested on a highly satisfactory self-appraisal of the time when we were still alive. Paradoxically, World War III cleaned up World War II.

In his wartime journey from Stalingrad to Ukraine, Vasily Grossman confronted very different scenarios about social interactions and untimely death that find no place in *Collier's*. Grossman made you look around, anxious; *Collier's* did not.

Grossman certainly paid attention to the power of the militarized state, which was why he came to align Stalin with Hitler, one totalitarian regime with another. By the time he wrote *Life and Fate*, Grossman had abandoned the idea that the Soviet armies fought on the side of life, while fascism incorporated death by invading peaceful towns and busting open the doors to drive people out of their "warm homes" onto "black autumn roads." But his observations did not emphasize the mechanics of the state as much as the sociology of the "Old Town" itself. What he came to fear was how the modern machinery of the government grew more powerful by incorporating the social discrimination of groups and by using the apparatus to make ethnic or religious differences concrete and to use them efficaciously.

The novelist was also keenly alert to twentieth-century science and technology; the main character in *Life and Fate*, Viktor

Shtrum, was a nuclear physicist. However, Shtrum came to realize that the problems of physics were ultimately sociological and
psychological and were in the realm of technique, not superior
technology itself. He considered how the laws of mechanical
motion measuring "individual entities" had given way to "laws
of probability" manipulating social "aggregates" such as racial
or class resentments. The bomb itself was not at the center of
Grossman's anxieties.

Grossman did not conceive mass death on many "square
miles of burnt-out wasteland." He imagined it along "the road to
Romanovka," which connected the Old Town to the ghetto and
the killing field. He considered the effacement of the graveyard,
not its vast or conspicuous features.[4]

In one outstanding case, *New York Times* correspondent
"Cy" Sulzberger, the nephew of the publisher, followed along
Grossman's road. At the end of the war, he made a sober analysis
of contemporary conditions based on hatreds in the towns rather
than on geopolitical conflicts among the Great Powers. "Hitler filled
Europe with all the horrors envisioned centuries before in the
Book of Revelation," he reported from the "new dark continent."
Hitler was not a warmongering genius but a personification of
long-standing aggressions in social and political life, the "villainies, deceptions, betrayals, thefts" that Tolstoy had described.[5]

World War II developed the most diverse human forms for
the Anti-Christ. Sulzberger surveyed homelessness and hunger
on the Continent, but he was most distressed by its murderous
dynamics. "Virtually every ancient hatred has been revived with
new intensity," he observed as the war came to an end in March
1945. The record confirmed that everyone "hates the German
with a personal frenzy," but "worse" was the hatred of "Serb for
Croat, Rumanian for Hungarian, Frenchman for Italian, Pole

for Russian," cruel animosities that cut across as much as they aligned with the Allied and Axis sides of the war. "Worst of all," he continued in his revelations, was the "fratricidal hatred of Greek for Greek, Frenchman for Frenchman, Serb for Serb and Pole for Pole, based on differing social and political conceptions fostered and encouraged by chaos and unleashed by the war." These hatreds overrode any romances such as the French resistance to the Nazis, and they tattered the ideological banners of the Allied nations.

Sulzberger pointed out that thousands of German prisoners of war held by the Allies had not been "able to see doom roll forward down the east and west and burst down out of the skies." They were an odd element in postwar Europe because their isolation made them "less convinced of the disaster to Hitler's philosophy." The prisoners remained captives of the Nazi worldview. More profoundly, however, they were representatives of a more general inability to comprehend the calamity of the militarization of collective life into the existential parts of "us" and "them."

Sulzberger's pessimistic outlook in 1945 was ameliorated by postwar developments in Europe. The destruction of the war animated efforts to establish economic security and regional cooperation. Postwar plans for social security envisioned by Britain's Beveridge Plan caught the world's imagination in 1942. In war-torn Europe and elsewhere, governments and the citizens they represented shouldered new responsibilities to secure domestic stability and preserve international peace. "Postwar" was in many ways just that: politics refracted and understood through the searing experience of the world wars. An unexpected process of moral reckoning took place. The ideas about security and sovereignty incorporated in the Atlantic Charter

mattered and pointed the way toward international cooperation. This is still our world, although the economic boom after
1945 expired long ago, and, in less auspicious times, globalism
in the form of neoliberal trade and fiscal policies and migration into Europe have stirred up deep anxieties about national
well-being. The nation-state has long been the site of political
reform, enfranchising voters and building up social and economic security; it is becoming the agitated line of defense in the
preservation of public goods, leading to a more fractured world
and a more impoverished and suspicious sense of the commons.
The public square and the public good they had once built up,
the nations are now dismantling.

Sulzberger's approach retains value precisely because he
examined conflict in World War II beyond the parameters of the
Great Powers. His report revealed how collective life was shaped
by the hyperactive mobilization of its social, ethnic, and religious parts. This mobilization is very much in play in national
and local politics today. Sulzberger's "dark continent" in 1945
anticipated disintegrative forces such as political nationalism,
economic deprivation, and climate change that, nearly a century
of progress after 1945, loom over local places without taking
the specific form of state or military threats. There is a growing sense of unsettlement and unfamiliarity when people think
about the present condition—and about future years. The effect
is often to create an immense outside that gathers up all sorts of
dangers and intrusions and raises alarms as if the global wars
of 1942 had sprung back to life. With its extravagant number of
civilian deaths, and "bewildered, driven people" "milling back
and forth," 1942 tells something about the winds of the present day, although people tend to concentrate on the unwanted

intruders at the borders and not on larger perils or the climates agitating them.[6]

World War II created its own atmospherics, its own weather. It came hot and cold and with moving fronts. Sundown took the form of the blackout. The bomber's moon eclipsed Juliet's "inconstant" one. Described as an "inferno" or "deluge," the global war was so forceful and combustible that it exceeded geopolitical boundaries or *Collier's* World War III. The global war in 1942 mobilized soldiers, but also armed partisans, local defenders, and vigilantes. What "one world, one war" conveys is not neatness all around, but the proliferation of danger in monstrous, protean forms reaching deep into the homeland.

War in 1942 is pertinent to perils in 2042 for two reasons: first, the positive example of the mobilization of cooperative effort and investment to vanquish dangerous threats; and second, the ample evidence of the consolidation of "us" in defense against "them" in countless divisive permutations of self-rule that defied the popular front or a common humanity. The all-out mobilization to win the war is an inspirational history. In many ways, the world war made "men feel the earth and the people upon it." There was a genuine sense of allies marching for shared aims. Yet the record of sheer loss and civil strife requires more gloomy recitations of the "good war." The outcome of any struggle against global danger depends on how the enemies or the fronts are defined: Who is the "we"? Is their march also ours?[7]

The contemporary world is ill-equipped to meet future disasters. In 1942, nation-states mobilized and aligned in the face of identifiable foreign adversaries, yet even then the number of domestic enemies imagined at home kept on being multiplied so that the state of war always generated corrosive and self-destructive tendencies. Moral righteousness was a source of huge amounts of energy in World War II, certainly for the Allies fighting Nazi Germany and Imperial Japan. But this sort of clarity does not apply nearly so well to widely dispersed and less defined threats such as climate change or challenges such as migration, which fortify parochial responses. Vigilance has in large measure replaced ideological beliefs and affiliations.

What does apply to the contemporary world, I think, is the response of the towns that in 1942 mobilized in self-defense, often dividing against themselves in order to do so. The refugees of 1942 were somewhat recognizable, but in 2042 refugees from the "Global South" will be more numerous and less familiar and will be made out to be dangerously foreign and intrusive. It is hard today to imagine refugees described as the *New York Times* did about the shipwrecked victims of the *Struma* in 1942: "They were the flesh and blood of the free peoples."[8] And even then, in the war against the Nazis, the Jewish refugees drowned. The energetic mobilizations in World War II against imperial and central authority, and the defense of religious and ethnic communalism as self-rule, indicate the long work of dispersive forces rather than unifying ones acting in the name of "our" humanity or "us" earthlings.

"The wars of peoples," Winston Churchill predicted when he was an impertinent young parliamentarian in 1901, "will be more terrible than those of kings." What he meant by "peoples" was the role of national publics and popular prejudices that combined to make military conflict more terribly violent and more emotionally rooted.[9] The "peoples" in 2042 will organize in their communities in self-defense against undefined but deeply felt threats, posed, first of all, by so-called strangers at the gate. The internationalist solidarities of the European Union, nurtured by memories of World War II and the postwar divisions of the Cold War, have shown limited reach when confronted with boat people crossing from the African rim of the Mediterranean— *Casablanca*'s escape routes in reverse. The pertinent lesson of 1942 when thinking about 2042 is the extravagance of purely local self-defense through the continuous manufacture of "us" against "them" and resistance to outsiders, however defined. Even the myth of World War II's shared purpose has disappeared sufficiently so that contemporaries today cannot even be faulted for their hypocrisy. What beckons are peoples' wars rather than the people's war, a total devaluation of forms of life and community beyond "our" defined borders. In time of crisis, self-rule will probably take the form of organized and violent mobilizations of the (still) secure parts of the world against the already insecure ones. It is difficult to imagine popular fronts cobbled together with so many "strangers" as opposed to "free peoples" on the move. The century of history since the united nations of 1942 has ended in sharpened parochialism, the tragic circumscription or simplification of the idea of self-rule.

In these conditions of radical and exclusive (gated) self-rule, the very notion of history falters. The role of collective history and narrative rests on creating connections and context that incorporate new elements. World War II did this work of global incorporation with the idea of "our war" and the "people's war," even as the stories left out groups who were abandoned, denationalized, and demilitarized. World War II energized useful, necessary myths, but the holes in those myths are about all we see today, the absence, not the deficits, of solidarity and connection. Sweat and toil, but actually blood and tears.

Thinking about climate change as "derangement," Amitav Ghosh provocatively asks whether modern storytelling ultimately requires "gradualism," the idea that "nothing could change otherwise than the way things were seen to change in the present." In the construction of incorporating narratives, catastrophe—in terms of "leaps," or basic permutations to nature and the land, to home and social units—was "un-modern," unworkable, otherworldly. In other words, history doesn't make sense if there is too much variation or discrepancy (or inequality) and too little incorporation. Today, the unincorporated, the "un-modern," the stranger, seems to be at the door.[10]

Gaia, goddess of life and of the earth itself, calls to "earthlings." Seen far away from outer space, the Earth looks whole, fragile, and beautiful. Seen in the continental storms, many of them forecast in 1942, life on Earth looks sinister and parsimonious, twisting into knots the appeal to "live, live, live for ever," to sway in solidarity rather than struggle for survival.

ACKNOWLEDGMENTS

As it took me some time to write this book, my debts became at once more widely dispersed and deeper. I sat around for long periods of time at my desk relying on my family at home to make do, and so my love is combined with gratitude, Franziska, Joshua, and Matteo. I was also fortunate to receive time off teaching from the University of Illinois, early on thanks to Humanities Release Time and, toward the end, with an appointment at the Center for Advanced Study. Very special thanks, as always over these last forty years, to the Interlibrary Loan office at the library at the University of Illinois. Along the way, I appreciated advice and counsel from Perry Anderson, Teresa Barnes, Jörg Echternkamp, Jerry Foster, Christian Gerlach, Michael Geyer, Benjamin Carter Hett, Samuel Kassow, Diane Koenker, Peter Limb, Jay Lockenour, John Lynn, Erik S. McDuffie, Richard Overy, David Roskies, Mark Steinberg, Jason Morgan Ward, and Gerhard Weinberg. A callout to my agent, Andrew Wylie, and also to his team. I have benefited so much from the editorial collaboration at Basic Books, again. Thank you, Brian Distelberg and Michael Kaler. My old comrade in arms, David Murphy, gave me broad and critical perspective.

NOTES

INTRODUCTION

1. Harry Brown, *A Walk in the Sun* (New York, 1944), p. 25; Helena Swanwick, *I Have Been Young* (London, 1935), pp. 500–501; Aldous Huxley, "Notes on the Way," *Time and Tide*, May 7, 1932; Bausch & Lomb advertisement, *New York Times*, Apr. 12, 1942.

2. Craig Symonds, *World War II at Sea: A Global History* (New York, 2018), p. xi.

3. "Atlas for the U.S. Citizen," *Fortune* (Sept. 1940).

4. "If New York City Were Besieged Stalingrad," *Richmond Independent*, Oct. 20, 1942.

5. Nelson Mandela, *Long Walk to Freedom* (Boston, 1994), p. 42; Natan Last, "Rearrangements," *New Yorker*, Dec. 25, 2023.

6. Anne O'Hare McCormick, "A Discoverer of the New World in the East," *New York Times*, Oct. 28, 1942.

7. *Bombay Chronicle* (1938), quoted in Deborah Cohen, *Last Call at the Hotel Imperial: The Reporters Who Took on a World at War* (New York, 2022), p. 259.

8. Alexander Werth, *The Year of Stalingrad* (London, 1946), p. 78; Alexander Werth, *Russia at War, 1941–1945* (New York, 1964), p. 414.

9. Dorothy Thompson, "Escape in a Frozen World," *Survey Graphic* 28 (Feb. 1939): p. 93.

10. Maurice Blanchot, *The Writing of the Disaster* (Lincoln, NE, 1986), p. 41.

CHAPTER 1: Five Days in December

1. Robert Hagy, "'The Worst News That I Have Encountered in the Last 20 Years,'" in *War Comes to the U.S.—Dec. 7, 1941: The First 30 Hours*, by Time-Life-Fortune News Bureau (New York, 1942); David Goodman, "Pittsburgh 1941: War, Race, Biography, and History," *Pennsylvania Magazine of History and Biography* 132 (2008): pp. 345, 347, 366, 368.

2. Quoted in John Gunther, *Inside U.S.A.* (New York, 1947), p. 288.

3. William H. Young and Nancy K. Young, *Music of the World War II Era* (Westport, CT, 2008), p. 2; "This Is What the Soldiers Complain About," *Life*, Aug. 18, 1941.

4. Halifax quoted in Richard M. Ketchum, *The Borrowed Years, 1938–1941: America on the Way to War* (New York, 1989), p. 602; Robert E. Sherwood, *Roosevelt and Hopkins: An Intimate History* (New York, 1950), p. 382.

5. "We All Have Only One Task," *Chicago Tribune*, Dec. 8, 1941; Fill Calhoun in Time-Life-Fortune News Bureau, *War Comes to the U.S.*, p. 65.

6. Entry for Dec. 10, 1941, Charles Kikuchi, *The Kikuchi Diary: Chronicle from an American Concentration Camp* (Urbana, 1995 [1973]), p. 45.

7. John Durant in Time-Life-Fortune News Bureau, *War Comes to the U.S.*, p. 157.

8. "Awake White America, the Hour Is at Hand" and "Army Rejects Negroes, First to Volunteer in Chicago," *Chicago Defender*, Dec. 13, 1941; on Tucker, Thomas A. Guglielmo, "'Red Cross, Double Cross': Race and America's World War II–Era Blood Donor Service," *Journal of American History* (2010): p. 168; Texas congressman John Rankin is quoted on pumping blood in Tracy Campbell, *The Year of Peril: America in 1942* (New Haven, CT, 2020), p. 25; on the American Medical Association and War Department, Rawn James Jr., *The Double V: How Wars, Protest and Harry Truman Desegregated America's Military* (New York, 2013), pp. 138–139.

9. Roy Wilkins quoted in James, *Double V*, p. 139.

10. "Little Tokyo Carries on Business as Usual," "Little Tokyo Banks and Concerns Shut," "Little Tokyo Lid Clamped," *Los Angeles Times*, Dec. 8, 9, and 14, 1941; entry for Dec. 9, 1941, Kikuchi, *Kikuchi Diary*, p. 44; James Matsumoto Omura, *Nisei Naysayer: The Memoir of Militant Japanese American Journalist Jimmie Omura*, edited by Arthur A. Hansen (Stanford, CA, 2018), p. 114.

11. "How to Tell Japs from the Chinese," *Life*, Dec. 22, 1941; "Not All Alike," *New York Times*, Dec. 22, 1941.

12. Chester Himes, *If He Hollers, Let Him Go* (New York, 2002 [1945]), p. 4; Chester Himes, *Lonely Crusade* (New York, 1997 [1947]), p. 44.

13. Tokugawa Musei quoted in Samuel Hideo Yamashita, "Popular Japanese Responses to the Pearl Harbor Attack: December 8, 1941, to January 8, 1942," in *Beyond Pearl Harbor: A Pacific History*, edited by Beth Bailey and David Farber (Lawrence, KS, 2019), p. 97.

14. "War Is On!," *Japan Times*, Dec. 8, 1941 (evening).

15. Robert Guillain, *I Saw Tokyo Burning: An Eyewitness Narrative from Pearl Harbor to Hiroshima* (London, 1981), pp. 1–2.

16. "Giant Rally at Hibiya Park Saturday afternoon," *Japan Times*, Dec. 14, 1941.

17. On turn: Kazushige Ugaki, "Message to Young Men," *Japan Times*, Dec. 8, 1941; bondage: "Prospect for Greater East Asia War," *Kokumin*, quoted in *Japan Times*, Dec. 30, 1941; axle: "History in Making as War Develops," *Japan Times*, Dec. 19, 1941.

18. "Toppling Britannia's Pride," *Japan Times*, Dec. 16, 1941; "When Japan Blasted Britain's Naval Hopes," *Japan Times*, Dec. 18, 1941; entry of Dec. 12, 1941, diary of Nagai Kafu, quoted in Donald Keene, ed., *So Lovely a Country Will Never Perish: Wartime Diaries of Japanese Writers* (New York, 2010), p. 12.

19. Dennis Showalter, "Storm over the Pacific: Japan's Road to Empire and War," in *The Pacific War: From Pearl Harbor to Hiroshima*, edited by Daniel Marston (Oxford, 2005), p. 28.

20. On Yamamoto's gambling, Ian W. Toll, *Pacific Crucible: War at Sea in the Pacific, 1941–1942* (New York, 2012), 73; "Japan's 'Full House' Beat America's 'Pair,' Writes Admiral Yamamoto to Poker Pals," *Japan Times*, Dec. 19, 1941; on Detroit and Texas, Ian W. Toll, *The Conquering Tide: War in the Pacific Islands, 1942–1944* (New York, 2015), p. 118.

21. Carl Boyd, *Hitler's Japanese Confidant: General Ōshima Hiroshi and Magic Intelligence* (Lawrence, KS, 1993), p. 5.

22. "Men Still Decide Outcome of Wars," *Japan Times*, Jan. 9, 1942; "Achieving the Objective of War," *Nichi Nichi*, quoted in *Japan Times*, Dec. 18, 1941; editorial, "Victory Day Speeches," *Japan Times*, Feb. 20, 1942.

23. Hideo Miyashita, "U.S. and Britain Must Be Crushed," *Japan Times*, Dec. 30, 1941; "War of Liberation Launched by Japan," *Japan Times*, Dec. 13, 1941; Klaus Meinert, "Every Corner of Globe at War," *Japan Times*, Mar. 3, 1942.

24. Peter Calvocoressi and Guy Wint, *Total War: Causes and Courses of the Second World War* (New York, 1972), p. 708; Tagore to Yone Noguchi, Sept. 1, 1938, in Zeljko Cipris, "Seduced by Nationalism: Yone Noguchi's 'Terrible Mistake.' Debating the China-Japan War with Tagore," *Asia-Pacific Journal* 5 (2007); Michael Bess, *Choices Under Fire: Moral Dimensions of World War II* (New York, 2006), p. 30.

25. Tokugawa Musei quoted in Yamashita, "Popular Japanese Responses to the Pearl Harbor Attack," in *Beyond Pearl Harbor*, edited by Bailey and Farber, p. 96.

26. Letters dated July 16, Aug. 26, and Sept. 28, 1941, in Helmuth James von Moltke, *Letters to Freya, 1939–1945* (New York, 1990), pp. 152, 155–156, 166.

27. Heinrich Haape, *Moscow Tram Stop: A Doctor's Experiences with the German Spearhead in Russia* (Guilford, CT, 2020 [London, 1957]), pp. 152, 215; entries for Dec. 25, 29, and 30, 1941, and Jan. 2, 1942, in Franz Halder, *Kriegstagebuch* (Stuttgart, 1964), pp. 3:366–371.

28. Letters dated Oct. 21 and Nov. 13, 1941, in Moltke, *Letters to Freya*, pp. 175, 182–183.

29. Letter dated Nov. 17, 1941, in Moltke, *Letters to Freya*, p. 187.

30. Letters dated Aug. 26 and Dec. 10, 1941, and Jan. 11, 1942, in Moltke, *Letters to Freya*, pp. 155–156, 193, 198.

31. Walter Warlimont, *Im Hauptquartier der deutschen Wehrmacht, 1939–1945: Grundlagen—Formen—Gestalten* (Frankfurt, 1962), p. 220.

32. Entries for Dec. 7 and 9, 1941, in Harald Sandner, *Hitler—Das Itinerar Band IV, 1940–1945* (Berlin, 2016), pp. 1976–1977; Warlimont, *Im Hauptquartier der deutschen Wehrmacht*, p. 221.

33. Entry for Dec. 11, 1941, *Die Tagebücher von Joseph Goebbels. Sämtliche Fragmente*, edited by Elke Fröhlich (Munich, 1994), pt. 2, vol. 2, p. 476.

34. Stenographic record, 7. Sitzung, Dec. 11, 1941, *Verhandlungen des Deutschen Reichstags, 4. Wahlperiode 1939, Band 460* (Berlin, 1942), pp. 93, 100, 104–106.

35. Schmidt quoted in Brendan Simms and Charlie Laderman, *Hitler's American Gamble: Pearl Harbor and Germany's March to Global War* (New York, 2022), p. 330.

36. Nicholas Henderson, "Hitler's Biggest Blunder and Germany's Declaration of War on the United States in December 1941," *History Today* (Apr. 1993); Sebastian Haffner, *The Meaning of Hitler* (Cambridge, MA, 1979), pp. 116–117, 120.

37. David Kennedy, *Freedom from Fear: The American People in Depression and War, 1929–1945* (New York, 1999), p. 524.

38. Entry for Dec. 13, 1941, *Die Tagebücher von Joseph Goebbels*, edited by Fröhlich, pt. 2, vol. 2, p. 498.

39. Regierungssitzung, Dec. 16, 1941, Hans Frank, *Das Diensttagebuch des deutschen Generalgouverneurs in Polen, 1939–1945*, edited by Werner Präg and Wolfgang Jacobmeyer (Stuttgart, 1975), p. 457.

40. Entries for Dec. 14 and 18, 1941, Heinrich Himmler, *Der Dienstkalender Heinrich Himmlers, 1941/42*, edited by Peter Witte et al. (Hamburg, 1999), pp. 290, 293–294.

41. Christian Gerlach, "The Wannsee Conference, the Fate of German Jews, and Hitler's Decision in Principle to Exterminate All European Jews," *Journal of Modern History* 70 (1998): p. 763.

42. Arvid Fredborg, *Behind the Steel Wall: A Swedish Journalist in Berlin, 1941-43* (New York, 1944); entry for Dec. 21, 1941, Matthias Joseph Mehs, *Tagebücher. Band 2, Januar 1936 bis September 1946*, edited by Günter Wein and Franziska Wein (Trier, 2011), p. 290; entry for Jan. 11, 1942, *Die Tagebücher von Joseph Goebbels*, edited by Fröhlich, pt. 2, vol. 3, p. 92.

43. Martin Rüther, *Köln im Zweiten Weltkrieg: Alltag und Erfahrungen zwischen 1939 und 1945* (Cologne, 2005), p. 149; "Es gibt heute nur noch Pflichten," *Westdeutscher Beobachter*, Apr. 27, 1942.

44. Warlimont, *Im Hauptquartier der deutschen Wehrmacht*, p. 223.

45. Entry for Dec. 7, 1942, *Die Tagebücher von Joseph Goebbels*, edited by Fröhlich, pt. 2, vol. 2, p. 453.

46. The equation in Robert E. Sherwood, *Roosevelt and Hopkins: An Intimate History* (New York, 1950), p. 301; villages in Calvocoressi and Wint, *Total War*, p. 709; J. M. Rose, "The World Has Become an Open Book," *Daily Mail* (Freetown), June 1, 1942.

47. Nehru quoted in Srnath Raghavan, *India's War: World War II and the Making of Modern South Asia* (New York, 2016), p. 209.

CHAPTER 2: Drawing a Map

1. Berggolts quoted in Anna Reid, *Leningrad: The Epic Siege of World War II, 1941–1944* (New York, 2011), p. 31.

2. "Quest for a Name" and "Public Calls It '2d World War,'" *New York Times*, Apr. 19 and 29, 1942.

3. "Roosevelt to Warn U.S. of Danger; Asks All to Trace Talk on Maps," *New York Times*, Feb. 21, 1941; "Clip and Save This Map for Use During President's Broadcast Tonight," *New York Times*, Feb. 23, 1942.

4. "President's Speech Causes Great Demand for Maps," *Publishers Weekly* 141 (Feb. 28, 1942): pp. 935–936; "Maps," *Consumer Reports* 8 (Nov. 30, 1943): pp. 291–295.

5. Eugene Staley, "The Myth of Continents," in *Compass to the World: A Symposium on Political Geography*, edited by Hans W. Weigert and Vilhjalmur Stefansson (New York, 1944), pp. 94–95.

6. Walter Warlimont, *Im Hauptquartier der deutschen Wehrmacht, 1939–1945: Grundlagen—Formen—Gestalten* (Frankfurt, 1962), pp. 232, 257; Leo Tolstoy, *War and Peace*, translated by Richard Pevear and Larissa Volokhonsky (New York, 2007), pp. 634, 773–774, 1025.

7. "Late—but Not Too Late," *New York Times*, Feb. 13, 1942; "The Solomons to the Volga," *New York Times*, Aug. 13, 1942; Timothy Barney, "Iron Albatross: Air-Age Globalism, the Maps of Richard Edes Harrison, and the Geographical Imagination of the Early Cold War," *Conference Papers—National Communication Association* (2008), p. 25.

8. "Late—but Not Too Late"; "The Solomons to the Volga"; Peter Schrijvers, *The GI War Against the Japanese* (New York, 2002), p. 6; Thomas Grady Gallant, *On Valor's Side* (New York, 1963), p. 179.

9. Hans Schwarz van Berk, "Auf weite Entfernung schlagen! Von der kleinen zur grossen Geographie," *Das Reich*, Jan. 4, 1942; Wolfgang Hirschfeld, *Feindfahrten: Das Logbuch eines U-Boot-Funkers* (Vienna, 1982), p. 320.

10. Editorial, "Colombo—a Step to Catastrophe," *Japan Times*, Apr. 10, 1942.

11. Maya Jasanoff, *The Dawn Watch: Joseph Conrad in a Global World* (New York, 2017), p. 282.

12. Richard Overy, *Why the Allies Won* (London, 1995), p. 27; John Deane Potter, *Pim and Churchill's Map Room* (Belfast, 2014), p. 20.

13. Theodor A. Wilson, *The First Summit: Roosevelt and Churchill at Placentia Bay, 1941,* rev. ed. (Lawrence, KS, 1991), p. 229; "The Rendezvous with Destiny," *New York Times,* Aug. 15, 1941; "Democratic Bomb," *New York Times,* Aug. 17, 1941.

14. Entry for Aug. 14, 1941, in John Barnes and David Nicholson, eds., *The Empire at Bay: The Leo Amery Diaries, 1929–1945* (London, 1988), p. 710; Richard Toye, *Churchill's Empire: The World That Made Him and the World He Made* (New York, 2010), p. 214.

15. Overall, see Zik's series, "Our Goodwill Tour," *West African Pilot* (Lagos), throughout February 1942.

16. Peter Alegi, *African Soccerscapes: How a Continent Changed the World's Game* (London, 2010), p. 40; "Warri People Pay £25 to Watch Zik's Athletic Club and W.A.F.A. Play Match," *West African Pilot,* Dec. 23, 1941.

17. Samuel Zipp, *The Idealist: Wendell Willkie's Wartime Quest to Build One World* (Cambridge, MA, 2020), pp. 204–205.

18. Zipp, *Idealist,* pp. 228–229, 249.

19. William Roger Louis, *Imperialism at Bay: The United States and the Decolonization of the British Empire, 1941–1945* (New York, 1978), p. 199n3.

20. Carl Schmitt, "Beschleuniger wider Willen oder: Problematik der westlichen Hemisphäre," *Das Reich,* Apr. 19, 1942.

21. "1941—Brilliant Year in History of Japan," *Japan Times,* Dec. 30, 1941; "The Assembly of the Greater East-Asiatic Nations," *Nippon Times,* Nov. 5, 1943; "The Voice of Asia," *Nippon Times,* Nov. 7, 1943.

22. "Dutch Suppress Education of Java Natives; Japanese Army Seeks to Reawaken People," *Japan Times,* Mar. 24, 1942.

23. Sven Saaler, "Pan-Asianism in Modern Japanese History: Overcoming the Nation, Creating a Region, Forging an Empire," in *Pan-Asianism in Modern Japanese History: Colonialism, Regionalism and Borders,* edited by Sven Saaler and J. Victor Koschmann (New York, 2007), pp. 12–13; Layton Horner, "Japanese Military Administration in Malaya and the Philippines" (PhD diss., University of Arizona, 1973), p. 8.

24. Eri Hotta, *Pan-Asianism and Japan's War, 1931–1945* (New York, 2007), p. 214; Toshi Go (the publisher of the *Nippon Times*), "The Call of Mother Asia," *Nippon Times,* Nov. 8, 1943.

25. Sugata Bose, *His Majesty's Opponent: Subhas Chandra Bose and India's Struggle Against Empire* (2011), p. 31.

26. M. R. Vyas, *Passage Through a Turbulent Era* (Bombay, 1982), p. 371;

David Motadel, "The Global Authoritarian Moment and the Revolt Against Empire," *American Historical Review* 124 (2019): p. 872.

27. "Aufzeichnungen Martin Bormanns über die Besprechung Adolf Hitlers mit seinen Mitarbeitern über die Ziele des Krieges gegen die Sowjetunion," July 16, 1941, in *Vom Generalplan Ost zum Generalsiedlungsplan*, edited by Czeslaw Madajczyk (Munich, 1994), pp. 16–18; Adam Tooze, *The Wages of Destruction: The Making and Breaking of the Nazi Economy* (New York, 2007), p. 467. On Riviera: entry for July 5–6, 1941, in Hugh Trevor-Roper, ed., *Hitler's Table Talk, 1941–1944* (London, 1953), pp. 4–5.

28. "Monolog Adolf Hitlers über das deutsche Besiedlungsbild im Osten, aufgezeichnet von Heinrich Heim," Oct. 17, 1941, and "Erinnerungen von Albert Speer an Äusserungen Adolf Hitlers über de Nutzung der besetzten Ostgebiete," Mar. 26, 1947, in *Vom Generalplan Ost zum Generalsiedlungsplan*, edited by Madajczyk, pp. 40, 291; on roads, entries for Feb. 26 and June 27, 1942, in Trevor-Roper, *Hitler's Table Talk*, pp. 338, 537–538; on millions, entry for May 24, 1942, *Die Tagebücher von Joseph Goebbels. Sämtliche Fragmente*, edited by Elke Fröhlich (Munich, 1994), pt. 2, vol. 4, p. 363; Richard Overy, *Blood and Ruins: The Great Imperial War, 1931–1945* (London, 2021), p. 216.

29. "Monolog Adolf Hitlers über das deutsche Besiedlungsbild im Osten, aufgezeichnet von Heinrich Heim," in *Vom Generalplan Ost zum Generalsiedlungsplan*, edited by Madajczyk, p. 24; entries for Oct. 17 and 26–27, 1941, in Trevor-Roper, *Hitler's Table Talk*, pp. 69, 93.

30. Vejas Gabriel Liulevicius, *War Land on the Eastern Front: Culture, National Identity, and German Occupation in World War I* (Cambridge, UK, 2000), p. 8; entry for May 17, 1942, in Trevor-Roper, *Hitler's Table Talk*, p. 489.

CHAPTER 3: Telling a Story

1. George Roeder, *The Censored War: American Visual Experience During World War II* (New Haven, CT, 1993), p. 83.

2. Gerd Horten, *Radio Goes to War: The Cultural Politics of Propaganda During World War II* (Berkeley, CA, 2003), pp. 13–14.

3. Isa to Fritz Kuchenbach, June 22 and 23, 1941, Kempowski Archive, 5483, Akademie der Künste, Berlin; Lidiya Ginzburg, *Blockade Diary* (London, 1984), p. 4.

4. Germaine de Staël, *Considerations on the Principal Events of the French Revolution*, 3 vols. (London, 1818), p. 3:136.

5. Erich Maria Remarque, *All Quiet on the Western Front* (New York, 1982), p. 167.

6. Jochen Hellbeck, *Stalingrad: The City That Defeated the Third Reich* (New York, 2015), p. 45.

7. "Late—but Not Too Late," *New York Times* editorial, Feb. 13, 1942; Anne

O'Hare McCormick, "There Is a Tide in the Affairs of Men," *New York Times*, July 1, 1942; "In the Iron Scale of War," editorial, *New York Times*, Sept. 3, 1942.

8. "Victory in Egypt May Be War Turning Point," *Los Angeles Times*, Nov. 6, 1942.

9. Entries for Feb. 16 and 26, 1942, in Paulheinz Wantzen, *Das Leben im Krieg. Ein Tagebuch* (Bad Homburg, 2000), pp. 1052, 1054.

10. "Grosskundgebung des Gaues Oberdonau der NSDAP zum 4. Jahrestag des 'Anschlusses,'" Linz, Mar. 15, 1942, in *Goebbels-Reden*, edited by Helmut Heiber, vol. 2, *1939–1945* (Düsseldorf, 1972), pp. 84–88.

11. "Kundgebung des Kreises Wuppertal der NSDAP," Nov. 17, 1942, in *Goebbels-Reden*, edited by Heiber, pp. 2:126–127, 137, 139–142, 144.

12. Letter dated Apr. 26, 1942, quoted in Martin Rüther, *Köln im Zweiten Weltkrieg: Alltag und Erfahrungen zwischen 1939 und 1945* (Cologne, 2005), pp. 164–165; entry for Sept. 17, 1942, in *Die Tagebücher von Joseph Goebbels. Sämtliche Fragmente*, edited by Elke Fröhlich (Munich, 1994), pt. 2, vol. 5, p. 516.

13. Entry for June 22, 1941, Wolfgang Hirschfeld, *Feindfahrten: Das Logbuch eines U-Boot-Funkers* (Vienna, 1982), p. 87.

14. Rodric Braithwaite, *Moscow 1941: A City and Its People at War* (New York, 2006), front matter.

15. David Stahel, *Retreat from Moscow: A New History of Germany's Winter Campaign, 1941–42* (New York, 2019), p. 366; "1812 und heute," *Völkischer Beobachter*, Sept. 30, 1941.

16. Hirschfeld, *Feindfahrten*, p. 87; Heinrich Haape, *Moscow Tram Stop: A Doctor's Experiences with the German Spearhead in Russia* (Guilford, CT, 2020 [London, 1957]), pp. 39–41.

17. Werner Hütter, letters dated July 14 and Dec. 10, 1941, Kempowski-Archive, 4627, Akademie der Künste, Berlin; Michael K. Jones, *The Retreat: Hitler's First Defeat* (New York, 2009), p. 152; Herman Wouk, *War and Remembrance* (New York, 1978), p. 212; Armand de Caulaincourt, *With Napoleon in Russia: The Memoirs of General de Caulaincourt, Duke of Vecenza* (New York, 1935), pp. 49, 155.

18. Herman Kruk, "Library and Reading Room in the Vilna Ghetto, Strashun Street 6," in *The Holocaust and the Book: Destruction and Preservation*, edited by Jonathan Rose (Amherst, MA, 2001), p. 194; James A. Michener, *Tales of the South Pacific* (New York, 1946), p. 45.

19. Konstantin Simonov, "On Reading Tolstoy," *Partisan Review* 38 (1971): p. 219; Ginzburg quoted in Braithwaite, *Moscow 1941*, p. 61.

20. Leo Tolstoy, *War and Peace*, translated by Pevear and Larissa Volokhonsky (New York, 2007), p. 165.

21. Tolstoy, *War and Peace*, translated by Pevear and Volokhonsky, pp. 775,

804; entries for Feb. 2 and Apr. 11, 1942, in Matthias Joseph Mehs, *Tagebücher*, vol. 2, *Januar 1936 bis September 1946*, edited by Günter Wein and Franziska Wein (Trier, 2011), pp. 296, 313–314.

22. Churchill quoted in Asa Briggs, *The War of Words: The History of Broadcasting in the United Kingdom* (London, 1970), p. 3:9. On events, Jeff Love, "The Great Man in *War and Peace*," in *Tolstoy on War: Narrative Art and Historical Truth in "War and Peace*," edited by Rick McPeak and Donna Tussing Orwin (Ithaca, NY, 2012), p. 92.

23. Tolstoy, *War and Peace*, translated by Pevear and Volokhonsky, p. 643; "U.S. Army Private Charles E. Teed of Effingham, Ill.," *Life*, Mar. 16, 1942.

24. Tolstoy, "A Few Words Apropos of the Book *War and Peace*," in *War and Peace*, translated by Pevear and Volokhonsky, p. 1220; Tolstoy, *War and Peace*, translated by Pevear and Volokhonsky, p. 1131; Mark Rawlinson, "Does Tolstoy's *War and Peace* Make Modern War Literature Redundant?," in *War and Literature*, edited by Laura Ashe and Ian Patterson (Cambridge, UK, 2014), p. 240.

25. Clifton Fadiman, foreword to Tolstoy, *War and Peace*, translated by Louise Maude and Aylmer Maude, Simon and Schuster's Inner Sanctum Edition (New York, 1942), pp. xxxix–xl.

26. Tolstoy, *War and Peace*, translated by Pevear and Volokhonsky, p. 944.

27. Maurice Blanchot, *The Writing of the Disaster* (Lincoln, NE, 1986), p. 41.

28. Mary L. Dudziak, *War Time: An Idea, Its History, Its Consequences* (New York, 2012), p. 7.

29. Gary Saul Morson, *Hidden in Plain View: Narrative and Creative Potentials in "War and Peace"* (Stanford, CA, 1987), p. 97.

30. Tolstoy, *War and Peace*, translated by Pevear and Volokhonsky, p. 603.

CHAPTER 4: "Road to Singapore"

1. Christopher Bayly and Tim Harper, *Forgotten Armies: The Fall of British Asia, 1941–1945* (London, 2004), p. 35; Frank S. Nugent, "The Screen," *New York Times*, Mar. 16, 1940.

2. "Drive to Singapore," *New York Times*, Dec. 20, 1941; Brian Farrell, *The Defence and Fall of Singapore, 1940–1942* (London, 2005), p. 312; Fran de Groen, "Made in England, 'The Road from Singapore,' and I Think I'll Live: Reflections on Mid-Twentieth Century National Identity," *Southerly* 67, nos. 1–2 (2007): 319–332.

3. Rupert Emerson, *Malaysia: A Study in Direct and Indirect Rule* (New York, 1937), pp. 11–41; Bayly and Harper, *Forgotten Armies*, p. 33.

4. Cecil Brown, *From Suez to Singapore* (New York, 1942), p. 151; Alan Warren, *Singapore 1942: Britain's Greatest Defeat* (London, 2002); James Leasor,

Singapore: The Battle That Changed the World (New York, 1968); Bayly and Harper, *Forgotten Armies*, p. 163.

5. Jules Verne, *Around the World in 80 Days*, edited by Frederick Paul Walker (Albany, NY, 2013), p. 90; Jean Cocteau, *Round the World Again in Eighty Days* (London, 1937), pp. 113–114; Bayly and Harper, *Forgotten Armies*, p. 50; entry for Aug. 3, 1941, in Brown, *From Suez to Singapore*, p. 127.

6. Verne, *Around the World in 80 Days*, edited by Walker, p. 90; Noel Barber, *A Sinister Twilight: The Fall of Singapore, 1942* (Boston, 1968), pp. 4–5.

7. George Orwell, *Burmese Days* (New York, 1963 [1934]), pp. 18, 61; Brown, *From Suez to Singapore*, p. 199; *Malaya Tribune*, Nov. 18, 1940, quoted in Hallett Abend, *Japan Unmasked* (New York, 1941), p. 96; "Colour Bar," *Straits Times*, Nov. 23, 1941.

8. R. C. H. McKie, *This Was Singapore* (Sydney, 1942), p. 19; entry for Nov. 29, 1941, in Brown, *From Suez to Singapore*, p. 273; Maye Wood, *Malay for Mems* (Singapore, 1958), pp. 8–9; Colin Smith, *Singapore Burning: Heroism and Surrender in World War II* (London, 2005), pp. 37, 451.

9. McKie, *This Was Singapore*, p. 94; "New World Cabaret," *Straits Times*, Aug. 7, 1941.

10. Abend, *Japan Unmasked*, pp. 100, 107.

11. Entries for Aug. 8, 11, and 20 and Nov. 3, 1942, in Brown, *From Suez to Singapore*, 142, 151–152, 160, 240; Paul Kennedy, *Victory at Sea: Naval Power and the Transformation of the Global Order in World War II* (New Haven, CT, 2022), p. 75.

12. See *Straits Times*, Aug. 22, Sept. 2, and Nov. 26, 1941; and John Gordon, "At Last," *Straits Times*, Nov. 24, 1941.

13. Lucian Zacharoff, "Japan's Bush League Air Force," *Air News* (Sept. 1941): pp. 4–8; Hallett Abend, "Yes, the Japs Can Fly," *Saturday Evening Post*, Apr. 19, 1941, pp. 29, 199–202; John R. Ferris, "Student and Master: The United Kingdom, Japan, Airpower, and the Fall of Singapore, 1920–1941," in *Sixty Years On: The Fall of Singapore Revisited*, edited by Brian Farrell and Sandy Hunter (Singapore, 2003), p. 103.

14. Spooner quoted in Richard B. Frank, *Tower of Skulls: A History of the Asia-Pacific War, 1937–1942* (New York, 2020), p. 336.

15. Smith, *Singapore Burning*, pp. 95, 122.

16. Entry for Dec. 8, 1941, in Brown, *From Suez to Singapore*, p. 297; O'Dowd Gallagher, *Retreat in the East* (London, 1942), p. 34.

17. Entries for Dec. 10, 1941, in Brown, *From Suez to Singapore*, pp. 315–320; Gallagher, *Retreat in the East*, pp. 50, 52.

18. Barber, *Sinister Twilight*, pp. 47–48; Arthur Bryant, *The Turn of the Tide: A History of the War Years Based on the Diaries of Field-Marshal Lord*

Alanbrooke (New York, 1957), p. 226; Winston S. Churchill, *The Grand Alliance* (Boston, 1951), p. 620.

19. Bayly and Harper, *Forgotten Armies*, p. 37; "Testing Times," *Straits Times*, Dec. 20, 1941.

20. "Raffles," *Straits Times*, Dec. 16, 1941; "Robinson's," *Straits Times*, Dec. 22, 1941; Bayly and Harper, *Forgotten Armies*, p. 120.

21. Masanobu Tsuji, *Japan's Greatest Victory, Britain's Worst Defeat* (New York, 1993 [1952]), p. 33; Bryant, *Turn of the Tide*, p. 235.

22. Smith, *Singapore Burning*, p. 258.

23. Farrell, *Defence and Fall of Singapore*, pp. 119–120.

24. Mollie Panter-Downes, *London War Notes, 1939–1945* (New York, 1971), p. 192.

25. Tsuji, *Japan's Greatest Victory, Britain's Worst Defeat*, pp. 149–150.

26. Smith, *Singapore Burning*, p. 430; Farrell, *Defence and Fall of Singapore*, p. 195.

27. Winston S. Churchill, *The Hinge of Fate* (Boston, 1950), p. 100; Raymond Callahan, "Churchill and Singapore," in *Sixty Years On*, edited by Farrell and Hunter, p. 158.

28. Bayly and Harper, *Forgotten Armies*, p. 132.

29. Barber, *Sinister Twilight*, p. 142.

30. Rupert Emerson, *Malaysia: A Study in Direct and Indirect Rule* (New York, 1937), pp. 31–33.

31. Louis Allen, *Singapore, 1941–1942* (Newark, NJ, 1977), p. 263.

32. Madhusree Mukerjee, *Churchill's Secret War: The British Empire and the Ravaging of India During World War II* (New York, 2010), p. 60; Allen, *Singapore, 1941–1942*, p. 260.

33. Allen, *Singapore, 1941–1942*, p. 260; Alan Warren, "The Indian Army and the Fall of Singapore," in *Sixty Years On*, edited by Farrell and Hunter, p. 285.

34. "Indians in Malaya to Hold Bumper Protest Meetings," *Shonan Times*, Aug. 12, 1942; "Indians Rally to Cause of Mother Country: Nippon's Help Recognized," *Shonan Times*, Aug. 13, 1942; "Gandhiji's Birthday Celebrated as Never Before in Malaya," *Shonan Times*, Oct. 4, 1942.

35. Tomoyuki Ishizu and Raymond Callahan, "The Rising Sun Strikes: The Japanese Invasions," in *The Pacific War: From Pearl Harbor to Hiroshima*, edited by Daniel Marston (Oxford, 2005), p. 56; "Anti-Japan Chinese Are Being Isolated," *Japan Times*, Feb. 22, 1942.

36. Henry F. Frei, *Guns of February: Ordinary Japanese Soldiers' Views of the Malayan Campaign and the Fall of Singapore, 1941–42* (Singapore, 2004), pp. 147–152; Mamoru Shinozaki, *Syonan—My Story* (Singapore, 1975).

37. Frei, *Guns of February*, pp. 153–154; Cheah Bon Kheng, "The Social

Impact of the Japanese Occupation of Malaya (1942–1945)," in *Southeast Asia Under Japanese Occupation*, edited by Alfred W. McCoy (New Haven, CT, 1980), p. 97.

38. Farrell, *Defence and Fall of Singapore*, p. 385.

39. Ashihei quoted in Eri Hotta, *Pan-Asianism and Japan's War, 1931–1945* (New York, 2007), p. 191; "The Historic Victory of Singapore," *Japan Times*, Feb. 17, 1942; "Foe Celebrates Singapore's Fall," *New York Times*, Feb. 19, 1942.

40. Robert Guillain, *I Saw Tokyo Burning: An Eyewitness Narrative from Pearl Harbor to Hiroshima* (London, 1981), p. 47.

41. Samuel Yamashita, *Daily Life in Wartime Japan, 1940–1945* (Lawrence, KS, 2013), pp. 18, 20; Harald Salomon, *Views of the Dark Valley: Japanese Cinema and the Culture of Nationalism, 1937–1945* (Wiesbaden, 2011), p. 173.

42. Entry for Feb. 14, 1942, in Panter-Downes, *London War Notes, 1939–1945*, p. 204.

43. Bryant, *Turn of the Tide*, pp. 268, 276; Lord Wedgewood quoted in Allen, *Singapore, 1941–1942*, p. 22; Orwell quoted in Yasmin Khan, *India at War: The Subcontinent and the Second World War* (New York, 2015), p. 93.

44. Entry for Feb. 20, 1942, in Panter-Downes, *London War Notes, 1939–1945*, pp. 207–208; Khan, *India at War*, p. 113.

45. Editorial, "China and India," *Times*, Feb. 28, 1942; Daniel Todman, "'The Worst Disaster': British Reactions to the Fall of Singapore," in *The World at War, 1911–1949: Explorations in the Cultural History of War*, edited by Catriona Pennell and Filipo Ribeiro DeMeneses (Leiden, 2019), p. 278; Margery Perham, "The Colonial Empire: II—Capital, Labour, and the Colour Bar," *Times*, Mar. 14, 1942.

46. Walter Lippmann, "The Post-Singapore War in the East," *Washington Post*, Feb. 21, 1942.

47. Pearl S. Buck, "The Race Barrier 'That Must Be Destroyed,'" *New York Times Magazine*, May 31, 1942.

CHAPTER 5: "On the Road to Mandalay"

1. Walter Baxter, *Look Down in Mercy* (London, 1951), p. 103.

2. Jack Belden, "The Fever of Defeat," *Time*, May 11, 1942.

3. Ba Maw, *Breakthrough in Burma* (New Haven, CT, 1968), p. 80.

4. Maw, *Breakthrough in Burma*, p. 47; Richard Toye, *Churchill's Empire: The World That Made Him and the World He Made* (New York, 2010), p. 218. On Nehru, see Gary J. Bass, *Judgment at Tokyo: World War II on Trial and the Making of Modern Asia* (New York, 2023), p. 211.

5. Colin Smith, *Singapore Burning: Heroism and Surrender in World War II* (London, 2005), p. 262; Louis Allen, *Singapore, 1941–1942* (Newark, NJ, 1977), pp. 257–258; Kent Fedorowich, "The Evacuation of Civilians from Hong Kong and Malaya/Singapore, 1939–42," in *Sixty Years On: The Fall of*

Singapore Revisited, edited by Brian Farrell and Sandy Hunter (Singapore, 2003), p. 135.

6.   Fedorowich, "Evacuation of Civilians," in *Sixty Years On*, edited by Farrell and Hunter, p. 140; Ronald W. Zweig, "British Plans for the Evacuation of Palestine in 1941–42," *Studies in Zionism* 8 (1983): p. 295.

7.   George Rodger quoted in Geoffrey Tyson, *Forgotten Frontier* (Calcutta, 1945), p. 19.

8.   H. E. Bates, *The Jacaranda Tree* (London, 1949), pp. 71–72, 192.

9.   "Indian Evacuees Witness Hellish Scenes," *Bombay Chronicle*, Apr. 10, 1942.

10.   "Indian Evacuees Witness Hellish Scenes"; Bates, *The Jacaranda Tree*, p. 266; Max Hastings, *Inferno: The World at War, 1939–1945* (New York, 2012), p. 223.

11.   Jack Belden, "Flight Through the Jungle," in *Reporting World War II: Part One, American Journalism, 1938–1944*, edited by Anne Matthews, Nancy Caldwell Sorel, and Samuel Hynes (New York, 1995), pp. 316–317.

12.   Christopher Bayly and Tim Harper, *Forgotten Armies: The Fall of British Asia, 1941–1945* (London, 2004), p. 252; "Tale of Japanese Cruelty," *Statesman* (Calcutta), Nov. 8, 1942.

13.   Basen Basu, *Rangrut* (Bombay, 1954 [Calcutta, 1950]), pp. 95, 103, 109; "Indian Evacuees Witness Hellish Scenes"; "Evacuation Scandals," *Bombay Chronicle*, Apr. 29, 1942.

14.   Gerhard L. Weinberg, *A World at Arms: A Global History of World War II* (New York, 1994), p. 327.

15.   Indivar Kamtekar, "The Shiver of 1942," in *War and Society in Colonial India*, edited by Kaushik Roy (New Delhi, 2006), pp. 333, 335, 355.

16.   See, for example, F. C. Jones, *Japan's New Order in East Asia* (London, 1954), pp. 402–403; and Weinberg, *A World at Arms*, p. 323.

CHAPTER 6: Spring Internment

1.   Dr. Seuss, "Waiting for the Signal from Home . . . ," *PM*, Feb. 13, 1942.

2.   Charles Hurd's Dec. 16, 1941, story in the *New York Times* featured a triple-decker headline: "Heroic Acts Cited; 2,897 Defenders Killed in Gallant Battle—Base Not 'on Alert'; Fifth Column Active."

3.   Arthur Krock, "A Candid Account of Losses at Pearl Harbor," *New York Times*, Dec. 16, 1941. On Norway, see Edwin L. James, "How Germany Repaid Norway's Hospitality," *New York Times*, Apr. 21, 1940; "Fifth Columns," editorial, *New York Times*, Apr. 21, 1940; Anne O'Hare McCormick, "Hambro Belittles Fifth-Column Idea," *New York Times*, July 12, 1940.

4.   Shotaro Frank Miyamoto, "Immigrants and Citizens of Japanese Origin," *Annals of the American Academy of Political and Social Science* 223 (Sept. 1942): p. 112.

5. Edgar Rice Burroughs, "Laugh It Off," *Honolulu Advertiser*, Dec. 15, 1941; "Text of Secretary Knox's Address to Annapolis Graduating Class," *New York Times*, Dec. 20, 1941.

6. Hurd, "Heroic Acts Cited"; Wallace Carroll, "Scope of Hawaii's Spy Army Told," *Los Angeles Times*, Dec. 31, 1941.

7. James Matsumoto Omura, *Nisei Naysayer: The Memoir of Militant Japanese American Journalist Jimmie Omura*, edited by Arthur A. Hansen (Stanford, CA, 2018), p. 16; "County Supervisors Map Emergency Measures, Steps Taken to Balk Sabotage," *Richmond Independent*, Dec. 8, 1941; "Welcome to Loyalty," *Richmond Independent*, Dec. 16, 1941.

8. "Many Aliens Finding Things Tougher in US," *Richmond Independent*, Dec. 10, 1941.

9. On "fact-finding," see "Eviction of Jap Aliens Sought," *Los Angeles Times*, Jan. 28, 1942; and "Bowron Asks Removal of All Japanese Inland," *Los Angeles Times*, Feb. 6, 1942. On uneasiness, see Patricia E. Roy, *The Triumph of Citizenship: The Japanese and Chinese in Canada, 1941–1967* (Vancouver, 2007), p. 28.

10. Miyamoto, "Immigrants and Citizens of Japanese Origin," p. 112; Kevin Allen Leonard, *The Battle for Los Angeles: Racial Ideology and World War II* (Albuquerque, 2006), p. 80.

11. H. M. Anderson, "The Question of Japanese-Americans," *Los Angeles Times*, Feb. 2, 1942.

12. "Bowron Asks Removal of All Japanese Inland"; Roger Daniels, *Concentration Camps USA: Japanese Americans and World War II* (Hinsdale, IL, 1971), p. 77.

13. Ayako Hagihara and Grace Shimizu, "The Japanese Latin American Wartime and Redress Experience," *Amerasia Journal* 28 (2002); John K. Emmerson, "Japanese and Americans in Peru, 1942–1943," *Foreign Service Journal* 54 (May 1977).

14. Ann Gomer Sunahara, *The Politics of Racism: The Uprooting of Japanese Canadians During the Second World War* (Toronto, 1981), pp. 31–32.

15. Edward Offley, *The Burning Shore: How Hitler's U-Boats Brought World War II to America* (New York, 2014), pp. 112, 184–187; "Liner Hit by U-Boat," *New York Times*, Jan. 29, 1942.

16. Franklin Odo, *No Sword to Bury: Japanese Americans in Hawai'i During World War II* (Philadelphia, 2004), p. 145; Beth Bailey and David Farber, *The First Strange Place: The Alchemy of Race and Sex in World War II Hawaii* (New York, 1992), pp. 8, 19, 23, 105.

17. "Persecutions in Barbaric America," editorial, *Japan Times*, Mar. 9, 1942.

18. Matthew M. Briones, *Jim and Jap Crow: A Cultural History of 1940s Interracial America* (Princeton, NJ, 2012), pp. 33, 93; Robert Hosokawa, "An American with a Japanese Face," *Christian Science Monitor*, May 22, 1943.

19. "Hundreds Hunt Bargains at Little Tokyo Sales," *Los Angeles Times*, Mar. 25, 1942.

20. Briones, *Jim and Jap Crow*, p. 136; Matthew Bodine, letter of May 11, 1942, quoted in Daniels, *Concentration Camps USA*, p. 87.

21. Hisaye Yamamoto quoted in Briones, *Jim and Jap Crow*, p. 123; "Eastward Ho," *Time*, Mar. 16, 1942; "Japanese Begin Work at New 'Colony' Homes," *Richmond Independent*, Mar. 24, 1942; "More Japs Leave Arcadia," *Los Angeles Times*, Sept. 26, 1942.

22. Mary Oyama, "When My Only Crime Is My Face," *Liberty: The Magazine of a Free People*, Aug. 14, 1943.

23. "Issei, Nisei, Kibei: The U.S. Has Put 100,000 People of Japanese Blood in 'Protective Custody,'" *Fortune* 29 (Apr. 1944); Roger Daniels, *The Decision to Relocate the Japanese Americans* (Philadelphia, 1975), p. 21; Leonard, *Battle for Los Angeles*, p. 141.

24. Ken Adachi, *The Enemy That Never Was: A History of the Japanese Canadians* (Toronto, 1976), pp. 279, 335.

25. Hosokawa, "An American with a Japanese Face."

26. Diary entries for Sept. 12 and Dec. 15, 1942, and Mar. 22, 1943, quoted in Briones, *Jim and Jap Crow*, pp. 16, 152, 154.

CHAPTER 7: Summer Offensive

1. Olivia Manning, *The Levant Trilogy* (New York, 1982), p. 80.

2. Christopher Browning, *Ordinary Men: Reserve Police Battalion 101 and the Final Solution in Poland* (New York, 1992), p. xv; Lewi Stone, "Quantifying the Holocaust: Hyperintense Kill Rates During the Nazi Genocide," *Science Advances* 5 (Jan. 2, 2019); "The New Plague in Egypt," editorial, *New York Times*, July 1, 1942.

3. Andreas Herberg-Rothe, "Tolstoy and Clausewitz: The Dialectics of War," in *Tolstoy on War: Narrative Art and Truth in "War and Peace,"* edited by Rickie Allen McPeak and Donna Tussing Orwin (Cornell, NY, 2012), p. 142.

4. Leo Tolstoy, *War and Peace*, translated by Richard Pevear and Larissa Volokhonsky (New York, 2007), p. 773.

5. "Text of Hitler's Address Reviewing the Course of the War and Explaining His Aims Opening of Winterhilfe at Sportpalast on 30.9.42," *New York Times*, Oct. 1, 1942; entry for Mar. 20, 1942, in *Die Tagebücher von Joseph Goebbels. Sämtliche Fragmente*, edited by Elke Fröhlich (Munich, 1994), pt. 2, vol. 3, p. 511.

6. Diary entries for Mar. 27, Apr. 20, and July 1, 1942, Klaus Budzinski, Kempowski Archive, 3585, Akademie der Künste, Berlin; entry for June 29, 1941, in Ruth Andreas-Friedrich, *Berlin Underground, 1938–1945* (New York, 1947), p. 69.

7. Robert M. Citino, *The Death of the Wehrmacht: The German Campaigns of 1942* (Lawrence, KS, 2007), pp. 11, 82.

8. For miles, Michael K. Jones, *The Retreat: Hitler's First Defeat* (New York, 2009), p. 19; flood, "Into the Caucasus," *Times*, Aug. 11, 1942; avalanche, Alexander Werth, *The Year of Stalingrad* (London, 1946), 159; stampede, Ilya Ehrenburg, *The War, 1941–45* (London, 1964), p. 73; propaganda, Stephen G. Fritz, *Ostkrieg: Hitler's War of Extermination in the East* (Lexington, KY, 2011), p. 283.

9. Vasily Grossman, *Stalingrad* (New York, 2019), pp. 130, 142; Leland Stowe, *They Shall Not Sleep* (New York, 1944), p. 232; Jochen Hellbeck, *Die Stalingrad-Protokolle: Sowjetische Augenzeugen berichten aus der Schlacht* (Frankfurt, 2012), p. 12.

10. Hans Doerr, *Der Feldzug nach Stalingrad* (Darmstadt, 1955), p. 42.

11. Citino, *Death of the Wehrmacht*, p. 267n89; Alexander Werth, *Russia at War, 1941–1945* (New York, 1964), p. 442; Grossman, *Stalingrad*, p. 60.

12. Christina Winkler, "Rostov-on-Don 1942: A Little-Known Chapter of the Holocaust," *Holocaust and Genocide Studies* 30, no. 1 (2016): pp. 105–130.

13. Diary entries for July 7 and 15 and Aug. 6–9, 1942, in Elena Skrjabina, *Siege and Survival: The Odyssey of a Leningrader* (Carbondale, IL, 1971), pp. 125, 128, 130, 137–142.

14. www.ww2online.org/image/arkansas-traveler-nose-art-north-africa-probably-1942.

15. Alan Moorehead, *African Trilogy* (London, 1944), pp. 21, 232; Eve Curie, *Journey Among Warriors* (Garden City, NY, 1943), p. 35.

16. Artemis Cooper, *Cairo in the War: 1939–1945* (London, 2006), p. 117.

17. Winston S. Churchill, *The Hinge of Fate* (Boston, 1950), pp. 383, 400–401.

18. Anne O'Hare McCormick, "There Is a Tide in the Affairs of Men," *New York Times*, July 1, 1942.

19. Richard Overy, *Why the Allies Won* (New York, 1995), p. 14; Citino, *Death of the Wehrmacht*, pp. 182, 214.

20. "We Are Losing the War," *Time*, Sept. 7, 1942; "The New Plague in Egypt," editorial, *New York Times*, July 1, 1942; Citino, *Death of the Wehrmacht*, p. 194.

21. Curie, *Journey Among Warriors*, p. 78.

22. Manning, *The Levant Trilogy*, p. 94; Cooper, *Cairo in the War*, p. 195; Cecil Beaton, *Near East* (London, 1943), p. 132.

23. Werth, *Russia at War*, pp. 232, 235; Rodric Braithwaite, *Moscow, 1941: A City and Its People at War* (New York, 2006), p. 222.

24. Klaus-Michael Mallmann and Martin Cüppers, *Nazi Palestine: The Plans for Extermination of the Jews in Palestine* (New York, 2010), pp. 107–108, 116–117.

25. Entry for June 14, 1940, in John Colville, *The Fringes of Power: 10 Downing Street Diaries, 1939–1955* (New York, 1985), p. 158; Erik Larson, *The Splendid and the Vile: A Saga of Churchill, Family and Defiance During the Blitz* (New York, 2020), p. 84; Manning, *The Levant Trilogy*, p. 37.

CHAPTER 8: America Prepares for War

1. Andrew Roberts, *The Storm of War: A New History of the Second World War* (New York, 2010), pp. 50–51; Joseph Goebbels, "Grosskundgebung des Gaues Oberdonau der NSDAP zum 4. Jahrestag des 'Anschlusses,'" Linz, Mar. 15, 1942, and "Kundgebung des Kreises Wuppertal der NSDAP," Wuppertal, Nov. 17, 1942, in Helmut Heiber, ed., *Goebbels-Reden*, vol. 2, *1939–1945* (Düsseldorf, 1972), pp. 104, 145; entry for Oct. 2, 1942, in *Die Tagebücher von Joseph Goebbels. Sämtliche Fragmente*, edited by Elke Fröhlich (Munich, 1994), pt. 2, vol. 6, p. 49.

2. Edward Alden Jewell, "Portrait of the Spirit of a Nation," *New York Times*, May 24, 1942; Edward Steichen and Carl Sandburg, "Road to Victory, a Procession of Photographs of the Nation at War," *Bulletin of the Museum of Modern Art* 9 (1942): pp. 2–17.

3. Kenneth Burke, "War and Cultural Life," *American Journal of Sociology* 48 (Nov. 1942): pp. 404–410; Catherine Bauer, "Cities in Flux," *American Scholar* 13 (Winter 1943–1944): pp. 70, 72.

4. "Willow Run: Ford Builds a Bombers' Hive," *Life*, Feb. 16, 1942; on the shovels, A. H. Raskin, "Mass Magic in Detroit," *New York Times*, Mar. 1, 1942; on the assembly lines, Richard Overy, *Why the Allies Won* (New York, 1995), p. 197; on jigsaw, "Auto War Orders Put at 12 Billion," *New York Times*, Feb. 11, 1942; the Canadian is quoted in Paul Fussell, *Wartime: Understanding and Behavior in the Second World War* (New York, 1989), p. 9.

5. George Roeder, *The Censored War: American Visual Experience During World War II* (New Haven, CT, 1993), p. 121; Richard R. Lingeman, *Don't You Know There's a War On? The American Home Front, 1941–1945* (New York, 1970), p. 109; Overy, *Why the Allies Won*, p. 197; Gerald Linderman, *The World Within War: America's Combat Experience in World War II* (New York, 1997), p. 341.

6. Doris Kearns Goodwin, *No Ordinary Time: Franklin and Eleanor Roosevelt; The Home Front in World War II* (New York, 1994), p. 23.

7. Edward Allen Jewell, "Portrait of the Spirit of the Nation," *New York Times*, May 24, 1942.

8. St. Clair McKelway, "U.S. Army Private," *Life*, Mar. 16, 1942.

9. Rick Atkinson, *An Army at Dawn: The War in North Africa, 1942–1943* (New York, 2002), p. 9; Lee Kennett, *G.I.: The American Soldier in World War II*

(New York, 1987), pp. 17–18, 60; Aaron Hiltner, *Taking Leave, Taking Liberties: American Troops on the World War II Home Front* (Chicago, 2020), p. 43.

10. Hiltner, *Taking Leave, Taking Liberties*, p. 22; Goodwin, *No Ordinary Time*, p. 217.

11. John Ellis, *The Sharp End: The Fighting Man in World War II* (New York, 1980), p. 13; Ronald Spector, *Eagle Against the Rising Sun: The American War with Japan* (New York, 1984), p. 10.

12. Roy Scranton, *Total Mobilization: World War II and American Literature* (Chicago, 2019), pp. 74–75, quoting Baldwin's *The Price of the Ticket* (1985).

13. George S. Schuyler, "Views and Reviews," *Pittsburgh Courier*, Jan. 24, 1942.

14. Tracy Campbell, *The Year of Peril: America in 1942* (New Haven, CT, 2020), pp. 22–23; Donny Gluckstein, *A People's History of the Second World War: Resistance Versus Empire* (London, 2012), p. 119.

15. Walter White, *A Man Called White: The Autobiography of Walter White* (New York, 1948), p. 194.

16. Matthew F. Delmont, *Half American: The Epic Story of African Americans Fighting World War II at Home and Abroad* (New York, 2023), p. 90.

17. Sarah Ayako Barksdale, "Prelude to a Revolution: African-American World War II Veterans, Double Consciousness, and Civil Rights, 1940–1955" (PhD diss., University of North Carolina, 2014), p. 33; Dudley Randall, "The Southern Road" (1943), in *Roses and Revolutions*, edited by Melba Joyce Boyd (Detroit, 2009), p. 70.

18. Ulysses Lee, *The Employment of Negro Troops* (Washington, DC, 1963), p. 300.

19. Ernie Pyle, *Here Is Your War* (New York, 1943), pp. 77–78; Morton Sosna, "The G.I.s' South and the North-South Dialogue During World War II," in *Developing Dixie: Modernization in a Traditional Society*, edited by Winfred B. Moore Jr. et al. (New York, 1988), p. 319.

20. On Georgia, Barksdale, "Prelude to a Revolution," p. 33; on overseers, Delmont, *Half American*, p. xviii; on polls, "What the Soldier Thinks" (Aug. 1943), in *What the Soldier Thinks: A Digest of War Department Studies on the Attitudes of American Troops*, by the War Department (Washington, DC, 1945), p. 57; on the medic, Elizabeth D. Samet, *Looking for the Good War: American Amnesia and the Violent Pursuit of Happiness* (New York, 2021), p. 249.

21. Joyce Thomas, "Double V Was for Victory: Black Soldiers, the Black Protest, and World War II" (PhD diss., Ohio State University, 1993), p. 144; Delmont, *Half American*, p. xvii.

22. Christopher Thorne, "Britain and the Black G.I.s: Racial Issues and Anglo-American Relations in 1942," *Journal of Ethnic and Migration Studies*

3, no. 3 (1974): p. 266; "U.S. Army Officers Spread Anti-Negro Feeling," *Pittsburgh Courier*, Mar. 20, 1943; Suke Wolton, *Lord Hailey, the Colonial Office, and the Politics of Race and Empire in the Second World War* (New York, 2000), p. 88.

23. Delmont, *Half American*, p. 38; Barksdale, "Prelude to a Revolution," p. 124.

24. Campbell, *Year of Peril*, p. x.

25. Herman Wouk, *War and Remembrance* (Boston, 1978); Robert Trumbull, "Army Fliers Blasted Two Fleets Off Midway," *New York Times*, June 12, 1942; Hanson Baldwin, "Our Naval Arm," *New York Times*, June 14, 1942; Walter Lord, *Incredible Victory: The Battle of Midway* (New York, 1967), p. 112, describing the horizon; Max Hastings, *Inferno: The World at War, 1939–1945* (New York, 2012), pp. 245–246, describing the explosions.

26. Matthew Stevenson, "Guadalcanal," *American Scholar* 59, no. 3 (1990): p. 363; Herbert L. Merillat, *The Island: A History of the First Marine Division on Guadalcanal, August 7–December 9, 1942* (Boston, 1944), p. 23.

27. Samuel Morison, *History of United States Naval Operations in World War II*, vol. 4, *Coral Sea, Midway and Submarine Actions, May 1942–August 1942* (Boston, 1950), p. 251.

28. Joseph Wheelan, *Midnight in the Pacific: Guadalcanal, the World War II Battle That Turned the Tide of War* (Boston, 2017), p. 98.

29. Hanson W. Baldwin, "Japan's Hold on West Pacific Not Broken in Almost a Year," *New York Times*, Oct. 23, 1942.

30. "Guadalcanal," *New York Times*, Oct. 16, 1942.

31. Herbert P. Bix, *Hirohito and the Making of Modern Japan* (London, 2000), p. 461.

32. Richard B. Frank, *Guadalcanal: The Definitive Account of the Landmark Battle* (New York, 1990), pp. 268, 534; Wheelan, *Midnight in the Pacific*, p. 267.

33. Wheelan, *Midnight in the Pacific*, pp. 230–231, 235; Hanson W. Baldwin, "The Navy's Battle Report, Volume III," *New York Times*, June 15, 1947.

34. John B. George, *Shots Fired in Anger* (Plantersville, SC, 1947), p. 65; Ellis, *Sharp End*, p. 95.

35. Robert Leckie, *Helmet for My Pillow* (New York, 1957), p. 88; Wheelan, *Midnight in the Pacific*, pp. 68, 70.

36. Leckie, *Helmet for My Pillow*, p. 88; Frank, *Guadalcanal*, p. 258; John Hersey, *Into the Valley: A Skirmish of the Marines* (New York, 1943 [Lincoln, NE, 2002]), pp. 48, 57; "The Psychiatric Toll of Warfare," *Fortune* (Dec. 1943): p. 278.

37. "Patch of Destiny," *Time*, Nov. 2, 1942.

38. David Stowe, *Swing Changes: Big-Band Jazz in New Deal America* (Cambridge, MA, 1994), p. 148; Mark Weiner, "Consumer Culture and Participatory

Democracy: The Story of Coca Cola During World War II," *Food and Foodways* 6 (1996): p. 113–114.

39. Stowe, *Swing Changes*, pp. 1, 25; Billy Rowe, "What Is This Thing Called Swing Music?," *Pittsburgh Courier*, Feb. 20, 1937.

40. "In Iceland, Too!," "Sweet Rose O'Day Digs Hot Today," "Jumpin' Jive Real Solid Way 'Down Under,'" *Yank*, Aug. 26 and Sept. 2, 1942; Jay L. Jenkins, letter to "Mom & folks," July 1942, in *Letters Home*, edited by Mina Curtiss (Boston, 1944), p. 70.

41. "Battle of Bands," *Bantu World* (Johannesburg), Dec. 20, 1941; "Nightlife Is Resurrected," *Manila Tribune*, July 12, 1942.

42. Entry for Jan. 1, 1942, in *Die Tagebücher von Joseph Goebbels*, edited by Fröhlich, pt. 2, vol. 3, pp. 34–35; letter to Erika, Oct. 3, 1942, in *Im Funkwagen der Wehrmacht durch Europa: Balkan, Ukraine, Stalingrad. Feldpostbriefe des Gefreiten Wilhelm Moldenhauer, 1940–1943*, edited by Jens Ebert (Berlin, 2008), p. 263.

CHAPTER 9: Stalingrad

1. Alexander Werth, *The Year of Stalingrad* (London, 1946), pp. 54–71.

2. Entry for Aug. 31, 1941, in Leon Werth, *Déposition: Journal, 1940–1944* (Paris, 1992), p. 343; Jochen Hellbeck, "Battles for Morale: An Entangled History of Total War in Europe, 1939–1945," in *The Cambridge History of the Second World War*, edited by Michael Geyer and Adam Tooze (Cambridge, UK, 2015), p. 3:336; A. Werth, *The Year of Stalingrad*, p. 158.

3. Entries for Sept. 12, 25, and 28 and Oct. 11 and 14, 1942, in Charles Rist, *Une saison gâtée: Journal de la guerre et de l'Occupation, 1939–1945* (Paris, 1983), pp. 272–280.

4. Anne O'Hare McCormick, "Why Stalingrad Produces So Much Emotion," *New York Times*, Sept. 30, 1942.

5. Robert M. Citino, *The Death of the Wehrmacht: The German Campaigns of 1942* (Lawrence, KS, 2007), p. 289.

6. Walter Graebner, "1,000 Miles Up the Volga," *Life*, Sept. 7, 1942; Jochen Hellbeck, *Stalingrad: The City That Defeated the Third Reich* (New York, 2015), p. 104.

7. Michael K. Jones, *Stalingrad: How the Red Army Triumphed* (Barnsley, UK, 2007), p. 57; Citino, *Death of the Wehrmacht*, p. 248.

8. Entry for Aug. 23, 1942, Wilhelm Hoffman diary, quoted in Vasili Chuikov, *The Beginning of the Road* (London, 1963), p. 249.

9. Letter to his brother Reinhard, Oct. 4, 1942, in Helmuth Groscurth, *Tagebücher eines Abwehroffiziers, 1938–1940: Mit weitern Dokumente zur Militäropposition gegen Hitler*, edited by Helmut Kruasnick and Harold C.

Deutsch (Stuttgart, 1970), p. 528; Heinz Schröter, *Stalingrad* (New York, 1958), p. 97.

10. Maurice Hindus, *Mother Russia* (London, 1943), p. 119.

11. A. Werth, *The Year of Stalingrad*, pp. 81–82.

12. Vyasheslav Molotov, *The Molotov Paper on Nazi Atrocities* (New York, 1942).

13. "How Russia Hit Back," *Times*, Mar. 11, 1942.

14. Konstantin Simonov, "Kill Him!," *Pravda*, July 14, 1942, and Ilya Ehrenburg in *Red Star*, Aug. 13, 1942, quoted in Alexander Werth, *Russia at War, 1941–1945* (New York, 1964), p. 414.

15. Simonov, "Kill Him!"; Hellbeck, *Stalingrad*, p. 35.

16. Chuikov, *Beginning of the Road*, pp. 206, 273.

17. Antony Beevor, *Stalingrad: The Fateful Siege, 1942–1943* (New York, 1998), p. 125; Leo Tolstoy, *War and Peace*, translated by Richard Pevear and Larissa Volokhonsky (New York, 2007), p. 1034; "Stalingrad and the Satellites," editorial, *Times*, Sept. 23, 1942.

18. Jones, *Stalingrad*, p. 138; Chuikov, *Beginning of the Road*, p. 180; Hitler speeches on Sept. 30 and Nov. 8, 1942, in Max Domarus, *Hitler: Reden und Proklamationen, 1932 bis 1945* (Leonberg, 1988), pp. 4:1912, 1938.

19. A. Werth, *The Year of Stalingrad*, p. 212.

20. *West African Pilot*, Sept. 24 and Oct. 6, 1942; *Richmond Independent*, Sept. 21 and 25, 1942; *New York Times*, Sept. 3, 5, 8, 9, 12, 14, and 20 and Oct. 16 and 18, 1942.

21. *Japan Times*, Sept. 9, 1942; *Rand Daily Mail* (Johannesburg), Sept. 5, 1942.

22. Entry for Sept. 16, 1942, in *Die Tagebücher von Joseph Goebbels. Sämtliche Fragmente*, edited by Elke Fröhlich (Munich, 1994), pt. 2, vol. 5, p. 507; Hans Doerr, *Der Feldzug nach Stalingrad* (Darmstadt, 1955), p. 52; "Reds Retake Stalingrad Streets," *Los Angeles Times*, Sept. 21, 1942.

23. Chuikov, *Beginning of the Road*, pp. 135–136; on the wave, Jones, *Stalingrad*, pp. 9–10; on crawling, Beevor, *Stalingrad*, p. 141.

24. Entries for Sept. 16, 18, 22, and 26 and Oct. 17, 1942, Hoffman diary, in Chuikov, *Beginning of the Road*, pp. 251–252.

25. Chuikov, *Beginning of the Road*, p. 97.

26. Entries for Nov. 14 and 29, 1942, in Lore Walb, *Ich die alte, ich, die junge: Konfrontation mit meinen Tagebüchern, 1933–1945* (Berlin, 1997), pp. 249, 253.

27. Chuikov, *Beginning of the Road*, pp. 187, 190; Beevor, *Stalingrad*, p. 173.

28. A. Werth, *The Year of Stalingrad*, pp. 305, 327; entries for Nov. 23 and 26, 1942, in *Die Tagebücher von Joseph Goebbels*, edited by Fröhlich, pt. 2, vol. 6, pp. 317, 335.

29. Theodore Plievier, *Stalingrad* (New York, 1984 [1948]), pp. 23–24, 26, 37.

30. See also letter to his brother Reinhard, Jan. 14, 1943, in Groscurth, *Tagebücher eines Abwehroffiziers*, edited by Kruasnick and Deutsch, p. 532.

31. A. Werth, *The Year of Stalingrad*, p. 428.

32. "Bericht der Feldpostprüfstelle des Panzer-Armeeoberkommandos 4 über die Feldpost aus dem Kessel von Stalingrad 22. Dezember–9. January 1943," Jan. 12, 1943, in *Stalingrad: Mythos und Wirklichkeit einer Schlacht*, edited by Wolfram Wette and Gerd Ueberschär (Frankfurt, 1992), p. 94.

33. Beevor, *Stalingrad*, p. 371.

34. Wolfram Wette, "Das Massenserben als 'Heldenepos. Stalingrad in der NS-Propaganda,'" in *Stalingrad*, edited by Wette and Ueberschär, pp. 50, 52, 55; entry for Jan. 23, 1943, in *Die Tagebücher von Joseph Goebbels*, edited by Fröhlich, pt. 2, vol. 7, pp. 172–175; *Völkischer Beobachter*, Feb. 4, 1943.

35. A. Werth, *The Year of Stalingrad*, p. 428.

36. Beevor, *Stalingrad*, p. 404; Sian Nicholas, *The Echo of War: Home Front Propaganda and the Wartime BBC, 1939–1945* (Manchester, 1996), p. 170.

37. "Bells Across the Meadow," *Times*, Nov. 17, 1942; "The World Hears Britain's Bells," *Times*, Nov. 16, 1942.

38. United States Army, "Biennial Report of the Chief of Staff of the United States Army, July 1, 1943, to June 30, 1945, to the Secretary of War," in *Biennial Reports of the Chief of Staff of the United States Army to the Secretary of War, 1 July 1939, to 30 June 1945* (Washington, DC, 1996), p. 107.

39. Williamson Murray and Allan R. Millett, *A War to Be Won: Fighting the Second World War* (Cambridge, MA, 2000), p. x.

40. "A Long War," editorial, *Richmond Independent*, Dec. 1, 1942; "'All Out with Halsey!,'" *New York Times*, Dec. 6, 1942.

41. Curzio Malaparte, *Kaputt* (New York, 2005), pp. 3, 37; Ernest Mandel, *The Meaning of the Second World War* (London, 1986), p. 162.

42. Les Daly, "Archeology with a Heart in Holland's Drained Inland Sea," *Smithsonian*, Apr. 1986, pp. 106–113; Victor Davis Hanson, *The Second World Wars: How the First Global Conflict Was Fought and Won* (New York, 2017), p. 67; "Vacation Days," *Time*, June 8, 1942.

CHAPTER 10: On Land

1. Jochen Hellbeck, *Stalingrad: The City That Defeated the Third Reich* (New York, 2015), p. 1.

2. "Fifteen Years or Six Months?," *Guardian* (Cape Town), Oct. 22, 1942.

3. James M. McPherson, *The Battle Cry of Freedom: The Civil War Era* (New York, 1988), pp. 698, 804.

4. John Hersey, *Into the Valley: A Skirmish of the Marines* (Lincoln, NE,

2002 [1943]), pp. 23, 42–43; on Texaco, David Shribman, "The Man Who Died for the Liberal Arts," *Atlantic*, May 2024.

5. "Im 'Kessel' von Wiborg," *Neue Zürcher Zeitung*, Sept. 21, 1941; Ernie Pyle, "Normandy Beachhead," June 12, 1944, in *Ernie's War: The Best of Ernie Pyle's World War II Dispatches*, edited by David Nichols (New York, 1986), pp. 277–280; Philip Shaw, *Waterloo and the Romantic Imagination* (London, 2002), p. 67.

6. David Stahel, *Retreat from Moscow: A New History of Germany's Winter Campaign, 1941–42* (New York, 2019), p. 242; Ortwin Buchbender and Reinhold Sterz, eds., *Das andere Gesicht des Krieges: Deutsche Feldpostbriefe 1939–1945* (Munich, 1982), p. 13; Brandon Schechter, *The Stuff of Soldiers: A History of the Red Army in World War II Through Objects* (Ithaca, NY, 2019), p. 196; J. B. Litoff and D. C. Smith, "'Will He Get My Letter': Popular Portrayals of Mail and Morale During World War II," *Journal of Popular Culture* 23 (1990): pp. 21–43; Robert L. Sherrod, *Tarawa* (Fredricksburg, 1973 [1944]), pp. 38–39.

7. Letter dated Nov. 3, 1942 in Sabine Rosemarie Arnold, "'Ich bin bisher noch lebendig und gesund': Briefe von den Fronten des sowjetischen 'Grossen Vaterländischen Krieges," in *Andere Helme—andere Menschen? Heimaterfahrung und Frontalltag im Zweiten Weltkrieg: Ein internationaler Vergleich*, edited by Detlef Vogel and Wolfram Wette (Essen, 1995), p. 144.

8. John Ellis, *The Sharp End: The Fighting Man in World War II* (New York, 1980), p. 110; Guy Sajer, *The Forgotten Soldier* (New York, 1971), pp. 84–85, 176.

9. Sadaki Tobishima, "The Pen and the Rifle," *Japan Times*, June 30, 1942; Stephen G. Fritz, *Frontsoldaten: The German Soldier in World War II* (Lexington, KY, 1995), p. 86.

10. Ortwin Buchbender and Reinhold Sterz, eds., *Das andere Gesicht des Krieges: Deutsche Feldpostbriefe 1939–1945* (Munich, 1982), p. 28.

11. Aaron William Moore, *Writing War: Soldiers Record the Japanese Empire* (Cambridge, MA, 2013), p. 14.

12. Klaus Latzel, *Deutsche Soldaten—nationalsozialistischer Krieg? Kriegserlebnis—Kriegserfahrung 1939–1945* (Paderborn, 1998), pp. 39–81.

13. Latzel, *Deutsche Soldaten*, pp. 90, 96–99.

14. Letter dated Nov. 12, 1941, Karl Fuchs, *Your Loyal and Loving Son: The Letters of Tank Gunner Karl Fuchs* (Washington, DC, 2003), 157; Fallnbigl in Omer Bartov, *Hitler's Army: Soldiers, Nazis, and War in the Third Reich* (New York, 1991), pp. 155–156.

15. Letter to Annemarie, Jan. 29, 1943, in Heinrich Böll, *Briefe aus dem Krieg 1939–1945*, edited by Jochen Schubert (Cologne, 2001), p. 1:599.

16. Entry for Oct. 3, 1941, diary of Wilhelm Prüller, quoted in Fritz, *Frontsoldaten*, p. 200; "Text of Reichsfuehrer's Hitler's Address Reporting Progress of

the Invasion of Russia," *New York Times*, Oct. 4, 1941; Latzel, *Deutsche Soldaten*, p. 297.

17. Albert Neuhaus to Agnes Neuhaus, Sept. 25 and Nov. 30, 1941, and Mar. 1, 1942, in Karl Reddemann, ed., *Zwischen Front und Heimat: Der Briefwechsel des Münsterischen Ehepaares Agnes und Albert Neuhaus 1940–1944* (Munster, 1996), pp. 323, 362–363, 433.

18. Albert Neuhaus to Agnes Neuhaus, Sept. 25 and Nov. 30, 1941, and Mar. 1, 1942, in Reddemann, *Zwischen Front und Heimat*, pp. 323, 362–363, 433; William L. Shirer, *"This Is Berlin": Radio Broadcasts from Nazi Germany, 1938–40* (New York, 1999), p. 328.

19. Letters to Erika dated July 28 and Dec. 8, 1941, in Jens Ebert, ed., *Im Funkwagen der Wehrmacht durch Europa: Balkan, Ukraine, Stalingrad. Feldpostbriefe des Gefreiten Wilhelm Moldenhauer 1940–1943* (Berlin, 2008), pp. 140, 179; Latzel, *Deutsche Soldaten*, p. 68; "Soldaten photographieren Soldaten," *Photoblätter* 18 (1941), quoted in Petra Bopp, *Fremde im Visier: Fotoalben aus dem Zweiten Weltkrieg* (Bielefeld, 2009), p. 38.

20. "Soldaten photographieren Soldaten," quoted in Bopp, *Fremde im Visier*, p. 38; Edward B. Westermann, *Drunk on Genocide: Alcohol and Mass Murder in Nazi Germany* (Ithaca, NY, 2021), p. 191.

21. Albert Neuhaus to Agnes Neuhaus, Mar. 19 and May 23, 1943, in Reddemann, *Zwischen Front und Heimat*, pp. 797, 851.

22. Felix Römer, *Kameraden: Die Wehrmacht von Innen* (Munich, 2012), p. 274.

23. H. M., letter dated Sept. 2, 1941, in Ortwin Buchbender and Reinhold Sterz, eds., *Das andere Gesicht des Krieges: Deutsche Feldpostbriefe 1939–1945* (Munich, 1982), pp. 79–80; J. H., letter dated Oct. 25, 1941, in Buchbender and Sterz, *Das andere Gesicht des Krieges*, p. 85; on endless war, entry for Nov. 29, 1942, in Walter Heller diary in *True to Type: A Selection from Letters and Diaries of German Soldiers and Civilians Collected on the Soviet-German Front* (London, n.d. [1943]), p. 67.

24. Sajer, *The Forgotten Soldier*, pp. 21, 36–37; Willy Peter Reese, *A Stranger to Myself: The Inhumanity of War, Russia, 1941–1944*, translated by Michael Hofmann (New York, 2005), p. 51.

25. Entry for Dec. 24, 1942, "Tagebuch Oberleutnant Bircher, 24.11.42–5.3.43," NL Eugen Bircher, 11.3.6.1, Archiv für Zeitgeschichte, Zurich.

26. Gottlob Herbert Bidermann, *In Deadly Combat: A German Soldier's Memoir of the Eastern Front*, edited by Derek S. Zumbro (Lawrence, KS, 2000), p. 52.

27. Letter to Ili dated Dec. 7, 1941, in Hellmuth Stieff, *Briefe*, edited by Horst Mühleisen (Berlin, 1991), p. 140.

28. Reese, *Stranger to Myself,* translated by Hofmann, pp. 52–53 56, 148, 159.

29. Gerald Linderman, *The World Within War: America's Combat Experience in World War II* (New York, 1997), p. 161; Richard B. Frank, *Guadalcanal: The Definitive Account of the Landmark Battle* (New York, 1990), p. 157; Ulrich Straus, *The Anguish of Surrender: Japanese POWs of World War II* (Seattle, 2003), pp. 21, 39–40; "Japanese Morale at Its Height in War with Idea of Sure Death," *Japan Times,* Jan. 13, 1942.

30. David C. Earhart, *Certain Victory: Images of World War II in the Japanese Media* (Armonk, NY, 2008), p. 393.

31. Shimizu Akira, "War and Cinema in Japan," in *The Japan-America Film Wars: WWII Propaganda and Cultural Contexts,* edited by Abe Mark Nornes and Yukio Fukushima (Chur, 1994), p. 19; Sarah Jane McClimon, "Music, Politics, and Memory: Japanese Military Songs in War and Peace" (PhD diss., University of Hawaii, 2011), pp. 19, 49–53.

32. Henry P. Frei, "The Island Battle: Japanese Soldiers Remember the Conquest of Singapore," in *Sixty Years On: The Fall of Singapore Revisited,* edited by Brian Farrell and Sandy Hunter (Singapore, 2003), p. 222.

33. McClimon, "Music, Politics, and Memory," pp. 81–83.

34. Eriko Ogihara-Schuck, "Subversive Tears? Tsujihara Minoru's Military Song 'Carrying My Comrade's Ashes' and the Submerged Memories of the Japanese Occupation of Singapore," *SOJOURN: Journal of Social Issues in Southeast Asia* 36, no. 3 (2021): pp. 417–447, here 420–423; Takao Fusayama, *Memoir of Takao Fusayama: A Japanese Soldier in Malaya & Sumatra* (Kuala Lumpur, 1997), pp. 106–107.

35. Aaron William Moore, *Writing War: Soldiers Record the Japanese Empire* (Cambridge, MA, 2013), p. 146.

36. Toyoji Hashiba, *Alas, Guadalcanal: A Record of Pacific War* (undated ms. [198?]), pp. 2–4.

CHAPTER 11: At Sea

1. Mark Parillo, "The Japanese Merchant Marine in World War II" (PhD diss., Ohio State University, 1987), p. 167.

2. Lothar-Günther Buchheim, *U-Boat War* (New York, 1978), n.p.

3. "News from Hollywood," *New York Times,* Dec. 29, 1942; Fred Stanley, "Hollywood Memoranda," *New York Times,* June 20, 1943; Philip K. Scheuer, "Director Pleads Off Poundage," *Los Angeles Times,* May 30, 1943. On the "tenth passenger," "Lifeboat Hitchcock Smash: Great Dramatic Triumph," *Variety,* Jan. 12, 1944.

4. "Rescue of Airman Delights Millions," *New York Times,* Nov. 15, 1942.

5. Winston Churchill, *Their Finest Hour* (New York, 1949), p. 529; Marc

Milner, "The Atlantic War, 1939–1945: The Case for a New Paradigm," in *Decision in the Atlantic: The Allies and the Longest Campaign of the Second World War*, edited by Marcus Faulkner (Lexington, KY, 2019), p. 34.

6. Milner, "Atlantic War," in *Decision in the Atlantic*, edited by Faulkner, p. 15.

7. "Hundred-mile mesh" and "On the march" in Buchheim, *U-Boat War*, n.p.

8. Felix Römer, *Kameraden: Die Wehrmacht von Innen* (Munich, 2012), pp. 252, 255.

9. Lothar-Günther Buchheim, *The Boat* (New York, 1975), pp. 136, 242; Timothy Mulligan, *Neither Sharks nor Wolves: The Men of Nazi Germany's U-Boat Arm, 1939–1945* (Annapolis, MD, 1999), p. 71.

10. Herbert Werner, *Iron Coffins: A Personal Account of the German U-Boat Battles of World War II* (New York 1969), pp. 52, 99, 140–141; Wolfgang Hirschfeld, *Feindfahrten: Das Logbuch eines U-Boot-Funkers* (Vienna, 1982), p. 51.

11. Werner, *Iron Coffins*, p. 54; Buchheim, *The Boat*, pp. 289–290, 370. Buchheim's postwar novel is based on his wartime experience; memoirs and Buchheim's historical account, *U-Boat War*, authenticate many of the novel's details.

12. Buchheim, *The Boat*, pp. 20–21, 59.

13. Nachman Ben-Yeduha, *Atrocity, Deviance, and Submarine Warfare: Norms and Practices During the World Wars* (Ann Arbor, MI, 2016), p. 209.

14. "The Last of the Convoy Sunk. Seas Littered with Survivors and Debris," *Manchester Guardian*, Mar. 6, 1943; M. Pratt, "Indescribable Carnage in Huon Gulf," *Sydney Morning Herald*, Mar. 5, 1943.

15. Buchheim, *The Boat*, p. 211.

16. Phil Richards and John J. Banigan, *How to Abandon Ship* (New York, 1942), p. 101; "The Torpedo Hop," *Pilot*, Nov. 6, 1942.

17. "Victims of U-Boat Trailed as Lure," *New York Times*, Apr. 4, 1942.

18. Archie Gubbs, "Four Days on a German Sub," *Life*, Aug. 24, 1942.

19. "Submarine Denies Water to Victims," *New York Times*, May 29, 1942; "U-Boat Commander Lectures Victims," *New York Times*, July 19, 1942; "13 Days Adrift: 'V' Sign to U-Boat," *Manchester Guardian*, Aug. 18, 1942.

20. "The Struma Disaster," *New York Times*, Mar. 13, 1942; "24 Days of Hunger and Madness: 'I Swore I Wouldn't Die,'" *Pilot*, Nov. 27, 1942; "MFOW Men Fight thru After 18 Days Adrift," *Pilot*, Jan. 15, 1943.

21. "Lifeboat," *Variety*, Jan. 12, 1944.

22. Bosley Crowther, "The Screen in Review," *New York Times*, Jan. 13, 1944; Crowther, "Adrift in 'Lifeboat': The New Hitchcock-Steinbeck Drama Represents Democracy at Sea," *New York Times*, Jan. 23, 1944; David Lardner, "The Current Cinema," *New Yorker*, Feb. 5, 1944, p. 65.

23. Alfred Hitchcock and Harry Sylvester, "Lifeboat," *Collier's*, Nov. 13, 1943, pp. 16–17, 52–58.

24. Hitchcock and Sylvester, "Lifeboat," pp. 16–17, 52–58; O'Dowd Gallagher, *Retreat in the East* (London, 1942), pp. 52–53.

25. Ralph Barker, *Goodnight, Sorry for Sinking You* (London, 1984), pp. 98–101; "Lucky Combination Saved Eleven Prusa Survivors," *Pilot*, May 15, 1942.

26. Noah Landau, "The Negro Seaman," *Negro Quarterly* 1 (1943): p. 341; Diane Kirby and Lee-Ann Monk, "Indian Seamen and Australian Unions Fighting for Labour Rights: 'The Real Facts of the Lascars' Case' of 1939," *Labour History* 113 (Nov. 2017): pp. 209–239; Donald Critchlow, "Communist Unions and Racism: A Comparative Study of the United Electrical, Radio, and Machine Workers and the National Maritime Union to the Black Question During World War II," *Labor History* 17 (1976): pp. 230–244; Arthur Carter, "Urges Full Participation of Negroes for Victory," *Pilot*, July 24, 1942; "No Room for Discrimination in a People's War!," *Pilot*, Dec. 11, 1942.

27. Hugh Mulzac, *A Star to Steer By: Captain of the Booker T. Washington* (New York, 1963), pp. 141, 147.

28. "Dinner to Mulzac, Crew Hails Advance in Unity," *Pilot*, Jan. 15, 1943.

29. "Boy, 17, Sole Survivor of Tanker Crew of 33, Watched Last 10 Die of Thirst in Lifeboat," *New York Times*, Mar. 25, 1942; "24 Days of Hunger and Madness."

CHAPTER 12: In the Air

1. Diary entry for Sept. 9, 1941, in Elena Skrjabina, *Siege and Survival: The Odyssey of a Leningrader* (Carbondale, IL, 1971), p. 26; Eric Taylor, *Operation Millennium: "Bomber" Harris's Raid on Cologne, May 1942* (London, 1987), p. xii.

2. Hans Erich Nossack, *The End: Hamburg, 1943* (Chicago, 2004), p. 23.

3. Aldous Huxley, "Notes on the Way," *Time and Tide*, May 7, 1932.

4. Mike Davis, *Dead Cities, and Other Tales* (New York, 2002), pp. 68, 81n3; Richard Overy, *The Bombers and the Bombed: Allied Air War over Europe, 1940–1945* (New York, 2013), pp. 136–137.

5. Nossack, *The End: Hamburg, 1943*, pp. 11–12; Overy, *Bombers and the Bombed*, p. 58.

6. Gerhart Weise, "Wo die Heimat zur Front Wird. Dr. Goebbels im Rheinland: 'Hier sind Kinder zu Helden geworden,'" *Das Reich*, Aug. 16, 1942.

7. "A Historic Raid" (editorial), *Bombay Chronicle*, June 2, 1942; Nossack, *The End: Hamburg, 1943*, p. 61.

8. "Wings over Germany" (editorial), *New York Times*, Feb. 10, 1945; "Doom over Germany" (editorial), *New York Times*, Feb. 16, 1945.

9. Max Hastings, "Censored for Days, This Picture Was Finally Published in the Mail," *Daily Mail*, Dec. 31, 2010; "War's Greatest Picture: St. Paul's Stands Unharmed in the Midst of the Burning City," *Daily Mail*, Dec. 31, 1940; *Berliner Illustrierte Zeitung*, Jan. 23, 1941; Tom Allbeson, "Visualizing Wartime Destruction and Postwar Reconstruction: Herbert Mason's Photograph of St. Paul's Reevaluated," *Journal of Modern History* 97 (Sept. 2015): p. 544.

10. Arthur Harris, *Bomber Offensive* (London, 1947), pp. 51–52.

11. Overy, *Bombers and the Bombed*, pp. 17–20, P. M. S. Blackett, "Thoughts on British Defense Policy," *New Statesman*, Dec. 5, 1959, p. 786.

12. Baldwin quoted in *House of Commons Debates*, vol. 270, cols. 631–632, Nov. 10, 1932.

13. Richard Overy, *Why the Allies Won* (New York, 1995), p. 105.

14. Overy, *Bombers and the Bombed*, p. 157; Mark Connelly, *Reaching for the Stars: A New History of Bomber Command in World War II* (London, 2001), p. 64; Robert E. Morseberger, "Adrift in Steinbeck's Lifeboat," *Literature/Film Quarterly* 4 (Oct. 1976): p. 334.

15. Max Hastings, *Bomber Command: Churchill's Epic Campaign* (New York, 1979), p. 126.

16. Connelly, *Reaching for the Stars*, p. 49; "Report by Mr. Butt to Bomber Command," Aug. 18, 1941, in *The Strategic Air Offensive Against Germany, 1939–1945*, by Charles Webster and Noble Frankland, vol. 4, *Annexes and Appendices* (London, 1961), pp. 205–213.

17. Noble Frankland quoted in Philip Kaplan and Jack Currie, *Round the Clock: The Experience of Allied Bomber Crews Who Flew by Day and by Night from England in the Second World War* (New York, 1993), p. 38.

18. Entries for June 12–13 and 19, 1944, in Campbell Muirhead, *The Diary of a Bomb Aimer* (Tunbridge Wells, 1987), pp. 38, 57.

19. Harris, *Bomber Offensive*, p. 109.

20. Norman Longmate, *The Bombers: The RAF Offensive Against Germany, 1939–1945* (London, 1983), pp. 218, 221; entry for July 18–19, 1944, in Muirhead, *Diary of a Bomb Aimer*, p. 97.

21. Eric Taylor, *Operation Millennium: "Bomber" Harris's Raid on Cologne, May 1942* (London, 1987), pp. 115–116; "Cologne Still Afire After 36 Hours," *Daily Telegraph*, June 2, 1942; "Burning Cologne Served as Beacon," *Palestine Post*, June 2, 1942.

22. "Chronik Volksschle Fühlingen" and "Chronist der Volksschule Lustheider Strasse" quoted in Martin Rüther, "Reaktionen und Folgen," in *Köln, 31. Mai 1942: Der 1000-Bomber Angriff*, edited by Martin Rüther (Cologne, 1992), pp. 58, 110.

23. "Cologne and Essen," *Times*, June 3, 1942; "BBC to Cologne: 'We Harden

Our Hearts,'" *Daily Mail*, June 1, 1942; Connelly, *Reaching for the Stars*, p. 101.

24. *Daily Mail*, June 1, 1942, quoted in Connelly, *Reaching for the Stars*, p. 74; A. C. Grayling, *Among the Dead Cities: The History and Moral Legacy of the WWII Bombings of Civilians in Germany and Japan* (New York, 2006), p. 169; John Keegan, "Flying Fortresses," in *Fields of Battle: The Wars for North America* (New York, 1996), p. 332.

25. Jörg Friedrich, *The Fire: The Bombing of Germany, 1940–1945* (New York, 2006), p. 98.

26. Mark Wells, *Courage and Air Warfare: The Allied Aircrew Experience in the Second World War* (London, 1995), p. 46; Harris, *Bomber Offensive*, p. 267; Don Charlwood, *No Moon Tonight* (Manchester, 2000 [1956]), p. 11.

27. On risk and strangers, Charlwood, *No Moon Tonight*, pp. 33, 115, 184; on prospects, Wells, *Courage and Air Warfare*, p. 102; on arithmetic, entry for July 18–19, 1944, in Muirhead, *Diary of a Bomb Aimer*, p. 97.

28. Flying Officer "X," *How Sleep the Brave, and Other Stories* (London, 1943), pp. 8–9; Miles Tripp, *The Eighth Passenger: A Flight of Recollection and Discovery* (London, 1969), pp. 145–146.

29. On running naked, Friedrich, *Fire*, p. 40; on Piccadilly, Wells, *Courage and Air Warfare*, p. 64; entry for Aug. 2, 1944, in Muirhead, *Diary of a Bomb Aimer*, p. 124.

30. Wells, *Courage and Air Warfare*, p. 99; Charlwood, *No Moon Tonight*, p. 131.

31. Entries for July 12–13, 18–19, and 25–26, 1944, in Muirhead, *Diary of a Bomb Aimer*, pp. 38, 96, 109.

32. Entry for Oct. 24, 1942, in Matthias Joseph Mehs, *Tagebücher*, vol. 2, *Januar 1936 bis September 1946*, edited by Günter Wein and Franziska Wein (Trier, 2011), p. 353.

33. Entry for Aug. 8, 1941, Paulheinz Wantzen, *Das Leben im Krieg. Ein Tagebuch* (Bad Homburg, 2000), p. 469; *Times*, July 22, 1942; Longmate, *Bombers*, p. 269.

34. Friedrich, *Fire*, p. 328; Muirhead, *Diary of a Bomb Aimer*, p. 158.

35. Entries for June 5, 6, and 11, 1942, in Wantzen, *Das Leben im Krieg*, pp. 851–852, 859.

36. Friedrich, *Fire*, p. 431; entry for Sept. 7, 1942, in Wantzen, *Das Leben im Krieg*, p. 944; Dietmar Süss, *Death from the Skies: How the British and Germans Survived Bombing in World War II* (New York, 2014), p. 376.

37. "Cologne Paper Calls City 'Lost,'" *New York Times*, June 6, 1942; Franz Berger, "Standhaft," *Kölnische Zeitung*, June 2, 1942.

38. Berger, "Standhaft"; *True to Type: A Selection from Letters and Diaries of*

German Soldiers and Civilians Collected on the Soviet-German Front (London, n.d. [1943]), p. 130.

39. Entry for Aug. 24, 1943, in Matthias Menzel, *Die Stadt ohne Tod: Berliner Tagebuch, 1943/45* (Berlin, 1946), p. 16.

40. Berger, "Standhaft"; Franz Berger, "In Köln," *Kölnische Zeitung*, June 5, 1942.

41. Anna Schmitz to Rudolf, June 6, 1942, in Martin Rüther, *Köln im Zweiten Weltkrieg: Alltag und Erfahrungen zwischen 1939 und 1945* (Cologne, 2005), p. 581; Rüther, "Reaktionen und Folgen," in *Köln, 31. Mai 1942*, edited by Rüther, p. 83.

42. Entries for Nov. 18, 1942, Nov. 24, 1943, and Jan. 25, 1944, in *Die Tagebücher von Joseph Goebbels. Sämtliche Fragmente*, edited by Elke Fröhlich (Munich, 1994), pt. 2, vol. 6, p. 307; vol. 10, p. 346; vol. 11, p. 166.

43. Hans Schwarz van Berk, "Unter den neuen Dächern. Von einer Reise zu den bombardierten Städten," *Das Reich*, Oct. 11, 1942.

44. Karola Fings, "Sklaven für die 'Heimatfront.' Kriegsgesellschaft und Konzentrationslager," in *Die Deutsche Kriegsgesellschaft 1939 bis 1945*, edited by Jörg Echternkamp, 2 vols. (Munich, 2004), pp. 1:220, 248, 260.

45. Entries for June 15 and July 7, 1942, in Markus Schmitz and Bernd Haunfelder, *Humanität und Diplomatie: Die Schweiz in Köln, 1940–1949* (Munster, 2001), pp. 178–181.

46. Entry for June 24, 1942, in Schmitz and Haunfelder, *Humanität und Diplomatie*, pp. 179.

47. Süss, *Death from the Skies*, pp. 185, 188; Rüther, "Reaktionen und Folgen," in *Köln, 31. Mai 1942*, edited by Rüther, pp. 195, 197.

48. Entry for Nov. 18, 1942, in Wantzen, *Das Leben im Krieg*, p. 1019.

49. Overy, *Bombers and the Bombed*, p. xvi; Connelly, *Reaching for the Stars*, p. 144.

50. Hans Schwarz van Berk, "Unsere aufgewühlte Welt. Die Wanderzüge der Völker," *Das Reich*, Aug. 30, 1942.

CHAPTER 13: Transit

1. Anthony Waine, "Anna Seghers's *Transit*: A Late Modern Thriller—Without Thrills," *Neophilologus* 89 (2005): p. 412; Anna Seghers, *Transit* (New York, 2013 [1944]), p. 78.

2. William du Bois, "A Refugee with a Visa to Nowhere," *New York Times*, May 14, 1944.

3. Rebecca Manley, *To the Tashkent Station: Evacuation and Survival in the Soviet Union at War* (Ithaca, NY, 2009), pp. 1–2.

4. Mark Edele, "The Second World War as a History of Displacement: The Soviet Case," *History Australia* 12 (2015): pp. 17–18; Huey Louis Kostanick,

"Soviet Territorial Annexations in Eastern Europe," *Yearbook of the Association of Pacific Coast Geographers* 13 (1951): pp. 14–18.

5. Andrew Pettegree, *The Book at War: How Reading Shaped Conflict and Conflict Shaped Reading* (New York, 2023), p. 174.

6. "The Camera Overseas: 136,000,000 People See This Picture of Shanghai's South Station," *Life*, Oct. 4, 1937.

7. Jack Belden, *Still Time to Die* (Philadelphia, 1943), pp. 179–180.

8. Di Wu, "The Cult of Geography: Chinese Riverine Defense During the Battle of Wuhan, 1937–1938," *War in History* 29 (2022): p. 199.

9. Belden, *Still Time to Die*, p. 180; Wu, "Cult of Geography," pp. 195–196; Lloyd Eastman, *Seeds of Destruction: Nationalist China in War and Revolution* (Stanford, CA, 1984), p. 134.

10. "Chinese Resigned to Flood Sacrifice to Check Invaders," *New York Times*, June 17, 1938; O. J. Todd, "The Yellow River Is 'Japan's Sorrow' Now," June 19, 1938; "Explorer Praises Chinese for River Trap," *New York Times*, July 11, 1938; Kathryn Jean Edgerton-Tarpley, "From 'Nourish the People' to 'Sacrifice for the Nation': Changing Responses to Disaster in Late Imperial and Modern China," *Journal of Asian Studies* 73 (May 2014): p. 462.

11. Diana Lary, *The Chinese People at War: Human Suffering and Social Transformation, 1937–1945* (Cambridge, UK, 2010), pp. 21–22; Ashihei Hino, *Wheat and Soldiers* (New York, 1939), p. 78; Richard B. Frank, *Tower of Skulls: A History of the Asia-Pacific War, 1937–1942* (New York, 2020), p. 88.

12. Micah S. Muscolino, *The Ecology of War in China: Henan Province, the Yellow River, and Beyond, 1938–1950* (Cambridge, UK, 2014), p. 2; Muscolino, "Violence Against People and the Land: The Environment and Refugee Migration from China's Henan Province, 1938–1945," *Environment and History* 17 (2011): pp. 298–299; Lary, *Chinese People at War*, p. 62.

13. Sun Yuanliang quoted in Hans van de Ven, *China at War: Triumph and Tragedy in the Emergence of the New China* (Cambridge, MA, 2018), p. 108.

14. "Explorer Praises Chinese for River Trap."

15. Graham Peck, *Two Kinds of Time* (Seattle, 2008 [Boston, 1950]), p. 311; Muscolino, *Ecology of War in China*; Eastman, *Seeds of Destruction*, p. 78.

16. E. P. Ashcraft to Arnold Vaught, Jan. 28, 1943, quoted in Erleen J. Christensen, *In War and Famine: Missionaries in China's Honan Province in the 1940s* (Montreal, 2005), p. 112; Muscolino, *Ecology of War in China*, pp. 102, 119, 143.

17. Eastman, *Seeds of Destruction*, pp. 148–152, 219; Theodore White and Annalee Jacoby, *Thunder Out of China* (New York, 1946), pp. 132–133.

18. Rana Mitter, *Forgotten Ally: China's World War II, 1937–1945* (Boston, 2013), p. 268; Muscolino, *Ecology of War in China*, p. 156.

19. White and Jacoby, *Thunder Out of China*, pp. 167–168; Muscolino, *Ecology of War in China*, p. 157.

20. White and Jacoby, *Thunder Out of China*, p. 169; Theodore H. White, *In Search of History: A Personal Adventure* (New York, 1978), p. 147.

21. Muscolino, *Ecology of War in China*, p. 163.

22. Theodore White, "Until the Harvest Is Reaped," *Time*, Mar. 22, 1943; Kathryn Edgerton-Tarpley, "Saving the Nation, Starving the People? The Henan Famine of 1942–1943," in *1943: China at the Crossroads*, edited by Joseph W. Escherick and Matthew T. Combs (Ithaca, NY, 2015), p. 337.

23. Edgerton-Tarpley, "Saving the Nation, Starving the People?," in *1943: China at the Crossroads*, edited by Escherick and Combs (Ithaca, NY, 2015), pp. 345–346, 361.

24. Micah S. Muscolino, "Refugees, Land Reclamation, and Militarized Landscapes in Wartime China," *Journal of Asian Studies* 69, no. 2 (2010): p. 466; Micah S. Muscolino, "Violence Against People and the Land: The Environment and Refugee Migration from China's Henan Province, 1938–1945," *Environment and History* 17 (2011): pp. 302–303; Mitter, *Forgotten Ally*, p. 363.

25. Muscolino, *Ecology of War in China*, p. 151; Belden, *Still Time to Die*, p. 180; Lary, *Chinese People at War*, pp. 51, 55, 57, 85–86, 93; R. Keith Schoppa, *In a Sea of Bitterness: Refugees During the Sino-Japanese War* (Cambridge, MA, 2011), p. 10.

26. Ba Jin, *Bitter Cold Nights*, in *Selected Works of Ba Jin* (Beijing, 1988), pp. 290, 377, 447.

CHAPTER 14: So Many Hungers

1. Amartya Sen, *Poverty and Famines: An Essay on Entitlement and Deprivation* (Oxford, 1981), p. 1.

2. Ian Stephens, *Monsoon Morning* (London, 1966), pp. 52–53.

3. Tarasankara Bandyopadhyaya, *Epoch's End* (Calcutta, n.d. [1945]), 13–14, 132–133.

4. Diya Gupta, *India in the Second World War: An Emotional History* (Oxford, 2023), p. 114; Bhabani Bhattacharya, *So Many Hungers!* (Bombay, 1947), p. 72; K. Santhanam, *The Cry of Distress: A First-Hand Description and an Objective Study of the Indian Famine of 1943* (New Delhi, 1944), p. 52.

5. Bandyopadhyaya, *Epoch's End*, p. 56.

6. Krishan Chandar, *I Cannot Die: A Story of Bengal* (Poona, [1943]), p. 41.

7. Chandar, *I Cannot Die*, p. 41.

8. Tarakchandra Das, *Bengal Famine (1943): As Revealed in a Survey of the Destitutes in Calcutta* (Calcutta, 1949), pp. 82–86.

9. Entries for "September 1942," "December 28, 1942–January 4, 1943,"

and Apr. 8, 1943, in Clive Branson, *British Soldier in India* (London, 1945), pp. 27, 44, 61.

10. "India's Food Supplies," editorial in *Statesman* (Calcutta), Nov. 21, 1943; "India's Food," editorial in *Statesman*, Dec. 13, 1942; Bhattacharya, *So Many Hungers!*, pp. 145–146.

11. Quoted in Madhusree Mukerjee, *Churchill's Secret War: The British Empire and the Ravaging of India During World War II* (New York, 2010), p. 170.

12. Bandyopadhyaya, *Epoch's End*, p. 277; Das, *Bengal Famine (1943)*, p. 3.

13. Amit Kumar Gupta, *Crises and Creativities: Middle-Class Bhadralok in Bengal c. 1939–52* (New Delhi, 2009), p. 143.

14. "Bengal's Foodless," *Statesman*, Aug. 22, 1943; "Bengal's Plight" and "An-All-India Disgrace," *Statesman*, Aug. 29, 1943; Bhattacharya, *So Many Hungers!*, pp. 227–228.

15. Chandar, *I Cannot Die*, pp. 15–16, 45; Bhattacharya, *So Many Hungers!*, p. 21.

16. Stephens, *Monsoon Morning*, p. 170; Chandar, *I Cannot Die*, p. 21; Rajender Kaur, "Interrogating the Limits of Bourgeois Radical Dissent: Nationalist Discourse in the Literature of the Bengal Famine of 1943" (PhD diss., Rutgers University, 2002), pp. 90, 92.

17. Stephens, *Monsoon Morning*, p. 184.

18. Mukerjee, *Churchill's Secret War*, p. ix.

19. "Die Stadt des langsames Todes," *Kölnische Zeitung*, Oct. 6, 1943; "Kolonialpolitik des Hungers," *Kölnische Zeitung*, Oct. 31, 1943.

20. William Fisher, "The Bengal Famine," *Life*, Nov. 22, 1943.

21. Bhattacharya, *So Many Hungers!*, p. 195.

22. Bhattacharya, *So Many Hungers!*, pp. 8, 22–24, 282.

23. Das, *Bengal Famine (1943)*, p. 9.

24. Alan Moorehead, "When Cripps Went to India," *Harper's Magazine*, May 1943, p. 615.

CHAPTER 15: Warsaw's Four Sons

1. "More Berlin Jews Shipped to Poland," *New York Times*, Oct. 30, 1941.

2. Richard B. Frank, *Tower of Skulls: A History of the Asia-Pacific War, 1937–1942* (New York, 2020), p. 92.

3. Arkadiusz Morawiec, *Polish Literature and Genocide* (New York, 2022), p. 86.

4. "Confidential Report on the Evacuation of Jews to Riga on 11–17 December 1941 by Police Captain Salitter, 26 December 1943," in *German Railroads, Jewish Souls: The Reichsbahn, Bureaucracy, and the Final Solution*, by Christopher Browning et al. (New York, 2020), pp. 80–86.

5. Karl Schlögel, *Im Raume Lesen wir die Zeit* (Munich, 2003), p. 54.

6. Varian Fry, "The Massacre of the Jews," *New Republic*, Dec. 21, 1942, p. 816.

7. Stenographic record, 7. Sitzung, Dec. 11, 1941, *Verhandlungen des Deutschen Reichtags, 4. Wahlperiode 1939, Band 460* (Berlin, 1942), pp. 93, 100, 104–106.

8. Entry for Mar. 27, 1942, *Die Tagebücher von Joseph Goebbels. Sämtliche Fragmente*, edited by Elke Fröhlich (Munich, 1994), pt. 2, vol. 3, p. 561.

9. Hans-Heinrich Wilhelm, "Hitlers Ansprache vor Generalen und Offizieren am 26. Mai 1944," *Militärgeschichtliche Mitteilungen* 20 (1976): pp. 155–156.

10. Lewi Stone, "Quantifying the Holocaust: Hyperintense Kill Rates During the Nazi Genocide," *Science Advances* 5, no. 1 (2019).

11. Sholem Asch, "In the Valley of Death," *New York Times Magazine*, Feb. 2, 1943.

12. "Text of Willkie's Address to the Nation Renewing His Plea for a Second Front," *New York Times*, Oct. 27, 1942; Calek Perechodnik quoted in Martin Winstone, *The Dark Heart of Hitler's Europe: Nazi Rule in Poland Under the General Government* (London, 2015), p. 160.

13. Kurt Pätzold and Erika Schwarz, *Auschwitz war für mich nur ein Bahnhof: Franz Novak, der Transportführer Adolf Eichmanns* (Berlin, 1994), pp. 104–105, 109; "Report of Police Lieutenant Westermann on Two Transports of Jews from Kolomea to Bełzec, 7–10 September 1942," Sept. 14, 1942, in *German Railroads, Jewish Souls*, by Browning et al., pp. 92–93.

14. David Carroll, *French Literary Fascism: Nationalism, Anti-Semitism, and the Ideology of Culture* (Princeton, NJ, 1995), p. 276n9.

15. Entries for Mar. 25 and 26, 1942, in Zygmunt Klukowski, *Diary of the Years of Occupation, 1939–44* (Urbana, IL, 1993), pp. 188–189.

16. Entries for Apr. 8 and Aug. 8, 1942, in Klukowski, *Diary of the Years of Occupation*, pp. 191, 209–210.

17. Entries for Oct. 21, 23, 26, and 27, 1942, in Klukowski, *Diary of the Years of Occupation*, pp. 219–222. On highways, Emanuel Ringelblum, "Oyneg Shabes," Jan. 1943, in *Voices from the Warsaw Ghetto: Writing Our History*, edited by David G. Roskies (New Haven, CT, 2019), p. 50.

18. Calel Perechodnik, *Am I a Murderer? Testament of a Jewish Ghetto Policeman* (Boulder, CO, 1996), pp. 72, 90.

19. Perechodnik, *Am I a Murderer?*, pp. 40–50; Albert Camus, *The Plague* (New York, 1972 [1948]), p. 229.

20. Hans Rothfels, "Kurt Gerstein's Eyewitness Report on Mass Gassings," *German Yearbook of Contemporary History* 1 (2016): pp. 78–79. For the English translation used at Nuremberg, see blob:https://nuremberg.law.harvard.edu/34656109-3fba-4430-b096-b872d92ed797.

21. Samuel D. Kassow, *Who Will Write Our History? Emanuel Ringelblum, the Warsaw Ghetto, and the Oyneg Shabes Archive* (Bloomington, IN, 2007), p. 319.

22. Peter Longerich, *"Davon haben wir nichts gewusst!": Die Deutschen und die Judenverfolgung 1933–1945* (Berlin, 2006), p. 7.

23. Peter Fritzsche, "Babi Yar, but Not Auschwitz: What Did Germans Know About the 'Final Solution'?," in *The Germans and the Holocaust: Popular Responses to the Persecution and Murder of the Jews*, edited by Susanna Schrafstetter and Alan E. Steinweis (New York, 2015), pp. 85–104.

24. Joseph Goebbels, "Gespräche mit Frontsoldaten," *Das Reich*, July 26, 1942.

25. Karl Dürkefälden, *"Schreiben wie es wirklich war . . .": Aufzeichungen Karl Dürkefäldens aus den Jahren 1933–1945*, edited by Herbert Obenaus and Sibylle Obenaus (Hannover, 1985), p. 110.

26. Entry for June 16, 1943, in Wilm Hosenfeld, *"Ich versuche jeden zu retten": Das Leben eines deutschen Offiziers in Briefen und Tagebüchern* (Munich, 2004), p. 719.

27. Raphael Lemkin, *Totally Unofficial: The Autobiography of Raphael Lemkin* (New Haven, CT, 2013), pp. 52, 55.

28. Norbert Elias's father on insisting to return to Breslau in Bernard Wasserstein, *On the Eve: The Jews of Europe Before the Second World War* (New York, 2012), p. 377.

29. Entries for Mar. 22, May 31, and June 3, 1942, in Chaim Kaplan, *Scroll of Agony: The Warsaw Diary of Chaim A. Kaplan*, edited by Abraham I. Katsh (Bloomington, IN, 1999), pp. 304, 345–346.

30. Entries for Sept. 14, 1939, and July 26, 1942, in Kaplan, *Scroll of Agony*, pp. 130, 383.

31. Jan Karski, *Story of a Secret State* (Boston, 1944), pp. 320–321.

32. "Idleness," Notebook A, in Oskar Rosenfeld, *In the Beginning Was the Ghetto: Notebooks from Lodz*, edited by Hanno Loewy (Evanston, IL, 2002), pp. 18–19.

33. Kassow, *Who Will Write Our History?*, p. 210.

34. Patrick Montague, *Chelmno and the Holocaust: The History of Hitler's First Death Camp* (Durham, NC, 2012), pp. 104–111; entry for July 11, 1942, in *Etty: The Letters and Diaries of Etty Hillesum, 1941–1943*, edited by Klaas A. D. Smelik, translated by Arnold J. Pomerans (Grand Rapids, MI, 2002), p. 485; entry for July 15, 1944, in Anne Frank, *The Diary of a Young Girl: The Definitive Edition* (New York, 1995), p. 332.

35. Quoted in Jacek Leociak, *Text in the Face of Destruction: Accounts from the Warsaw Ghetto Reconsidered* (Warsaw, 2004), p. 101.

36. Jarecka quoted in Kassow, *Who Will Write Our History?*, p. 6; Emanuel

Ringelblum, "Oyneg Shabbes," in *The Literature of Destruction*, edited by David G. Roskies, p. 386; entry for June 11, 1942, in Lucjan Dobroszycki, ed., *The Chronicle of the Lodz Ghetto, 1941–1944* (New Haven, CT, 1984), p. 204.

37. Leociak, *Text in the Face of Destruction*, pp. 101, 266.

38. Entry for July 31, 1942, in Kaplan, *Scroll of Agony*, p. 335.

39. Auerbach quoted in Philip Friedman, *Martyrs and Fighters: The Epic of the Warsaw Ghetto* (London, 1954), p. 136; Szlengel in Kassow, *Who Will Write Our History?*, pp. 316–317.

40. Saul Friedländer, *The Years of Extermination: Nazi Germany and the Jews, 1939–1945* (New York, 2007), p. xxvi; Leociak, *Text in the Face of Destruction*, pp. 103–104.

41. "Terror Against Jews," *Times*, Dec. 7, 1942; Laurel Leff, *Buried by the Times: The Holocaust and America's Most Important Newspaper* (New York, 2005), p. 4. On Sweden, see Hadley Cantril, ed., *Public Opinion, 1935–1946* (Princeton, NJ, 1951), p. 153.

42. "How Hitler's Mass Murders Are Germanizing Europe," *PM*, Oct. 7, 1942; "The Verified Record of Hitler's Massacre of the Jews as Told to FDR," *PM*, Dec. 9, 1942.

43. The stories appeared in the *New York Times* in order on Feb. 13, Sept. 19, Apr. 24, and Aug. 7, 1942.

44. "They Die for France," *Life*, May, 25, 1942.

45. Editorial, "This Was Lidice," *New York Times*, June 14, 1942; "Walls Will Enclose Warsaw Jews Today; 500,000 Begin 'New Life' in Nazi-Built Ghetto," *New York Times*, Nov. 26, 1940.

46. Chad Bryant, *Prague in Black: Nazi Rule and Czech Nationalism* (Cambridge, MA, 2007), p. 172; Joseph Wechsberg, "The Children of Lidice," *New Yorker*, May 1, 1948, pp. 34–51.

47. On the debates, see Michael Burleigh, *Moral Combat: A History of World War II* (London, 2010), pp. 277–296, 305.

48. "Hitler Wipes Out Czech Village; Kills All Men in Hangman Revenge," *Los Angeles Times*, June 11, 1942; "Horror for Horror?," *Time*, June 22, 1942; Knox in Nicholas G. Balint, *Lidice Lives Forever* (New York, 1942), p. 65.

49. "Hitler Wipes Out Czech Village"; editorial, "Lidice, in Illinois," *New York Times*, July 14, 1942; Gerald Kersh, *The Dead Look On* (New York, 1943), p. 17.

50. Editorial, "Lidice the Immortal," *New York Times*, June 12, 1942; "1,000,000 Jews Slain by Nazis, Report Says," and editorial, "Lidice, Illinois," *New York Times*, June 30, 1942.

51. "Extinction Feared by Jews in Poland," *New York Times*, Mar. 1, 1942; editorial, "The First to Suffer," *New York Times*, Dec. 2, 1942.

52. William Cantuar, "Nazi War on Jews," *Times*, Dec. 5, 1942.

53. Jan Karski, *Story of a Secret State: My Report to the World* (Washington, DC, 2013 [1944]), p. 311; Richard Brody, "The Unicorn and the 'Karski Report,'" *New Yorker*, Dec. 15, 2010.

54. Edward Said, *Reflections on Exile, and Other Essays* (Cambridge, MA, 2000), p. 174; Dwight Garner, "Again and Again, Literature Provides an Outlet for the Upended Lives of Refugees," *New York Times*, Mar. 7, 2022.

CHAPTER 16: Richmond, California

1. Ulrich Herbert, *Hitler's Foreign Workers: Enforced Foreign Labor in Germany Under the Third Reich* (Cambridge, UK, 1997), pp. 201, 214.

2. Entry for Jan. 1–3, 1943, in Lisa de Boor, *Tagbuchblätter: Aus den Jahren, 1938–1945* (Munich, 1963), p. 127.

3. Ba Maw, *Breakthrough in Burma* (New Haven, CT, 1968), p. 305.

4. David Killingray, "Labor Mobilization in British Colonial Africa for the War Effort, 1939–46," in *Africa and the Second World War*, edited by David Killingray and Richard Rathbone (Basingstoke, 1985), pp. 76, 86.

5. Cyprian Ekwensi, *Lokotown, and Other Stories* (London, 1966), p. 2.

6. John McNulty, "Bartender Here Takes Dislike to 'Deep in the Heart of Texas,'" *New Yorker*, May 2, 1942, p. 15.

7. Bill C. Malone and Tracey E. W. Laird, *Country Music USA* (Austin, TX, 2018 [1968]), p. 219.

8. Marilynn S. Johnson, *The Second Gold Rush: Oakland and the East Bay in World War II* (Berkeley, CA, 1993), p. 2; Roger W. Lotchin, ed., *The Way We Really Were: The Golden State in the Second World War* (Urbana, IL, 2000), p. 92; James A. McVittie, *An Avalanche Hits Richmond: A Report* (Richmond, CA, 1944); Gerald Nash, *The American West Transformed: The Impact of the Second World War* (Bloomington, IN, 1985), p. 25.

9. "Townsendites Enjoy Barn Dance Here," *Richmond Independent*, Mar. 21, 1942; "20–30 Club Barn Dance This Evening," *Richmond Independent*, Nov. 14, 1942; "Sam Lico, 1916–2014," *Contra Costa Times*, Jan. 6, 2015.

10. Johnson, *Second Gold Rush*, p. 138.

11. Hubert Owen Brown, "The Impact of War Worker Migration on the Public School System of Richmond, California, from 1940–1945" (PhD diss., Stanford University, 1973), p. 169; Johnson, *Second Gold Rush*, p. 46; "Richmond Took a Beating," *Fortune* 31 (Feb. 1945): pp. 262–269.

12. Brown, "Impact of War Worker Migration," p. 143.

13. John Dos Passos, "Gold Rush Down South: Mobile, Alabama, March 1943," in *State of the Nation* (Boston, 1944), p. 89; William Martin Camp, *Skip to My Lou* (New York, 1943), p. 193; Margaret Walsh, *Making Connections: The*

Long-Distance Bus Industry in the USA (Aldershot, 2000), p. 27; Johnson, *Second Gold Rush*, p. 54.

14. Dos Passos, "Gold Rush Down South," in *State of the Nation*, pp. 91–92; Johnson, *Second Gold Rush*, p. 147.

15. "Lucky Opens New Market," *Richmond Independent*, Apr. 17, 1942.

16. "New Theater Sets Opening," *Richmond Independent*, Jan. 16, 1942; "Lippert to Open New Showhouse on MacDonald," *Richmond Independent*, May 20, 1942; "'V' Theatre to Open at Point Richmond," *Richmond Independent*, Aug. 3, 1942.

17. "Sears Roebuck to Open Store in Richmond," *Richmond Independent*, Mar. 24, 1942; "New Victory Liquor Stores Here Opens," *Richmond Independent*, July 10, 1942; "New Marlene's Apparel Shop Opens Here Tomorrow," *Richmond Independent*, Mar. 11, 1942.

18. "Richmond Took a Beating," *Fortune* 31 (Feb. 1945): pp. 262–269; Johnson, *Second Gold Rush*, pp. 145–149; "Holiday for Nitwits," editorial, *Richmond Independent*, Feb. 26, 1942; Brown, "Impact of War Worker Migration," pp. 142, 144.

19. Johnson, *Second Gold Rush*, pp. 85, 109; Brown, "Impact of War Worker Migration," p. 121; Nash, *American West Transformed*, p. 70.

20. McVittie, *Avalanche Hits Richmond*, p. 20; Helm's testimony, Apr. 15, 1943, in *Investigation of Congested Areas: Hearing Before a Subcommittee of the Committee on Naval Affairs, House of Representatives, Seventy-Eighth Congress, First Session* (Washington, DC, 1943), p. 3:884; Charles Wollenberg, ed., *Photographing the Second Gold Rush: Dorothea Lange and the Bay Area at War* (Berkeley, CA, 1995), p. 86.

21. Johnson, *Second Gold Rush*, p. 175.

22. Johnson, *Second Gold Rush*, p. 118; "Sailor's Lonely Wife Asks If It Is Wrong to Date," *Detroit Free Press*, Jan. 4, 1942; "Dear Miss Alden," *Detroit Free Press*, Jan. 6, 1942; Robert L. McLaughlin and Sally E. Parry, *We'll Always Have the Movies: American Cinema During World War II* (Lexington, KY, 2006), p. 262; John Dos Passos, "Pacific Waterfront," in *State of the Nation* (Boston, 1944), p. 310.

23. Kevin Starr, *Embattled Dreams: California in War and Peace, 1940–1950* (New York, 2002), p. 158.

24. Joseph Fabry, "Romance on a Liberty," in *Swing Shift* (San Francisco, 1982), p. 150.

25. "Perry Launched in 4½ Days," *Richmond Independent*, Nov. 12, 1942; "Kaiser Launches a Ship in 4⅔ Days," *New York Times*, Nov. 13, 1942; J. H. Walker, "Hatching the *Ugly Ducklings*," *Popular Science*, Sept. 1942, pp. 81–87.

26. Alex Lichtenstein and Eric Arnesen, "Labor and the Problem of Social

Unity During World War II: Katherine Archibald's *Wartime Shipyard* in Retrospect," *Labor: Studies in Working-Class History of the Americas* 3 (2006): p. 127; Henry J. Kaiser, *Building a Ship in 4 Days, 15 Hours, 25 Minutes* (n.p., 1943); "Kaiser's Circus," *Time*, Nov. 23, 1942.

27. Lichtenstein and Arnesen, "Labor and the Problem of Social Unity," pp. 115, 119, 124; Joseph Fabry, "There She Goes, My Wonderboat," in *Swing Shift* (San Francisco, 1982), pp. 199–200.

28. Katherine Archibald, *Wartime Shipyard: A Study in Social Disunity* (Berkeley, CA, 1947).

29. Archibald, *Wartime Shipyard*, pp. 18, 22.

30. Lichtenstein and Arnesen, "Labor and the Problem of Social Unity," p. 136.

31. Archibald, *Wartime Shipyard*, pp. 63–65.

32. Archibald, *Wartime Shipyard*, pp. 63–65; Lichtenstein and Arnesen, "Labor and the Problem of Social Unity," p. 145; Kevin Starr, *Embattled Dreams: California in War and Peace, 1940–1950* (New York, 2002), p. 96.

33. Shirley Ann Wilson Moore, *To Place Our Deeds: The African-American Community in Richmond, California, 1910–1963* (Berkeley, CA, 2000), pp. 63–64; Archibald, *Wartime Shipyard*, pp. 73, 104.

34. Chester Himes, *If He Hollers, Let Him Go* (New York, 2002 [1945]), pp. 14–15, 103.

35. Chester B. Himes, "Zoot Riots Are Race Riots," *Crisis*, July 1943, pp. 200–201, 222; Aaron Hiltner, *Taking Leave, Taking Liberties: American Troops on the World War II Home Front* (Chicago, 2020), p. 9.

36. Dominic J. Capeci Jr., *Race Relations in Wartime Detroit: The Sojourner Truth Housing Controversy of 1942* (Philadelphia, 1984), p. 67; Thomas E. Hachey, "The Wages of War: A British Commentary on Life in Detroit in July 1943," *Michigan History* 59 (1975): p. 234; Sarah Frohardt-Lane, "Race, Public Transit, and Automobility in World War II Detroit" (PhD diss., University of Illinois, 2011), pp. 33, 36.

37. Frohardt-Lane, "Race, Public Transit, and Automobility," pp. 58, 63, 79.

38. John Temple Graves, "The Southern Negro and the War Crisis," *Virginia Review* 18 (Autumn 1942): p. 502; Jason Morgan Ward, *Hanging Bridge: Racial Violence and America's Civil Rights Century* (New York, 2016), p. 95; Howard W. Odum, *Race and Rumors of Race* (Chapel Hill, NC, 1943), p. 59.

39. Bryant Simon, introduction to *Race and Rumors of Race*, by Howard W. Odum (Baltimore, 1997), p. x.

40. Simon, introduction to *Race and Rumors of Race*, by Odum, p. xxiii; Odum, *Race and Rumors of Race*, p. 3.

41. Edwin C. Berry, "Profiles: Portland," *Journal of Educational Sociology* 19 (Nov. 1945): p. 158.

42. Joyce Thomas, "Double V Was for Victory: Black Soldiers, the Black Protest, and World War II" (PhD diss., Ohio State University, 1993), p. 56.

43. Harvard Sitkoff, "Racial Militancy and Interracial Violence in the Second World War," *Journal of American History* 58, no. 3 (1971): p. 665; Luis Alvarez, *The Power of the Zoot: Youth Culture and Resistance During World War II* (Berkeley, CA, 2008), p. 20; Richard M. Dalfiume, "The 'Forgotten Years' of the Negro Revolution," *Journal of American History* 55 (1968): p. 91.

44. "Billion of Colored Peoples to be Freed by War," *Pittsburgh Courier*, Apr. 4, 1942.

45. "Should I Sacrifice to Live 'Half-American'?," *Pittsburgh Courier*, Jan. 31, 1942.

46. George S. Schuyler, "'Make Democracy Real,' Says Double V Originator," *Pittsburgh Courier*, Apr. 11, 1942.

47. "The Truth Slips Out," editorial, *Michigan Chronicle*, Nov. 21, 1942.

48. Capeci, *Race Relations in Wartime Detroit*, pp. 88, 92.

49. Arthur Krock, "Detroit's Achievement: American Industry Proves That Adolf Hitler Was Wrong," *New York Times*, Apr. 1, 1942; "Detroit Is Dynamite," *Life*, Aug. 17, 1942.

50. "'Jitterbugs' Are Lauded as Race Heroes" and "Nazis Capture Detroit," editorial, *Michigan Chronicle*, Mar. 7, 1942; on arrests, see Capeci, *Race Relations in Wartime Detroit*, pp. 105–106.

51. "Nazis Capture Detroit"; "Negro Morale," editorial, *Michigan Chronicle*, Mar. 28, 1942; and "The Truth Slips Out."

52. "No Blackout!," editorial, *Pittsburgh Courier*, May 30, 1942; Edgar T. Rouzeau, "Black Americans Willingly Offer Services for Democracy," *Pittsburgh Courier*, Mar. 14, 1942.

53. Albert Deutsch, "Kid-Lynchers: Federal Action Needed to Halt Lynching Atrocities," *PM*, Oct. 13, 1942.

54. Lillian Smith, *Strange Fruit* (New York, 1972 [1944]), p. 364.

55. Ward, *Hanging Bridge*, pp. 124, 151; John W. Dower, *War Without Mercy: Race & Power in the Pacific War* (New York, 1986), p. 177.

56. "2 Negro Boys Lynched," *New York Times*, Oct. 13, 1942; "Mississippi Lynching," editorial, *New York Times*, Oct. 17, 1942; "Negro Balance Sheet," *New York Times*, Oct. 18, 1942.

57. Victor Bernstein, "How *damyankees* Foster Race Hate in South: A Seven-Page Survey of the Negro Question," *PM*, Sept. 9. 1942.

58. Hughes in "Let's Face the Race Question," *Town Meeting* (Feb. 17, 1944): p. 5.

59. Victor Bernstein, "Mississippi Laments Lynchings—but Doing Something About Them Is Another Matter," *PM*, Oct. 28, 1942.

60. J. Ron Davis, "Here's Real Story of Lynching of Children," *Baltimore Afro-American*, Oct. 31, 1942; Ward, *Hanging Bridge*, pp. 52, 80.

61. Dabney quoted in Dalfiume, "'Forgotten Years' of the Negro Revolution," p. 101; Horace Clayton, "Mark Etheridge," *Pittsburgh Courier*, July 4, 1942.

62. Odum, *Race and Rumors of Race*, 79; Dan J. Puckett, "Hitler, Race and Democracy in the Heart of Dixie: Alabamian Attitudes and Responses to the Issues of Nazi and Southern Racism, 1933–1946" (PhD diss., Mississippi State University, 2005), p. 15.

63. Jason Morgan Ward, "'A War for States' Rights': The White Supremacy Vision of Double Victory," in *Fog of War: The Second World War and the Civil Rights Movement*, edited by Kevin M. Kruse and Stephen Tuck (New York, 2012), pp. 135, 137.

64. On folkways, Odum, *Race and Rumors of Race*, pp. 7, 21; on dream world, Joel Williamson, *The Crucible of Race: Black-White Relations in the American South Since Emancipation* (New York, 1982), p. 479; on primaries, Turner Catledge, "'White Supremacy' Issue Revived in the South," *New York Times*, Aug. 28, 1938.

65. Graves in "Let's Face the Race Question," p. 7; "An (Axis?) Axe to Grind," *Meridian Star*, Oct. 20, 1942, quoted in Jason Morgan Ward, "Saving Segregation: Southern Whites, Civil Rights, and the Roots of Massive Resistance, 1936–1954" (PhD diss., Yale University, 2008), pp. 97–98.

66. Office of War Information, "Intelligence Report: White Attitudes Toward Negroes," May 8, 1942.

CHAPTER 17: Johannesburg, South Africa

1. Peter Abrahams, *Song of the City* (London, 1943), pp. 70–72; Modikwe Dikobi, *The Marabi Dance* (London, 1973), pp. 6–7.

2. David Coplan, *In Township Tonight! South Africa's Black City Music and Theater*, 2nd ed. (Chicago, 2008), p. 159.

3. Christopher Ballantine, *Marabi Nights: Jazz, "Race," and Society in Early Apartheid South Africa* (Scottsville, South Africa, 2012 [1993]), pp. 6–7, 17.

4. Todd Matshikiza quoted in Coplan, *In Township Tonight!*, p. 129; *Bantu World*, Feb. 2, 1935, quoted in Ballantine, *Marabi Nights*, p. 75.

5. The 1922 Stallard Commission quoted in David Harrison, *The White Tribe of South Africa: South Africa in Perspective* (Berkeley, CA, 1981), p. 83.

6. Jonathan Hyslop, "'Segregation Has Fallen on Evil Days': Smuts' South Africa, Global War, and Transnational Politics, 1939–1946," *Journal of Global History* 7 (2012): p. 439.

7. "Sunday Drive," *Guardian* (Cape Town), May 14, 1942.

8. Peter Alexander, *Workers, War and the Origins of Apartheid: Labor and Politics in South Africa, 1939–1948* (Athens, OH, 2000), pp. 17–19; Baruch Hirson, *Yours for the Union: Class and Community Struggles in South Africa* (London, 1990), pp. 53–55.

9. "The Evil of Intolerance," editorial, *Bantu World*, July 25, 1942; "The New World," Oct. 31, 1942; "The Natives' Attitude," editorial, *Rand Daily Mail* (Johannesburg), Dec. 14, 1942.

10. "Native Loiterers at the Station," letter to the *Rand Daily Mail*, Mar. 31, 1939.

11. Angry Citizen, "House in State of Siege. Prowling Gangs of Natives," *Rand Daily Mail*, June 23, 1942; Deon van Tonder, "'First Win the War, Then Clear the Slums': The Genesis of the Western Areas Removal Scheme, 1940–1949," in *Apartheid's Genesis, 1935–1962*, edited by P. L. Bonner et al. (Johannesburg, 1993).

12. E'skia Mphahlele, "Grieg on a Stolen Piano," in *In Corner B, and Other Stories* (Nairobi, 1967), p. 41; E'skia Mphahlele, *Down Second Avenue* (Berlin, 1962 [1959]), pp. 101–102, 169.

13. Abrahams, *Song of the City*, pp. 9, 174; Peter Abrahams, *Tell Freedom: Memories of Africa* (New York, 1954), p. 197.

14. Mphahlele, "Grieg on a Stolen Piano," p. 47; Ballantine, *Marabi Nights*, p. 88; Mphahlele, *Down Second Avenue*, pp. 39, 43; Coplan, *In Township Tonight!*, p. 129.

15. Dikobi, *The Marabi Dance*, p. 1.

16. Department of Native Affairs, *Report of the Inter-Departmental Committee on the Social, Health and Economic Conditions of Urban Natives* (Pretoria, 1942), p. 2.

17. Harrison, *White Tribe of South Africa*, p. 83.

18. Abrahams, *Tell Freedom*, pp. 172–174.

19. Hirson, *Yours for the Union*, p. 65.

20. Entry for Nov. 28, 1937, in Robert R. Edgar, ed., *The Travel Notes of Ralph J. Bunche: 28 September 1937–1 January 1938* (Athens, OH, 1992), p. 192; Peter Abrahams, *Return to Goli* (London, 1953), pp. 71–74.

21. Entry for Dec. 9, 1937, in Edgar, *Travel Notes of Ralph J. Bunche*, p. 249.

22. Abrahams, *Tell Freedom*, pp. 138, 185–186, 191, 194.

23. "Spotlight on Social Events," *Bantu World*, Oct. 31, 1942.

24. Gideon Roos, "The Great Trek," *Australian Quarterly* 22 (Dec. 1950): p. 38; Jennifer Crwys-Williams, *A Country at War: The Mood of a Nation, 1939–1945* (Rivonia, South Africa, 1992), p. 8.

25. Roos, "The Great Trek," pp. 35, 37; Harrison, *White Tribe of South Africa*, pp. 110–111.

26. Lindie Koorts, *D. F. Malan and the Rise of Afrikaner Nationalism* (Cape Town, 2014), p. 326; Harrison, *White Tribe of South Africa*, p. 112.

27. Koorts, *D. F. Malan and the Rise of Afrikaner Nationalism*, p. 329; on brown children, Richard Steyn, *Seven Votes: How World War II Changed South Africa Forever* (Johannesburg, 2020), p. 111.

28. Hermann Giliomee, "The Making of the Apartheid Plan, 1929–1948," *Journal of South African Studies* 29 (2003): pp. 373–374; Koorts, *D. F. Malan and the Rise of Afrikaner Nationalism*, p. 369.

29. See T. R. H. Davenport, "South Africa's Janus Moment: The Schizophrenic 1940s," *South African Historical Journal* 52 (2005): pp. 191–205.

30. Smuts to M. C. Gillett, May 12, 1940, in Jean van der Poel, *Selections from the Smuts Papers*, vol. 6, *December 1934–August 1945* (Cambridge, UK, 1973), p. 222.

31. Dan J. Puckett, "Hitler, Race and Democracy in the Heart of Dixie: Alabamian Attitudes and Responses to the Issues of Nazi and Southern Racism, 1933–1946" (PhD diss., Mississippi State University, 2005), p. 25.

32. W. K. Hancock, *Smuts: The Field of Force, 1919–1950* (Cambridge, UK, 1968), p. 333.

33. "Incendiary Bombs at Cavalcade," *Rand Daily Mail*, May 27, 1942; "Planes Will 'Bomb' Cavalcade To-Night," *Rand Daily Mail*, May 28, 1942.

34. Hyslop, "'Segregation Has Fallen on Evil Days.'"

35. "Nats Condemn Proposal to Arm Natives," *Rand Daily Mail*, Mar. 24, 1942.

36. Steyn, *Seven Votes*, p. 109; Jan Smuts, "The Basis of Trusteeship in African Native Policy," Jan. 21, 1942, reprinted in *Selections from the Smuts Papers*, edited by Jean van der Poel (Cambridge, UK, 1973), document 556, pp. 6:331–343.

37. "Pro-Japanese," editorial, *Guardian* (Cape Town), Mar. 12, 1942; Smuts letter, June 7, 1942, quoted in Christopher Thorne, *Allies of a Kind: The United States, Britain, and the War Against Japan, 1941–1945* (New York, 1978), p. 8; Davenport, "South Africa's Janus Moment," p. 203.

38. Social and Economic Planning Council, *The Economic and Social Conditions of the Racial Groups in South Africa* (Pretoria, 1948), p. 109.

39. Harrison, *White Tribe of South Africa*, p. 152.

40. Peter Walshe, *The Rise of African Nationalism in South Africa: The African National Congress, 1912–1952* (Berkeley, CA, 1971), p. 267; "Africans Are Entitled to Know," editorial, *Bantu World*, Feb. 28, 1942.

41. Robert Edgar, "Changing the Old Guard: A. P. Mda and the ANC Youth League, 1944–1945," in *South Africa's 1940s: Worlds of Possibilities*, edited by Saul Dubow and Alan Jeeves (Cape Town, 2005), p. 155.

42. Anne O'Hare McCormick, "A Discoverer of the New World in the East," *New York Times*, Oct. 28, 1942.

43. Cyprian Ekwensi, *People of the City* (New York, 2020 [1954]), p. 13.

CHAPTER 18: "Quit India"

1. "Text of Willkie's Address to the Nation Renewing His Plea for a Second Front," *New York Times*, Oct. 27, 1942.

2. Entries for Feb. 27 and Mar. 4, 1942, in Anne Frank, *The Diary of a Young Girl*, edited by Otto H. Frank and Mirjam Pressler (New York, 1991), pp. 87–88; entry for Aug. 5, 1942, in Dawid Sierakowiak, *The Diary of Dawid Siera-kowiak: Five Notebooks from the Lodz Ghetto*, edited by Alan Adelson (New York, 1996), p. 203; Khubchand Samtani, "The Greatest Man of the Age," *Manila Tribune*, Oct. 2, 1942; "'Saint Gandhi': Man of the Year, 1930," *Time*, Jan. 5, 1931.

3. "An Open Letter from the Editors of LIFE to the People of England," *Life*, Oct. 12, 1942.

4. Paul Scott, *The Jewel in the Crown*, in *The Raj Quartet* (New York, 1976), p. 258.

5. Penny M. Von Eschen, *Race Against Empire: Black Americans and Anti-Colonialism, 1937–1957* (Ithaca, NY, 1997), p. 34.

6. Margery Perham, "The Aftermath of Mr. Willkie's Broadcast," *Times* (London), Nov. 20, 1942; Lloyd C. Gardner, "The Atlantic Charter: Idea and Reality, 1942–1945," in *The Atlantic Charter*, edited by Douglas Brinkley and David R. Facey-Crowther (New York, 1994), p. 63.

7. Entry for Dec. 1, 1941, in *The Empire at Bay: The Leo Amery Diaries, 1929–1945*, edited by John Barnes and David Nicholson (London, 1988), p. 751; Amery to Linlithgow, Nov. 25, 1941, quoted in Christopher Thorne, *Allies of a Kind: The United States, Britain, and the War Against Japan, 1941–1945* (New York, 1978), p. 62; Frederick Cooper, *Decolonization and African Society: The Labor Question in French and British Africa* (Cambridge, UK, 1996), p. 112; Samuel Zipp, *The Idealist: Wendell Willkie's Wartime Quest to Build One World* (Cambridge, MA, 2020), p. 205.

8. Goebbels quoted in Romain Hayes, *Subhas Chandra Bose in Nazi Germany* (New York, 2011), p. 92.

9. P. F. Clarke, *Cripps Version: The Life of Sir Stafford Cripps, 1889–1952* (London, 2002), p. 305; "Message to India," editorial, *New York Times*, Apr. 2, 1942; Daniel Todman, *Britain's War: A New World, 1942–1947* (Oxford, 2020), p. 143.

10. Andrew N. Buchanan, "The War Crisis and the Decolonization of India, December 1941–September 1942: A Political and Military Dilemma," *Global War Studies* 8, no. 2 (2011): p. 18.

11. Francis G. Hutchins, *India's Revolution: Gandhi and the Quit India Movement* (Cambridge, MA, 1973), p. 261.

12. Srnath Raghavan, *India's War: World War II and the Making of Modern South Asia* (New York, 2016), pp. 260–262.

13. Ashley Jackson, *The British Empire and the Second World War* (London, 2006), p. 362.

14. "Viceroy's Message to People of India," *Times of India*, Sept. 4, 1939; "Gandhi Urges Britain to 'Liberate' India," *New York Times*, Sept. 17, 1939.

15. Sumit Sarkar, *Modern India, 1885–1947* (Delhi, 1983), p. 376; Kaushik Roy, "Military Loyalty in the Colonial Context: A Case Study of the Indian Army During World War II," *Journal of Military History* 73, no. 2 (2008): p. 503.

16. Ayesha Jalal, *The Sole Spokesman: Jinnah, the Muslim League, and the Demand for Pakistan* (Cambridge, UK, 1985).

17. "Pakistan Is Our Sacred Creed," *Bombay Chronicle*, Dec. 25, 1941.

18. Madhusree Mukerjee, *Churchill's Secret War: The British Empire and the Ravaging of India During World War II* (New York, 2010), pp. 67–68; "Princes' 'Stan'?," editorial, *Bombay Chronicle*, July 7, 1942.

19. "Not the Right Way," editorial, *Bombay Chronicle*, Apr. 4, 1942.

20. Indivar Kamtekar, "The Shiver of 1942," in *War and Society in Colonial India*, edited by Kaushik Roy (New Delhi, 2006), p. 333; Sarkar, *Modern India, 1885–1947*, p. 388; A. C. Bhuyan, *The Quit India Movement, the Second World War, and Indian Nationalism* (New Delhi, 1975), p. 7.

21. Francis G. Hutchins, *India's Revolution: Gandhi and the Quit India Movement* (Cambridge, MA, 1973), pp. 197, 201.

22. "The Finger of Fate," editorial, *Statesman* (Calcutta), July 30, 1942.

23. "Frogs in a Well," *Time*, Aug. 17, 1942.

24. David Hardiman, "The Quit India Movement in Gujarat," in *The Indian Nation in 1942*, edited by Gyanendra Pandey (Calcutta, 1988), p. 84.

25. "A Barren Tract," editorial, *Statesman*, Aug. 14, 1942; Hardiman, "Quit India Movement in Gujarat," in *Indian Nation in 1942*, edited by Pandey, pp. 111–112.

26. R. H. Niblett: *The Congress Rebellion in Azamgarh: August & September 1942, as Recorded in the Diary of R. H. Niblett*, edited by S. A. A. Rizvi (Allahabad, 1957), pp. 11, 13, 40.

27. Sarkar, *Modern India, 1885–1947*, p. 390.

28. Hardiman, "Quit India Movement in Gujarat," in *Indian Nation in 1942*, edited by Pandey, pp. 83, 109–113, 116–117.

29. "Shahed," "Dar-El-Islam," *Statesman*, Sept. 6, 1942.

30. Richard Toye, *Churchill's Empire: The World That Made Him and the World He Made* (New York, 2010), p. 225.

31. Sarkar, *Modern India, 1885–1947*, p. 396.

32. Sugata Bose, *His Majesty's Opponent: Subhas Chandra Bose and India's Struggle Against Empire* (Cambridge, MA, 2011), pp. 3, 9.

33. Kirsten Sellars, "Meanings of Treason in a Colonial Context: Indian Challenges to the Charges of 'Waging War Against the King' and 'Crimes Against Peace,'" *Leiden Journal of International Law* 30 (2017): pp. 827–828, 831, 833.

34. R. B. Pal, *International Military Tribunal for the Far East: Dissentient Judgment of Justice R. B. Pal* (Calcutta, 1953), p. 114.

CHAPTER 19: The People's War in the Philippines

1. Pankay Mishra, *From the Ruins of Empire: The Revolt Against the West and the Remaking of Asia* (London, 2012), p. 8.

2. Entries for Jan. 6 and Feb. 12, 1942, in Victor Buencamino diary, https://philippinediaryproject.com.

3. John W. Dower, *War Without Mercy: Race & Power in the Pacific War* (New York, 1986), p. 176.

4. Entries for Nov. 8, 1943, and Mar. 15, 1944, in Leocadio De Asis, *From Bataan to Tokyo: Diary of a Filipino Student in Wartime Japan, 1943–1944* (Lawrence, KS, 1979), pp. 77, 122.

5. "Declaration of the Commander of the Nippon Army, Tomoyuki Yamashita," *Shonan Times*, Feb. 20, 1942; Willard H. Elsbree, *Japan's Role in Southeast Asian Nationalist Movements, 1940 to 1945* (New York, 1953), p. 79.

6. Victor Gosiengfiao, "The Japanese Occupation: 'The Cultural Campaign,'" *Philippine Studies* 14 (1966): pp. 230, 237.

7. Goh Sin Tub, "Sayonara Sensei," in *The Ghost Lover of Emerald Hill, and Other Stories* (Singapore, 1987), pp. 109, 122.

8. Yoji Akashi, "Japanese Cultural Policy in Malaya and Singapore, 1942–45," in *Japanese Cultural Policies in Southeast Asia During World War 2*, edited by Grant K. Goodman (New York, 1991), p. 147.

9. Quoted in Ian Buruma, "The Battered Bride," *New York Review of Books*, June 1, 1989.

10. Entry for July 21, 1942, in Juan Labrador, *A Diary of the Japanese Occupation* (Manila, 1989), p. 122.

11. Entry for May 10, 1942, in Pacita Pestano-Jacinto, *Living with the Enemy: A Diary of the Japanese Occupation* (Pasig City, Philippines, 2002), p. 40.

12. Entries for Jan. 5 and 12, 1942, in Buencamino diary; entry for Dec. 8, 1943, in Labrador, *Diary of the Japanese Occupation*, p. 181.

13. Fernando J. Manalac, *Manila: Memories of World War II* (Quezon City, 1995), p. 63.

14. Entry for Jan. 22, 1943, Pestano-Jacinto, *Living with the Enemy*, pp. 115–117; Manalac, *Manila*, p. 68.

15. Entry for July 8, 1942, in Buencamino diary.

16. Entry for Jan. 17, 1942, in Pestano-Jacinto, *Living with the Enemy*, p. 16; Theodore Friend, *The Blue-Eyed Enemy: Japan Against the West in Java and Luzon, 1942–1945* (Princeton, NJ, 1988), pp. 144, 188–189.

17. Entry for Apr. 3, 1942, in Buencamino diary.

18. Entries for Feb. 19 and Mar. 7, 1942, in Buencamino diary.

19. Entry for Feb. 21, 1942, in Buencamino diary.

20. Entry for Mar. 7, 1942, in Buencamino diary; entry for July 29, 1942, in Labrador, *Diary of the Japanese Occupation*, p. 227.

21. Entry for Apr. 26, 1942, in Buencamino diary; entry for May 27, 1942, in Labrador, *Diary of the Japanese Occupation*, p. 104; Manalac, *Manila*, pp. 23–24, 33.

22. Entries for June 25 and 26 and July 31, 1942, in Buencamino diary.

23. "Japan Promises P.I. Independence," *Manila Tribune*, Jan. 22, 1942; "Vargas, Aquino Urge Full Collaboration," *Manila Tribune*, Jan. 23, 1942.

24. "2,000 Attending Nippongo Classes," *Manila Tribune*, Nov. 27, 1942; entry for Nov. 23, 1943, in Pestano-Jacinto, *Living with the Enemy*, p. 117.

25. Charles Nell, "Drums: A Short Story of Malayan Magic," *Shonan Times*, Apr. 11, 1942; advertisement for the Peacock Garden Night Club, *Manila Tribune*, Oct. 10, 1942.

26. Entry for Apr. 17, 1942, in Pestano-Jacinto, *Living with the Enemy*, p. 33.

27. Entry for Feb. 7, 1942, in Pestano-Jacinto, *Living with the Enemy*, p. 125; "Officials to Lead 100,000 Marchers in Dec. 8 Parade," *Manila Tribune*, Dec. 5, 1942; "Civic Body Organized," *Manila Tribune*, Dec. 7, 1942.

28. Michael Lucken, *The Japanese and the War: From Expectation to Memory* (New York, 2017), p. 69; "Old, Young Enjoy Radio Taiso," *Manila Tribune*, Oct. 15, 1942.

29. Entries for Sept. 4, 5, and 9 and Oct. 14, 1942, in Labrador, *Diary of the Japanese Occupation*, pp. 168–170, 176; "Flags Ready for Distribution," *Manila Tribune*, Oct. 9, 1943; "Republic Inaugurated Before 500,000 People," *Manila Tribune*, Oct. 15, 1943.

30. "Here at Last!," editorial, *Manila Tribune*, Oct. 14, 1943.

31. Entry for Feb. 14, 1942, in Buencamino diary.

32. Entry for Apr. 18, 1944, in Pestano-Jacinto, *Living with the Enemy*, p. 211.

33. Entry for Mar. 12, 1942, in Buencamino diary.

34. James Kelley Morningstar, "War and Resistance: The Philippines, 1942–1944" (PhD diss., University of Maryland, 2018), p. 246; T. D. Agcaoili, "Tenderness," reprinted in *Philippine Short Stories, 1941–1955*, edited by Leopoldo Y. Yabes, pt. 1 (Quezon City, 1981), pp. 475–480; Jaime Laid An Lim, "Literature and Politics: The Colonial Experience in the Philippine Novel" (PhD diss., Indiana University, 1989), pp. 211–212.

35. Entries for Nov. 21 and Dec. 14, 1942, in Labrador, *Diary of the Japanese Occupation*, pp. 143, 147.

36. David Joel Steinberg, *Philippine Collaboration in World War II* (Ann Arbor, MI, 1967), p. 57; Stanley Karnow, *In Our Image: America's Empire in the Philippines* (New York, 1989), p. 311.

37. Quoted in Gary J. Bass, *Judgment at Tokyo: World War II on Trial and the Making of Modern Asia* (New York, 2023), p. 7; Hiroyuki Mizuguchi, *Jungle of No Mercy: Memoir of a Japanese Soldier* (Manila, 2010).

38. Stevan Javellana, *Without Seeing the Dawn* (Boston, 1947), pp. 270, 284–286.

39. Morningstar, "War and Resistance," p. 120; Jeremy Yellen, *The Greater Asian Co-Prosperity Sphere: When Total Empire Met Total War* (Ithaca, NY, 2019), p. 122.

40. F. Sionil José, *Ermita* (Manila, 1988); Buruma, "The Battered Bride."

CHAPTER 20: The "Old Town" in Ukraine

1. Jochen Hellbeck, *Stalingrad: The City That Defeated the Third Reich* (New York, 2015), p. 68; Richard Overy quoted in Catherine Merridale, *Ivan's War: Life and Death in the Red Army, 1939–1945* (New York, 2006), p. 6.

2. Anna Reid, *Leningrad: The Epic Siege of World War II, 1941–1944* (New York, 2011), pp. 15, 25–27.

3. Entry for June 16, 1941, in *Die Tagebücher von Joseph Goebbels. Sämtliche Fragmente*, edited by Elke Fröhlich (Munich, 1994), pt. 1, vol. 4, p. 695; Jacob Gerstenfeld-Maltiel, *My Private War: One Man's Struggle to Survive the Soviets and the Nazis* (London, 1993), p. 73; Mark Edele, *Stalinism at War: The Soviet Union in World War II* (London, 2021), p. 77.

4. Jochen Hellbeck, "*War and Peace* in the Twentieth Century," *Raritan* 26 (2007): p. 37; Ilya Ehrenburg, *The War, 1941–45* (London, 1964), p. 12.

5. Alexandra Popoff, *Vasily Grossman and the Soviet Century* (New Haven, CT, 2019), p. 122; Antony Beevor and Luba Vinogradova, eds., *A Writer at War: Vasily Grossman with the Red Army, 1941–1945* (London, 2005), p. 123; Timothy Snyder, *Bloodlands: Europe Between Hitler and Stalin* (New York, 2010), p. 308.

6. Snyder, *Bloodlands*, p. 392.

7. Snyder, *Bloodlands*, p. 182.

8. Karel Berkhoff, *Harvest of Despair: Life and Death in Ukraine Under Nazi Rule* (Cambridge, MA, 2004), pp. 173, 183.

9. Snyder, *Bloodlands*, p. 244; Berkhoff, *Harvest of Despair*, p. 262.

10. Vasily Grossman, "Ukraine Without Jews" [1943], *Jewish Quarterly* 217 (Spring 2011): pp. 12–13.

11. Aleksandr Dovzhenko quoted in Ostap Kin, ed., *Babyn Yar: Ukrainian Poets Respond* (Cambridge, MA, 2023), p. 15.

12. "Diary of Unknown Soldier" and entry for Mar. 9, 1942, diary of Friedrich Schmidt, in *True to Type: A Selection from Letters and Diaries of German Soldiers and Civilians Collected on the Soviet-German Front* (London, n.d. [1943]), pp. 48, 51.

13. Bernhard Chiari, *Alltag hinter der Front. Besatzung, Kollaboration und Widerstand in Weissrussland, 1941–1944* (Düsseldorf, 1998), p. 5.

14. Chiari, *Alltag hinter der Front*, pp. 257–259; Berkhoff, *Harvest of Despair*, p. 78.

15. Chiari, *Alltag hinter der Front*, pp. 155–156.

16. Snyder, *Bloodlands*, pp. 243–244.

17. Vasily Grossman, "The Old Teacher" [1943], in *The Road: Stories, Journalism, and Essays* (New York, 2010), p. 106.

18. Vasily Grossman, *Life and Fate* (New York, 2006), p. 410.

19. John Garrard and Carol Garrard, *The Bones of Berdichev: The Life and Fate of Vasily Grossman* (New York, 1996), p. 138.

20. Vasily Grossman, *Stalingrad* (New York, 2019), pp. 8–9, 25, 292.

21. Grossman, *Life and Fate*, p. 94; Grossman, *Stalingrad*, p. 236.

22. Grossman, *Life and Fate*, pp. 54–55, 395, 860; Grossman, "With the Khasin Tank Brigade," in *Writer at War*, edited by Beevor and Vinogradova.

23. Grossman, "Ukraine Without Jews," 12–18.

24. Grossman, "Ukraine Without Jews"; Vasily Grossman, "The Murders of the Jews in Berdichev," in *The Black Book: The Ruthless Murder of Jews by German-Fascist Invaders Throughout the Temporarily-Occupied Regions of the Soviet Union and in the Death Camps of Poland During the War of 1941–1945*, edited by Vasily Grossman and Ilya Ehrenburg (New York, 1980 [1946]), p. 18.

25. Grossman, "Ukraine Without Jews"; Grossman, preface to *Black Book*, edited by Grossman and Ehrenburg, p. xxxvii.

26. Alexandra Popoff, *Vasily Grossman and the Soviet Century* (New Haven, CT, 2019), p. 133.

27. Vasily Grossman, "The Old Teacher," in *Road*, pp. 84–115.

28. Robert Chandler, "Mother and Son; Life and Fate," *Granta*, June 6, 2019, at https://granta.com/mother-and-son-life-and-fate/; Grossman, *Stalingrad*, pp. 334–351.

29. Grossman, *Stalingrad*, p. 351.

30. Grossman, *Life and Fate*, pp. 80–93.

31. Grossman, "Murders of the Jews in Berdichev," in *Black Book*, edited by Grossman and Ehrenburg, p. 20.

32. Grossman, *Life and Fate*, p. 841.

33. Grossman, *Life and Fate*, pp. 410, 860.

CONCLUSION

1. Spencer Weart, *Nuclear Fear: A History of Images* (Cambridge, MA, 1988), pp. 104–107; William Faulkner on Dec. 10, 1950, www.nobelprize.org/prizes/literature/1949/faulkner/speech/.

2. "National Affairs: World War III?," *Time*, Nov. 3, 1941; "Foreign News: World War III?," *Time*, Mar. 22, 1943.

3. D. F. Fleming, "*Collier's* Wins World War III," *Nation*, Nov. 10, 1951; John Morano, "*Collier's* Magazine: *Preview of the War We Do Not Want*," *War, Literature, and the Arts* 5 (1993): pp. 39–46.

4. Vasily Grossman, *Life and Fate*, translated by Robert Chandler (New York, 1980), pp. 79, 91.

5. C. L. Sulzberger, "Europe: The New Dark Continent," *New York Times*, Mar. 18, 1945.

6. C. L. Sulzberger, "Grim Winter Marches on Torn Europe," *New York Times*, Nov. 18, 1945.

7. Richard Wright, "I Tried to Be a Communist," *Atlantic Monthly*, Sept. 1944, p. 54.

8. "The Struma Disaster," editorial, *New York Times*, Mar. 13, 1942.

9. Benjamin Carter Hett, *The Nazi Menace: Hitler, Churchill, Roosevelt, Stalin, and the Road to War* (New York, 2020), p. 65.

10. Amitav Ghosh, *The Great Derangement: Climate Change and the Unthinkable* (Chicago, 2016), pp. 20–23.

INDEX

Index